# Fighting for Time

# Fighting for Time

## Shifting Boundaries of Work and Social Life

Cynthia Fuchs Epstein
and
Arne L. Kalleberg
Editors

Russell Sage Foundation • New York

# The Russell Sage Foundation

The Russell Sage Foundation, one of the oldest of America's general purpose foundations, was established in 1907 by Mrs. Margaret Olivia Sage for "the improvement of social and living conditions in the United States." The Foundation seeks to fulfill this mandate by fostering the development and dissemination of knowledge about the country's political, social, and economic problems. While the Foundation endeavors to assure the accuracy and objectivity of each book it publishes, the conclusions and interpretations in Russell Sage Foundation publications are those of the authors and not of the Foundation, its Trustees, or its staff. Publication by Russell Sage, therefore, does not imply Foundation endorsement.

**Library of Congress Cataloging-in-Publication Data**

Fighting for time : shifting boundaries of work and social life / Cynthia Fuchs Epstein and Arne L. Kalleberg, editors.
    p. cm.
    Includes bibliographical references and index.
    ISBN 0-87154-286-2
      1. Time management. 2. Hours of labor. 3. Work and family. 4. Time measurements.
5. Time—Social aspects. 6. Work—Social aspects. I. Epstein, Cynthia Fuchs. II. Kalleberg, Arne L.

HD69.T54R48 2004
650.1'1—dc22

2004046632

The paper used in this publication meets the minimum requirements of American National Standard for Information Sciences—Permanence of Paper for Printed Library Materials. ANSI Z39.48-1992.

Text design by Suzanne Nichols.

RUSSELL SAGE FOUNDATION
112 East 64th Street, New York, New York 10021
10 9 8 7 6 5 4 3 2 1

For the generation that preceded us, and the generations
who will follow us,

Cynthia dedicates this book to Jesse and Birdie Fuchs and
Jesse Epstein,

and

Arne dedicates this book to Ted and Solveig Kalleberg,
and to Kathryn, Jonathan, and Kari Kalleberg

# Contents

# Contributors

**Cynthia Fuchs Epstein** is Distinguished Professor in the Department of Sociology at the Graduate Center of the City University of New York.

**Arne L. Kalleberg** is Kenan Distinguished Professor of Sociology at the University of North Carolina at Chapel Hill.

**Mary Blair-Loy** is associate professor of sociology at the University of California at San Diego.

**Allen C. Bluedorn** is the Emma S. Hibbs Distinguished Professor and chair of the Department of Management at the University of Missouri-Columbia.

**David L. Collinson** is Foundation for Management Professor of Strategic Learning and Leadership at Lancaster University Management School.

**Margaret Collinson** is senior research fellow in the Centre for Excellence in Leadership at Lancaster University Management School.

**Rudy Fenwick** is associate professor of sociology at the University of Akron.

**Stephen P. Ferris** is the James Harvey Rogers Chair of Money, Credit, and Banking, director of the Financial Research Institute, and professor of finance at the University of Missouri-Columbia.

**Kathleen Gerson** is professor of sociology at New York University.

**Jerry A. Jacobs** is Merriam Term Professor of Sociology at the University of Pennsylvania.

**Peter Levin** is assistant professor of sociology at Barnard College and faculty fellow in the Institute for Social and Economic Research and Policy at Columbia University.

**Harriet B. Presser** is distinguished university professor in the Department of Sociology at the University of Maryland.

**Ofer Sharone** is a doctoral candidate in sociology at the University of California at Berkeley.

**Benjamin Stewart** is a doctoral candidate in the Department of Performance Studies at New York University.

**Mark Tausig** is professor of sociology at the University of Akron.

— Chapter 1 —

# Time and Work: Changes and Challenges

## Cynthia Fuchs Epstein and Arne L. Kalleberg

TIME IS A basic human concern. It orders the lives of all individuals and groups. Time differentiation is a basic component of social structure and of the cultural value system: time designations structure human effort, experience, and expectations, and cultural values are embedded in them (Durkheim 1902/1947; Merton 1984; Sorokin and Merton 1937).

Throughout history claims on people's time have come from formal and informal authorities—from the state, from the church, from the firm and corporation, and from the family. The "natural" pace of life, in earlier times determined by the rising and setting of the sun, has given way to an ordering by church bells, bugles, factory whistles, and alarm clocks, all sending messages to engage in or cease various activities. Technology—from the invention of the incandescent light to the computer chip—has extended the possibility of work beyond the daylight hours and through time zones (Melbin 1987). Time frames are internalized in individuals' psyches, structured as time frames are by social conditioning and cultural perspectives.

Social scientists, historians, philosophers, and of course writers of fiction—particularly science fiction—have considered the issue of time in various ways through the ages and some have jostled our imaginations. Historical memory is located in identified periods—for example, the Reformation, the Hundred Years war, the Enlightenment, the Great Depression—and "progress" has been defined as a

1

movement through time. Individuals born in different generations may view the same experiences through different lenses (Mannheim 1952). Today time boundaries and their significance are often contested (Jameson 1994; Scott 1988; Fukuyama 1992; Veyne 1984; Ermath 1991; Braudel 1982–84/1992), and thus we are drawn to analyze time structures in new and different ways.

In modern societies, time designations are often contested both by scholars and by ordinary actors in daily life. In fact, the time demands of people's work lives and their private lives have become a persistent topic of debate and negotiation, the subject of books and conferences and private discussion.

What has fueled these debates and discussions? One source of concern is a perception by many of a speedup in the pace of work and an increase in hours worked. The anxiety over an intensification of work has been fueled by corporate restructurings such as downsizing and has been supported by feelings of economic insecurity on the part of employees who have survived layoffs. Such intensification and insecurity constituted a "dark side" to the booming American economy of the 1990s and are reflected in part today by an increase in workloads for formerly privileged white-collar workers (Kalleberg and Epstein 2001). Some writers (see Fraser 2001) have even used the metaphor of the sweatshop to describe the deterioration of white-collar work that has accompanied the greater time pressures resulting from corporate restructuring. The intensification of white- as well as blue-collar work has been facilitated by technological developments that have enabled employers to become increasingly sophisticated in their ability to monitor and control the amount of time workers spend at work and their activities at the workplace.

Associated with increases in work hours are the growing demands of family obligations, a trend due largely to continued increases in female labor-force participation and in the number of dual-career families. These perceptions of a time squeeze on families have been given voice by a highly articulate and visible segment of the public, leading scholars and laypersons to question the legitimacy of time demands at work, the sacrifice of other values to the ever-faster production of goods and services, and the resulting burden placed on the family and the health of citizens.

As Jerry Jacobs and Kathleen Gerson point out in chapter 2, time pressure is experienced by vast numbers of people, not only professionals and managers whose hours at work have increased and workers at lower strata who often have to work two or more jobs to make a decent living, but also those in the workforce who are not working longer hours than they did a decade ago. Jacobs and Gerson point out that the sources of the pressure is that families now typically comprise a husband and wife who are each bound by the demands of their jobs, unlike their own fathers and mothers; typically their fathers worked outside the home but their mothers stayed home. Children's schedules, too, have become more demanding, especially in middle-class families (see Lareau 2003), and parents today are expected to participate in their school, sports, and social-enrichment activities. The belief of many that the home is no longer "a haven in a heartless world" (Lasch 1977; Hochschild 1997) reflects the reality that the family as a unit may have little time that is not programmed with a variety of activities. This perception of time demands as oppressive has attracted a good deal of attention in academic research and in the popular press.

Work restructuring and greater economic insecurity have also given rise to debates about the reasons for and implications of the growth in temporary work arrangements (see, for example, Kalleberg, Reskin, and Hudson 2000). Employers and workers can no longer assume that their employment relations are permanent but rather must assume that they are contingent and depend primarily on how long employers need their employees. Concerns about the quality of jobs associated with temporary work as well as with the need for individuals to obtain flexible or nonstandard work schedules (such as part-time work, shift work, and weekend and evening work) have come to occupy a prominent place in debates about the regulation of working time and the evolving nature of employment relations.

These changes underscore the importance of reconsidering time at work as we begin the twenty-first century. The authors of the essays collected consider various aspects of time evaluation, time pressures, and time realities. These essays address not only the current crises but also reconsider more basic issues related to the creation and implementation of time norms as one of the central control systems in social life. Many scholars have investigated the processes involved in the social and political construction of time, particularly the domination of workers' time by employers. On the other hand, relatively few theorists have considered the elemental place of time norms in structuring social behavior and attitudes and in maintaining the boundaries of gender, race, and class.

Time norms are part of the formal rule system that governs our everyday lives. What we should be doing at any time of the day is barely a matter of personal option once we have chosen to go to school, to have a job, or to have children. And the simple fact of being a man or woman, or of being a young, middle-aged, or older person carries time prescriptions that become internalized so that people think about the scheduling of their lives according to culturally set values.

This book brings together the work of social scientists whose research and writing address a variety of issues raised by the connections between time and work. The authors examine ways in which time interacts with other factors such as professional and gender roles, and the organization and control of work. They focus on the ways in which time is ordered in the workplace, the implications of this ordering for other domains of society, and the conditions under which it is manipulated or controlled. The book includes essays that also suggest alternative ways of framing the concepts whereby time is understood, for example, by deconstructing concepts such as the workweek, part-time work, and work-family conflict and looking at how various assessment systems motivate or undercut work efforts.

The essays also question certain assumptions embedded in current views about the use of time at work and the economics of productivity. They emphasize the manipulation of time as a social-control mechanism that not only keeps individuals' noses to the grindstone at their jobs by measuring their output per minute, hour, or day but also reinforces the boundaries that define the sexual division of labor through the assignment of different time priorities for men and women, the division between skilled and unskilled labor based on measurements of activity, and experiences of autonomy and control at work. These writers address the human costs and social consequences of the timing of work and social life, and they document the realities of the ways in which people are asked to use their time, and the consequences that flow from various kinds of work arrangements. What, for example, asks Harriet Presser, are the effects of overtime work, night and split shifts, and mandatory overtime on individuals' mental health and marital stability?

Time measurement is another issue we explore with regard to its cultural and political overtones. As many sociologists have pointed out, individuals and groups determine how time is measured. Whether a social group measures performance at work or in other spheres of life by the minute, hour, day, or project may valorize work or may make it drudgery. And once set in place, systems of time control become institutionalized. When time clocks are installed and keystrokes per minute are calculated by the computer or billable hours become the measure of assessment of work effort, individuals have little autonomy with regard to the use of their work time.

This volume also explores individuals' agency in interpreting the meaning of time in their workplaces and in adapting to or transforming their work experience. Individuals may conform or rebel when confronted with time disciplines. They may mobilize with others to control the pace of work and beat the system with clever ploys, or they may act independently yet be co-opted as when they "make out"—a process that Michael Burawoy (1979) describes in *Manufacturing Consent* (reproducing the work of Donald Roy) to denote the "games" workers play to achieve levels of production that earn incentive pay.

Thus, we are suggesting that the sociology of time incorporates both the cultural and structural elements related to time in society (Coser and Coser 1963; Nowotny 1992). As we noted above, far from accepting time as an absolute, humans have defined, altered, and stretched it (Zerubavel 1981; Adam 1995). People attribute spiritual as well as practical meanings to time, and hierarchies of control and power are reflected in its distribution.

Although the chapters focus on the use and meaning of time in the workplace, they also have wider relevance for other sectors of social life. Indeed, the analyses show how conceptions regarding time measurement at work are embedded in larger structures and interact with other parts of the social system. Some of these papers propose to dispel myths about time, some offer a different angle of vision that makes us question widely accepted categorizations, and some inform us about the ways in which time is used as a social mechanism.

We have grouped the chapters loosely in three, somewhat overlapping, sections. The first section contains three chapters that address debates about changes in the hours that people work and the scheduling of these hours, and the impacts of these changes on workers and their families. The chapters in the second section discuss how issues of time are related to the organization and control of work. Time is a key component of managerial strategies that, for example, encourage employees to work hard and that emphasize, alternately, long or short planning horizons. The third group of chapters examines how ideologies of time, or "time norms," influence the conceptualization and consequences of gender and work.

Here we offer an overview of the issues and chapters included in each of these sections.

## CHANGES IN WORKING TIME AND TIMING AND CONSEQUENCES FOR INDIVIDUALS AND FAMILIES

How hard do people actually work? In this "good-time" culture in which TV ads bombard us with images of people on the beach, drinking Coke or beer, or going on cruises, television does not show many individuals burning the midnight oil on a work project unless they are nerds who will be saved by the sponsor's product, such as a cell phone company or Federal Express. Only mad scientists in films offer a picture of the work-obsessed individuals who today are well represented in professional and technical workplaces. Yet we all know individuals (perhaps they are we?) who engage in work heroics such as working in marathon sessions on a computer project or a film, writing a book, or building something. What drives them? Some are seeking fame or fortune. Others, having internalized the "Protestant Ethic," work hard as a way of life, or they may feel that it is a professional obligation to work very hard. Some are not interested in leisure-time activities. Or, perhaps they are escaping the humdrum or stress of family life (Hochschild 1997).

Are most people working harder and longer than ever before? Is there less free time to devote to family and leisure activities? Jacobs and Gerson summarize the key findings from their project on changes in paid working time and its consequences for work and family in the United States. They briefly review the debate over trends in working time: whereas Juliet Schor (1991) argues that working time has increased at the expense of leisure, John Robinson and Geoffrey Godbey (1999) respond that leisure time has actually expanded. Jacobs and Gerson argue that no single trend, neither the growth of leisure nor the rising time demands of work, can be said to characterize the whole U.S. economy. Instead, social changes in the organization of work and family life have affected different groups of workers and those living in different family situations in disparate ways. To support their argument, they show the following:

The length of the work week (rather than the work year) is the key to understanding pressures on working families.

Average working time has remained relatively constant over the last several decades, but the dispersion of the time different workers spend on the job has increased: some are working very long hours, while others face shortened workweeks.

Differences in working time are linked to sharp and growing educational disparities, with well-educated workers more likely to put in very long work weeks.

The dramatic shift from single- to dual-income households has created a marked increase in the joint paid working time of couples and a decrease in the time that neither spouse is working, thus creating a "leisure pinch" for many American families.

Couples in the United States tend to face significantly longer work weeks than their European counterparts.

A significant proportion of American workers, and especially those who have very long work weeks, would prefer to work less.

Jacobs and Gerson's analysis points to the need to abandon the search for one overarching trend in favor of theoretical explanations that examine how economic transformations have created varied time constraints and dilemmas for workers and their families. It also suggests that most Americans do not wish to avoid family life through work, but rather are seeking a reasonable, if elusive, balance between paid work and family pursuits.

Although most research on working time has focused on how many hours people work, a growing number of studies have emphasized the importance of considering the timing of those hours. The latter focus is represented by the other two chapters in this section, which address the question of people's work schedules. These authors suggest that the timing of work—not so much the number of hours one works—is important for the quality of family and personal life: working forty hours on a nine-to-five, Monday-through-Friday schedule has very different implications for one's health and the ability to participate in family activities than working forty hours on the night shift or irregularly during the month. Particularly salient for an individual's health and quality of family relations is the degree to which workers are able to control their work schedules.

Harriet Presser's chapter draws on her research and new book on the "24/7 economy" (Presser 2003). She discusses recent national data on nonstandard work schedules such as evening and night shifts and varying and rotating hours in the United States. She notes that in the late 1990s, less than a third of employed Americans worked a "standard workweek," defined as thirty-five to forty hours a week. Only slightly more than half regularly worked a fixed daytime schedule, on all five weekdays, for a specific number of hours. She argues that the expansion of nonstandard work schedules results from at least three interrelated factors: a changing economy, especially the growth of the service sector; demographic changes such as the postponement of marriage and the rise in real family income that has accompanied dual-earner households, developments that have increased the demand for entertainment and recreation during late hours and weekends; and new technologies such as computers, cell phones, and faxes, which have made it possible for people to work on a twenty-four–seven basis. She then highlights some of the social implications of the growth of nonstandard work schedules, such as their often negative impact on a variety of aspects of family life. Presser finally identifies key elements of a research agenda that is needed to understand better the advantages and costs of non-standard work schedules.

Of particular importance for understanding the consequences of working nonstandard schedules is the individual's degree of control over when he or she works. Workers who can control when they work have more flexibility and thus tend to experience fewer of the negative effects associated with working nonstandard schedules. Rudy Fenwick and Mark Tausig (chapter 4) examine the consequences of various types of shift work and schedule flexibility on the physical and mental health of workers as well as their families and social lives outside work. They begin by reviewing and evaluating previous research into these subjects along two distinct paths. The first is an epidemiological literature that focuses on the physiological adjustment problems faced by workers on nonstandard shifts, particularly those working nights or rotating shifts. Workers on these shifts have been found to be at increased risk of having various health problems because of disruptions to their circadian rhythms and sleeping and eating patterns. A second research path has investigated the social and psychological adjustment problems of shift work for workers. These problems are seen as especially acute for workers in particular types of families and family roles—for example, single mothers and dual-career parents—because of increased difficulties of coordinating work and family roles and activities. On the other hand, coordination between work and family is enhanced and stress is reduced when workers have some choice or flexibility about when to start and end their shifts. Furthermore, as Fenwick and Tausig suggest, the effects of scheduling flexibility on reducing worker stress go beyond coordination. Flexibility gives workers some control over their work time, and this control in itself is beneficial. Thus, flexibility and control over one's time can be conceptualized as a dimension of "job control" that is similar in its positive effects on workers to the effects of control over one's work content—for both social life and health. Using this broader conceptualization of flexibility they then compare its effects on worker stress (as measured by health and family outcomes) to the effects of actual clock times worked, using illustrative data such as the 1977 Quality of Employment Survey and the 1997 National Study of the Changing Workforce. These data also enable them to look at changes in work schedules and their effects on worker stress over the past quarter century.

## TIME AND THE ORGANIZATION OF WORK

Time is central to a number of features of the employment relationship and the organization and control of work. Power relations at work inevitably have a temporal component, and social scientists have long recognized that control over the use of time underlies the organization of production practices and power relations in the workplace (see the reviews in Blyton, Hassard, Hill, and Starkey 1989 and Hassard 1990). The realization that time is a potentially valuable resource—Benjamin Franklin long ago noted that time is money—led managers to try to maximize the amount of work expected of their employees in a given unit of work time by means of the so-called "scientific management" of work procedures and the design of work organizations to elicit as much labor as possible for given units of labor power. Workers have often resisted this, and questions about who controls the amount of time workers spend at work have been central to labor-management struggles concerning the definition and length of the workday.

The writers in this section broaden the concepts defining our experience with time and the organization and control of work. They question accepted categories that are time-linked. They probe the ways in which time categories alter people's sense of themselves and whether they feel comfortable or uncomfortable with it. Further, they examine the consequences of managerial strategies designed around notions of time.

Allen Bluedorn and Stephen Ferris (chapter 5) propose the concept "temporal depth" to describe a perspective people have when contemplating past events or when proposing activities and plans for the future. When managers are able to plan ahead, their notion of "the future" is calculated according to cultural views of what is the proper, relevant time period. For example, managers in Japanese firms typically have been able to think long-term, unlike American managers, who are more often subjected to short-run pressures generated by investors who keep a close eye on quarterly stock market returns. Moreover, managers' time perspectives are also affected by the age of their organization; managers in firms with a long history may plan for a longer future than firms created recently. People in old organizations, Bluedorn and Ferris note, see themselves as part of an ongoing and continuous historical process, so the decisions they make about the future may be different than those made by persons who see themselves as creatures of the moment. Thus the calculus about the pay-off for investments may have different meanings for individuals in organizations of different ages. Bluedorn and Ferris demonstrate that temporal depth "matters": they find that after they controlled for organizational size, age, and the dimensions of the organizational environment, temporal depth was significantly related to measures of organizational performance such as capital expenditures and one financial performance ratio, earnings per share.

As in the rest of life, organizational time is measured not only in years, but by quarters, months, weeks, days, hours, and minutes. Depending on the organization, each measure carries value beyond that of money. Prestige, satisfaction, and commitment are also associated with the performance of activity (work) within the parameters of a time period.

Individuals and groups determine how time is measured and the value attached to its pace. One of the newest forms of measurement—one that is loaded with symbolism and has the consequence of controlling people at work—is the billable hour. Now used by law firms and consulting firms to charge clients for service and also to evaluate the productivity of their staffs, the billable hour has become fraught with meaning. The number of billable hours a person accrues and whether or not the number is above, at, or below the norm has a lot to do with whether a person is defined as being on a partnership track, doing excellent work, and being committed to the work organization. Many observers (Galanter and Palay 1991; Epstein et al. 1995; Yakura 2001) have illustrated how billable hours become a proxy for excellence and commitment. The commodification of time may have many and far-reaching unintended consequences (see Yakura 2001).

The commodification of time in another domain is the theme of Benjamin Stewart's (chapter 6) discussion of the urban bicycle messenger industry, an industry that produces the commodity—speed. He shows that the low-tech bicycle offers considerable advantages over other forms of delivery and is actually the fastest mode of transportation in congested urban areas. Bicycle messengers are continually urged to go faster in order to deliver their packages. This need for speed, coupled with the congestion and other difficulties characteristic of the urban environment, lead to physical and emotional stresses on the messengers. One way stress is reduced—and messengers maintain their interest in their work—is by game-like activities such as riding bicycles without brakes and trying to figure out the optimal ways to reach a destination. In addition, messenger races (known as "alley cats") provide a way that messengers can obtain recognition for their speed-riding skills. These races contribute to the establishment of a bicycle messenger culture that illustrates vividly how work behaviors may spill over into nonwork activities.

While most of the studies on work intensification have sought to identify trends and assess their consequences, relatively few have attempted to explain the causes of these trends. This is the focus of Ofer Sharone's (chapter 7) research on high-tech software engineers in a large American technology firm, which seeks to explain the causes of the increase in work hours that has been documented by Jacobs and Gerson, among others. He shows how workers in this industry, although theoretically free to work at their own pace, tend to extend their work hours, putting in fifty-to-seventy-hour weeks. Building on the work of Michael Burawoy (1979) and Gideon Kunda (1992), which demonstrated that some workers exceed management standards because of competition with their own performances, or because of a culture that places a high valence on exacting standards, Sharone shows how a culture of excellence and a structure of comparative performance create the individual "choice" to work very hard. The pattern he observes of "competitive self-management" has established itself in many organizational settings. His in-depth interviews suggest that the rapidly spreading management practice of assigning employees relative performance "scores" along a bell-shaped curve—a normal distribution curve—is an important cause of long work hours. He claims that the practice of curved grading generates intense anxiety among the engineers regarding their relative professional status, which in turn drives them to self-impose long work hours. Like the study by Mary Blair-Loy (chapter 10), Sharone concludes that the seemingly independent "choices" of individuals to work hard emanate from highly structured cultural mandates and social norms. Both these scholars observe how people often base their feelings of self-esteem on fulfilling socially structured evaluation systems.

Time boundaries of age have multiple consequences in today's economy. This is illustrated by David Collinson and Margaret Collinson's (chapter 8) examination of the multiple consequences of age and gender boundaries in a downsizing economy. Drawing on their research in the financial services sector in Britain, they explore some of the ways that temporality and power intersect within organizational and managerial practices. They first look at restructuring and the layoffs that result in management grades, noting these have created much shorter tenures within the organization. They note the concentration of layoffs (the "delayering" of management) among people over the age of forty, with the result that managers over fifty are becoming a rarity in many sectors. This has consequence for the rising significance of a management youth culture in which attributes of youth are privileged, celebrated, and valorized and attributes of higher age are devalorized. They then examine work intensification for all levels of employees. Flatter hierarchies and leaner management in terms of numbers result in the need for managerial survivors to work longer hours and have an almost "permanent" presence within the organization. This time-related mandate of work intensification reinforces the masculine culture within management. Finally, the authors consider the issue of a balance between work and home obligations, exploring the industry under analysis to see what kinds of managerial survival strategies are employed to meet the requirements of the work environment.

## TIME NORMS, GENDER, AND WORK

Time norms have consequences for role behaviors during specific time periods. It is obvious that people assume their roles as managers, teachers, or factory workers when they go to the workplace at a particular time of day. Work "starts" at a time set by tradition or rules, and people become workers when they set foot in the door of the office or factory, often behaving differently than they would if they were acting as a coach for their child's soccer team or helping to fix a car as a neighbor. Similarly, when work ends, and they leave their places of work and go home, they assume their "nonwork" roles. Of course, people in some occupations or at various levels of the work hierarchy may take work home, carrying papers in their briefcases, or staying on call through their cell phones or pagers. Thus, time boundaries may activate social roles and terminate them, although there is considerable opportunity for spillover effects. In these instances time boundaries and activation of roles are highly articulated.

Time norms not only set boundaries around work activity but also, when they interact with factors related to gender, age, and race, contribute to keeping people in their place socially and even literally. When German women are required to be at home because their children's school day ends at one P.M. this has an impact on their ability to pursue demanding work in the economy; when older people are reminded that they are blocking the ascent of talented young people in a university and should retire, they may feel forced to do so while they still have contributions to make; when African Americans must work late but cannot find adequate transportation home because taxi drivers do not wish to go into black neighborhoods, this may limit their work opportunities. These examples illustrate how time boundaries enforce various social statuses.

The three chapters in this section examine how time norms influence conceptions of gender and consequences such as overwork and the ability of people to cross boundaries that define what is appropriate for men and women.

Peter Levin's chapter on commodity traders presents a microcosm of time-related social boundaries that make gender very salient in a work situation (chapter 9). He demonstrates how, in the commodities exchange he studied, behavior repertoires become activated or deactivated depending on the pace of work. There, women and men traders, engaged in high-demand work that requires constant alertness, worked side by side and behaved very much the same. The setting was dominated by a male culture in which ribald humor and off-color comments peppered discourse, and women engaged in similar behavior and were treated rather alike. During busy times references to gender were framed in language that conceptualized the trading floor as gender-neutral even as it privileged a particular form of dominant masculinity. When things slowed down, the dynamic changed. Levin's contribution to our understanding of time-activating sequences is his noticing that when the pace eased up on the trading floor, many men referred to the women in their midst in gender-related terms, commenting on their sexual attributes and highlighting sex difference. The change of pace allowed men to consider women as sex objects rather than as coworkers doing the same tasks.

Time norms enforce gender distinctions in other ways. Time priorities and gender are always linked. What men and women do at various time of the day is guided by expectations and controls, as we shall discuss later. But even cultural views about what people ought to be able to do within a time period have their consequences.

Holding social statuses defined as being disharmonious may make individuals feel anxious. Today, as the media focus on problems women may encounter combining jobs and motherhood, women become anxious about time management. The power of conceptualization of time allocation has been suggested by Jeffrey Thompson and J. Stuart Bunderson (2001) in a paper questioning the concept of work-family conflict. They point out that some individuals with a large number of time demands may feel stressed while others with the same amount may feel productively busy. Certainly whether we like what we are doing and whether people close to us think we are doing the "right" thing has something to do with this. Today, women in particular, but also families in which both parents are in the workforce are said to face stress through role overload because of the conflict between the time demands of work and family. In the workplace, the media, and the academy attention is directed at the proper "balance" of time allotted to carrying out the obligations and responsibilities created by work and family roles. However, little attention is paid to the success stories of families in which men and women manage work and family obligations successfully (Barnett and Baruch 1985; Moen 2003). Certainly the work-family conflict model has become a hot-button topic, especially for women, as evidenced by the many conferences devoted to this issue and magazine articles that suggest that women who work are invariably under stress.

Curiously, the notion of work-family conflict is a relatively new one. It was not generated simply by women's entry into the paid labor market—women were there long before the term was used to describe the problem. Were our great-grandmothers faulted, or did we feel sympathy for them when they worked on the family farm, cooked for the farm hands, raised chickens, and took care of babies? We regarded what they did as natural. Only when women began to take on high-profile work assignments for high pay did the idea that work and family are inevitably in conflict become a matter of public attention. If what we do is self-affirming and consistent or supportive of our identities then we will not experience conflict but may see our lives as multifaceted and rich.

Although some time norms are informally drawn or seem to arise automatically from work situations, others are highly specified. Required hours of work, such as the eight-hour day and the five-day workweek, determine formal boundaries, and often in addition reinforce a standard by which a worker is deemed to be a good worker and to be doing his or her fair share of the work. Organizations have, therefore, a standard by which "overtime" or "part-time" may be determined. Furthermore, individuals are often evaluated according to whether they work over or under the standard. Thus they may be called overachievers, or workaholics or, at the other end of the continuum, shirkers, lacking ambition, or off-track in their careers. These issues are of deep concern today as the standard workweek for some categories of workers, such as managers and professionals, has been steadily increasing. Yet as more and more women are coming into the work place, these time demands may conflict with family roles and also the needs of children. For women more than men, part-time work schedules offer the opportunity both to work productively although at a decelerated pace and to spend time with children. It often costs them career advancement, however (Epstein et al. 1999).

The matter of how hard people work is to some extent gendered: generally it is men rather than women who represent the overachievers and workaholics who put in the long hours. Of course, some women also fit this profile, although there are not believed to be many of them. Women who are overachievers in their unpaid work at home are regarded as engaging in appropriate activity, but men are regarded as strange if they are invested in home-based work to the exclusion of compensated work. Thus we see that individuals' choices are hardly a product only of their own personalities and history but rather are heavily affected by social values and norms.

Mary Blair-Loy notes the competition between devotion to work and to motherhood for many women who have successful careers in finance. She discusses how the seemingly independent "choices" of individuals to work hard emanate from highly structured cultural mandates and social norms (which she calls schemas) that inspire, organize, and justify work dedication, whether in the home or at the workplace. Although women who work as homemakers often view their choice as "natural," it is often the case that they have left the paid workforce to work uncompensated at home. She maintains that the cultural facets of structure help define people's moral identities and their desires about how to spend their waking hours. The pressures on mothers to reduce work hours and spend more on mothering follow a cultural prescription that may not bring them fulfillment but that does reduce their guilt. Mothers who do not reduce their work hours conform to a work-devotion schema, but have to tolerate their own feelings of guilt, which may contribute to their sense of work-family conflict.

Blair-Loy's analysis questions scholars' implicit equation of long work hours with "overwork" as well as the assumptions, embedded in the terms "work-life balance" and "work-life conflict," that work is *not* one's life and that long work hours sap one's life. She illustrates some of the conditions under which these assumptions do and do not hold true for the case of women finance executives, whose schema demands long work hours, allegiance, and single-minded dedication while promising them financial rewards, social status, warm collegial relationships, interesting work, intensity, and even transcendence. Respondents do not experience long work hours as "overwork" as long as their faith in the work-devotion schema remains strong. Immersion in work allows them to transcend ordinary time and exalts them to an almost timeless realm of purpose and meaning. To say that these women lack "work-life balance" is beside the point; work *is,* in large part, their life. Yet about half of Blair-Loy's sample members have lost their faith in the schema and have come to resent the time their careers demand. For them, work ceases to provide "an adrenaline flow" of meaning and becomes grueling. Whether or not respondents retain faith in this schema is associated with whether they have reached very senior positions or have languished at mid-senior levels. A robust faith in the work-devotion schema is likely both a cause and a consequence of career advancement.

Cynthia Fuchs Epstein (chapter 11) explores how the link between time norms in society and gender roles makes it difficult for individuals to cross the occupational and social boundaries associated with their sex. She points out that professional women with heavy work schedules and men oriented to sharing child care in the home each face social disapproval for spending "too much" time at activities not regarded as their primary obligation. Even women who work part-time find they elicit disapproval from their fellow workers; and men who take off time during the workday to engage in child care find that their loyalty and competence is challenged by their superiors at work and by stay-at-home mothers in their communities. Epstein analyzes the ordering of time priorities and flexibility in deviating from cultural norms, and notes how time norms control an individual's ability to privately negotiate time allocations and solve time conflicts in innovative ways.

## CONCLUSION

The analysis of time and its relationship to work and the workplace has a long history and no doubt will inspire thoughtful consideration in the future. The essays extend our thinking about some issues that have been inspired by the social conditions of our day—the acceleration of demands at work and in the home, the control and evaluation of work effort, and the appropriateness of the work activity and social supports for it. In doing so they identify basic issues such as the ways we think about the value of work performed at particular places and times of the day, and by individuals who belong to particular groups or social categories. The essays also focus on the power of particular concepts or metaphors (such as work-family conflict) as we plan and evaluate the scholarship on time that appears in professional journals and in the popular media. These chapters thus offer new ways to think about time as a variable in analyzing the workplace and its impact on and interaction with other cultural and structural factors in society.

The chapters also have implications for public policy designed to regulate time at work and its consequences. In particular, policies designed to give workers greater control over the scheduling of their work are likely to alleviate some of the pressures associated with work intensification.

As noted, these essays certainly will not be the last word on the areas where they direct our attention. Nevertheless, these writers inform us of some of the central theoretical and policy-relevant issues raised by the intersection of time and work—issues that are

likely to grow in importance as the twenty-first century progresses—
and contribute to the lively and ongoing discussion.

## REFERENCES

Adam, Barbara. 1995. *Timewatch: The Social Analysis of Time*. New York: Polity Press.

Barnett, Rosalind, and Grace Baruch. 1985. "Women's Involvement in Multiple Roles and Psychological Distress." *Journal of Personality and Social Psychology* 49(1): 135–48.

Blyton, Paul, John Hassard, Stephen Hill, and Ken Starkey. 1989. *Time, Work, and Organization*. New York: Routledge.

Braudel, Fernand. 1982–84/1992. *Civilization and Capitalism*. Translated from the French by Sian Reynolds. Berkeley: University of California Press.

Burawoy, Michael. 1979. *Manufacturing Consent: Changes in the Labor Process Under Monopoly Capitalism*. Chicago: University of Chicago Press.

Coser, Lewis, and Rose Laub Coser. 1963. "Time Perspectives and Social Structure." In *Modern Sociology,* edited by Alvin Gouldner and Helen Gouldner. New York: Harcourt Brace Jovanovich.

Durkheim, Emile. 1902/1947. *The Division of Labor in Society*. Reprint, Glencoe, Ill.: Free Press.

Epstein, Cynthia Fuchs. 2002. "Stricture and Structure: The Social and Cultural Context of Pro Bono Work in Wall Street Firms." *Fordham Law Review* 70(5, April): 1689–98.

Epstein, Cynthia Fuchs, and Arne L. Kalleberg. 2001. "Time and the Sociology of Work: Issues and Implications." *Work and Occupations* 28(1): 5–16.

Epstein, Cynthia Fuchs, and Robert Sauté, Bonnie Oglensky, and Martha Gever. 1995. "Glass Ceilings and Open Doors: Women's Mobility in the Legal Profession." *Fordham Law Review* 64(2): 291–449.

Epstein, Cynthia Fuchs, Carroll Seron, Bonnie Oglensky, and Robert Sauté. 1999. *Paradox: Time Norms, Professional Life, Family, and Gender*. New York: Routledge.

Ermath, Elizabeth Deeds. 1991. *Sequel to History: Postmodernism and the Crisis of Representational Time*. Princeton: Princeton University Press.

Fraser, Jill Andresky. 2001. *White-Collar Sweatshop: The Deterioration of Work and Its Rewards in Corporate America*. New York: Norton.

Fukuyama, Francis. 1992. *The End of History and the Last Man*. New York: Penguin.

Galanter, Marc, and Thomas M. Palay. 1991. *Tournament of Lawyers: The Transformation of the Big Law Firm*. Chicago: University of Chicago Press.

Hassard, John. 1990. "Introduction: The Sociological Study of Time." In *The Sociology of Time*. New York: St. Martin's Press.

Hochschild, Arlie R. 1997. *The Time Bind: When Work Becomes Home and Home Becomes Work*. New York: Metropolitan Books.

Jameson, Frederic. 1994. *The Seeds of Time*. New York: Columbia University Press.

Kalleberg, Arne L., and Cynthia Fuchs Epstein. 2001. "Temporal Dimensions of Employment Relations." *American Behavioral Scientist* 44(7): 1064–75.

Kalleberg, Arne L., Barbara F. Reskin, and Ken Hudson. 2000. "Bad Jobs in America: Standard and Nonstandard Employment Relations and Job Quality in the United States." *American Sociological Review* 65(2): 256–78.

Kunda, Gideon. 1992. *Engineering Culture: Control and Commitment in a High Tech Corporation*. Philadelphia: Temple University Press.

Lareau, Annette. 2003. *Unequal Childhoods: Class, Race, and Family Life*. Berkeley: University of California Press.

Lasch, Christopher. 1977. *Haven in a Heartless World: The Family Besieged*. New York: Basic Books.

Mannheim, Karl. 1952. "The Problem of Generation." In *Essays in the Sociology of Knowledge,* edited by Paul Kecskemeti. London: Routledge & Kegan Paul.

Melbin, Murray. 1987. *Night as Frontier: Colonizing the World After Dark*. New York: Free Press.

Merton, Robert K. 1984. "Socially Expected Durations: A Case Study of Concept Formation in Sociology." In *Conflict and Consensus: A Festschrift in Honor of Lewis A. Coser,* edited by Walter W. Powell and Richard Robbins. New York: Free Press.

Moen, Phyllis. 2003. *It's About Time: Couples and Careers*. Ithaca, N.Y.: Cornell University Press.

Nowotny, Helga. 1992. "Time and Social Theory: Towards a Theory of Time." *Time and Society* 1(3): 421–54.

Presser, Harriet B. 2003. *Working in a 24/7 Economy: Challenges for American Families*. New York: Russell Sage Foundation.

Robinson, John, and Geoffrey Godbey. 1999. *Time for Life: The Surprising Ways Americans Use Their Time*. 2nd ed. University Park: Pennsylvania State University Press.

Schor, Juliet. 1991. *The Overworked American: The Unexpected Decline of Leisure*. New York: Basic Books.

Scott, Joan Wallach. 1988 *Gender and the Politics of History*. New York: Columbia University Press.

Sorokin, Pitirim A., and Robert K. Merton. 1937. "Social Time: A Methodological and Functional Analysis." *American Journal of Sociology* 42(5): 615–29

Thompson, Jeffrey A., and J. Stuart Bunderson. 2001. "Work-Nonwork Conflict and the Phenomenology of Time: Beyond the Balance Metaphor." *Work and Occupations* 28(1): 17–39.

Veyne, Paul. 1984. *Writing History: Essay on Epistemology*. Translated by Mina Moore-Rinvolucri. Middletown, Conn.: Wesleyan University Press.

Yakura, Elaine K. 2001. "Billables: The Valorization of Time in Consulting." *American Behavioral Scientist* 44(7): 1076–95.

Zerubavel, Eviatar. 1981. *Hidden Rhythms: Schedules and Calendars in Social Life*. Chicago: University of Chicago Press.

# — PART I —

# CHANGES IN WORKING TIME AND TIMING AND CONSEQUENCES FOR INDIVIDUALS AND FAMILIES

— Chapter 2 —

# Understanding Changes in American Working Time: A Synthesis

## Jerry A. Jacobs and Kathleen Gerson

TIME ON THE job is a central and increasingly contested terrain in the lives of Americans. Working time sets the framework for both work and family life, and since time is not an expandable resource, long hours at the workplace must inevitably take time away from the rest of life. Long schedules of sixty hours a week or more mean that a worker is forced to scramble for time at home, inevitably missing even simple daily rituals such as breakfast or dinner with family and friends. Yet short workweeks of thirty hours or less, which offer more time for private pursuits, are not likely to provide the financial support most families need. Working time is thus basic to understanding broader aspects of changes in work-family relationships.

Many Americans appear to feel more pressed for time than ever before. Since the early 1990s, when Juliet Schor's *The Overworked American* (1991) hit a nerve in the American imagination, popular and academic concern about the time squeeze has continued to grow. The sense that the pace of life is increasingly hectic has prompted a burgeoning field of research on the difficulties facing contemporary workers as they try to resolve the competing demands of work and family.

Curiously, despite the concern for time-squeezed Americans, official statistics suggest that little if any change has occurred in the average workweek over the last several decades. Some time-diary researchers, such as John Robinson and Geoffrey Godbey (1999), have even argued that a more important trend is the growth of leisure time. Does this mean that the common perception is simply wrong? Are the statistics skewed for some reason? Do the time squeezes of contemporary life stem from other social changes rather than from working time per se? How can we reconcile these divergent views?

This essay offers a framework for resolving these debates and apparent contradictions. Drawing on findings presented in our book, *The Time Divide: Work, Family and Gender Inequality* (Jacobs and Gerson 2004), it presents some of our most central conclusions about how to understand the causes, contours, and consequences of changes in working time over the last several decades.[1] In so doing, we aim to offer a more inclusive and coherent picture of these important social trends. Our analysis shows that time pressures are indeed real, but they have different roots than those suggested by Schor. We also find that no single trend can capture the variety of changes that characterize the labor force as a whole. Instead, it is more useful to see time as a new form of social inequality that is dividing a number of groups in our society—the overworked and the underemployed, men and women, and parents and nonparents, to mention a few. For this reason, it is crucial to move beyond a focus on national averages to look carefully at the way work is increasingly divided into longer and shorter workweeks. We also need to pay attention to the ways that family change has created different time pressures for different types of households. Across occupational contexts and demographic groups there is growing variation in the time demands confronting workers and their families. Once we pay attention to the complexity of our increasingly diverse labor force and family structures, the pieces of the puzzle fall into place.

## TRENDS IN THE WORKWEEK

Although it may come as a surprise to most, the average length of the workweek has remained remarkably constant over the last thirty years. According to our analysis of the March Current Population Survey, a large national survey conducted monthly that forms the basis for many of the nation's labor-force data, the average man worked about 43.5 hours a week for pay in 1970; his counterpart in

2000 worked 43.1 hours. For employed women, the average work-week was 37.0 hours in 1970 and 37.1 hours in 2000 (see table 2.1).

We know that working time partly reflects the state of the economy, with the workweek shrinking during a recession and expanding during boom times, but what is remarkable is how slight these variations have been despite large changes in the nature of American economic life.[2] Reflecting the sluggish economy, from 2000 to 2002 men's average working hours declined less than one hour per week (0.7 hours), and women's hours declined less than half an hour (0.4 hours).[3] Even during the more severe recession of the early 1980s, the average workweek for men lost just over one hour per week and that for women, less than half an hour.

Another important component of working time is vacation time, which has grown slightly for some groups and remained roughly constant for others. In 1997, those with one year of service with a firm received an average of just under two weeks of vacation time, while those with five years of service received 13.8 vacation days on average, up from 12.4 days in 1980. Those with ten years of service received just over three weeks of vacation, and those with twenty years of service received four weeks on average. Thus, it typically takes American workers twenty years of continuous service with one firm to obtain four weeks of paid vacation, and many

TABLE 2.1  **Hours Worked per Week by Male and Female Nonfarm-Wage-Earning and Salaried Workers, 1970 and 2000**

|  | Total Hours Worked (Mean) | Percentage Working Less Than Thirty Hours per Week | Percentage Working More Than Fifty Hours per Week |
|---|---|---|---|
| Men |  |  |  |
| 1970 | 43.5 | 4.5% | 21.0% |
| 2000 | 43.1 | 8.6 | 26.5 |
|  |  |  |  |
| Women |  |  |  |
| 1970 | 37.0 | 15.5 | 5.2 |
| 2000 | 37.1 | 19.6 | 11.3 |

*Source:* Authors' estimates based on the March 1970 and 2000 Current Population Survey data.

never attain this degree of continuity in employment. Even those who do enjoy substantially less vacation time than workers in many European countries, where five- and six-week vacations are the legal standard for most. The vacation time enjoyed by American workers is surely paltry compared to that of other postindustrial nations, but it does not appear to have worsened substantially in recent years. Of course, we cannot know if changes have occurred in American workers' use of the vacation time they have accrued, but we have found that most employees take most of the time that they are offered.

## The Growing Dispersion of Working Time

Though the length of the average workweek and average vacation time have changed only slightly, this overall stability can be misleading. The puzzle remains: If there is no substantial change in these averages, why do so many people feel so busy? In fact, the unchanging average masks a number of important changes that explain why large and growing groups of Americans are more squeezed for time than ever before.

One important trend is the growing dispersion—or variability—in the workweek among different types of jobs and workers. As jobs have diversified, the notion of an average workweek has less meaning than in the past (see table 2.1). In 1970, just under half of both men (48.2 percent) and women (48.5 percent) reported working forty hours a week. By 2000, these figures had dipped to just over two in five (41.0 percent for both men and women). In the same time period, the proportion working very long weeks has increased. In 1970, 21.0 percent of men worked fifty or more hours per week; by 2000, this figure had climbed to 26.5 percent. Among working women, the percentage working fifty or more hours per week rose from 5.2 to 11.3 percent during the same time period. Simultaneously, the percentage of workers who put in relatively short workweeks has also risen.

The busiest occupational groups tend to be professionals and managers. Over one in three men (37.2 percent) who work in professional, technical, or managerial occupations put in fifty hours or more per week on the job, compared to one in five (21.3 percent) in other occupations. For women, the comparable figures are one in six for those in professional and managerial positions, compared to fewer than one in fourteen for other occupations. The gap in working time between the college-educated and those with more limited educational credentials has also grown since 1970. If life seems increasingly fast-paced to the many scholars and observers who write and read about these matters, it is partly because they are members of the group where this experience is indeed quite common.

Thorstein Veblen, writing in 1899, highlighted leisure as a defining feature of an elite lifestyle. By midcentury, however, this long-standing pattern had been reversed, as Harold Wilensky noted in 1963. During the decades since Wilensky wrote about this reversal, the gap between the amount of leisure that the poor have compared to the better-off has grown, with the poor and less educated having more leisure time—whether chosen by them or imposed on them.[4] Thus, life feels busier and is busier for many Americans, especially those in the most highly rewarded occupations, yet alongside this development, a countervailing trend has left other American workers with less time at work than they might need and prefer.[5]

## The Transformation of Family Life

A second, even more fundamental, change has occurred in the demographic composition of American families. Working time looks and feels different from the point of view of whole households than it does from the point of view of individuals. Yet the standard analyses of working time focus on the schedules of individual workers. Although individual schedules are surely the obvious place to start, time squeezes are created and experienced in the context of family units rather than of isolated individuals. A sixty-hour workweek takes on a different meaning for a husband married to a woman who also puts in sixty hours a week on the job than it does for a neighbor with the same working hours whose wife is not employed, or for a single parent, or for a single woman or man. Examining the workweek from the point of view of the whole family, rather than the individual, provides important insights into the way time pressures are experienced.

When we combine the hours of paid work for married couples (see table 2.2), we find that the length of the paid workweek has indeed increased from 52.5 hours per week in 1970 to 63.1 hours

TABLE 2.2  Trends in Joint Hours per Week of Paid Work by Nonfarm Husbands and Wives Aged Eighteen to Sixty-Four, 1970 and 2000

| | Mean Total Hours Worked | Percentage Working Less Than Seventy Hours | Percentage Working More Than One Hundred Hours | Husband's Hours | Wife's Hours |
|---|---|---|---|---|---|
| 1970 | | | | | |
| All couples | 52.5 | 63.4% | 3.1% | 38.9 | 33.6 |
| Both work (35.9 percent) | 78.0 | 24.9 | 8.7 | 44.1 | 33.9 |
| Husband only works (51.4 percent) | 44.4 | 96.0 | 0.0 | 44.4 | 0.0 |
| Wife only works (4.6 percent) | 35.5 | 99.6 | 0.0 | 0.0 | 35.5 |
| Neither works (8.2 percent) | 0.0 | 0.0 | 0.0 | 0.0 | 0.0 |
| 2000 | | | | | |
| All couples | 63.1 | 53.7% | 9.3% | 41.5 | 26.4 |
| Both work (59.6 percent) | 81.6 | 18.9 | 14.5 | 45.0 | 36.6 |
| Husband only works (26.0 percent) | 44.9 | 95.2 | 0.0 | 44.9 | 0.0 |
| Wife only works (7.1 percent) | 37.2 | 97.9 | 0.0 | 0.0 | 37.2 |
| Neither works (7.2 percent) | 0.0 | 100.0 | 0.0 | 0.0 | 0.0 |

*Source:* Authors' estimates based on the March 1970 and 2000 Current Population Survey data.

per week in 2000. This leads to a paradox: the average individual workweek has not changed substantially for either men or women, but the paid workweek of many families has changed significantly. Why? Primarily because women's labor-force participation, particularly married women's, has grown dramatically. In 1970, male-breadwinner families (in which the husband worked for pay and the wife did not) represented a majority, though a small one, of married couples (51.4 percent). By 2000, this group represented barely more than one quarter of married couples (26.0 percent). Dual-earner couples have risen to predominance. In 1970, dual earners represented just over one third of married couples (35.9 percent). By 2000, they represented three in five (59.6 percent). In fact, dual-earner couples today are more common than were male-breadwinner couples thirty years ago.

The workweek of dual-earner couples today is quite similar to that of such couples several decades ago, but there are many more dual-earner couples than there used to be. The vast majority of the change in working time over the last thirty years can be traced to changes in the kinds of families that predominate, rather than changes in working time within these groups. Moreover, in addition to the large change in family types, there also has been a small increase in the workweek for each type of family. Dual-earner families thus put in 81.6 hours per week on the job in 2000, compared with 78.0 hours per week in 1970. Male breadwinners worked 44.4 hours per week on average in 1970 and 44.9 hours per week in 2000.

Single parents, who are overwhelmingly mothers, constitute another important group whose members are truly caught in a time bind. Over one-fifth (21.9 percent) of families were headed by women in 2000, more than double the 1970 percentage (9.9 percent) (U.S. Bureau of the Census 2002). But despite the fact that the proportion of families living in these circumstances rose dramatically, their average workweek actually remained unchanged over three decades: 38.5 hours per week. Although single fathers constitute a much smaller group than single mothers, it is a rapidly growing one, and these men face the same time dilemmas as single mothers. The proportion of families headed by single fathers doubled from 1.2 percent in 1970 to 2.4 percent in 2000 (U.S. Bureau of the Census 2002). Single dads thus work about the same average workweeks as single moms—36.8 hours per week for single fathers in 2000, which represents a drop of two hours since 1970. Here again, despite relatively unchanging average workweeks, the dispersion of working time has grown for single fathers and mothers, as it has for other groups. Being a single parent poses daunting time dilemmas that a growing group of mothers and fathers cannot escape.

## BEYOND WORKING TIME

Changes in the configuration of working time, along with changes in family structure, are central to understanding how and why Americans feel overworked and time-squeezed. Furthermore, the influence of these forces is magnified by other social changes that may be less obvious but are equally important. Some of these changes are linked to ways that jobs are structured, regardless of how much time they demand. Some are linked to changes in private life that have added intensifying time pressures. At the workplace, aspects of work such as intensity, scheduling, and flexibility may matter as much as the time a job takes, especially for those in time-consuming occupations. At home, the social and cultural organization of child care and housework are equally consequential. Changes in working time, then, are best understood as part of a much larger picture.

### Intensity of Work

The intensity of work can be as important as the amount of time it takes. Although it is difficult to measure, work demands may well have intensified in recent decades. Comparatively small changes in working time may thus obscure more subtle changes in the effort, energy, and concentration expected on the job.

Over the course of the twentieth century, the rise of new technologies fueled improvements in labor productivity as they helped raise living standards for most Americans. These changes allowed workers to produce more in a shorter period of time, but they also likely contributed to increasing expectations for more concentrated effort on the job.[6] Corporate downsizing may also have increased the scope of many white-collar jobs, as fewer employees have had to assume broader responsibilities. Thus, a range of factors make it reasonable to conclude that many late-twentieth and early-twenty-first-century workers are putting in more concentrated effort than their counterparts in earlier generations.

Thus, a high-performance employment system that puts pressure on fewer employees to produce more has emerged alongside the growth of dual-earner couples, many of whom are likely to hold such high-demand positions. The result is a collision between the expectations of employers and the ability of workers to maintain the pace that has come to be expected.

## Job Schedules and Evening and Weekend Work

Changes in the way that work is organized, and especially the emergence of "nonstandard" work shifts, add to the growing complexities of balancing work and family time. Work is increasingly taking place at times that were formerly considered private time, such as at night and on weekends. Indeed, Harriet Presser (2003) maintains that we are moving toward a twenty-four-hour, seven-day-a-week economy in which employees are more likely than at any other time since the rise of industrialism to work evenings, nights, rotating shifts, and weekends. Nearly one-fourth of all married couples with at least one earner contain a spouse who works nonstandard hours. That percentage is even higher for those with children, and it rises to 30.6 percent for couples with children under age five. Whether they lack child-care options or the funds to pay for them or simply believe that children should be cared for by their own parents, these couples are crafting a strategy of tag-team parenting to counter the work demands they face. Yet these strategies can exact a toll on relationships and are in fact associated with elevated rates of separation and divorce. Shifting work schedules, along with new technologies such as email and cell phones, contribute to the sense that work increasingly spills over into family life, even as the needs of children become more diffuse and complex.

## Flexibility on the Job

Although the debate over work and family change in America has focused largely on the issue of overwork, amount of time spent working is not the whole story in the workplace, just as it is not the whole story at home. Working time, however important, is only one of several ingredients contributing to both work-family conflict and gender inequality. Workplace structure and culture matter, and workers who enjoy job flexibility and employer support are clearly better off than those who do not.

Thus, flexibility matters. Like actual working time, flexibility also is distributed unequally. Professional jobs tend to make more time demands, but they also offer more flexibility than other jobs, leaving many middle-class and working-class families facing different, if equally perplexing, challenges. Professional workers often put in longer hours, but they have more control and autonomy on the job and more economic resources with which to cope (including hiring help). Working-class families are less likely to put in the longest workweeks, but their jobs are also less likely to afford a flexible weaving of family and work obligations, and they can rely on fewer economic resources to cover the gaps.

Gender is another factor. Even though women and men face many similar personal dilemmas, women also face their own, for inequality persists at the workplace and in the home, leaving women more exposed to the conflicts and pressures of balancing work and family. As women build ever-stronger ties to the workplace and families confront the time squeezes posed by dual-earning arrangements, mothers and fathers must cope with conflicts that are structured not simply by family demands, but more fundamentally by intransigent job constraints. When women and men face similar opportunities, they tend to respond in similar ways. Yet the organization of gender means that, more often than not, the situations confronting women and men present different options and pressures. In the struggle to resolve work-family conflicts, persisting gender inequality continues to place women at a disadvantage. Women not only shoulder more responsibility for domestic work, but also face larger obstacles at the workplace, including less autonomy and flexibility on the job and more pressure to make career sacrifices by cutting back temporarily on time at work in the face of family contingencies.

This pattern also reflects differences in the opportunities and constraints they face. The organization of economic and family life leaves women with both greater pressures and more options to pull back from work. Although the gender gap in earnings has declined and a rising proportion of wives earn as much as or more than their husbands, most couples do not fit this pattern. In about one dual-earner household in five, the wife earns more than her husband, and some of these cases may represent temporary fluctuations in earnings rather than an enduring role reversal.[7] The more common context, in which a husband earns more, encourages mothers to reduce their time at work and fathers to maximize their earnings by working more.

### The Cumulative Influence of Rising Work Pressures

Other aspects of work in addition to the actual time a job demands are adding to the time pressures experienced by American workers. Some jobs require an intensifying work effort; others are structured around nonstandard schedules; and still others involve both inconvenient hours and intense pressures. Control over the conditions of work, especially in the form of autonomy and flexibility on the job, can alleviate some of these strains, especially for those who must put in very long workdays. But these work advantages are distributed unequally, leaving many—especially women and employed parents—with less opportunity to organize their work and family lives as they would prefer.

## BEYOND THE WORKPLACE: INTENSIFYING FAMILY PRESSURES

The other element in the debate as to whether Americans are overworked or in fact have more leisure time than in the past requires looking more closely at basic trends in housework and child care. These family demands and responsibilities pose challenges that are added on to pressures at work.

### Housework and Child Care

At first glance, it might be tempting to conclude that domestic pressures have lessened in recent decades, especially since time-diary studies find that the number of hours spent in housework and child care have dropped. Indeed, the purported growth in leisure discovered by Robinson and Godbey (1999) can be understood principally as a decline in time spent in housework rather than a change in the length of the paid workweek. Thus, it may appear that some groups have experienced a decline in the total amount of paid and unpaid work. A deeper look, however, reveals a more complex picture.

Time-diary studies provide an in-depth picture of the changing contours of housework and thus complement the findings of surveys and census materials.[8] Their finding of a decline in the time families spend in housework can be partly explained by the rise of smaller families and the later ages of first marriage. Since wives spend more time on housework than do single women, delayed marriage contributes to the growth in the population of single women who spend less time doing household chores.

The size of the housework load also depends on family size, and the average number of children in American households has declined since the 1950s. Between 1955 and 1959, the average woman in the United States could expect to have 3.7 children. Today, this figure, known to demographers as the total fertility rate, is at 2.1 (U.S. Bureau of the Census 1979, 2002). Parenting is a time-intensive responsibility, and fewer children means less time spent in child care.

Even so, some offsetting trends have dampened the effect that smaller families might be expected to have on time squeezes. Although people are having fewer children, parents are spending more time with each child (Bianchi 2000). Children are spending less time playing with other children and more time with parents. First, fewer brothers and sisters and fewer children in the neighborhood means less unsupervised play time for groups of children. Concerns about crime also make parents more watchful, even in neighborhoods with relatively low crime rates. More programmed activities for children, especially in the middle class, require more time shuttling them between sports games, music lessons, play dates, and other organized activities, further disrupting a more informal, unstructured flow of family time (Lareau 2002). Alongside these trends there appears to be a growing emphasis on "intensive mothering," which also is concentrated among middle-class families (Hays 1997).

Rising pressures at work thus combine with increasing expectations for parenting to reinforce the time pressures already confronting American families. These pressures are especially concentrated among employed parents. Middle-class families bear the brunt of these new time demands and expectations, but they also are more likely to have flexibility at work, as well as more economic resources to ease the burden in various ways. Working-class families are more likely to have jobs with limited, if any, flexibility and limited financial resources to cushion the parental burden.

## Paid Help, Immigrants, and Child Care

The time pressures experienced by dual-earner and single-parent families require rethinking the demands of the workplace. Indeed, the gap between the demands of the job and the contours and needs of family life has grown increasingly wide. For example, current labor regulations date back to the Fair Labor Standards Act of 1938, when the male-breadwinner family predominated, and even this legislation does not cover most professional and managerial workers. The time has come to restructure paid work to create a far better fit with the needs of contemporary families.

Yet work restructuring, however important, cannot provide a complete resolution to the binds facing families. Alongside more genuinely family-friendly and gender-equal workplaces, parents also need to be able to depend on help from other dedicated, qualified, and well-rewarded caretakers. Twenty-first-century parents cannot realistically provide the sole care for their children and must increasingly turn for help to others, whether in the form of day care outside the home or paid child care within it.

Traditionally, conservatives, uneasy with women's march into the workplace, have raised concerns about the propriety of relying on paid caregivers to help rear children. Recently, however, some feminists have joined the chorus of critics who worry about this strategy. This perspective focuses on how the expansion of opportunities for professional women in the United States and other countries has fueled a demand for nannies and other caretakers, especially in the absence of widely available high-quality publicly sponsored child care. Increasingly, these caretakers are drawn from the ranks of immigrants from poorer countries. It is thus not surprising that attention has turned to concern for the perils posed by an expanded market for domestic workers.[9] From this perspective, immigration is seen more as a new dimension of economic colonialism than as an age-old pursuit of opportunity by poor women and their families. Rich countries—in particular affluent groups within those countries—that once drained poor countries of natural resources and brainpower now are seen to extract caregiving while the children of the immigrants are left behind. Working parents, especially full-time employed mothers, are seen as accomplices in a new form of international exploitation.[10]

In a society that fails to assign appropriate social or economic value to the care of children, all child-care workers, like all involved parents, face disadvantage and discrimination. Indeed, immigrants and other women who work as nannies in private households may be even more vulnerable than those who care for children in public settings, especially if they do not speak English and can count on few friends or relatives for support. Like their American-born counterparts, immigrant domestic workers may be not be paid fairly or regularly and may be physically or emotionally abused. Furthermore—and unlike their American peers—they may also be threatened with deportation if they protest. In addition, the problems facing private domestic workers, whether or not they are immigrants, are especially prone to invisibility because their isolation limits the options for organizing as a group or informing others of their plight.[11]

Though some may be tempted to do so, the deficiencies and dangers of an inadequate child-care system should not be blamed on employed mothers, who all confront perplexing obstacles. Such an approach pits women against each other, making it seem that the economic independence of middle-class women can only come at the expense of poor immigrant women and their children. By framing paid caretaking as the "commodification" of care, this perspective adds to the critique facing all women who hold paid jobs, whether in public workplaces or private homes.[12]

The focus on private child care obscures the more widespread trend toward greater reliance on child-care centers, where the conditions of work and the rights of workers are more visible. In fact, the rise of the rate of employment among middle-class women does not inevitably create a major infusion of foreign nannies. Indeed, published statistics on the U.S. labor force suggest that the largest increase in child-care employment has occurred among workers in child-care centers, not among domestic workers in private households. (Since an unknown portion of domestic workers are undocumented, it is difficult to calculate these comparisons precisely.) Most child-care workers are also born in the United States, with immigrants making up a substantial yet minority proportion only among domestic workers in private households.

Moreover, private household workers constitute a small and declining segment of the U.S. labor force. Table 2.3 shows that the number of domestic workers peaked in 1940 at 2.4 million and declined sharply during the 1960s. It fell below one million for the first time in 2000 and now represents less than 1 percent (0.66 percent) of the labor force. It appears, then, that the prevalence of nannies declined just as married women entered the labor force in ever-growing numbers. Furthermore, of those who work in private households, many are not directly providing child care. In 2000, roughly 275,000 were doing child care in private household settings, whereas the rest were performing other forms of domestic service, such as cooking and cleaning. All of these workers deserve good pay and working conditions, but they are not all caring for children.

These recent labor-force statistics probably miss some immigrants, but they are also more complete than those of earlier censuses. The level of underreporting would have had to grow at a

**TABLE 2.3  Number of Workers in Private Household Employment, 1900 to 2000**

| Year | Private Household Workers | Total Labor Force | Percentage of Labor Force Working in Private Households |
|------|---------------------------|-------------------|--------------------------------------------------------|
| 1900 | 1,579 | 29,030 | 5.44% |
| 1910 | 1,851 | 37,291 | 4.96 |
| 1920 | 1,411 | 42,206 | 3.34 |
| 1930 | 1,998 | 48,686 | 4.10 |
| 1940 | 2,412 | 51,742 | 4.66 |
| 1950 | 1,539 | 58,999 | 2.61 |
| 1960 | 1,825 | 67,990 | 2.69 |
| 1970 | 1,204 | 80,603 | 1.49 |
| 1980 | 1,229 | 97,279 | 1.26 |
| 1990 | 1,023 | 117,914 | 0.87 |
| 2000 | 894 | 135,208 | 0.66 |

*Source:* Census and Current Population Survey data.
*Note:* In thousands.

remarkable rate to offset the marked declines the figures show. These declines can also be found in other studies. Surveys that look at who is taking care of children reinforce the view that nannies represent a small slice of the child-care pie. According to U.S. Census information, 4.8 percent of preschool children in 1991 were cared for in the child's home by a non–family member. The U.S. Census Bureau's 1998 statistics show a downward trend in this arrangement, from 7.0 percent in 1977 to 5.1 percent in 1994 (U.S. Bureau of the Census 1998, 2002). Sandra Hofferth and Deborah Phillips (1987) also report a decline in nanny care between 1965, 1977, and 1982. Clearly, the growth of mothers' labor-force participation has not depended on a growing pool of nannies, whether they are from this country or from poorer countries. Child-care centers have absorbed much of the growing demand for child-care services, and these centers principally employ U.S.-born women workers. Our preliminary estimates from the 2000 census suggest that nearly 90 percent of employees in child-care centers were born in the United States, and about 30 percent of nannies are foreign-born.

There are surely many heart-wrenching cases of immigrant women who leave their own families to care for other people's children, but these cases are not the norm and cannot tell the complete, more complex, story of child care. Rather, most child-care workers are not immigrants, and most immigrants come to the United States seeking opportunities they could not find in their native land. They also are likely to be embedded in a process of chain migration, in which they join a spouse or family member who has already established a base and aid in the effort to bring other family members to their newly chosen home. Indeed, many immigrant women are married either to an immigrant husband also residing in the United States or to a native-born American. Many also either bring their children with them or send for them once they feel settled and secure. To be sure, the wages of all domestic workers in the United States are far too low, but even these modest wages typically exceed what immigrant women could have expected to earn in their country of origin. For these reasons, the image of exploitation also needs to be balanced with a parallel story of opportunity for immigrant women.

All child-care workers, native- and foreign-born, should receive a living wage as well as fair and just working conditions. Living wages for paid caretakers benefit the children as well as the workers. Fair wages reduce turnover, create more satisfied employees, and promote durable relationships that are a key to high-quality care. Unfortunately, American society has yet to provide these conditions in a consistent and egalitarian fashion.

The contours of the child-care quandary are far broader and more complicated than images of disadvantaged foreign workers can capture. American women are coping as best they can within the confines of a system that provides few supports for working mothers, whether they work in an office, a child-care center, or at home. Not a certain subgroup of employed mothers but American society as a whole is responsible for the failure to create child-care supports on a wide scale. Certainly, all care work cannot and need not be done by working parents, and there is nothing inherently wrong with hiring domestic help. If those workers are well paid and respected, they and their families can benefit from the job opportunities afforded by the rise of paid employment for all women.

## SOLVING THE TIME-SQUEEZE PUZZLE

The sense that Americans are overworked and time-squeezed is rooted in basic social changes that are placing increasing pressures on workers and their families. Focusing on average changes in working time contributes to misunderstanding the sources and shape of these new time squeezes, since we find that the average workweek for individual workers has changed very little in the last several decades. This apparent stability, however, masks important changes in the ways that jobs and families are structured. An increasingly heterogeneous workforce has been accompanied by a dispersion in working time, with more jobs requiring either very long or short workweeks. This time divide among jobs tends to be reflected in an occupational divide, with long workweeks concentrated among managerial and professional workers and shorter ones more likely to be found among workers with more modest educational and occupational credentials. To some extent, this occupational divide mirrors a sharpening in income inequality and is linked to other broad institutional shifts in the structure of the workplace such as downsizing, the decline in manufacturing, and the rise of service work.[13]

A second factor contributing to increasing time pressures can be found in the transformation of family life. Even though individual workers may not be putting in significantly longer days at the workplace, family time is squeezed because more household members are employed. The rise of dual-earning couples has contributed to a large increase in the combined working time of married couples, and the rise of single-parent homes has created more households in which one worker is solely responsible for both breadwinning and domestic caretaking.

These developments go a long way to explaining why Americans are more pressed for time, and other work and family changes add additional pressures. Beyond the issue of working time, job structure matters. Job intensity may have increased in many occupations, as nonstandard work schedules have expanded for a growing number of workers. For those in high-pressure jobs, flexibility, autonomy, and control over the conditions of work help ease the difficulties posed by long workweeks, but these privileges tend to be reserved for those at the higher levels of bureaucratic hierarchies. Yet gaining access to these jobs is especially hard for the workers who most need these supports, such as mothers and other women as well as involved parents of either sex.

The other factor in the time squeeze is the configuration of non-work time, for domestic life also involves increasing pressures. Parenting norms emphasizing "intensive" caretaking create unattainable standards for employed mothers and fathers. In the absence of widely available high-quality child care, parents must develop private strategies for coping, including hiring others to care for their children. Though necessary, this strategy has triggered criticism across the political spectrum, adding to the pressures facing middle- and working-class parents alike.

The basic forces creating these time pressures are deeply anchored in our social and economic arrangements. Thus, as we argue in *The Time Divide* (2004), finding solutions will depend on developing broad policies geared to the new needs of twenty-first-century families by altering the basic organization of our work and community institutions, including moving toward a shorter work-week norm, developing a wide array of child-care services and supports, and mandating more family-friendly and gender-equal workplaces. These changes will not be easy to achieve, but they are our best hope for providing genuine resolutions to the time squeezes that confront growing numbers of Americans.

## NOTES

1. For a full presentation of our argument, findings, and analysis, see Jacobs and Gerson (2004).
2. The correlation between the unemployment rate and the length of the workweek is −0.6.
3. These statistics were provided by Randy Ilg of the Bureau of Labor Statistics.
4. Leisure may be a misnomer in this context, since we find that many of these workers would prefer to work more.
5. In *The Time Divide: Work, Family and Gender Inequality,* we show that workers putting in relatively short workweeks (less than thirty-five hours) would generally prefer to work more, while those putting in excessive hours at work (fifty hours or more per week) would generally prefer to work more.
6. The British labor historian Chris Nyland (1989) has suggested, for example, that historical reductions in working time have involved a gradual and concomitant rise in the intensity of work.
7. This figure is based on our estimate using information from the 1997 National Study of the Changing Workplace (Bond, Galinsky, and Swanberg 1998).
8. These different methodologies and data sources have offsetting strengths and weaknesses. For an in-depth discussion of the methodological factors in the measurement of time use by time-diaries, surveys, and other methods, see Jacobs and Gerson (2004).
9. See, for example, Barbara Ehrenreich and Arlie R. Hochschild (2002) and Pierrette Hondagneu-Sotelo (2001).
10. Ehrenreich and Hochschild (2002, 3–4) call this "the female underside of globalization, whereby millions of Josephines from poor countries in the south migrate to do the 'women's work' of the north—work that affluent women are no longer able or willing to do. These migrant workers often leave their own children in the care of grandmothers, sisters and sisters-in-law. . . . The lifestyles of the First World are made possible by a global transfer of the services associated with a wife's traditional role—child care, homemaking, and sex—from poor countries to rich ones."
11. See Hondagneu-Sotelo (2001) and Judith Rollins (1985).

12. The commodification of housework is part of a long history of post-industrial development. New ways of producing domestic goods and services may appear controversial at the outset, but ultimately become widely accepted. We no longer expect mothers to sew their children's clothes, for example, yet we do not define the purchase of clothing as a commodification of care. Similarly, in countries where public childcare is widely available and respected, such as France or Denmark, paying for care is not deemed harmful to the well-being of either children or the people who take care of them.

13. For a discussion of the rise in income inequality, see Robert Lerman (1997).

## REFERENCES

Bianchi, Suzanne M. 2000. "Maternal Employment and Time with Children: Dramatic Change or Surprising Continuity?" *Demography* 37(4): 401–14.

Bond, James T., Ellen Galinsky, and Jennifer E. Swanberg. 1998. *The 1997 National Study of the Changing Workforce.* New York: Families and Work Institute.

Ehrenreich, Barbara, and Arlie R. Hochschild, eds. 2002. *Global Women: Nannies, Maids, and Sex Workers in the New Economy.* New York: Metropolitan Books.

Hays, Sharon. 1997. *The Cultural Contradictions of Motherhood.* New Haven, Conn.: Yale University Press.

Hofferth, Sandra L., and Deborah A. Phillips. 1987. "Child Care in the United States, 1970 to 1995." *Journal of Marriage and the Family* 49(4):559–71.

Hondagneu-Sotelo, Pierrette. 2001. *Domestica: Immigrant Workers Cleaning and Caring in the Shadows of Affluence.* Berkeley and Los Angeles: University of California Press.

Jacobs, Jerry A., and Kathleen Gerson. 2004. *The Time Divide: Work, Family, and Gender Inequality.* Cambridge, Mass.: Harvard University Press.

Lareau, Annette. 2002. "Invisible Inequalities: Class, Race and Child Rearing in Black Families and White Families." *American Sociological Review* 67(5): 747–76.

Lerman, Robert I. 1997. "Is Earnings Inequality Really Increasing?" In *Economic Restructuring and the Job Market.* Brief no. 1 (March). Washington, D.C.: Urban Institute.

Nyland, Chris. 1989. Reduced Worktime and the Management of Production. Cambridge: Cambridge University Press.

Presser, Harriet B. 2003. *Working in a 24/7 Economy: Challenges for American Families.* New York: Russell Sage Foundation.

Robinson, John P., and Geoffrey Godbey. 1999. *Time for Life: The Surprising Ways Americans Use Their Time.* 2nd ed. University Park: Pennsylvania State University Press.

Rollins, Judith. 1985. *Between Women: Domestics and Their Employers.* Philadelphia: Temple University Press.

Schor, Juliet. 1991. *The Overworked American: The Unexpected Decline of Leisure.* New York: Basic Books.

U.S. Bureau of the Census. 1979. *Statistical Abstract of the United States.* Washington: U.S. Government Printing Office.

————. 1998. *Who's Minding the Kids? Child Care Arrangements.* Washington: U.S. Government Printing Office (Spring).

————. 1999. *Who's Minding the Kids? Child Care Arrangements.* Washington: U.S. Government Printing Office (Spring).

————. 2002. *Statistical Abstract of the United States.* Washington: U.S. Government Printing Office.

Veblen, Thorstein. 1899/1994. *The Theory of the Leisure Class.* New York: Penguin Books.

Wilensky, Harold. 1963. "The Uneven Distribution of Leisure: The Impact of Economic Growth on 'Free Time.' " In *Work and Leisure,* edited by Erwin O. Smigel. New Haven, Conn.: College and University Press.

—— Chapter 3 ——

# Employment in a 24/7 Economy: Challenges for the Family

## Harriet B. Presser

O VER RECENT DECADES, the U.S. labor force has been experiencing greater temporal diversity in the nature of employment. The total number of weekly hours people are employed has been spreading to both ends of the continuum, so that more people are working very few as well as very many hours (Smith 1986; U.S. Department of Labor 2002). Which hours people are working has also been changing with flextime on the rise (Golden 2001; U.S. Department of Labor 1998) and more people working the "fringe times"—several hours before or after the traditional nine-to-five workday (Hamermesh 1999). It is interesting that the increasing diversity in the actual time frame of work hours—called temporal diversity—has been occurring while the cumulative number of weekly hours people are employed has remained virtually unchanged between 1970 and 2001 (Rones, Ilg, and Gardner 1997; U.S. Department of Labor 2002).[1]

An important but often neglected aspect of temporal diversity is employment that occurs mostly in the evening or night, or on a rotating basis around the clock. Although we do not have comparable data over time to rigorously assess the trend in nonday work shifts, there are strong indications that such employment is on the rise as we move toward a twenty-four-hour, seven-days-a-week economy. As of 1997, only 29.1 percent of all Americans worked the "standard" workweek: working mostly during the daytime, thirty-five to forty

46

hours per week, Monday through Friday. If one removes the limitation of thirty-five to forty hours and includes those working part-time and overtime, the percentage increases to 54.4 percent—a bare majority (Presser 1999).[2]

As consumers, we witness the movement toward an all-day, every-day economy by observing that stores are increasingly open evenings and nights, it is easier to make travel reservations or order goods with a live voice on the phone at any time of the day or week, and we increasingly expect medical care and other services to be available to us at all times. A new phrase, "24/7" has quickly become common parlance to denote around-the-clock availability. From a consumer perspective, there seem to be few complaints about "colonizing the world after dark," to borrow Murray Melbin's (1987) phrase.

But what does this expansion of economic activity around the clock mean for workers who provide their labor in the evenings, nights, and weekends? And what does it mean for families? While there is a considerable body of research on the individual consequences of shift work, particularly its health consequences (for reviews, see U.S. Congress 1991; Wedderburn 2000), there is a paucity of research on the family consequences of late-hour shifts and weekend employment—what I mean by nonstandard schedules.

In this chapter, I document the prevalence of nonstandard work schedules among employed Americans and consider what this implies for the functioning and stability of family life, drawing primarily on findings from my new book, *Working in a 24/7 Economy: Challenges for American Families* (Presser 2003a), my earlier publications, and reviewing the work of others. The challenges that families with preschool- and school-age children face when parents work nonstandard schedules is discussed in the context of these findings, particularly as they relate to low-income families. I also list some important research needs to fill major gaps in our knowledge.

It is important to acknowledge at the outset that the temporal nature of work life for families is being driven primarily by factors external to the family. As I have described elsewhere (Presser 1999), there are at least three interrelated factors that increase the demand for Americans to work late or rotating shifts and to work on weekends: a changing economy, changing demography, and changing technology. The growth of the service sector of the economy (which has higher proportions working nonstandard schedules than the goods-producing sector) is a critically important factor underlying all of these changes. This growth has been remarkable: in the 1960s, employees in manufacturing greatly exceeded those in service industries, whereas by 1999, the percentage was over twice as high in services as in manufacturing (Hatch and Clinton 2000; Meisenheimer 1998). A related change has been the dramatic increase in women's labor-force participation during this period, especially among married women with children, 70 percent of whom are now employed (U.S. Bureau of the Census 2001, table 578). Not only have women moved disproportionately into the service sector, responding to the growing demand for such workers, but their increased employment in all sectors contributed to this growing demand, as people needed more services at late hours and weekends. For example, the decline in full-time homemaking with greater daytime employment of women has generated an increase in the extent to which family members eat out and purchase other homemaking services. (For elaboration of other relevant factors, see Presser 2003a.)

We have, then, a process whereby macro changes external to the family affect the temporal nature of employment, offering more job opportunities at late and rotating hours as well as on weekends. Out of necessity or preference—and the data suggest mostly the former (Presser 1995, 2003a)—employees increasingly take such jobs, which in turn affect the temporal nature of family life, particularly the "at home" structure of American families in the evenings and nights and on weekends. This is the context in which we should view the challenges of American families generated by the 24/7 economy.

## PREVALENCE OF
## NONSTANDARD WORK SCHEDULES:
## MAY 1997 CURRENT POPULATION SURVEY

National studies describing the prevalence of shift workers—those who work most of their hours in the evening or at night—go back to the early 1970s and are based primarily on special supplements added to the U.S. Census Bureau's Current Population Surveys, or CPS (see, for example, Hedges and Sekscenski 1979). These surveys are based on very large samples (over 50,000 households), making them ideal for assessing prevalence. Over the years, however, the way the work-schedule questions have been asked and the response options allowed have often changed, precluding a rigorous determination of trends over time in the prevalence of work schedules.[3] Also, no questions about weekend employment were asked until 1991. I report here what we know about the prevalence of nonstandard work schedules in 1997—both with regard to shifts and weekend employment.

## Definitions of Work Schedules

First, an important note about defining work schedules. As used in this chapter, work shifts refer to the time period when people work most of their hours. Accordingly, people who work mostly in the day, but also in the evening or night, are considered here to be daytime workers. Estimates of the extent to which people work evenings and nights, whether or not they primarily work days, would be substantially larger than the estimates for evening and night shifts shown here. I prefer to define work shifts as the shift in which most hours are worked, as this provides a sharper distinction between various patterns of employment around the clock, differences that are expected to substantially alter the temporal nature of family life.

In determining what constitutes a specific shift, I have modified the definition used by the Bureau of Labor Statistics of the U.S. Department of Labor (Hedges and Sekscenski 1979; U.S. Department of Labor 1981) to include the recently "hours vary" response option used in 1997.[4]

> *Fixed day:* At least half the hours worked most days in the prior week fall between 8:00 A.M. and 4:00 P.M.
>
> *Fixed evening:* At least half the hours worked most days in the prior week fall between 4:00 P.M. and midnight.
>
> *Fixed night:* At least half the hours worked most days in the prior week fall between midnight and 8:00 A.M.
>
> *Rotating:* Schedules change periodically from days to evenings or nights.
>
> *Hours vary:* An irregular schedule that cannot be classified in any of the above categories.

I define persons as working nonstandard hours when they work other than fixed-day schedules the previous week on their principal job.[5] (The percentage of the employed who are multiple job holders is 7.6 percent; inclusion of the hours of employment on secondary jobs would make little difference in designating shifts, since the definition refers to most hours worked.)

The specific days of the week worked were asked for the principal job, although no reference to last week or usual week is included in the question.[6] However, this information was asked after other questions relating to the usual week were asked. The specific workdays are categorized by specific weekday or weekend combinations. Those who work nonstandard days (weekends) are defined as working on Saturday or Sunday.

It should be noted that we are not addressing here the issue of flextime, in which employees are given the option to vary their beginning and ending hours within a confined range according to their personal preferences. Rather, we are considering the work shift that is typically mandated by employers.

## Estimates of Prevalence of Nonday Employment

Table 3.1 shows, in terms of these definitions, the prevalence of nonday employment for all employed Americans aged eighteen and over in 1997. One-fifth of the employed do not work a fixed daytime schedule on their principal job. Two-fifths of the employed do not work five days a week, Monday through Friday. Part-time workers (those who work fewer than thirty-five hours a week on all their jobs) are more likely than full-time workers to work nonstandard hours and days. Most of the diversity in work schedules, however, is contributed by full-timers because part-timers make up less than one-fourth of all employed.

Although the labor force is highly segregated occupationally by gender (Reskin and Roos 1990), gender differences in work-schedule behavior among all those employed are not great. With regard to hours, men are somewhat more likely than women not to work fixed daytime schedules (21.1 percent and 19.6 percent, respectively). The gender difference is seen specifically in the higher percentages of men than women working fixed nights and variable and rotating hours. There is no gender difference in the prevalence of evening work (both 8.1 percent). Among part-time workers of both sexes, substantial proportions work evenings (15.2 percent of men and 14.0 percent of women). Part-time workers are the subgroup showing the highest percentages who work variable hours.

As for workdays, men are only slightly more likely than women to work during nonstandard times—that is, not to work a five-day workweek, Monday through Friday (39.7 percent and 38.9 percent, respectively). The distribution of nonstandard workdays varies considerably by gender, however. In particular, men are more likely than women to work weekends (34.9 percent and 27.9 percent, respectively); women are more likely than men to work weekdays but fewer than five days a week (11.0 percent vs. 5.3 percent, respectively). Very few employed Americans, men or women, work weekends only. As might be expected, workdays are most likely to be nonstandard when people work part-time.

When work hours and days are combined, table 3.1 shows the figure cited earlier—that only 54.4 percent of employed Americans work Monday through Friday, five days a week, on a fixed day schedule. The counterpart is that 45.6 percent do not: 47.1 percent of men and 43.8 percent of women. Moreover, the large majority of part-timers work other than this five-day weekday pattern.

If individuals have this high prevalence of nonstandard schedules, it follows that there will be a higher prevalence of couples as a unit with a spouse working such schedules—since both spouses are "at risk." We see in table 3.2 that almost one-fourth (23.8 percent) of all couples with at least one earner have at least one spouse who works a nonday shift. The percentages are higher for those with children, and particularly for those with preschool-age children (30.6 percent).

When focusing on dual-earner couples only, the prevalence of nonday shifts is higher than for all couples, since in all cases, two spouses are "at risk" of working nondays. Over one-fourth (27.8 percent) of dual-earner couples have a spouse who works a nonday shift. Again, those with children are most likely to have such a schedule, and particularly those with preschool-aged children (34.7 percent). Rarely do both spouses work nonday shifts. Although there are usually some overlapping hours of employment among couples in which one spouse works nondays, there

**TABLE 3.1  Percentage Distribution of Work Schedules Among Employed Americans Age Eighteen and over, by Gender and Number of Hours Worked (Current Population Survey, May 1997)**

| Work Schedules | Total | | | Males | | | Females | | |
| --- | --- | --- | --- | --- | --- | --- | --- | --- | --- |
| | Total | More Than 35 Hours | Less Than 35 Hours | Total | More Than 35 Hours | Less Than 35 Hours | Total | More Than 35 Hours | Less Than 35 Hours |
| Hours | | | | | | | | | |
| Fixed day | 80.1% | 83.0% | 70.4% | 78.9% | 81.1% | 67.5% | 81.4% | 85.9% | 72.0% |
| Fixed evening | 8.1 | 6.3 | 14.4 | 8.1 | 6.9 | 15.2 | 8.1 | 5.5 | 14.0 |
| Fixed night | 4.1 | 4.3 | 3.7 | 4.5 | 4.5 | 4.5 | 3.7 | 3.9 | 3.3 |
| Hours vary | 4.2 | 3.2 | 7.7 | 4.4 | 3.7 | 8.5 | 3.9 | 2.5 | 7.2 |
| Rotating[a] | 3.6 | 3.2 | 3.8 | 4.1 | 4.0 | 4.4 | 2.8 | 2.2 | 3.5 |
| N | 49,570 | 38,272 | 11,201 | 25,916 | 22,067 | 3,800 | 23,654 | 16,205 | 7,401 |
| Days | | | | | | | | | |
| Weekday only, five days | 60.3 | 65.7 | 42.4 | 59.7 | 62.3 | 45.6 | 61.1 | 70.6 | 40.6 |
| Weekday only, less than five days | 8.0 | 3.6 | 22.9 | 5.3 | 3.4 | 16.1 | 11.0 | 3.9 | 26.6 |
| Seven days | 7.9 | 7.7 | 8.0 | 8.7 | 8.4 | 9.5 | 6.9 | 6.7 | 7.2 |

| | | | | | | | | | |
|---|---|---|---|---|---|---|---|---|---|
| Weekday and weekend, less than seven days | 23.1 | 22.9 | 24.3 | 25.7 | 25.8 | 26.2 | 20.1 | 18.7 | 23.3 |
| Weekend only, one or two days | 0.7 | 0.1 | 2.4 | 0.5 | 0.1 | 2.6 | 0.9 | 0.1 | 2.2 |
| N | 50,275 | 37,827 | 10,771 | 26,167 | 21,802 | 3,635 | 24,108 | 16,025 | 7,136 |
| Combination | | | | | | | | | |
| Fixed day, weekdays only, five days | 54.4 | 59.6 | 36.5 | 52.9 | 55.5 | 38.6 | 56.2 | 65.4 | 35.3 |
| Rotators or hours vary and weekend[a] | 5.3 | 4.6 | 7.2 | 5.9 | 5.4 | 8.6 | 4.5 | 3.5 | 6.5 |
| All others | 40.3 | 35.8 | 56.3 | 41.1 | 39.2 | 52.8 | 39.3 | 31.1 | 58.2 |
| N | 48,672 | 37,813 | 10,765 | 25,469 | 21,790 | 3,631 | 23,203 | 16,203 | 7,134 |

*Source:* Presser (1999).

*Notes:* The total number of cases is more than the sum of those working thirty-five or more hours last week and less than thirty-five hours because of missing data on the number of hours worked last week on all jobs. Also, differences in number of cases by type of work schedules are due to missing data for these variables. All percentages are weighted for national representativeness; the number of cases reports unweighted samples for each category. Percentages may not add exactly to 100.0 because of rounding.

[a]This includes seventy-four individuals designated as twenty-four-hour workers.

TABLE 3.2 **Percentage of Married Couples with at Least One Spouse Who Works Nonday Shifts by Family Type and Age of Youngest Child (Current Population Survey, May 1997)**

| Family Type and Age of Youngest Child | Percentage Nonday |
|---|---|
| At least one earner[a] | 23.8% |
| At least one earner and a | |
| Child under the age of fourteen | 25.8 |
| Child under the age of five | 30.6 |
| Two earners only[b] | 27.8 |
| Two earners and a | |
| Child under the age of fourteen | 31.1 |
| Child under the age of five | 34.7 |

*Source:* Author's analysis.
*Note:* Nonday shifts include work schedules in which the hours most days of the reference week were between 4 P.M. and 8 A.M., rotating hours, and those too variable to classify.
[a]Couples with at least one employed spouse on the job during the reference week in a nonagricultural occupation, including all rotators, and both spouses aged eighteen and over.
[b]Couples with both spouses on the job during the reference week, including all rotators, both in nonagricultural occupations and aged eighteen and over.

is considerable nonoverlap, and thus it is appropriate to characterize such couples as essentially working "split shifts." (An alternative term in use is "tag-team couples.")

Single mothers (nonmarried and separated or divorced) are more likely to work nonstandard schedules than married mothers—as well as longer hours. Among single mothers with children under age 14, 20.8 percent work nonstandard hours and 33.2 percent work weekends; for married mothers with children under age 14, it is 16.4 percent and 23.9 percent, respectively (Presser 2003a). For both marital statuses, having younger children and having low earnings both increase the percentages.

With such widespread prevalence of nonstandard work schedules among American families, what do we know about the consequences? I address this issue first with regard to the existing literature, and then report on some findings from my own research.

## SOCIAL CONSEQUENCES
## OF NONSTANDARD SCHEDULES:
## A REVIEW OF THE LITERATURE

Although there is an abundant literature on the effect of women's employment per se on family life, particularly relating to issues of marital quality, child care, and child well-being, there is a more limited body of research on the effects of employment at nonstandard work schedules (by either employed mothers or fathers) on the family. The following reviews many of these findings for the United States.[7]

### Quantitative Studies

The most thorough national study, and one that considered weekend employment as well as nonday shifts, is based on data now twenty-five years old, the 1977 U.S. Quality of Employment Survey (Staines and Pleck 1983). The authors found that for all married couples as well as dual-earner couples specifically, shift work was associated with difficulties in scheduling family activities; moreover, working weekends and variable days was linked with less time in family roles and higher levels of work-family conflict and problems of family adjustment. Some of the negative family outcomes were reduced when a worker's control over his or her work schedule was taken into account.[8] This study was an ambitious effort to explore the impact of work schedules on families, although the way nonday shifts were defined and grouped together is problematic as was the different sampling procedure for main respondents and spouses.[9]

Another, less intensive, national study that considered the relationship between nonstandard work schedules and family life was the longitudinal study of the effects of shift work on marital quality and stability by Lynn White and Bruce Keith (1990), which was based on a 1980 survey with a follow-up component in 1983 (White and Keith 1990). This study also has definitional problems.[10] The study found that marital happiness, sexual problems, and child-related problems were negatively affected by shift work, although the effects were of relatively low magnitude. The longitudinal analysis revealed that among marriages that remained intact over the three-year period, entry into shift work significantly increased marital disagreements and exiting shift work significantly increased marital interaction and decreased child-related problems. Looking specifically at marital breakup, the investigators found that being a shift-work couple in 1980 significantly increased the likelihood of divorce by 1983—from 7 percent to 11 percent.

Neither of these two studies was designed to study shift work in depth; rather, they were secondary analyses of surveys undertaken for more general purposes. Another secondary analysis by Sampson Lee Blair (1993), based on the National Survey of Families and Households (the same survey to be reported in the next section), considered the effects of employment (and family) characteristics on various dimensions of marital quality for both husbands and wives, and included shift status as one aspect of employment. The operational definition of shift status (a dichotomous variable) is not provided, but working a "shift" was found to significantly reduce marital quality only in terms of "daily contact" (not other measures considered). A smaller longitudinal study of ninety-two working-class dual-earner couples recruited from prenatal classes at hospitals in western New England, about one-half with spouses working the same shift and one-half, different shifts (Perry-Jenkins and Haley 2000) showed that during the first year of parenthood, working different shifts helped couples manage child care but often had negative consequences for the mental health of the parents and their marital relationship.

Empirical studies designed specifically to study the impact of shift work on employees, although not national in scope, suggest some negative family effects. The most extensive U.S. study of this type dates back to the early 1960s (Mott et al. 1965), and was designed to investigate the social, psychological, and physical consequences of shift work for white male blue-collar workers in selected continuous processing industries. Analyzing three dimensions of marital quality, the investigators concluded that shift work led to "some reduction in marital happiness and an even greater reduction in the ability to co-ordinate family activities and to minimize strain and friction among family members" (Mott et al. 1965, 146).

More recently, some empirical studies have addressed issues of parent-child interaction and child-care use as related to nonstandard work schedules in studies of the family life of certain populations. With regard to parent-child interaction, the 1999 National Survey of America's Families (Phillips 2002), which focuses on low-income households, found that married couples with children aged six to eleven who worked late hours were more likely to be involved in their children's school, but the children of such parents were less likely to be engaged in extracurricular activities. This study does not distinguish type of shift, defining "night hours" as employment mostly from 6:00 P.M. to 6:00 A.M. Another study, more broadly inclusive of all married couples (not just low-income), is based on the 1981 Study of Time Use; this study found little relationship between work schedules—the amount of minutes husband and wife are employed within certain ranges of hours around the clock—and the amount of parental time spent with children, but children here include all those under age twenty (Nock and Kingston 1988).

The type of child-care arrangements that people working nonstandard hours make for their children has been studied at the national level, and shows a heavy reliance on care by relatives. Among dual-earner couples, much of this relative care is by resident fathers (Brayfield 1995, Casper 1997, O'Connell 1993, Presser 1986). This is essentially "split-shift" parenting, whereby mothers and fathers work very different hours, one mostly days and the other mostly nondays. Only a minority of parents report "better child-care arrangements" as their main reason for working nonstandard hours, but among those who do so, mothers are more likely than fathers to give this reason. But most parents report reasons for working nonstandard hours that are related to their jobs, not their families (Presser 1995).

We know very little about child outcomes related to shift work, either from quantitative or qualitative studies. A cross-tabular analysis of data from the National Longitudinal Survey of Youth (Heymann 2000), without controls, showed that school-age children who had poor educational outcomes in 1996 were more likely to have parents who worked evening shifts some or all of their working years between 1990 and 1996 than were other children. (Evening shifts are reported by respondents without their specifying which hours they mean.)

A three-city study (Boston, Chicago, and San Antonio) of low- and moderate-income families in 1999 found more problem behaviors and fewer positive behaviors among children aged two to four when parents worked nonstandard hours or weekends (the two nonstandard work times were grouped together) compared to those whose parents worked fixed daytime schedules (Bogen and Joshi 2001). Multivariate analyses suggested that nonstandard schedules may not only affect children directly but also have a small indirect effect on children by increasing parenting challenges as a consequence of decreasing satisfaction with their own parenting and increasing stress levels.

### Qualitative Studies

Qualitative studies on how families cope when one or both parents work nonstandard schedules are rare. Lillian Rubin (1994), in her study of 162 working-class and lower-middle-class families in the United States, discusses the pressures on time for both husbands and wives when they work different shifts (about one-fifth of her couples). She notes the lack of child-care options that results in each parent's caring for the children while the other parent is employed.

Other qualitative studies offer a mixed message about positive and negative aspects of parents working nonstandard schedules. For example, Francine Deutsch's study (1999) of thirty dual-earner couples working different shifts finds parents speaking positively about such work schedules because they allow both spouses to rear their children and have a joint income. Yet the author concludes, "The loss of time together was a bitter pill to swallow. The physical separation symbolized a spiritual separation as well" (Deutsch 1999, 177).

Anita Ilta Garey's (1999) interviews with seven nurses working the night shift full-time indicated that these mothers liked the fact that this late work schedule allowed them to maximize family time and do traditional maternal tasks at home, as though they were full-time "at-home moms." Such tasks included helping with homework and being able to participate or facilitate children's school and extracurricular activities. Moreover, they preferred night to evening shifts because they were able to supervise their children's dinner and bedtime and, for married interviewees, have more time with their spouses. The cost to these mothers, which they were all willing to assume, was considerable sleep deprivation: most of them got four to five hours of sleep a night.

Problems of sleep deprivation among shift workers and the desire to be a "good mother" by working late hours are also relayed in interviews with women in the Midwest, in a study (Hattery 2001) in which the sample size was not provided. Another qualitative study of ninety male security guards on rotating shifts found that many fathers also deprived themselves of sleep in order to participate in family life, eating meals with their family "out of sync with their biological rhythm" (Hertz and Charlton 1989, 502).

## SOCIAL CONSEQUENCES OF NONSTANDARD WORK SCHEDULES: THE NATIONAL SURVEY OF FAMILIES AND HOUSEHOLDS, 1986 TO 1987 AND 1992 TO 1994

Building on this body of research, I have analyzed data from the National Survey of Families and Households (NSFH) on the relationship between nonstandard work schedules and family life. I present here some highlights of these findings relating to marital quality, marital instability, gender division of household labor, parent-child interactions, and child-care arrangements (for more details, see the references cited).

First, a note on the NSFH. This representative survey of all American families was conducted in two waves; the first set of interviews of individuals, both married and unmarried, during the years 1987 to 1988 (N = 13,007), and the second, between 1992 and 1994 (N = 10,007). Spouses and partners were asked to complete a separate questionnaire, so that researchers can obtain couple data on selected variables.[11] The findings reported here are based on the data from wave 1, with an analysis of wave 2 when marital instability is considered, and relies on data from both spouses among those married. The shift definition is the same as that reported earlier for the CPS, except that "Hours vary" is not a response option to questions about work, and thus all nonstandard work shifts are "nonday" (see note 5, on shift definitions). For some analyses, nonday shifts had to be combined as a single group because of the small numbers in each type of shift. In analyses that permit a separate examination of different nonday shifts, the results typically present a complex picture.

## Marital Quality

Four dimensions of marital quality at wave 1 were examined as separate dichotomous dependent variables in regressions: general marital unhappiness, low amount of quality time, marriage in trouble, and an assessment that there is a fifty-fifty or higher chance of divorce. The shift patterns worked by the couples (nondays grouped) and the family type were key independent variables. Control variables included the number of hours each spouse worked, the education level of both spouses, the number of times each spouse has been married, whether either spouse cohabited, difference in age between spouses, duration of marriage, the presence of children under age nineteen in the household, and, for some models, gender ideology of each spouse and the age of the wife. The results can be summarized as follows, separately for married single-earner couples (one-fifth of these single earners are wives) and dual-earner couples.

Among single-earner couples, nonday shifts and weekend employment seem to pose a risk to the quality of the marriage as compared to daytime employment—but only when it is the wife who is the single earner, not the husband. The negative relationships for wives are stronger when children are present.

Among dual-earner couples, couples with a spouse working nonstandard hours generally have higher levels of marital dissatisfaction than those in which both spouses work fixed days, but these relationships are specific to certain couples' work schedules and certain indicators of marital quality. In most instances the relationships are stronger when children are present. Interestingly, adding the control for gender ideology of the spouses did not significantly alter these relationships for couples with or without children. Weekend employment was not significantly associated with marital dissatisfaction.

## Marital Instability

Among couples married at wave 1, their marital status at wave 2—about five years later—was assessed in regression analyses that considered the work shifts and weekend employment of both spouses (with similar controls as above). It was found that only for couples with children did nonstandard work schedules increase the likelihood of marital instability—and this, only when the husband or wife worked the night shift. (There are some additional conditions relating to duration of marriage; see Presser 2000). One could speculate that this result occurs because spouses who choose to work late-night hours are especially likely to be in troubled marriages before making this decision, but a separate analysis of the quality of marriages among those who started to work nonday shifts between waves 1 and 2 does not support this view (Presser 2000).

## Gender Division of Household Labor

The NSFH data suggest that the functioning as well as the stability of family life is affected by nonstandard work schedules. An important family function is household labor. Focusing specifically on dual-earner households, regression analyses show that when husbands work a nondaytime or rotating shift and their wives work a day shift, the men are significantly more likely to do traditionally female household tasks than couples in which both spouses work day shifts. These tasks include preparing meals, washing dishes and cleaning up after meals, cleaning house, and washing, ironing, and mending clothes (Presser 1994). The control variables included the husband's education, occupation, and earnings, both absolute and relative to his wife, the gender ideologies of both spouses, and their stage in the life course, including the number of preschool and school-age children they have.

## Parent-Child Interaction

Other aspects of family functioning include the frequency of parent-child interaction. In the NSFH, data are available on the extent to which married and custodial unmarried parents eat meals with their children and do various one-on-one activities together.

Having dinner together is an especially important day-to-day ritual in most families. Both mothers and fathers who work evenings and rotating shifts are significantly less likely to have dinner with their children than parents who work days. Working nights, however, does not show less frequent family involvement in dinner relative to days (Presser 2003b). When it comes to breakfast, by contrast, nonstandard work schedules are associated with parents' eating breakfast with their children more frequently, but this association differs by the gender of parent and in the case of the mother, by her being single or married (Presser 2003a).

As for one-on-one parent-child interaction, the NSFH asked questions about the frequency of the following parental activities with children ages five to eighteen: leisure activities outside the home, work on projects, private talks, and help with homework. Overall there is a mixed picture, and differences are evident by gender of the parent and the marital status of mothers. The findings (Presser 2003a) suggest the following: Working nights may minimize the frequency of leisure activities outside the home for mothers, both single and married; rotating shifts seem to do this for married fathers and single mothers. The frequency of parents' working on projects with children is higher when dual-earner mothers work rotating shifts and single mothers work evenings, as compared to days; shift status is not associated with this activity for fathers, with the exception of one near-significant relationship. As for the frequency of private talks, there is a relationship to shift status in the case of single, but not married, mothers: such talks are more frequent when they work evenings and nights rather than days, less frequent when they rotate. Married fathers show a reverse pattern from single mothers: such talks are less frequent with evening work and more frequent with rotating shifts. As for help with homework, the significant relationships for mothers of both marital statuses are negative when they are on rotating shifts, and positive for fathers when they work night shifts. The few significant or near-significant relationships with regard to weekend employment also show a mixed picture: only some activities are seemingly related and there are differences in direction by gender of parent. This is a very complex set of results, suggesting that nonday shifts have both positive and negative effects for parent-child interactions, but the different effects of different shifts, as well as the gender differences, are hard to interpret and need further study.

## Child-Care Arrangements

Parents who work nonstandard hours and weekends rely more heavily on relatives for child care for their preschool-age children when mothers are employed. When mothers are married and working nonstandard schedules, the most frequent "relative" providing care is the child's father, clearly increasing that form of parent-child interaction. When mothers are not married and are working nonstandard schedules, the most frequent relative providing care is the grandparent. While this greater reliance on relatives when working nonstandard hours has been shown with other national data sources, as previously noted, analysis of the NSFH data takes into account weekend employment as well as work shifts and also considers patterns of multiple child-care use. Those working nonstandard schedules, weekends as well as nonday, are more likely to make multiple types of arrangements (Presser 2003a). This fact, along with the heavier reliance on informal providers, makes for more complex child-care arrangements for such parents, both married and single.

Among school-age children five to eleven years old, the presence of parents at home when children leave for and return from school is generally enhanced when mothers work evenings and nights, a clear advantage of such schedules. This relationship obtains for single mothers, but the overall presence of a parent at home during such times is less than for married mothers—which is to be expected, given that the child's father is usually not living in these nonmarried households. For both family types, we do not know if the parents working late hours are awake or asleep before and after school. Typically, other child-care arrangements are made when parents are not present. However, about 15 percent of parents report their children aged five to eleven in self-care before school, and about 10 percent, after school. Self-care is reported less by parents who work late rather than work daytime hours, but if parents working nights are more likely to be asleep when the child leaves and returns from school, parental supervision of children may be lacking, and the level of self-care of such children may be greatly underestimated.

## IMPLICATIONS FOR LOW-INCOME FAMILIES

Both the existing research and my new NSFH-based findings, summarized here, suggest that employment at nonstandard times presents some major challenges to U.S. families. Despite the possible advantages of such work schedules, the data suggest that in many ways employment at nonstandard hours and weekends adds extra stress to families with children, and night work may actually substantially increase the risk of separation or divorce among the married. There has been no research to date that rigorously assesses how low-income families cope with nonstandard schedules compared to those with higher incomes. In fact, few researchers have rigorously compared how people working nonstandard schedules cope compared to those working at standard times, regardless of income. Some of the qualitative studies are insightful but they report on too few cases for analysts to be able to draw conclusions.

We know that although employment at nonstandard times occurs at all levels of income, it is disproportionately found among those with low incomes. For example, the top five occupations of nonday workers are cashier, truck driver, waiter and waitress, cook, and janitor or cleaner. It is not just that these jobs are low-paying in general—they are even more low-paying if you have these occupations and work at nonstandard times (Presser 2003a). Thus, people who work nonstandard hours have to deal with the joint stresses of managing with such low pay and with being "out of sync" temporally with other family members, including their children. As noted earlier, it does not appear that parents who work nonstandard schedules generally find this the preferred mode of child rearing, despite the advantage of reduced child-care costs and greater involvement of fathers in child rearing. Single mothers of low income, who generally do not benefit from sharing child care with fathers, would seem to find working nonstandard schedules especially problematic.

It thus seems appropriate to conclude that while some parents may prefer such schedules, employment at nonstandard times is driven by demand and generally recruits those with limited job possibilities. This includes mothers moving from welfare to work, who often experience a misfit between their required hours and days of employment and the availability of formal child care, and have to put together a patchwork of informal arrangements to hold on to their jobs. My analysis of mothers in the labor force in 1997 with characteristics similar to those moving from welfare to work (high school education or less, aged eighteen to thirty-four, with at least one child under age fourteen) revealed that about two-fifths of these employed mothers did not work a fixed-day schedule on weekdays only (Presser 2003a). Moreover, many of those working fixed days had hours that extended into the "fringe": they started very early in the morning or ended in the evening, times when formal daytime child care is typically not available.

The minimal attention to such issues reflects the general lack of attention in the social policy arena to the temporal conflicts between work and family life that occur as a consequence of the widespread engagement of employed parents in nonstandard schedules. In terms of parent-child interaction, two-parent families often look much like one-parent families, and single-parent families much like no-parent families. Presumably "intact" families often are composed of spouses who hardly see each other. We need to be concerned about the special needs such situations generate for low-income families and how they might be addressed. One way to find this out is to do research that focuses specifically on this issue.

## NEED FOR FURTHER RESEARCH

It is clear from the research to date that investigating the social consequences of nonstandard work schedules for individuals and their families is not an easy task. There are different work shifts, there is weekend employment, and the cumulative number of hours people work needs to be taken into account. Moreover, the consequences may be different for families with children than for those with no children, and for those with preschoolers as compared to those with older children. On top of such considerations are the special problems of low-income parents, particularly single mothers. And there is the question of short-term benefits versus long-term costs (for example, enhanced father-child interaction when spouses work split shifts, but increased odds of divorce if one of the spouses works nights).

Such considerations reflect complex situations that need further study, and there are many ways to approach this. I offer my assessment of some important considerations for future research as specified in my book (Presser 2003a), recognizing that we need many studies with multiple approaches.

*We need to do focused studies on the costs and benefits of working nonstandard schedules.* As we have seen, most of the research to date on the consequences of working nonstandard schedules has not been designed with this focus, but rather has been based on secondary analyses of large-scale surveys or on special cases that show up in qualitative studies of the stresses of work and family life more generally. Thus we know very little about why people work these schedules, their perceived trade-offs, and the perceived impact on their lives and those of family members. It would be highly relevant to consider gender differences here as well as distinctions between single and married mothers, particularly with regard to the trade-offs being made.

*We need to distinguish different work shifts in studies of the consequences of nonstandard work schedules.* As the findings presented in this chapter suggest, different nonstandard work shifts may have different effects on family life and on children. To better assess this, we need large-scale studies that oversample those working nonstandard shifts so that there are sufficiently large numbers to enable researchers to make comparisons between those working evenings, nights, and rotating shifts, as well as days.

*We need precise measures of work shifts.* It has been noted that many of the shift-work studies use ambiguous definitions of work shifts, often defined by the respondent without clear instruction from the interviewer. It would seem best to ask people the specific times when their work begins and ends (daily or for most days during a reference week), plus whether they rotate, and leave the derivation of the definitions of day, evening, and night shifts to the investigator (which is then reported with the findings). This approach would also allow investigators to compare different studies by deriving similar definitions of work shifts.

*We need to study the movement of employees in and out of different work schedules.* Studies of shift work have generally been cross-sectional rather than longitudinal, yet there is undoubtedly considerable flow in and out of different work schedules. It is important to know the duration of shift work for employees, and particularly employed parents, and the ways movement in and out of nonstandard work shifts relates to family concerns, employer demands, and the lack of alternative daytime job opportunities.

*We need to explore the effects of nonstandard work schedules on the physical and emotional health of individuals and how these effects on individual well-being interact with the functioning of family life.* Given the paucity of knowledge on this interaction, it would seem appropriate to start with intensive qualitative studies of families working late and rotating shifts. It would be especially interesting to explore the extent to which those working such schedules suffer from sleep deprivation, and the process by which this may interact with family functioning, affecting the quality and stability of marriages as well as the care of children. In the latter regard, it is important to know how well preschool-age children are being cared for during the day by parents who work nights or rotating shifts.

*We need research on married fathers who care for their children during most of the hours that mothers are employed.* It would be revealing to know how distinctive these fathers are from other fathers and the consequences (positive and negative) that they perceive for themselves of having taken on this responsibility as well as the actual consequences. In the latter context, it would be especially fruitful to have longitudinal data to assess change over time.

*We need intensive research on the reasons people work nonstandard work schedules, particularly those of parents with children.* To date, we rely on one question in the CPS for our knowledge of reasons people work nonstandard hours. Qualitative studies refer to some couples who report either positive or negative consequences of shift work, but we have no research that probes in depth as to why substantial numbers of parents have chosen these schedules or whether it is really a choice, not a necessity. In addition to some preferring to arrange child care this way (given the options and their income status), there may be other caregiving reasons that merit exploration, such as better arrangements for the care of disabled persons and the elderly. Also, it would be good to know what people really mean when they say their main reason is that it is a job requirement, and if there are gender differences in this meaning.

*We need more research on the effects of nonstandard work schedules on children, including their development and school achievement.* Although we have moved forward over the past decade in gaining a better understanding of the effect of child care on child development, we have generally ignored the issue of how the non-standard work schedules of parents, and the need for more complex child-care arrangements that this generates, affects child outcomes. This issue calls for studies of the children in addition to the parents, and of both the frequency and quality of parent-child interactions as well as of child-care quality. Such research would require substantial sample sizes in order to rigorously compare children of different ages and the different work schedules of parents. Good measures of child outcomes are also important.

## FUTURE EXPECTATIONS

Filling these research needs is important not only to better understand today's families, but to better anticipate future consequences, as the number of American households with parents working non-standard hours increases. I predict this increase will be experienced disproportionately by employed women, and to a lesser extent by employed blacks and Hispanics. This prediction is supported by job-growth projections to the year 2010, although I recognize that such projections essentially are educated guesses, subject to error.

Table 3.3 shows the top ten occupations that as of 2000 were projected by the Bureau of Labor Statistics to have the largest job growth between 2000 and 2010 (Hecker 2001, table 4). Using the May 1997 CPS data, I have calculated the percentage of workers in these top growth occupations who work nonstandard schedules. (As noted in table 3.3's footnote, given the difference in occupational codes used for the projections and for the CPS, the matching of some occupations is not precise, and for one it is not possible.)

What we see is that for most of these occupations—namely, food preparation and serving workers, registered nurses, retail salespersons, cashiers, security guards, and waiters and waitresses—a disproportionately high percentage of the workers do not work a fixed day (far exceeding the overall average for all occupations of 19.9 percent). The same occupations that are disproportionately high on nonstandard hours are disproportionately high on weekend employment.

We also see in table 3.3 (far right) the percentage of the workers who are female, black, and Hispanic in these top growth occupations. These percentages can be compared with the percentages in all occupations for the groups shown in the column headings. When the percentages for specific occupations exceed that for all occupations, the subgroups are disproportionately in those occupations.

This comparison reveals that the top growth occupations that are high on nonstandard work schedules also have high percentages of female workers, the one exception being security guards.[12] The picture is more mixed for blacks and Hispanics, who are overrepresented in the top growth occupations of food preparer and server, cashier, and security guard, and, for Hispanics, of waiters and waitresses. Hispanics are underrepresented as registered nurses; blacks, as waiters and waitresses.

In conclusion, employment in a 24/7 economy presents many challenges for U.S. families. The research to date hints at many of these, but we have much more to learn. We should not be turned away by the complexity of the issue. Indeed, I contend that when work and family research does not take into account the nonstandard work schedules of employed family members, it is likely to be missing some important explanatory variables for the outcomes of interest. Moreover, work and family policies cannot continue to ignore the temporal diversity of work schedules for working families, especially those of low income. Failure to explicitly acknowledge such diversity compromises the effectiveness of such policies, as exemplified by the misfit between child-care availability and the work hours of many mothers moving from welfare to work.

The movement toward a 24/7 economy will not, in my view, be reversed in the decades ahead. It may slow in pace or even be stalled by a weakening economy, but I believe the long-term trend is toward more employment around the clock, particularly in the service sector. I hold this view because the 24/7 economy is driven by factors external to the family that are not likely to change in the foreseeable future. For better or worse, families will increasingly need to respond to these challenges. And so will we as scholars.

**TABLE 3.3  Largest Projected Job Growth Occupations (2000 to 2010) and Their Work Schedule, Gender, and Race Characteristics**

| Job Growth Rank | Occupation[b] | Employment (in Thousands) | | Percentage in Occupation Working Nonstandard Schedules (CPS, May 1997) | | | Percentage of Group in Occupation (CPS, May 1997) | | |
|---|---|---|---|---|---|---|---|---|---|
| | | 2000 | 2010[a] (Projected) | Percentage Other Than Fixed Day (a) | Percentage Weekend (b) | Percentage (a) or (b) (c) | Percentage Female (All Occupations = 46.0) | Percentage Non-Hispanic Black (All Occupations = 10.5) | Percentage Hispanic (All Occupations = 9.8) |
| 1 | Food preparation and serving workers, including fast food[c] | 2,206 | 2,879 | 45.8% | 55.0% | 68.0% | 51.5% | 11.8% | 24.2% |
| 2 | Customer service representatives[d] | 1,946 | 2,577 | n.a. | n.a. | n.a. | n.a. | n.a. | n.a. |
| 3 | Registered nurses | 2,194 | 2,755 | 34.6 | 42.9 | 55.1 | 94.5 | 7.5 | 3.2 |
| 4 | Retail salespersons | 4,109 | 4,619 | 32.2 | 62.9 | 70.6 | 55.3 | 7.7 | 8.7 |
| 5 | Computer support specialists[e] | 506 | 996 | 20.0 | 15.9 | 26.5 | 56.1 | 19.9 | 3.1 |

| 6 | Cashiers, except gaming | 3,325 | 3,799 | 50.4 | 71.0 | 80.1 | 77.2 | 15.6 | 12.3 |
| 7 | Office clerks, general | 2,705 | 3,135 | 16.2 | 15.7 | 23.5 | 76.3 | 13.6 | 8.9 |
| 8 | Security guards[f] | 1,106 | 1,497 | 57.0 | 55.8 | 73.9 | 22.8 | 19.4 | 13.0 |
| 9 | Computer software engineers, applications[g] | 380 | 760 | 5.2 | 13.5 | 16.9 | 31.5 | 6.6 | 2.4 |
| 10 | Waiters and waitresses | 1,983 | 2,347 | 65.1 | 79.0 | 89.5 | 78.8 | 3.1 | 12.6 |

*Source:* Presser (2003).

*Note:* n.a. = not available.

[a] Projections are derived by the Bureau of Labor Statistics (Hecker 2001, table 4).

[b] The BLS occupational classifications for job projections is based on the National Industry-Occupation Employment Matrix (NIOEM) and do not always correspond exactly with the CPS occupational classifications, as noted in these footnotes.

[c] This category includes kitchen workers, food preparation and miscellaneous food preparation occupations in the CPS.

[d] There is no separate classification in the CPS for this category.

[e] This category corresponds to computer equipment operators in the CPS.

[f] This category includes guards and police, except public service and protective service occupations, not elsewhere classified in the CPS.

[g] This category includes computer system analysis and scientists and operations and systems researchers and analysts in the CPS.

This chapter has been reprinted with the permission of Lawrence Erlbaum Associates. Harriet B. Presser. 2004. "Employment in a 24/7 Economy: Challenges for the Family." In Ann C. Crouter and Alan Booth, eds. *Work-Family Challenges for Low-Income Parents and Their Children*. Mahwah, N.J.: Lawrence Erlbaum Associates.

---

I am grateful to Kei Nomaguchi and Lijuan Wu for their very able research assistance in generating the data both for this chapter and for my other publications upon which this chapter draws. The analysis of the NSFH data summarized here was supported in large part by the W. T. Grant Foundation and a visiting scholarship at the Russell Sage Foundation.

## NOTES

1. As Jerry Jacobs and Kathleen Gerson (1998) note, the changes in cumulative work time have been essentially in the number of weeks worked per year, and the extent of this increase is the subject of considerable debate.
2. Data for 2001 have recently become available, but have not yet been analyzed in detail. It appears that there has been little change in overall prevalence during the four-year period, but the work-schedule questions changed, particularly with regard to the reference period, precluding definitive comparisons with 1997 or previous survey years (see note 3).
3. For example, between 1973 and 1980, people were asked the hours they began and ended working most days in the prior week but there was no question as to whether they are rotators who happen to be on the day shift in the prior week. Since about one-third of those who work other than fixed daytime schedules are rotators, this seriously underestimates the prevalence of nonday shifts. Changes in the CPS were made in 1980 so that workers were asked specifically about shift rotation, but the response options on hours work began and ended varied in other ways in the special CPS supplements on work schedules that followed (1985, 1991, and 1997), presenting comparability problems. In spite of this issue, which has been ignored, the data have been presented as if they showed that there has been little change in shift work between 1985 and 1997 (Beers 2000). I do not believe one can draw this conclusion from these data.

4. The BLS used these shift definitions when analyzing only full-time wage and salary workers. I use this designation for all workers, both full- and part-time and both self-employed and wage and salary workers.

5. The shift definition used for my analysis of data from the National Survey of Families and Households, to be discussed later in this chapter, excludes "hours vary," as detailed information on work schedules for every day of the week were provided without this response option, permitting the allocation of individuals into the other categories as appropriate.

6. The question reads, "Which days of the week (do you/does name) work [ON THIS JOB/FOR THIS BUSINESS] [ONLY]?" "Check all that apply."

7. For a more extensive review of the literature on shift work, separately by topic, see Presser 2003a.

8. Using the same data source, Kingston and Nock (1985) found among dual-earner couples that there was no strong relationship between the combined number of hours couples worked or the amount of time one or both spouses worked and marital or family satisfaction. (This study excludes those who work "irregular hours," and thus presumably excludes rotators.)

9. Those working afternoon schedules were combined with evening and night workers, and together they all were categorized as nonday shift workers. Those working in the morning were considered to be among the day workers. The effects of different nonday shifts were not separately considered, nor was the gender of the shift worker. Also, the main respondents in the sample were eligible only if they worked at least twenty hours a week, but the number of hours of employment was not restricted for spouses.

10. The researchers asked respondents if they were shift workers but did not define the range of hours that constitute a shift nor the type of shift.

11. For further methodological details, see James Sweet, Larry Bumpass, and L. Vaughn Call (1988), and http://www.ssc.wisc.edu/nsfh/home.htm.

12. Although the focus here is on job growth with regard to occupations (and the characteristics of individuals in these occupations), an analysis of projected industrial changes would undoubtedly show certain service industries (personal and distributive) to be exceptionally high on future growth and on employment at nonstandard times. For a tabulation of industry by work schedule status in 1997, see Presser (2003a, chapter 2).

## REFERENCES

Beers, Thomas. 2000. "Flexible Schedules and Shift Work: Replacing the '9-to-5' Workday?" *Monthly Labor Review* 123(6): 33–39.

Blair, Sampson Lee. 1993. "Employment, Family, and Perceptions of Marital Quality Among Husbands and Wives." *Journal of Family Issues* 14(2): 189–212.

Bogen, Karen, and Pamela Joshi. 2001. "Bad Work or Good Move: The Relationship of Part-Time and Nonstandard Work Schedules to Parenting and Child Behavior in Working Poor Families." Paper presented at the Conference on Working Poor Families: Coping as Parents and Workers. National Institutes of Health, Bethesda, Md. (November 13–14, 2001).

Brayfield, April A. 1995. "Juggling Jobs and Kids: The Impact of Employment Schedules on Fathers' Caring for Children." *Journal of Marriage and the Family* 57(2): 321–32.

Casper, Lynne M. 1997. "My Daddy Takes Care of Me! Fathers as Care Providers." *Current Population Reports,* series P70, no. 59 (September). Washington: U.S. Government Printing Office for Bureau of the Census.

Deutsch, Francine M. 1999. *Halving It All: How Equally Shared Parenting Works*. Cambridge, Mass.: Harvard University Press.

Garey, Anita Ilta. 1999. *Weaving Work and Motherhood*. Philadelphia: Temple University Press.

Golden, Lonnie. 2001. "Flexible Work Schedules." *American Behavioral Scientist* 44(7): 1157–78.

Hamermesh, Daniel S. 1999. "The Timing of Work Over Time." *The Economic Journal* 109(January): 37–66.

Hatch, Julie, and Angela Clinton. 2000. "Job Growth in the 1990s: A Retrospect." *Monthly Labor Review* 123(12): 3–18.

Hattery, Angela. J. 2001. "Tag-Team Parenting: Costs and Benefits of Utilizing Nonoverlapping Shift Work in Families with Young Children." *Families in Society: The Journal of Contemporary Human Services* 82(4): 419–27.

Hecker, Daniel E. 2001. "Occupational Employment Projections to 2010." *Monthly Labor Review* 124(11): 57–84.

Hedges, Janice N., and Edward S. Sekscenski. 1979. "Workers on Late Shifts in a Changing Economy." *Monthly Labor Review* 102(9): 14–22.

Hertz, Rosanna, and Joy Charlton. 1989. "Making Family Under a Shiftwork Schedule: Air Force Security Guards and Their Wives." *Social Problems* 36(5): 491–507.

Heymann, Jody. 2000. *The Widening Gap: Why America's Working Families Are in Jeopardy and What Can Be Done About It*. New York: Basic Books.

Jacobs, Jerry A., and Kathleen Gerson, 1998. "Who Are the Overworked Americans?" *Review of Social Economy* 56(4): 442–59.

Kingston, Paul W., and Steven L. Nock. 1985. "Consequences of the Family Work Day." *Journal of Marriage and the Family* 47(3): 619–29.

Meisenheimer, Joseph R. 1998. "The Service Industry in the 'Good' Versus 'Bad' Debate." *Monthly Labor Review* 121(2): 10–21.

Melbin, Murray. 1987. *Night as Frontier: Colonizing the World After Dark.* New York: Free Press.

Mott, Paul E., Floyd C. Mann, Quain McLoughlin, and Donald P. Warwick. 1965. *Shift Work: The Social, Psychological, and Physical Consequences.* Ann Arbor: University of Michigan Press.

Nock, Steven L., and Paul William Kingston, 1988. "Time with Children: The Impact of Couples' Work Time Commitments." *Social Forces* 67(1): 59–85.

O'Connell, Martin. 1993. *Where's Papa? Father's Role in Child Care.* Population Trends and Public Policy Report no. 20. Washington, D.C.: Population Reference Bureau.

Perry-Jenkins, Maureen, and Heather-Lyn Haley. 2000. "Employment Schedules and the Transition to Parenthood: Implications for Mental Health and Marriage." Paper presented at the annual meeting of the National Council on Family Relations. Minneapolis, Minn. (November 10–13).

Phillips, Katherine Ross. 2002. "Parent Work and Child Well-Being in Low-Income Families." Occasional Paper no. 56. Washington, D.C.: Urban Institute.

Presser, Harriet B. 1986. "Shift Work Among American Women and Child Care." *Journal of Marriage and the Family* 48(3): 551–63.

———. 1994. "Employment Schedules Among Dual-Earner Spouses and the Division of Household Labor by Gender." *American Sociological Review* 59(3): 348–64.

———. 1995. "Job, Family, and Gender: Determinants of Nonstandard Work Schedules Among Employed Americans in 1991." *Demography* 32(4): 577–98.

———. 1999. "Toward a 24-Hour Economy." *Science* 284(June 11): 1778–79.

———. 2000. "Nonstandard Work Schedules and Marital Instability." *Journal of Marriage and the Family* 62(1): 93–110.

———. 2003a. *Working in a 24/7 Economy: Challenges for American Families.* New York: Russell Sage Foundation.

———. 2003b. "Toward a 24-Hour Economy: Implications for the Temporal Structure and Functioning of Family Life." In *Ages, Generations et Contrat Social,* edited by Jacques Véron, Jacques Légaré, Sophie Pennec, and Marie Digoix. Paris: Institut National d'Études Démographiques.

Reskin, Barbara F., and Patricia A. Roos. 1990. *Job Queues, Gender Queues.* Philadelphia: Temple University Press.

Rones, Philip L., Randy E. Ilg, and Jennifer M. Gardner. 1997. "Trends in Hours of Work Since the Mid-1970s." *Monthly Labor Review* 120(4): 3–14.

Rubin, Lillian. B. 1994. *Families on the Fault Line.* New York: Harper-Perennial.

Smith, Shirley J. 1986. "The Growing Diversity of Work Schedules." *Monthly Labor Review* 109(11): 7–13.

Staines, Graham L., and Joseph H. Pleck. 1983. *The Impact of Work Schedules on the Family.* Ann Arbor: University of Michigan, Institute for Social Research.

Sweet, James, Larry Bumpass, and L. Vaughn Call. 1988. *The Design and Content of the National Survey of Families and Households.* Madison: University of Wisconsin, Center for Demography and Ecology.

U.S. Bureau of the Census. 2001. *Statistical Abstract of the United States: 2001.* Washington: U.S. Government Printing Office.

U.S. Congress. Office of Technology Assessment. 1991. *Biological Rhythms: Implications for the Worker.* Publication no. OTA-BA-463. Washington: U.S. Government Printing Office.

U.S. Department of Labor. Bureau of Labor Statistics. 1981. "Workers on Late Shifts." Summary 81-13 [September]. Washington: U.S. Government Printing Office.

———. 1998. *Workers on Flexible and Shift Schedules.* Labor Force Statistics from the CPS, publication no. USDL98-119. Washington: U.S. Government Printing Office.

———. 2002. "Labor Force Statistics from the Current Population Survey: Household Data Annual Averages." Available at http://www.bls.gov/cps/cpsaat19.pdf. Accessed on October 7, 2002.

Wedderburn, Alexander, ed. 2000. "Shift Work and Health." Special issue of *Bulletin of European Studies on Time* (Luxembourg: Office for Official Publications of the European Communities), vol. 1, available at http://www.eurofound.ie.

White, Lynn, and Bruce Keith. 1990. "The Effect of Shift Work on the Quality and Stability of Marital Relations." *Journal of Marriage and the Family* 52(2): 453–62.

— Chapter 4 —

# The Health and Family-Social Consequences of Shift Work and Schedule Control: 1977 and 1997

## Rudy Fenwick and Mark Tausig

R ECENT CHANGES IN the U.S. economy and labor force have led to great diversity in the time workers spend on the job. The increased diversity refers not only to changes in the absolute number of working hours, as many workers work more hours per week and many others work fewer hours, but also to which hours and days they are working and how much flexibility they have in determining which hours they work. The so-called "standard shift"—thirty-five to forty hours per week, nine to five, Monday through Friday—has increasingly become the exception rather than the standard, since fewer than one in three American workers now work that shift (Presser 1999; chapter 3, this volume). Much of this change can be accounted for by the growth of part-time and contingent employment, but even among full-time workers one in six work nonstandard hours (U.S. Department of Labor 1998).

With an increasing number of workers on nonstandard shifts comes an increasing concern with the harmful effects of non-standard work schedules on workers and on their families. A number of studies have linked working nonstandard shifts to increased risks of physical and mental health problems (see Akerstedt 1990; Barton 1994; Kawachi et al. 1995; Parkes 1999; Karlsson, Knuttson, and Lindahl 2001). Other research has found a link between nonstandard shifts and increased problems in workers' family and personal lives (see, for example, Staines and Pleck 1983; Kingston and Nock 1985; White and Keith 1990; Kinnunen and Mauno 1998; Presser 2000). On the other hand, this research has also suggested that flexibility in scheduling, because it provides workers with some choice as to when they begin and end work, has positive effects on workers' health and on their family and social lives. Flexible scheduling is related to lower perceived job stress, especially among those working nonstandard schedules (see, for example, Fast and Frederick 1996; Benach et al. 2002; Ala-Marsula et al. 2002; Griffin et al. 2002), and to decreased work-family conflict (Staines and Pleck 1983, 1986; Fast and Frederick 1996).

In this chapter we investigate the effects of working different job schedules and the degree to which workers have control or choice over their schedules and the effect of this level of control on their physical and mental health and on their family and personal lives. Does the diversity of work schedules pose greater problems for American workers at the beginning of the millennium than in the 1970s, when working the standard shift and "traditional" single-earner families were more prevalent? If so, to what extent do increased problems of shift work reflect increases in the number of Americans working nonstandard schedules, and to what extent do they reflect changes in who is working nonstandard shifts?

We address these issues by analyzing two data sets obtained twenty years apart that are representative samples of the U.S. labor force and contain necessary controls for other relevant individual, job, and family characteristics. The data sets we use are the 1977 Quality of Employment Survey (QES), conducted by Robert Quinn and Graham Staines (1979) on behalf of the U.S. Department of Labor, and the 1997 National Study of the Changing Workforce (NSCW), conducted by James T. Bond, Ellen Galinsky, and Jennifer Swanberg (1998) for the Families and Work Institute. Using these data sets we will test the assumptions that negative health and family and social outcomes of shift work are due to problems of physiological, psychological, and social adjustments to the times worked, or to the inability to control times worked. In light of the fact that the prevalence of shift work varies by occupation and by demographic characteristics of workers, the inclusion of relevant individual, job, and family controls will enable us to see how much differences in scheduling and scheduling control add to our knowledge of the health and family and social relations of workers. In particular, given the focus of previous research, we will be able to see whether these outcomes vary by gender and by family structure, and whether changing occupational and family structures have influenced the effects of shift work on workers.

## ADJUSTMENT TO SHIFT WORK

The most pervasive result from research on the effects of shift work is that working nonstandard schedules is undesirable and harmful to workers because it creates physiological, psychological, and family-social adjustment problems. The results are pervasive because they cover a wide range of outcomes among a variety of occupations in countries around the globe. A substantial body of epidemiological research has linked working nonstandard times to disruptions of circadian rhythms and sleeping and eating patterns (Akerstedt 1990; Bohle and Tilley 1990; Parkes 1999); two groups that have been studied are Italian police (Gabarino et al. 2002) and North Sea oil-platform workers (Bjorvatn, Keclund, and Akerstedt 1998). Other research has found shift work to be related to increased risk for cardiovascular and coronary heart disease (CHD) morbidity and mortality. Populations studied include female nurses in the United States (Kawachi et al. 1995), male workers in a Swedish paper mill (Knuttson et al. 1986), factory workers of both genders in the Netherlands (van Amelsvoort et al. 2001), and office workers in Japan (Murata, Yano, and Shinozaki 1999). Moreover, these relationships have been found to be independent of the effects of the workers' individual characteristics, such as age, medical history, and health-related behaviors, such as smoking or alcohol use (see Kawachi et al. 1995; Knuttson et al. 1986). On the other hand, shift work has been linked to these and other causative factors that increase the risk of cardiovascular and coronary problems, such as hypertension; diabetes; increased levels of serum cholesterol, glucose, uric acid, and adrenaline (De Backer et al. 1984; Kawachi et al. 1995; Knuttson et al. 1986; Thelle et al. 1976;

Theorell and Akerstedt 1976); and the incidence of obesity (Karlsson, Knuttson, and Lindahl 2001).

Beyond its links to circadian disruptions and cardiovascular and coronary disease, shift work has been found to increase digestive and gastrointestinal problems (Zober et al. 1998; Smith et al. 1999) as well as headaches, musculoskeletal problems, and work-related injuries (Parkes 1999). Other health outcomes of shift work include increased incidence of neurotic disorder (Costa et al. 1989), as well as lower levels of psychological well-being (Bohle and Tilley 1990), higher levels of perceived stress (Coffey, Skipper, and Jung 1988), and chronic malaise (U.S. Congress 1991).

Adjustment problems associated with shift work extend to family and social life and relationships. Working nonstandard hours or days generally means that one's availability for social interaction and participation is out of sync with that of others (Carpenter and Cazamian 1977; U.S. Congress 1991). Family relations in particular suffer, and especially so if there are children. Graham Staines and Joseph Pleck (1983, 1984, 1986) found that married couples and single mothers who worked nonstandard shifts had problems scheduling family activities and spent less time in family roles. They also found that working nonstandard shifts increased the level of work-family conflict and reduced the level of family adjustment, as reflected in feelings of marital satisfaction, marital happiness, and satisfaction with family life. Lynn White and Bruce Keith (1990) also found that shift work reduced marital happiness while increasing couples' sexual problems and parents' problems with their children, all of which culminated in an increased likelihood of divorce within three years. As with the health effects of shift work, the effects on family relations are cross-cultural, with similar results reported for Canada (Fast and Frederick 1996), Australia (Vandenheuvel and Wooden 1995), Great Britain (Colligan and Rosa 1990), and Finland (Kinnunen and Mauno 1998).

Although shift work has been found to be a problem for both men and women, there is evidence that the effects on women are somewhat more adverse, for women's relations with their families are strongly affected by their shift work. The primary reason is that women retain higher levels of family obligation, such as child care, even when employed outside the home. Thus, shift work creates greater work-family role conflict for women (Staines and Pleck

1984) because it interferes with their more-involved family roles (Kinnunen and Mauno 1998). Attempts to balance work-family role demands can lead to higher rates of job absenteeism for female workers (Vandenheuvel and Wooden 1995). However, there is no general consensus with regard to these results. For example, White and Keith (1990) found no differences by gender in the effects of shift work on measures of marital satisfaction and family problems.

There is more of a consensus that the increased participation of women in the labor force, together with changing family structures, has substantially increased concerns over shift work because of the increased difficulties of balancing work and family demands. The percentage of women in the U.S. labor force increased by almost 50 percent from the 1970s to the late 1990s, from making up 43 percent of the labor force to making up 60 percent (Fullerton 1999). An even greater percentage—almost 75 percent—of married women with dependent children is engaged in paid employment, and two-fifths worked full-time, year-round (Bianchi and Spain 1996). Although roughly one-third of both men and women full-time workers—those who work thirty-five or more hours per week—work nonstandard shifts, there are demographic differences in these shift workers that suggest the greater need for women to balance work and home. Marital status and the presence of children affect the likelihood of women's working nonstandard shifts but have no effect for men (Presser 1995, 1999). Marriage reduces shift work for women but not for men. Married or not, women with preschool-age children (five and younger) are more likely to work nonstandard shifts than those without children, but those with school-age children (aged five to eighteen) are less likely to do so. For men, the presence of children of any age has no effect on the likelihood of working nonstandard shifts (Hamermesh 1996; Presser 1995, 1999).

The concern with work-family balance among female workers is also reflected in reasons workers give for working nonstandard schedules (Presser 1995). In a 1991 Current Population Survey (CPS), two-thirds of male respondents gave "job requirements" as the primary reason for working nonstandard shifts, but only about half of female respondents did so. Other reasons commonly given for working nonstandard schedules included child-care arrangements and schooling. Indeed, among women with preschool children, child-care arrangements were reasons as important as job requirements for working nonstandard shifts.

## SCHEDULE FLEXIBILITY AND CONTROL

These responses from the 1991 CPS clearly indicate that many workers, especially women, work irregular shifts out of *choice* rather than because of job or employer requirements. This runs counter to the assumption underlying much of the above literature that shift work is harmful to workers because they must adjust to working nonstandard times that are *imposed* upon them. Rather, it is consistent with the evidence that American workers have greater access to and are increasingly taking advantage of nonstandard and flexible scheduling options as a means of reducing harmful effects of working times on family or personal life. A number of recent surveys show substantial increases during the 1990s of employers offering some form of flexible scheduling, ranging from flexibility in starting and quitting times for workers on a standard eight-hour workday (usually a one- or two-hour window of choice) to allowing workers to change their starting and quitting times on a daily basis (Golden 2001). Many of these plans have been implemented as part of employer attempts to create "family-friendly" workplaces in response to increased labor-force participation among women and concern with managing both work and family demands (Bond, Galinsky, and Swanberg 1998). But, because many of these plans are discretionary on the part of employers, are not offered to all employees of the firm, and are often perceived by employees as detrimental to their careers if they actually take advantage of them, only a small percentage of eligible workers actually report working on flexible schedules. Nonetheless, the percentage of workers who work nonstandard schedules has increased substantially, from 12 percent in 1985 to almost 28 percent by 1997 (Beers 2000; Golden 2001).

It is not clear how many "flextime" plans offer workers choices among different shifts, such as working nights versus days, rather than just when to start their shift within a one- or two-hour window. However, their increasing availability raises the question of whether it is really schedule choice or control (or the lack of it) that determines whether shift work is harmful, rather than adjustments to working nonstandard times. If workers choose to work nonstandard schedules, are the effects harmful or as harmful as those for whom shift work is imposed? Does flexibility of scheduling mediate the supposedly harmful effects of nonstandard schedules or, does flexibility have an effect independent of the shifts worked?

There is limited but consistent evidence that worker choice, or schedule flexibility, is an important determinant of whether shift work is disruptive and harmful. For example, in Great Britain, Jane Barton (1994) found that among nurses of both genders, those who chose to work night shifts had significantly lower symptoms of cardiovascular disease and had fewer "non-domestic" disruptions (running personal errands, such as going to the doctor or to the bank) than those who did not choose their night-shift schedules. Staines and Pleck (1986) found that ability to change work schedules ("schedule flexibility") not only reduced but in many cases reversed the negative effects of working nonstandard shifts on measures of the quality of family life among married couples and single parents in the United States. Cynthia Negrey (1993) found that schedule control increased the well-being of women workers on the work site she studied because it increased the predictability of participating in nonwork social activities and roles. Data from the 1992 Canadian General Social Survey (Fast and Frederick 1996) found that "flextime" (workers choose when they begin and end their workday) reduced perceived "time stress" (a scale measuring time demands at work and the extent to which they interfere with time spent with family and friends). And, as with the negative effects of shift work per se, the positive effects of schedule flexibility on family outcomes have generally been found to be greater for women than men (Fast and Frederick 1996; Staines and Pleck 1986). As conceptualized in these studies, schedule flexibility and choice have positive effects on well-being and family life because they provide workers with the ability to adjust to potentially conflicting time demands.

Beyond this line of research, however, there is reason to believe that schedule flexibility and choice could benefit all workers, not just those who face problems of adjustment or conflicting demands brought on by working nonstandard shifts. By providing some degree of control over when work is done, flexibility and choice can be conceptualized more broadly as a dimension of overall job control (Christensen and Staines 1990; Loscocco 1997; Parasuraman and Simmers 2001). Since the 1970s, an increasing body of research in North America and Europe has consistently shown that having control over various aspects of one's job, such as the use of one's skills and the sequencing of different tasks, significantly reduces the risks of various illnesses. These include both direct and indirect risk factors in coronary heart disease and cardiovascular diseases such as high blood pressure, serum cholesterol, and smoking (Alfredsson, Spetz, and Theorell 1985; Haan 1985; Karasek 1979, 1989; Karasek and Theorell 1989; La Croix and Haynes 1984) and the rates of attempted suicide and psychiatric, gastrointestinal, and alcohol-related illnesses (Karasek and Theorell 1989). Job control also has been found to be inversely related to the incidence of self-reported anxiety and depression in the United States (Fenwick and Tausig 1994) and Great Britain (Griffin et al. 2002). Beyond these health outcomes, Linda Duxbury, Christopher Higgins, and Catherine Lee (1994) found that job control reduced family conflicts among their sample of workers in Canada. In turn, job control can also be seen as a component of the even broader concept of personal control that is strongly related to psychological well-being (Mirowsky and Ross 1989; Ross and Sastry 1999).

Overall, this line of research presents an additional way of thinking about the negative health and family outcomes associated with shift work: Rather than resulting from physiological, psychological, and family and social difficulties in adjusting to the actual clock time worked, these are the results of the lack of control over the time worked. Recent research has directly linked the degree of control over worktime to both health and family outcomes. For example, Leena Ala-Marsula et al. (2002) found that the level of "work time control" was related to levels of self-reported health, psychological distress, and "sickness absence rates" among female municipal employees in Finland. Rudy Fenwick and Mark Tausig (2001), using data from a 1992 national representative survey, found that the degree of "control over scheduling" (from "none" to "complete flexibility") was positively related to a number of positive family and health outcomes among U.S. workers of both genders. The strength and directions of these effects did not vary by gender, family structure (for example, single parent, dual earners, no children), or by shift worked. Control over work schedules was important for all workers.

In the analysis that follows, we will examine the adjustment and job control propositions in detail, specifically, proposition 1, that negative family and health outcomes associated with working nonstandard shifts such as non-weekday, night, or rotating shifts are consequences of the problems of adjustment to the actual times worked; proposition 2, that these negative outcomes are consequences of the lack of control or choice over the hours worked, independent of schedule; and proposition 3, that the level of schedule control mediates the negative effects of working nonstandard schedules by allowing workers to choose their schedules.

We will also examine whether shift work and schedule control are more consequential for some types of workers than others. In particular, the above discussion suggests proposition 4, that because of greater potential stress associated with working nonstandard schedules, control would have greater effects on those working nonstandard shifts than those on the standard day shift.

The prominence of gender differences and differences in family roles in the literature leads to proposition 5, that working nonstandard shifts and the degree of schedule control are more consequential for women and, proposition 6, working nonstandard shifts is more consequential for workers most in need of coordinating their job schedules with the needs of other family members: dual-career and single parents.

Finally, by looking at data sets from 1977 and 1997, we will be able to evaluate whether the changing demographics of shift work—what shifts are worked and who works them—have changed and how much shift work affects the health and family and personal lives of workers.

## DATA AND MEASURES

As stated above, our analysis uses data from two studies, the 1977 Quality of Employment Survey (QES), conducted on behalf of the U.S. Department of Labor, and the 1997 survey of the National Study of the Changing Workforce (NSCW) conducted by the Families and Work Institute. The QES data are from a national probability sample of persons 16 years old and older who were working for pay for 20 or more hours per week. There were 1,515 completed interviews. The NSCW data consist of responses to telephone interviews with a randomly selected national sample of employed adults over 18 years old. A total of 3,551 interviews were completed. Only persons who worked 35 or more hours per week (at all jobs) in either 1977 or 1997 are studied here. We choose to study only full-time workers because issues of time and time management are likely to be most salient for those working longer hours than for the typical part-time employee. In 1977 this results in 1,314 cases and in 1997 there are 3,036 cases for analysis.

Each of these data sets contains information on the health and family-social adjustment of workers, their work schedules, schedule control, work characteristics, and personal and family characteristics. Indeed, the 1997 NSCW survey was designed in part to permit direct comparison with the 1977 QES data. However, differences in sample characteristics and variable measurement limit the ways we can compare findings across data sets. The age criterion differs for the two samples, but there are few full-time workers aged sixteen or seventeen (N = 11) in the 1977 sample. Using only workers who average thirty-five hours per week or more excluded similar proportions of the original samples (12.2 and 13.5, respectively), but excluded a larger percentage of women in both data sets. This restriction does not affect the proportions of workers in each family structure we measure, except that married workers with children and a nonworking spouse in both data sets are more likely to work over 35 hours per week.

The definitions and measurement of shifts by the U.S. government and researchers has varied over time, and this prevents precise comparisons of change in the prevalence of schedule alternatives. In our study, differences in the measurement of shifts across data sets means that we must also be cautious in the way we interpret changes in the prevalence of shift alternatives. Similarly, since measures of health and family-social adjustment differ in 1977 and 1997, we will make no claims that the precise relationship between health and family-social outcomes and shifts has changed. Our comparison strategy is to evaluate broad patterns of relationships across survey years for a large variety of outcome measures. The analyses that follow are not in the strict sense longitudinal, since we will not conduct statistical tests between data sets nor attempt to explain change by computing change scores. However, we argue that changes or consistencies in patterns of relationships across surveys can be meaningfully interpreted.

## Dependent Variables: Health and Family-Social Adjustment

The reported effects of scheduling variations include a range of physical, psychological, and family-social adjustment outcomes. In 1977 we measured three physical or psychological health outcomes: distress, general health status, and dissatisfaction with life. (Details of measurement can be found in the table 4.1 for all dependent measures.) In 1997 we measured four physical or psychological health outcomes: distress, days ill (indicated by absence from work in past three months), dissatisfaction with life, and burnout.

In 1977 we measured three outcomes related to family-social adjustment: interference between job and free time, satisfaction with spare time, and work-family life interference. In 1997 we measured four outcomes related to family-social adjustment: interference between job and free time, conflict balancing work and personal life, negative spillover from home to job, and negative spillover from work to home.

## Independent Variables: Work Schedules

In both the 1977 and 1997 data sets, four dummy variables were created to categorize work-shift schedules. "M–F, day shift" (standard day shift) refers to workers who reported regular Monday- to Friday-daytime work hours. This dummy variable is the omitted comparison category in regression analysis. "Nonday shift" distinguishes workers reporting "regular evening" or "regular night" shift schedules (in 1997) from those reporting any other form of work schedule (for 1977, this shift includes workers who start work after noon). "Non–Monday–Friday shift" ("Non–M–F") distinguishes workers who report working any schedule that is other than Monday through Friday from respondents reporting any other form of work schedule.

TABLE 4.1  **Summary of Measures of Dependent Variables and Work, Family, and Individual Control Variables, 1977 and 1997**

Dependent Variables
1977
  Health-related
    Distress                      Nine items: physical symptoms of anxiety or depression[a]

    General health status       Single item: scale of 1 to 7
    Dissatisfaction with life    Single item: three levels (complete, not very)

  Family and social adjustment
    Interference between job and free time    Single item: how much interference

    Satisfaction with spare time    Single item: how satisfied
    Work-family life interference    Single item: how much

1997
  Health-related
    Distress                      Two items, minor health problems, stressed

    Ill days                     Single item: days missed work in three months

    Dissatisfaction with life    Single item: four levels
    Burnout                  Four items, used up, drained, tired, burned out[a]

  Family and social adjustment
    Interference between job and free time    One item: same as 1977

    Conflict balancing work and personal life    One item: how much conflict

    Negative spillover from home to job    Five items: family life prevents work involvements[a]

    Negative spillover from work to home    Five items: work prevents family involvements[b]

Work, Family, and Individual Control Variables
1977 and 1997
  Work-related
    Professional              Legal, medical, teaching, engineering and like occupations (omitted category)

    White collar            Managers or administrators, technical, sales, clerical

    Blue collar             Craft, operator, skilled and manual labor
    Service                 Service

(*continued*)

**TABLE 4.1** *Continued*

| | |
|---|---|
| Core | Manufacturing, transportation, finance, business services, health services, construction industries |
| State | Educational services, social services, public administration |
| Periphery | Wholesale and retail trade, other services, mining, agriculture, forestry, fishing (omitted category) |
| Self-employed | Single item |
| Hours per week | Actual hours worked in average week |
| Size | Natural log of number of employees at workplace |
| Union | Union member (yes, no) |
| Family and individual | |
| Gender | Male = 0, female = 1 |
| Race | White = 0, nonwhite = 1 |
| Education | Categories from less than high school to post-B.A. |
| Age | Years |
| Family structure | |
| | No children, unmarried (omitted category) |
| | No children, married, spouse not working |
| | No children, married, spouse works |
| | Single parent |
| | Two parents, married, spouse not working |
| | Two parents, married, spouse works |

*Source:* Authors' compilation.
[a]$\alpha = 0.81$.
[b]$\alpha = 0.85$.

"Rotating shift" distinguishes workers who work any form of rotating shift from those reporting any other work schedule. In the 1997 data we were also able to create an additional schedule type, "flexible schedule," which distinguishes workers who reported having a "flexible or variable schedule with no set hours" from those reporting any other work schedule.

## Schedule Control

In 1977, schedule control is measured as the mean of responses to three items:

> "How difficult do you think it would be for you to get the days you work changed permanently if you wanted them changed?"

> "How hard is it for you to take time off during the workday to take care of personal or family matters?"

> "How hard would it be for you to get the hours you begin and end work changed permanently?"

Cronbach's alpha for this set of items is 0.56 (Cronbach 1951). In 1997 we measured worker schedule control on the basis of a single item: "Overall, how much control would you say you have in scheduling your work hours: none, very little, some, a lot, or complete control?" Since we will not specifically compare coefficients for schedule control in 1977 and 1997, the differences in the way schedule control is measured are not as important as the similarity of the concept in both surveys.

## Control Variables: Work-Related, Family, and Individual Characteristics

In the 1977 and 1997 data sets we were able to measure work-related characteristics in identical ways. We measured occupational and industrial categories, self-employment, average hours worked per week, size of the workplace, and union membership (details of all measures of work-related and family and individual variables can be found in table 4.1).

In the 1977 and 1997 data we also have identical measures of a number of personal and family-related characteristics that we include as control measures. We measured respondents' gender, race, education, age, and family status (combination of marital, parental, and spouse work status).

## Interaction Terms

We constructed two-way interaction terms to investigate how schedule type and schedule control might interact. Separate terms for each schedule type by schedule control were computed for each data set. We also constructed two-way interaction terms for respondent family status by schedule type and by schedule control. These latter terms permit us to test whether the effects of schedules and schedule control are more salient to workers depending on their marital, parental, and family situation. Finally, we computed interaction terms for gender by shift and by schedule control to examine the hypothesis that the impact of schedules is different for men and women.

## ANALYSIS

Table 4.2 reports the means for independent variables by schedule type and for those with high schedule control in 1977 and 1997, respectively. Overall there were substantial changes in the composition of the full-time labor force in this twenty-year span. Between 1977 and 1997 the labor force aged slightly. It became more female, included more nonwhites, was better educated, and included more parents and dual-income families. Workers averaged more hours on the job per week in 1997 and they were less likely to be members of labor unions. In 1997 workers were less likely to work in blue-collar occupations and more likely to work in professional occupations. They were also more likely to be self-employed and to work in core industries. These changes in the labor force have been well documented by others. By themselves these differences suggest that time might become a more salient factor for workers because they spend more time at work and because more workers have children.

It is more difficult to assess changes in the distribution of the labor force across various shifts because of the different ways shifts were measured in 1977 and 1997. Most notably, "flexible schedule" was measured only in 1997. In addition, respondents can have work schedules with more than one shift characteristic (rotating and non–Monday-to-Friday); thus, the proportion of workers across shifts adds to more than 100 percent. Nonetheless, comparisons showed no dramatic changes in the distribution of shift work. Most workers employed thirty or more hours per week continued to work the standard day shift in 1997 (70 percent, compared to 68 percent in 1977). Likewise, the percentages of workers on non–Monday-to-Friday

TABLE 4.2  Means for Independent Variables by Schedule Type and Schedule Control, 1977 and 1997

| Variables | All | | Regular Monday to Friday Day | | Non-Monday to Friday Day | | Nonday[a] | | Rotating | | Flexible[b] | High Control | |
|---|---|---|---|---|---|---|---|---|---|---|---|---|---|
| | 1977 | 1997 | 1977 | 1997 | 1977 | 1997 | 1977 | 1997 | 1977 | 1997 | 1997 | 1977 | 1997 |
| n | 1,147 | 3,030 | 784 | 2,174 | 346 | 856 | 136 | 226 | 56 | 166 | 407 | 137 | 565 |
| | | | (68.4) | (71.7) | (30.2) | (28.3) | (11.9) | (7.5) | (4.9) | (5.5) | (13.4) | (11.9) | (18.6) |
| Age | 38.50 | 40.99 | 38.93 | 41.00 | 38.43 | 40.90 | 32.65 | 38.08 | 36.75 | 38.18 | 41.07 | 39.32 | 43.41 |
| Sex (percentage female) | 0.33 | 0.47 | 0.37 | 0.48 | 0.24 | 0.44 | 0.34 | 0.45 | 0.21 | 0.42 | 0.35 | 0.23 | 0.39 |
| Race (percentage nonwhite) | 0.10 | 0.20 | 0.12 | 0.21 | 0.08 | 0.18 | 0.19 | 0.34 | 0.07 | 0.23 | 0.12 | 0.07 | 0.20 |
| Less than high school | 0.21 | 0.06 | 0.21 | 0.05 | 0.23 | 0.07 | 0.21 | 0.08 | 0.23 | 0.07 | 0.06 | 0.15 | 0.07 |
| High school graduate | 0.37 | 0.29 | 0.35 | 0.27 | 0.40 | 0.33 | 0.46 | 0.45 | 0.41 | 0.38 | 0.25 | 0.27 | 0.29 |
| Some college | 0.23 | 0.32 | 0.22 | 0.31 | 0.22 | 0.34 | 0.22 | 0.35 | 0.27 | 0.37 | 0.29 | 0.34 | 0.31 |
| Bachelor's degree | 0.09 | 0.21 | 0.10 | 0.23 | 0.08 | 0.17 | 0.09 | 0.09 | 0.09 | 0.11 | 0.25 | 0.12 | 0.21 |
| Post-baccalaureate | 0.10 | 0.12 | 0.13 | 0.13 | 0.07 | 0.08 | 0.01 | 0.03 | 0 | 0.06 | 0.16 | 0.12 | 0.11 |
| Single, no children | 0.26 | 0.26 | 0.26 | 0.25 | 0.29 | 0.28 | 0.38 | 0.32 | 0.12 | 0.36 | 0.28 | 0.26 | 0.20 |
| Single parent | 0.05 | 0.11 | 0.05 | 0.11 | 0.03 | 0.13 | 0.07 | 0.17 | 0.04 | 0.15 | 0.08 | 0.01 | 0.12 |
| No children, spouse working | 0.13 | 0.17 | 0.14 | 0.17 | 0.11 | 0.15 | 0.06 | 0.10 | 0.14 | 0.10 | 0.17 | 0.16 | 0.16 |

| No children, spouse not working | 0.12 | 0.06 | 0.12 | 0.05 | 0.11 | 0.08 | 0.04 | 0.07 | 0.20 | 0.06 | 0.07 | 0.12 | 0.10 |
|---|---|---|---|---|---|---|---|---|---|---|---|---|---|
| Children, spouse working | 0.20 | 0.28 | 0.21 | 0.30 | 0.18 | 0.25 | 0.24 | 0.20 | 0.18 | 0.21 | 0.27 | 0.15 | 0.29 |
| Children, spouse not working | 0.24 | 0.12 | 0.22 | 0.12 | 0.28 | 0.11 | 0.21 | 0.14 | 0.32 | 0.12 | 0.13 | 0.30 | 0.13 |
| Core | 0.56 | 0.62 | 0.63 | 0.66 | 0.39 | 0.51 | 0.74 | 0.71 | 0.57 | 0.40 | 0.58 | 0.50 | 0.60 |
| State | 0.18 | 0.15 | 0.23 | 0.18 | 0.08 | 0.07 | 0.09 | 0.08 | 0.16 | 0.16 | 0.09 | 0.13 | 0.08 |
| Periphery | 0.25 | 0.23 | 0.14 | 0.16 | 0.52 | 0.41 | 0.18 | 0.20 | 0.27 | 0.44 | 0.34 | 0.37 | 0.32 |
| Self-employed | 0.13 | 0.17 | 0.06 | 0.12 | 0.32 | 0.30 | 0 | 0.09 | 0.02 | 0.11 | 0.46 | 0.39 | 0.42 |
| White collar | 0.40 | 0.46 | 0.36 | 0.48 | 0.49 | 0.43 | 0.26 | 0.24 | 0.27 | 0.41 | 0.46 | 0.55 | 0.53 |
| Professional | 0.14 | 0.18 | 0.18 | 0.20 | 0.06 | 0.12 | 0.07 | 0.07 | 0.05 | 0.11 | 0.19 | 0.09 | 0.14 |
| Blue collar | 0.37 | 0.26 | 0.40 | 0.26 | 0.32 | 0.27 | 0.51 | 0.49 | 0.48 | 0.31 | 0.24 | 0.27 | 0.23 |
| Service | 0.11 | 0.09 | 0.05 | 0.06 | 0.13 | 0.17 | 0.22 | 0.20 | 0.20 | 0.16 | 0.11 | 0.09 | 0.09 |
| Hours per week | 46.2 | 49.8 | 42.9 | 48.5 | 53.0 | 53.0 | 43.8 | 47.7 | 44.9 | 51.6 | 56.7 | 48.8 | 52.5 |
| Multiple jobs | 0.15 | 0.16 | 0.14 | 0.15 | 0.15 | 0.19 | 0.12 | 0.16 | 0.18 | 0.17 | 0.24 | 0.12 | 0.20 |
| Size of firm | 4.43 | 4.45 | 4.69 | 4.54 | 3.67 | 4.20 | 5.71 | 5.24 | 5.07 | 4.74 | 3.85 | 3.36 | 3.76 |
| Union member | 0.26 | 0.15 | 0.29 | 0.18 | 0.20 | 0.14 | 0.44 | 0.27 | 0.41 | 0.21 | 0.08 | 0.10 | 0.06 |
| Schedule control[c] | 2.15 | 3.05 | 2.10 | 2.95 | 2.32 | 3.29 | 2.08 | 2.65 | 1.87 | 2.67 | 3.76 | 3.36 | 3.76 |

*Source:* Authors' analyses. 1977 data are from Quinn and Staines (1979); 1997 data are from Bond, Galinsky, and Swanberg (1998).

*Note:* Numbers in parentheses are percentages.

[a]Nonday shift is regular evening or night shift in 1997 and in 1977 includes those who start work after noon.

[b]Flexible schedules were not measured in 1977.

[c]Schedule control is measured differently in 1977 and 1997 (see text). The values cannot be compared directly.

and rotating shifts remained roughly the same at around 30 percent and 5 percent, respectively. Those who reported working nonday shifts actually declined from 12 percent to just over 7 percent, but this may be an artifact of differences in the way nonday shifts are computed in our analysis. Just over 13 percent of respondents in 1997 reported working flexible shifts. Finally, there was an increase in workers reporting a "high" level of schedule control: from 12 percent in 1977 to almost 19 percent in 1997, but different measures of control were used in each year.

Overall, changes in the characteristics of the workers on the various shifts mirrored changing characteristics of the general labor force. For example, as the percentage of the total labor force with college and graduate degrees increased, the percentages of these workers in each shift category also increased. The most significant exception involves women workers, who increased from 33 to 47 percent of the total labor force between 1977 and 1997. However, in 1977, women were substantially underrepresented among workers on non–Monday-to-Friday and rotating shifts: 24 and 21 percent of these shifts, respectively. By 1997, the percentages of women on these shifts nearly doubled, to 44 and 42 percent, respectively, thus becoming nearly proportional to their overall rate of labor-force participation. This change in the distribution of women across job shifts was consistent with the increasing concerns about the effects of shift work on women workers.

Although the category "flexible shift" was not measured in 1977, it is worth describing the type of worker with this schedule in 1997. These workers were more likely to be male and white and to have higher levels of education. They were slightly less likely to be single parents, but otherwise family structure does not affect the likelihood of having this schedule. Self-employed workers and workers in peripheral industries were much more likely to have flexible schedules. Those with flexible schedules worked more hours each week and were more likely to have multiple jobs and to work in smaller firms and were least likely to be union members. Workers with flexible schedules also reported the highest level of schedule control.

Finally, in 1997 workers who reported high levels of schedule control were proportionately older. Whereas educational level was positively associated with high control in 1977, there was no relationship to control in 1997. In 1997, workers with high schedule control worked more hours and were more likely to have multiple jobs. In both 1977 and 1997, they worked for the smallest firms.

Results for the multivariate analyses of the effects of job schedules and schedule control on family-social and health outcomes in 1977 and 1997 are presented in tables 4.3A and 4.3B, respectively. To control for the potential spuriousness of these effects as a result of their common associations with characteristics of individuals (age, education, gender, race), families (marital and parental status), and work (occupation, industry), we have included these variables in our regression equations. However, because the specific effects of these control variables are not central to our analysis or discussion, we will not report them here (the tables are available on request). Briefly, we note that the effects of these variables are consistent across time and consistent with previous research. In both surveys, family-social and health problems are related primarily to being younger, being female, and working longer hours. Parents, and especially single parents in 1997, report more family-social problems, but also (with the exception of single parents) lower dissatisfaction with life than nonparents.

Tables 4.3A and 4.3B present the multivariate effects of schedule type and schedule control on family-social and health outcomes net of the effects of the individual, family, and work variables. In addition to the regression coefficients for the schedule and control variables in each equation, we present a measure of R-squared change that shows the increase in explained variance when schedule types and schedule control were added to the effects of the covariates. We also present an adjusted overall R-squared that shows the total amount of explained variance when both the schedule variables and covariates are included in the equation. These results enable us to test our first three propositions, that these outcomes are the result of (1) working nonstandard shifts and (2) the lack of control over work schedules, and (3) that the effects of working nonstandard schedules are mediated by the level of schedule control. In order to test this third proposition, we have entered these variables into the regression equations in two stages: (1) schedule type and (2) schedule control. If mediation occurs, significant effects of schedule type should reduce to nonsignificance when schedule control is entered.

TABLE 4.3A  The Effects of Schedule Type and Schedule Control on Job–Free Time Interference, Work-Family Interference, Dissatisfaction with Spare Time, Distress, Dissatisfaction with Life and General Health Status (Controlling for Individual, Family, and Work and Employment Variables), 1977

| | Dependent Variables | | | | | | | | | | | |
|---|---|---|---|---|---|---|---|---|---|---|---|---|
| Independent Variables | Job–Free-Time Interference | | Work-Family Interference | | Dissatisfaction with Spare Time | | Distress | | Dissatisfaction | | General Health Status | |
| Schedule types | | | | | | | | | | | | |
| Nonday | .319*** | .345*** | .506*** | .529*** | .253*** | .277*** | .167 | .239 | .029 | .037 | -.100 | -.115 |
| | (.092) | (.094) | (.109) | (.112) | (.072) | (.074) | (.514) | (.526) | (.049) | (.051) | (.097) | (.100) |
| Not Monday to Friday | .132+ | .152* | .104 | .127 | .043 | .052 | .423 | .620 | .056 | .071+ | -.158* | -.181* |
| | (.069) | (.071) | (.076) | (.079) | (.054) | (.055) | (.387) | (.395) | (.037) | (.038) | (.072) | (.074) |
| Rotating | .054 | .037 | .472*** | .449*** | -.023 | -.023 | 1.503* | 1.312+ | -.032 | -.048 | .042 | .047 |
| | (.130) | (.131) | (.131) | (.133) | (.101) | (.102) | (.713) | (.719) | (.069) | (.070) | (.135) | (.138) |
| Schedule control | | | | | | | | | | | | |
| Schedule control | | -.129*** | | -.111** | | -.056+ | | -.829*** | | -.066*** | | .089* |
| | | (.038) | | (.042) | | (.029) | | (.210) | | (.020) | | (.040) |
| Change in R-squared[a] | .009 | .004 | .028 | .003 | .010 | .006 | .005 | .014 | .000 | .006 | .004 | .000 |
| Total adjusted R-squared[b] | .091 | .095 | .150 | .153 | .049 | .054 | .043 | .057 | .030 | .036 | .053 | .053 |

*Source:* Authors' analyses of data from Quinn and Staines (1979).

*Notes:* Numbers in parentheses are standard errors. N = 1,250. The equation for work-family interference contains 928 cases (the dependent variable was not measured for single individuals or marrieds without children). Under each dependent variable, the first column of figures represents regression effects and R-squared with just schedule-type variables. The second column represents schedule type and control.

[a] R-squared changes when schedule types and control are added to the equation with covariates.

[b] Includes schedule types and covariates in equation.

+ p < .10   * p ≤ .05   ** p ≤ .01   *** p ≤ .001

TABLE 4.3B  The Effects of Schedule Type and Schedule Control on Job–Free Time Interference, Conflict Balancing Work and Personal Life, Negative Spillover from Home to Work, Negative Spillover from Work to Home, Distress, Dissatisfaction with Life, and Days Ill in the Past Three Months (Controlling for Individual, Family and Work, and Employment Variables), 1997

Dependent Variables

| Independent Variables | Job–Free-Time Interference | | Conflict Balancing Work and Personal Life | | Negative Spillover from Home to Work | | Negative Spillover from Work to Home | | Burnout | | Distress | | Dissatisfaction with Life | | Days Ill in Past Three Months | |
|---|---|---|---|---|---|---|---|---|---|---|---|---|---|---|---|---|
| **Schedule types** | | | | | | | | | | | | | | | | |
| Nonday | .203** | .211** | .176* | .184+ | .050 | .054 | .112 | .111 | -.015 | -.011 | .059 | .064 | .053 | .052 | -.833* | -.836* |
| | (.078) | (.078) | (.089) | (.089) | (.054) | (.054) | (.075) | (.074) | (.080) | (.079) | (.076) | (.076) | (.055) | (.055) | (.409) | (.412) |
| Not Monday to Friday | .065 | .067 | .016 | .017 | -.063 | -.062 | -.030 | -.021 | -.055 | -.047 | -.041 | -.035 | .058 | .061 | .447 | .447 |
| | (.053) | (.053) | (.061) | (.060) | (.037) | (.037) | (.051) | (.051) | (.055) | (.054) | (.052) | (.052) | (.038) | (.037) | (.280) | (.282) |
| Rotating | .281** | .257** | .263** | .228* | .100 | .093 | .302*** | .260** | .149 | .104 | .010 | -.018 | .054 | .022 | -.893+ | -.895+ |
| | (.089) | (.089) | (.102) | (.101) | (.101) | (.062) | (.086) | (.085) | (.092) | (.090) | (.087) | (.087) | (.064) | (.063) | (.469) | (.471) |
| Flexible | .034 | .058 | .095 | .127 | -.030 | -.022 | -.019 | .021 | -.029 | .015 | .013 | .042 | -.037 | -.013 | .260 | .262 |
| | (.070) | (.070) | (.080) | (.079) | (.049) | (.048) | (.067) | (.066) | (.072) | (.071) | (.069) | (.068) | (.050) | (.049) | (.368) | (.371) |
| **Schedule control** | | | | | | | | | | | | | | | | |
| Schedule control | | -.073*** | | -.100*** | | -.016 | | -.128*** | | -.139*** | | -.091*** | | -.092*** | | .004 |
| | | (.016) | | (.018) | | (.011) | | (.015) | | (.016) | | | | (.025) | | (.084) |
| Change in R-squared[a] | .006 | .009 | .003 | .012 | .002 | -.001 | .003 | .028 | -.003 | .028 | -.001 | .013 | .000 | .025 | .001 | .000 |
| Total adjusted R-squared[b] | .055 | .064 | .078 | .090 | .042 | .041 | .079 | .107 | .046 | .074 | .052 | .065 | .047 | .072 | .009 | .009 |

Source: Authors' analyses of data from Bond, Galinsky, and Swanberg (1998).

Notes: Numbers in parentheses are standard errors. N = 2,556.

[a] R-squared changes when schedule types and control are added to the equation with covariates.

[b] Includes schedule types and covariates in equation.

+ p < .10   * p ≤ .05   ** p ≤ .01   *** p ≤ .001

However, while the results from tables 4.3A and 4.3B show consistent significant effects for both work schedules and schedule control, the effects appear to be independent of each other. There is no evidence that control mediates the effects of schedules. The effects of work schedules were almost entirely limited to family-social outcomes in 1977 and 1997. In both surveys, working either "nonday" or "rotating" shifts increased family and social adjustment problems. In 1977, working "nonday" shifts increased all three of the measures "job–free-time interference," "work-family interference," and "dissatisfaction with spare time," while "rotating shift" increased "work-family interference." In 1997, "rotating" shifts significantly increased three of the four measures of family-social adjustment problems: "job–free-time interference," "conflict balancing work and family life," and "negative work-to-home spillover." Working "nonday" shifts increased "job–free-time interference." All of these effects remained significant when schedule control was entered into the equations. By contrast, different work schedules had few and inconsistent effects on health adjustment problems in either survey: working "nonday" shifts reduced "general health status" in 1977, but actually reduced the number of reported days ill in 1997, as did (modestly) working "rotating" shifts. The one type of irregular schedule touted to have positive effects on workers—"flexible"—had no effects at all.

On the other hand, the effects of schedule control were consistent in both surveys and across both family-social and health outcomes. In 1977, schedule control had significant effects on all three family-social outcomes and all three health outcomes. Control reduced both "job–free-time" and "work-family" interference, and (marginally) "dissatisfaction with spare time." It also reduced "distress" and "life dissatisfaction," while improving "general health." In 1997, control had significant effects on three of the four family-social outcomes and three of the four health outcomes. It reduced "job–free-time interference" (as in 1977), as well as "conflict balancing work and personal life" and "negative work-to-home spillover." Among health outcomes, it reduced "distress" and "dissatisfaction with life," as in 1977, as well as "burnout."

In tables 4.4A and 4.4B we test proposition 4, that schedule control moderates the stressful family-social and health outcomes for those working nonstandard schedules, and thus should be more

**TABLE 4.4A  Nonlinear Effects of Schedule Type and Schedule Control, 1977**

| Interaction of Terms | Job–Free-Time Interference | Work-Family Interference | Dissatisfaction with Spare Time | Distress | Dissatisfaction | General Health |
|---|---|---|---|---|---|---|
| Schedule multiplied by control | | | | | | |
| Nonday multiplied by control | -.094 | -.217 | -.256** | -.018 | .026 | -.017 |
| | (.124) | (.150) | (.097) | (.702) | (.067) | (.133) |
| Not Monday to Friday multiplied by control | -.059 | .154+ | -.007 | .446 | .012 | .055 |
| | (.076) | (.085) | (.060) | (.425) | (.041) | (.081) |
| Rotating multiplied by control | -.220 | -.276 | -.185 | .601 | .006 | -.035 |
| | (.175) | (.169) | (.137) | (.962) | (.094) | (.184) |
| Change in R-squared[a] | .000 | .004 | .005 | -.001 | -.002 | -.002 |
| Total adjusted R-squared[b] | .095 | .157 | .059 | .056 | .034 | .051 |

*Source:* Authors' analyses of data from Quinn and Staines (1979).

*Notes:* Numbers in parentheses are standard errors. N = 1,250. The equation for work-family interference contains 928 cases (the dependent variable was not measured for single persons or marrieds without children).

[a]Increment in R-squared is from the equation with covariates, schedule and control (table 4.3A).

[b]Includes schedule types and covariates in equation.

+ p < .10   *p < .05   **p < .01

**TABLE 4.4B  Nonlinear Effects of Schedule Type and Schedule Control, 1997**

| Interaction Terms | Job–Free-Time Interference | Conflict Balancing Work and Personal Life | Negative Spillover from Home to Work | Negative Spillover from Work to Home | Burnout | Distress | Dissatisfaction with Life | Days Ill in Past Three Months |
|---|---|---|---|---|---|---|---|---|
| Schedule multiplied by control | | | | | | | | |
| Nonday multiplied by control | .008 | -.004 | .004 | -.019 | .039 | .025 | .004 | -.203 |
| | (.056) | (.063) | (.039) | (.052) | (.056) | (.054) | (.039) | (.303) |
| Not Monday to Friday multiplied by control | -.054 | -.049 | -.032 | -.072+ | -.046 | .015 | .022 | .462* |
| | (.039) | (.044) | (.027) | (.037) | (.039) | (.038) | (.027) | (.211) |
| Rotating multiplied by control | -.027 | -.033 | .020 | .061 | .030 | .023 | -.068 | -.359 |
| | (.066) | (.075) | (.046) | (.063) | (.067) | (.065) | (.046) | (.361) |
| Flexible multiplied by control | -.175*** | -.208*** | -.067** | -.246*** | -.272*** | -.210*** | -.149*** | -.288 |
| | (.033) | (.038) | (.023) | (.031) | (.034) | (.032) | (.023) | (.181) |
| Change in R-squared[a] | .010 | .010 | .004 | .026 | .027 | .014 | .010 | .002 |
| Total adjusted R-squared[b] | .074 | .100 | .045 | .133 | .101 | .079 | .082 | .011 |

*Source:* Data from Bond, Galinsky, and Swanberg (1998).
*Notes:* Numbers in parentheses are standard errors. N = 2,556.
[a]Increment in R-squared is from the equation with covariates, schedule and control (table 4.3B).
[b]Includes schedule types and covariates in equation.
+ p < .10  * p < .05  ** p < .01  *** p < .001

significant for those workers than for those on the standard day shift. We do so by examining the interactions between control and the various types of schedules. Results indicate little evidence for moderation—with one glaring exception: the significant interaction effects between flexible work schedules and schedule control in 1997 (table 4.4B). Increasing levels of schedule control significantly reduced the negative family-social and health outcomes for workers on "flexible" schedules in seven of the eight equations (excepting "days ill"). These results raise serious questions about the tendency of much of the previous literature to equate flexible scheduling with some degree of worker control over schedules. However, as pointed out in the review of the literature, "flexible scheduling" is a term that covers a wide variety of scheduling practices that offer workers more or less worker choice as to when they work (Golden 2001). And, as measured in 1997, the "flexible schedule" category includes workers on "variable schedules with no set hours," a term that would include workers who are "on call" and have little choice as to how they respond to the call. It is clear that in 1997, respondents made the distinction between these "flexible schedules" and having "control" over them.

The last part of our analysis concerns proposition 5, that both shift work and schedule control have differential effects on women workers, and proposition 6, that both shift work and schedule control have differential effects on single and dual-career parents because these groups have more extensive family obligations and greater difficulties in coordinating these obligations with the obligations of work. We tested these propositions by creating interaction terms for each schedule type by each family status and terms for each family status and high schedule control. Interaction terms for gender by schedule type and control were also computed. In both 1977 and 1997 there were few significant interaction terms with gender (gender by schedule type, gender by schedule control). Hence, these results are not shown and the significant interactions that were observed can be attributed to chance.

The same situation pertains to the effects of computed interactions for family status by schedule type or control in 1977. Only seven of ninety-six interaction terms were found to be significant at $p < .05$. In table 4.5, however, we summarize the findings from analysis of interaction terms crossing family status by schedule and

**TABLE 4.5  Summary of Significant Family Status by Shift, Family Structure by Schedule Control Interactions (Controlling for Individual, Family, Work and Employment Variables, Schedule Type, and Control), 1997**

| Outcome Interaction[a] | Burnout | Stress | Dissatisfaction | Days Ill | Job Versus Free Time | Work-Personal Balance | Spillover from Home to Job | Spillover from Job to Home |
|---|---|---|---|---|---|---|---|---|
| Flexible schedule multiplied by | | | | | | | | |
| No kids, spouse works | − | | | | − | | | − |
| No kids, spouse does not work | | | | | − | − | | − |
| Single parent | − | | | + | | | | |
| Two parents, spouse works | − | − | | | − | − | − | |
| Two parents, spouse does not work | − | − | | | − | | − | |
| Rotating schedule multiplied by | | | | | | | | |
| No kids, spouse does not work | − | | | | | − | | |
| Single parent | − | | | − | | | − | |

| | | | | | |
|---|---|---|---|---|---|
| **Not Monday to Friday schedule multiplied by** | | | | | |
| No kids, spouse does not work | | − | | + | |
| Single parent | + | | − | | |
| **Non-day schedule multiplied by** | | | | | |
| Two parents, spouse works | | + | + | | + |
| **High schedule control multiplied by** | | | | | |
| No kids, spouse works | + | | + | | |
| No kids, spouse does not work | − | | − | | |
| Single parent | + | | | | |

*Source:* Authors' analyses of data from Bond, Galinsky, and Swanberg (1998).

[a]Only these specific interaction terms had significant coefficients (p < .05) with the outcome variables.

by schedule control in the 1997 data. For this analysis, thirty-eight of a possible two hundred interaction terms were significant. In table 4.5 significant coefficients for interaction terms are indicated by a plus or minus sign, depending on their relationship with the dependent variable. Interestingly, and in contrast to the results in tables 4.3B and 4.4B, "flexible schedules" per se have the most consistent effects in reducing the negative outcomes associated with shift work. Regardless of family status, excepting the reference category "not married and no children," workers with flexible schedules reported lower levels of family-social adjustment and health problems. The sole exception is that single parents with flexible schedules reported more days ill in the past three months. Among other schedule types, with the exception of nonday schedules among dual-career households, significant interactions also reduce negative family-social and health outcomes. This suggests that families can use schedule options to their benefit, although the benefits are not widespread by schedule type or across outcomes. It is also clear that workers with nonday schedules in dual-career households are at risk for increased adjustment and health problems. This is the sole condition in which the interaction of schedule and family status appears to consistently create problems.

## DISCUSSION

The preceding analysis provides mixed support for the various propositions relating nonstandard and flexible job schedules to family-social and health outcomes. Results from 1977 and 1997 (tables 4.3A and 4.3B) are consistent with those of previous research that have found nonstandard shifts, especially nonday and rotating, to be disruptive of family and social life (proposition 1). However, we found no substantial effects for nonstandard job schedules on health outcomes at either time (proposition 1). Although this is at variance with much previous research, the variance could be accounted for by differences in sampling and health measures. Much previous research used large, in-depth, and often longitudinal samples (for example, Kawachi et al. 1995) to capture medically diagnosed illnesses (CHD, CV) that are relatively rare in the overall population. In contrast, we have used representative samples of the entire workforce to examine more general and subjectively measured health outcomes.

The benefits of working on a "flexible" schedule are also supported by our results from 1997 (table 4.5), and these benefits extend beyond dual-career and single-parent households (proposition 6). All workers with either children or a spouse or partner benefit; only those who have neither children nor a spouse or partner do not benefit. Working on a "flexible" schedule not only reduces disruptions to one's family and social life but also reduces one's level of stress and burnout. Otherwise, the effects of nonstandard and flexible schedules do not differ systematically by gender (proposition 5), or by family type (proposition 6).

Likewise, the effects of schedule control are more general and more important than the way they are generally portrayed in the literature. Consistent with the job-control literature (proposition 2), the effects of schedule control are linear and independent of job schedules. Schedule control matters for all workers: those on standard shifts as well as those on nonstandard shifts; men as well as women; workers in "traditional" single-breadwinner families as well as single and dual-career parents. Schedule control also matters for both family-social and health outcomes. Schedule control had significant positive effects on all six family-social outcomes measured in 1977 and six of eight outcomes measured in 1997 (tables 4.3A and 4.3B). These findings support our earlier argument that schedule control might best be regarded as a dimension of job control rather than as a dimension of flexible scheduling. Both the ability to choose a work schedule and to control starting and ending times within that schedule may reflect the underlying issue of autonomy in the workplace.

This interpretation of the meaning of schedule control is reinforced by the lack of evidence that it either mediates (proposition 3) or moderates (proposition 4) the effects of working nonstandard shifts, or that it is especially beneficial to workers thought to be most vulnerable to the negative consequences of shift work: women (proposition 5) and single and dual-career parents (proposition 6). The one exception concerns the significant interactions between schedule control and working flexible schedules. As discussed above, this result is suggestive of a great range of "control" that workers have over their "flexible" schedules, and cautions against conflating "flexible" scheduling with having schedule "control."

Schedule control should properly be regarded as a dimension of overall job control that is in turn related to worker well-being. This view has received scant attention in the literature on shift work. Instead, control is often conceived as a mediating or moderating factor between schedule type and well-being, a view that obscures its direct effect on well-being. This has allowed the discussion about shift work and schedule flexibility to center on issues of individual (especially women with children) worker adjustment as opposed to issues of the organization of work and the contested terrain of the workplace. Our results indicate that in 1977, control over one's schedule had substantial and direct effects on well-being; despite changes in the composition of the workforce by 1997 and characteristics of workers in schedule alternatives at that time, control still has substantial and direct effects on worker well-being. Hence, the more general issue of who controls a worker's labor and what effects such control has on worker well-being need to reenter discussions of the consequences of the changing nature of work, especially as it relates to changing job schedules. In the present instance, the "gender" issue of creating family-friendly workplaces by providing flextime schedules obscures the continuing issue of work control that is faced by all workers. To be sure, many workers face adjustment problems that are directly related to the physical, emotional, and family-related strains caused by work schedules. But the impact of schedules must include as well consideration of the fundamental issue of control over work.

---

We would like to thank Corina Graif for her assistance with the data analysis. We also thank the Families and Work Institute, New York City, for permitting the use of their data, and the Inter-University Consortium for Political and Social Research for making the Quality of Employment Survey data available. The authors of this study are solely responsible for any conclusions or opinions expressed herein.

## REFERENCES

Akerstedt, Torbjorn. 1990. "Psychological and Physiological Effects of Shiftwork." *Scandinavian Journal of Work and Environmental Health* 16(1): 67–73.

Ala-Marsula, Leena, Jussi Vahtera, Mika Kivimaki, May V. Kevin, and Jossi Pentti. 2002. "Employee Control over Working Times: Associations with Subjective Health and Sickness Absences." *Journal of Epidemiology and Community Health* 56(4): 272–8.

Alfredsson, Lars, Curt L. Spetz, and Töres Theorell. 1985. "Type of Occupation and Near-future Hospitalization for Myocardial Infarction and some Other Diagnoses." *International Journal of Epidemiology* 14(3): 378–88.

Barton, Jane. 1994. "Choosing to Work at Night: A Moderating Influence on Individual Tolerance to Shift Work." *Journal of Applied Psychology* 79(3): 449–54.

Beers, Thomas M. 2000 "Flexible Schedules and Shift Work: Replacing the '9-to-5' Workday?" *Monthly Labor Review* 123(6): 33–40.

Benach Joan, M. Amable, Carles Mutaner, and Fernando G. Benavides. 2002. "The Consequences of Flexible Work for Health: Are We Looking at the Right Place?" *Journal of Epidemiology and Community Health* 56(6): 405–6.

Bianchi, Suzanne M., and Daphne Spain. 1996. "Women, Work, and Family in America." *Population Bulletin* 51(3): 2–48.

Bjorvatn, Bjorn, Goran Keclund, and Torbjorn Akerstedt. 1998. "Rapid Adaptation to Night Work on an Oil Platform, but Slow Readaptation After Returning Home." *Journal of Occupational and Environmental Medicine* 40(7): 601–8.

Bohle, Phillip, and Andrew J. Tilley. 1990. "The Impact of Night Work on Psychological Well Being." *Ergonomics* 32(9): 1089–99.

Bond, James T., Ellen Galinsky, and Jennifer Swanberg. 1998. *The 1997 National Study of the Changing Work Force.* New York: Families and Work Institute.

Carpenter, James, and Pierre Cazamian. 1977. "Night Work: Its Effects on the Health and Welfare of the Worker." Geneva: International Labour Office.

Christensen, Kathleen E., and Graham L. Staines. 1990. "Flextime: A Viable Solution to Work/Family Conflict." *Journal of Family Issues* 11(4): 455–76.

Coffey, Linda C., James K. Skipper, and Fred D. Jung. 1988. "Nurses and Shift Work: Effects on Job Performance and Job-Related Stress." *Journal of Advanced Nursing* 13(2): 245–54.

Colligan, Michael J., and Rodger R. Rosa. 1990. "Shift Work Effects on Social and Family Life." *Occupational Medicine* 5(2): 301–22.

Costa, Giovanni, Francesca Lievore, Giovanni Casaletti, Edoardo Gaffuri, and Simon Folkard. 1989. "Circadian Characteristics Influencing Inter-Individual Differences in Tolerance and Adjustment to Shift Work." *Ergonomics* 32(4): 373–85.

Cronbach, Lee J. 1951. "Coefficient Alpha and the Internal Structure of Tests." *Psychometrika* 16(3): 297–334.

De Backer, Guy, Marcel Kornitzer, H. Peters, and M. Dramaix. 1984. "Relationship Between Work Rhythm and Coronary Risk Factors." *European Heart Journal* 5(suppl. 1): 307.

Duxbury, Linda, Christopher Higgins, and Catherine Lee. 1994. "Work-Family Conflict: A Comparison by Gender, Family Type and Perceived Control." *Journal of Family Issues* 15(3): 449–66.

Fast, Janet E., and Judith A. Frederick. 1996. "Untitled Canadian Social Trends Backgrounder." *Canadian Social Trends* 43(Winter): 15–19.

Fenwick, Rudy, and Mark Tausig. 1994. "The Macroecomonic Context of Job Stress." *Journal of Health and Social Behavior* 35(3): 266–82.

———. 2001. "Scheduling Stress: Family and Health Outcomes of Shift Work and Schedule Control." *American Behavioral Scientist* 44(7): 1179–98.

Fullerton, Howard N. 1999. "Labor Force Projections to 2008: Steady Growth and Changing Composition." *Monthly Labor Review* 122(11): 19–32.

Gabarino, Sergio, Lino Nobili, Manolo Beelke, Vincenzo Balestra, Alessandro Cordelli, and Franco Ferrillo. 2002. "Sleep Disorders and Daytime Sleepiness in State Police Shiftworkers." *Archives of Environmental Health* 57(2): 167–73.

Golden, Lonnie. 2001. "Flexible Work Schedules: Which Workers Get Them?" *American Behavioral Scientist* 44(7): 1157–78.

Griffin, Joan M., Rebecca Fuhrer, Stephen A. Stansfeld, and Michael Marmot. 2002. "The Importance of Low Control at Work and Home on Depression and Anxiety: Do These Effects Vary by Gender and Social Class?" *Social Science and Medicine* 54(5): 783–98.

Haan, Mary. 1985. "Job Strain and Cardiovascular Disease: A Ten-year Prospective Study." Paper presented at the eighteenth annual meeting of the Society for Epidemiologic Research, Chapel Hill, N.C. (June 13–16).

Hamermesh, Daniel S. 1996. *Work Days, Work Hours and Work Schedules: Evidence for the United States and Germany.* Kalamazoo, Mich.: W. E. Upjohn Institute for Employment Research.

Karasek, Robert A. 1979. "Job Demands, Job Decision Latitude, and Mental Strain: Implications for Job Redesign." *Administrative Quarterly* 24(2): 285–306.

———. 1989. "Control in the Workplace and Its Health-Related Aspects." In *Job Control and Worker Health,* edited by Steven L. Sauter, Joseph J. Hurrell, and Cary L. Cooper. Chichester, U.K.: Wiley.

Karasek, Robert A., and Töres Theorell. 1989. *Healthy Work.* New York: Basic Books.

Karlsson, Bengt, Anders Knuttson, and Bjorn Lindahl. 2001. "Is There an Association between Shift Work and Having a Metabolic Syndrome? Results from a Population Based Study of 27,485 People." *Occupational and Environmental Medicine* 58(11): 747–52.

Kawachi, Ichiro, Graham A. Colditz, Meir J. Stampfer, Walter C. Willett, JoAnn E. Manson, Frank E. Speizer, and Charles H. Hennekens. 1995. "Prospective Study of Shift Work and Risk of Coronary Heart Disease in Women." *Circulation* 92(11): 3178–82.

Kingston, Paul W., and Steven L. Nock. 1985. "Consequences of the Family Work Day." *Journal of Marriage and the Family* 47(3): 619–29.

Kinnunen, Ulla, and Saija Mauno. 1998. "Antecedents and Outcomes of Work-family Conflict Among Employed Women and Men in Finland." *Human Relations* 51(2): 157–77.

Knuttson, Anders, Torbjorn Akerstedt, Bjorn G. Jonsson, and Kristina Orth-Gomer. 1986. "Increased Risk of Ischemic Heart Disease in Shift Workers." *Lancet* 498(2): 89–92.

La Croix, Andrea Z., and Suzanne G. Haynes. 1984. "Occupational Exposure to High Demand/Low Control Work and Coronary Heart Disease Incidence in the Framingham Cohort." Presented at the seventeenth annual meeting of the Society for Epidemiologic Research, Houston (June 14–17).

Loscocco, Karen A. 1997. "Work-Family Linkages Among Self-Employed Women and Men." *Journal of Vocational Behavior* 50(2): 204–26.

Mirowsky, John, and Catherine E. Ross. 1989. *Social Causes of Psychological Distress*. New York: Aldine de Gruyter.

Murata, Katsuyuki, Eijiy Yano, and Toshiaki Shinozaki. 1999. "Cardiovascular Dysfunction Due to Shiftwork." *Journal of Occupational and Environmental Medicine* 41(9): 748–53.

Negrey, Cynthia. 1993. *Gender, Time, and Reduced Work*. Albany: State University of New York Press.

Parasuraman, Saroj, and Claire A. Simmers. 2001. "Type of Employment, Work-Family Conflict and Well-being: A Comparative Study." *Journal of Organizational Behavior* 22(5): 551–68.

Parkes, Katherine R. 1999. "Shiftwork, Job Type, and the Work Environment as Joint Predictors of Health-Related Outcomes." *Journal of Occupational Health Psychology* 4(3): 256–68.

Presser, Harriet B. 1995. "Job, Family and Gender: Determinants of Nonstandard Work Schedules Among Employed Americans in 1991." *Demography* 32(4): 577–95

———. 1999. "Toward a 24-hour Economy." *Science* 284(June 11): 1778–79.

———. 2000. "Nonstandard Work Schedules and Marital Instability." *Journal of Marriage and the Family* 62(1): 93–110.

Quinn, Robert, and Graham Staines. 1979. *Quality of Employment Survey, 1977: Cross-Section*. Ann Arbor, Mich.: Inter-university Consortium for Political and Social Research.

Ross, Catherine E., and Jaya Sastry. 1999. "The Sense of Personal Control." In *Handbook of the Sociology of Mental Health,* edited by Carol S.

Aneshensel and Jo Phelan. New York: Kluwer Academic Publishers/Plenum.

Smith, Carlla, S. Chet Robie, Simon Folkard, Jane Barton, Ian Macdonald, Lawrence Smith, Evelien Spelten, Peter Totterdell, and Giovanni Costa. 1999. "A Process Model of Shiftwork and Health." *Journal of Occupational Health Psychology* 4(3): 207–18.

Staines, Graham L., and Joseph H. Pleck. 1983. *The Impact of Work Schedules on the Family.* Ann Arbor: Institute for Social Research, University of Michigan.

———. 1984. "Nonstandard Work Schedules and Family Life." *Journal of Applied Psychology* 69(3): 515–23.

———. 1986. "Work Schedule Flexibility and Family Life." *Journal of Occupational Behaviour* 7(2): 147–53.

Thelle, Dag S., Olav H. Forde, K. Try, and Egil H. Lehman. 1976. "The Tromsø Heart Study." *Acta Medica Scandinavica* 200(2): 107–18.

Theorell, Töres, and Torbjorn Akerstedt. 1976. "Day and Night Work: Changes in Cholesterol, Uric Acid, Glucose and Potassium in Serum and Circadian Patterns of Urinary Catecholamine Excretion." *Acta Medica Scandinavica* 200(1): 47–57.

U.S. Congress. Office of Technology Assessment. 1991. *Biological Rhythms: Implications for the Worker.* OTA-BA-463. Washington: U.S. Government Printing Office.

U.S. Department of Labor. Bureau of Labor Statistics. 1998. "Workers on Flexible and Shift Schedules in 1997." Report no. 98–119. Washington: U.S. Government Printing Office.

Vandenheuvel, Audrey, and Mark Wooden. 1995. "Do Explanations of Absenteeism Differ for Men and Women?" *Human Relations* 48(11): 1309–29.

Van Amelsvoort, Ludovic G., Evert G. Schouten, Arie C. Maan, Cees A. Swenne, and Frans J. Kok. 2001. "Changes in Frequency of Premature Complexes and Heart Rate Variability Related to Shift Work." *Occupational and Environmental Medicine* 58(10): 678–81.

White, Lynn, and Bruce Keith. 1990. "The Effect of Shift Work on the Quality and Stability of Marital Relations." *Journal of Marriage and the Family* 52(2): 453–62.

Zober, Andreas, Dieter Schilling, M. Gerald Ott, Peter Schauwecker, Jurgen F. Riemann, and P. Messerer. 1998. "*Helicobacter pylori* Infection: Prevalence and Clinical Relevance in a Large Company." *Journal of Occupational and Environmental Medicine* 40(7): 586–94.

# — PART II —

# TIME AND THE
# ORGANIZATION OF WORK

— Chapter 5 —

# Temporal Depth, Age, and Organizational Performance

## Allen C. Bluedorn and Stephen P. Ferris

T HE FIRST AUTHOR once toured a manufacturing plant in the United States that was owned and operated by a Japanese company. After guiding him on the tour, the facility's Japanese manager said, "I have an advantage over my American counterparts: they are expected to show a profit every quarter, but I have years to develop this business before my company expects my operation to be profitable." The comment could have come from the pages of William Ouchi's best-seller, *Theory Z* (1981), which proposed, as did this Japanese businessman, that a long-term perspective gives companies a competitive advantage. Indeed, John Kotter and James Heskett's (1992) benchmark study of organizational culture and financial performance reported a belief among industry financial analysts that an emphasis on short-term results harms a company's performance (47)—a notable belief, given the institutional pressures on American managers, such as concern over quarterly reports and daily stock prices, to emphasize the short term. And the beliefs about the salutary effects of a long-term orientation are not without theoretical foundation, for, according to the resource-based theory of the firm, "Some resources and capabilities can only be developed over long periods of time (i.e., path dependence) because it may not always be clear how to develop those capabilities in the short to medium term" (Barney 2001, 645).

113

Thus according to this theory, some "resources and capabilities" will never be developed, will never achieve their potential, unless organizations provide adequate time (a long-term commitment) for their managers to do so. This means that by definition, a long-term orientation is necessary to develop and fully benefit from such resources and capabilities. And the more resources a company can benefit from more completely, the greater its performance should be.

As these conclusions attest, a strong belief has developed in both the managerial and academic communities that a long-term perspective is better for companies than a short-term one (see also Deal and Kennedy 1999, 43–62). Surprisingly, however, there is little empirical evidence to support this belief. Further, it is unclear what constitutes a short-term or long-term perspective. Yet it is clear that individuals and societies vary considerably in their temporal depths: how far into the future and the past their interests and horizons extend. As one of the authors reported elsewhere, American time capsules are usually intended to be opened in one hundred years, whereas in Japan some time capsules specify they are to be opened in five thousand (Bluedorn 2002, 118–19, 286–87). So the distances into the past and the future vary considerably, and investigating these time spans seems as though it should be straightforward.

The concepts involved do seem intuitively straightforward, but as recent work indicates (Bluedorn 2000; Judge and Spitzfaden 1995), conceptions of past and future temporal depths are much more complex than they appear on casual inspection. Perhaps because these constructs have only been inspected casually, they have received insufficient conceptual and empirical attention. This neglect served as the major motivation for the research presented in this chapter. More specifically, we provide a more developed concept of temporal depths and use a measure of temporal depths to answer the following and related questions:

1. What intervals into *both* the future and the past do American companies use to define temporal depths?
2. How are these temporal depths related to each other and to possible determinants such as organizational age and environmental dynamism?

3. How do temporal depths relate to organizations' capital expenditures and performance, as the resource-based theory of the firm suggests they do, if they are related to them at all?

## CONCEPTS AND QUESTIONS

We examined several questions about temporal attributes of organizations in this research. To make this discussion of the relevant concepts and their related research questions more accessible for quick referencing, we have grouped the variables investigated into four categories: temporal variables, an organizational investment variable, environmental variables, and organizational performance variables.

### Temporal Variables

Two temporal concepts were examined in this research: temporal depth and organizational age. Indeed, they are the topics of primary interest.

*Temporal Depth*   The recently introduced concept of temporal depth (Bluedorn 2000, 124–25; see also Bluedorn 2002, 111–45) is defined as *the combined distance into the past and future that individuals and organizations consider when contemplating events that have happened, may have happened, or may happen.* (Technically, this is the definition of *total temporal depth* because it includes the sum of the distances into both the past and the future.) The overall concept of total temporal depth is defined as the *combined* distance into the past and future, and the terms "future temporal depth" and "past temporal depth" are appropriate for referring to these components separately, should one or the other component be the point of interest. As should be apparent, temporal depth's conceptual antecedents are the planning horizon (see, for example, Barringer and Bluedorn 1999; Das 1986, 1987), the similar time horizon concept (see Ebert and Piehl 1973), and William Judge and Mark Spitzfaden's (1995) expansion of the unitary time horizon idea into the concept of a portfolio of time horizons. Although *past* time horizons are seldom considered—Omar El Sawy (1983) and Laurie Larwood et al. (1995) being rare exceptions who do consider them—total temporal depth does include the length of the past horizons as well as of future horizons.

Another conceptual antecedent of temporal depth, albeit more of a metaphorical one, is the depth-of-field concept in optics and photography. Depth of field is the distance in front of and behind the object on which a camera is focused in which other objects will appear to be in focus at different camera settings (see London and Upton 1994, 50). The greater the depth of field, the greater the distance in front of and behind the object on which the camera is focused in which other objects will be in focus; the shorter the depth of field, the shorter the distances in front of and behind the object that will be in focus. To follow through on this metaphor, the individual or organization at the present moment would correspond to the object on which the camera is focused, and temporal depth, like depth of field, is the total distance in front of (into the future) and behind (into the past) that individuals or organizations typically consider when they think about things that have happened or may happen.

The metaphor extends even further in that objects within a specific depth of field are not all in equally clear focus: objects closer to the object on which the camera is focused are in better focus than objects farther from it. Similarly, events that have occurred recently or are envisioned to occur soon are likely to be remembered or envisioned more clearly and in greater detail (be in clearer focus) than events farther into the past or the future.

The depth-of-field metaphor may be particularly apt, because if it holds, it also suggests that the past and future components of temporal depth will be positively correlated. For within the range of the typical distances over which photographs are taken, most camera lenses reveal a depth of field with about one-third of the depth of field in front of the object on which the camera is focused (technically the plane of critical focus) and two-thirds of the depth of field behind it (see London and Upton 1994, 50–51). If this 1:2 ratio remains constant over a range of distances, the greater the depth of field in front of the object on which the camera is focused, the greater the distance of the depth of field behind the object: a positive correlation.

And the positive correlation for temporal depth-of-field components anticipated by the depth-of-field metaphor appears to be an accurate anticipation. For example, data from the individual level of analysis reveal positive correlations between individuals' past and future temporal depths in several samples (Bluedorn 2002, 117, 270–71; El Sawy 1983): the longer the future temporal depth, the longer the expected past temporal depth; thus, the longer the future temporal depth, the longer the total temporal depth as well. But these studies were conducted on the individual as the subject of investigation and as the unit of analysis. To assume that the same relationships would be found at both the individual and organizational levels of analysis would be an ecological fallacy (Robinson 1950). These relationships must be demonstrated empirically at the organizational level, which is why we investigated them in our sample of organizations.

But aside from reasoning by analogy from the individual to the organizational level of analysis and by metaphor from the depth-of-field phenomenon, are there other reasons to expect a positive correlation between the past and future components of temporal depth at the organizational level of analysis? Larwood et al. (1995, 758) found a positive correlation between how long a company had held its current vision and how far that vision extended into the future, which when combined with Allen Bluedorn's (2002) findings, suggests a positive correlation between the two components of temporal depth across levels of analysis. Indeed, James March (1999) reached a similar conclusion about the correlation between past and future depths in general, which he expressed strongly: "It is hard to imagine a long future without a long past" (74–75). Further, he formally proposed, "Long time perspectives for the past encourage long time perspectives for the future" (March 1999, 74). A key aspect of his rationale for this proposition was the importance of seeing oneself as part of an ongoing historical process: connections made with historical continuity as perceived in the past will tend to promote similar connections with the future (March 1999, 75). Here can be seen a larger base of reasons for anticipating similar relationships at the organizational level, and perhaps even some theoretical bases in March's work. We will present results from an empirical examination of this relationship later in this chapter.

An even more straightforward question about temporal depth is the important descriptive question concerning the distances into the past and the future firms consider when they make decisions and plans. Ross Webber (1972, 130) noted that managers tend to be influenced by the financial investment tradition, which defines the short-term future as less than one year, the intermediate future as ranging from one to five years, and the long-term as over five years. Similarly, Michael Hay and Jean-Claude Usunier (1993, 319) described a more fine-grained set of future horizons in which the near future was defined as ranging from one to three years, the intermediate future from two to five years, and the distant future from five to ten years. But what do managers themselves say about how they and people in their firms define these future depths? Do they still see them in terms of the traditional investment horizons or as Hay and Usunier described them? And what about past temporal depths? As noted, past temporal depths have been almost completely ignored in organizational research, but as Bluedorn has argued forcefully, the past is likely to hold strategic importance for both individuals and organizations. Bluedorn's recent research (2002) on college students in the United States revealed substantial divergence from the investment-based definitions of short, intermediate, and long terms, but again, these are findings about individuals. Our question is: Do organizations, that is, organizational cultures and their temporal parameters, reveal similar temporal depths? The results we present later provide an answer to this question and by doing so provide empirical benchmarks against which subsequent comparisons can be made.

Before moving on to a discussion of the other variables included in our study, we will explain our approach to measuring temporal depth because to do so will help provide a better understanding of the concept, the central variable in this investigation. Bluedorn (2002, 265–72) developed the six-item Temporal Depth Index (TDI) to measure individuals' sense of temporal depth. We modified and adapted the TDI to measure perceptions of top managers about the time spans into the past and future that people in their companies generally used in planning and decision making for the company. Thus we modified the TDI to measure perceptions of these time spans as attributes of the companies' cultures (see Bluedorn 2000, for a discussion of time as an attribute of organizational culture). In this modified version of the TDI, respondents were asked about the temporal distances most people in their companies typically employ when they consider the short-term, mid-term, and long-term futures and pasts. For example, the TDI questionnaire contained the item "When we think about the short-term future, we usually think about things this far ahead," and two comparable items about the mid-term and long-term future. Respondents answered each item with choices, on a fifteen-point scale, ranging from "one day" to "more than twenty-five years." Similarly, respondents were asked to respond to three items about events in the past that had happened recently, a middling time ago, and a long time ago, again using the 15-point scale that ranged from "one day" to "more than twenty-five years."

The validity and reliability of a measure are, of course, essential for assessing the results obtained when using it. As noted previously, Bluedorn (2002, 265–72) developed the TDI to measure the temporal depths of *individuals*. In that work, Bluedorn conducted several investigations of both validity and reliability, including successful tests of both convergent and discriminant validity (Kerlinger 1973) for the TDI. We repeated several of these tests with our modified version of the TDI and found results that parallel strikingly the results obtained with the original TDI, that is, strong evidence of both convergent and discriminant validity and of good reliability (internal consistency). Principal-components analysis results indicated the correct items loaded on future and past depth factors, respectively, without any cross-loadings, as well as a strong single-factor solution, all of which indicate convergent validity. The general lack of correlations between each of the six modified TDI items and six parallel items asking about the importance the organization attached to the different distances into the past and future indicated discriminant validity, and alpha coefficients (Cronbach 1951) ranging from 0.79 to 0.88 reveal a high level of reliability (internal consistency). Details about these analyses and the measures of the other variables in this study are presented in the appendix.

*Organizational Age*   The age of an organization is determined by the date of the organization's founding. But far from being a solely objective issue, the date organization members regard as the organization's founding date is a social construction, as are all collective views of the past (Bluedorn 2002, 123), so a socially constructed event should provide a significant temporal benchmark for anchoring the past temporal depth members use when they think about the past in their organization's frame of reference. And as El Sawy's (1983) experiments on executives revealed, past temporal depth appears to be a determinant of future temporal depth, but the relationship does not appear to be reciprocal because future temporal depth does not appear to determine past temporal depth. Thus the date of the organization's founding (hence its age), however it is constructed and defined, appears likely to determine, at least in part, the total temporal depth of an organization because—if El Sawy's findings extend to the organizational level—past temporal depth is a determinant of future temporal depth.

Unfortunately, just as the past component of temporal depth has seldom been considered in organizational research, organizational age has also been neglected. It is not completely absent, however, because organizational age is implicitly included in concepts of the organizational life cycle (compare Kimberly and Miles 1980; Quinn and Cameron 1983), albeit as more of an ordinal, qualitative factor than as a ratio-scale continuous variable. Further, age occupies a prominent position in the organizational ecology paradigm, where it has played a significant role in important theoretical statements and constructs (for example, the liability of newness, the liability of adolescence), theoretical issues that have generated a significant amount of empirical research (see Baum 1996, 79–83; also Carroll and Hannan 2000). Nevertheless, outside the ecology paradigm little work has been done to investigate the main effects of organizational age on other organizational variables. And when age has occasionally been included in a study outside the ecology paradigm, it has usually been employed in the secondary role of a control variable (for example, May, Stewart, and Sweo 2000), although Pradip Khandwalla's (1977) work is an exception to this practice. We define organizational age as the number of years since the organization's founding and have measured it accordingly (see the appendix).

A key factor in thinking about the past is the degree of detail with which this temporal domain is conceived (Weick 1979, 196–97), and a salient detail about any organization is the date of its founding. Even if the past is not attended to overly much in an organization, a general knowledge of the organization's age will be created by the social construction of an accepted founding date, a construction likely to be manifested in cultural artifacts. Given the likely determinant role of the organization's age for the length of its past temporal depth, should organizational age also be positively correlated with future temporal depth as well as past temporal depth? If so, this should lead to a positive correlation of organizational age with total temporal depth.

## Environmental Dimensions

The concept of organizational environments is perhaps the core concept in traditional organization theory (for example, Burns and Stalker 1961; Lawrence and Lorsch 1967; Thompson 1967). Today, the concept is described and studied in terms of three dimensions: environmental munificence, dynamism, and complexity (Bluedorn 1993; Dess and Beard 1984). Environmental munificence is the extent to which the environment can support sustained growth (Dess and Beard 1984, 55). Environmental dynamism is the extent to which the environment is unstable, hence the extent to which change in the environment is unpredictable (Dess and Beard 1984, 56). Environmental complexity is the degree to which the elements in the environment are homogeneous and concentrated (Dess and Beard 1984, 56–57).

Of particular interest is environmental dynamism. Rosalie Tung (1979) found that the length of a department's planning horizon (its future temporal depth) was negatively related to perceived environmental uncertainty (similar to environmental dynamism); William Lindsay and Leslie Rue (1980) found limited support for a similar relationship in a sample of American and Canadian companies; and Mansour Javidan (1984) likewise found a negative relationship between decision-making horizon and a proxy for environmental uncertainty (1984, 389), although it was not statistically significant. Although the results are not unanimous, they appear to indicate that organizations in more dynamic environments might have adjusted to such conditions by shortening their future temporal depths. Extending this reasoning, organizations in more dynamic environments may also shorten their past temporal depths as they scan for more recent patterns and solutions to address the issues they will face in their rapidly changing environments. Shorter future depths are adopted for the future because the volatility of history (in other words, a dynamic environment) makes the future "unpredictable," and a shallower past is used because the many changes have made much of the past "irrelevant" (March 1999, 73). Thus we ask whether environmental dynamism is negatively related to past, future, and total temporal depth? We investigated this question in our sample of organizations. (See the appendix for measurement details.)

## Organizational Investments

A large set of variables describe organizational functioning (Donaldson 2001), but we have elected to focus on one such variable, capital investment, because of its potential for being directly related to organizational age and temporal depth. Capital investment is *the amount of funds the firm has invested in long-term projects that will serve as the sources of future corporate profitability.* (See the appendix for measurement details.) Clearly infused with temporality ("long-term approach," "future corporate profitability"), capital investment seems especially promising as an important organizational phenomenon likely to be related to both temporal depth and organizational age. And beyond simple intuition, there is even the beginning of a theoretical rationale for looking for relationships between capital investments and temporal depth.

By their nature and definition, capital expenditures are large investments whose paybacks will occur over many years, making capital expenditures investments in "capabilities" that "can only be developed over long periods of time" (Barney 2001, 645). Moreover, March (1999, 75) concluded that "involvement in the past leads to concern about the future," which in turn produces a greater likelihood that the firm will "invest in activities with long term results." Since capital expenditures are so clearly "activities with long term results," and given the possible, even likely, relationship between temporal depth and organizational age, it seems reasonable to investigate the questions: Are capital investments related to temporal depth and organizational age? And if so, how are they related to them?

## Organizational Performance

Though sometimes criticized (for example, by Siehl and Martin 1990), a major focus of organization theory and strategic management research is the attempt to explain organizations' financial performance. Consistent with this focus, we define an organization's performance as its annual financial performance, as indicated by several financial ratios: earnings per share (EPS), return on assets (ROA), return on equity (ROE), and return on sales (ROS); see the appendix for measurement details. Such performance is of interest.

Starting, perhaps, with Ouchi's (1981) inclusion of time horizon (future temporal depth) in *Theory Z,* it has become almost a truism that a long-term orientation will ultimately benefit organizational performance (see Collins and Porras 1997; Deal and Kennedy 1999). But if so, why? What is the advantage of a long-term perspective? It seems likely that *not* all opportunities a company might take advantage of can be exploited in the short run (see Laverty 1996). This conclusion is consistent with the resource-based perspective presented earlier, that not only are some capabilities and resources developable in the long term only, but they *must* be developed in the long term if they are to be realized at all because of uncertainty about how to develop them in the short or medium terms (Barney 2001, 645). Thus, there are rationales and there is even some indirect empirical evidence that supports the received wisdom that longer future temporal depths provide positive benefits for organizational performance. But is this true generally? Is it even so within limited conditions? The lack of genuine empirical findings that deal with these claims directly led us to examine them in our sample of organizations.

And as discussed earlier, organizational age has generally been neglected in empirical studies of organizations. However, organizational age has consistently been negatively related to organizational mortality rates (Carroll and Hannan 2000), hence the liability-of-newness perspective within the organizational ecology paradigm, whereby the younger the company, the greater the likelihood of it "dying." Given this relationship between age and organizational mortality, it is reasonable to expect a comparable but positive relationship between age and a company's financial performance. If not, why would age be negatively correlated with firms' death rates? The relationships between organizational age and both death rates and financial performance should be parallel, albeit with opposite signs. Consequently, there are potentially important results that could inform the organizational ecology paradigm if organizational age is related to financial indicators of organizational performance, which is why we investigated these possible relationships in our sample of organizations.

However, we decided to examine the possibilities of even more complex relationships among temporal depth, organizational age, and both capital investments and the indicators of financial performance. For if older organizations tend to possess longer temporal horizons and younger ones tend toward shorter ones, what are the consequences for relationships with other variables if an old organization has a shallow temporal depth, or a young one, a great depth? In other words, is there a statistical interaction between age and temporal depth such that relationships between either variable and a third variable are contingent upon the other? And if so, what is the nature of these interactions?

## EMPIRICAL INVESTIGATION AND RESULTS

We sought answers to the questions raised in the preceding discussions by collecting data about a representative sample of all publicly traded companies in the United States. Questionnaires were sent to the CEOs and one other top executive of over 1,300 randomly selected publicly traded American companies, a sampling plan that produced responses from 15.1 percent of the companies contacted (N = 193 companies). This response rate is comparable to that obtained in studies that have asked for responses from comparable high-ranking executives (Hambrick, Geletkanycz, and Fredrickson 1993, 407). Several analyses revealed only one difference between responding and nonresponding firms (see the appendix for details), an indication that our sample of responding companies is representative of the population of publicly traded companies in the United States. The questionnaires asked for responses about how things were done and seen in the company as a whole and provided us with information about each company's temporal depth and age. Data about all of the other variables involved in this analysis—organizational size, capital investments, earnings per share (EPS), return on assets (ROA), return on equity (ROE), return on sales (ROS), and environmental dynamism, complexity, and munificence—were obtained from a publicly accessible database (the 1999 Compustat database). Please refer to the appendix for details about the sampling procedure and the measurement of the variables.

In the following sections we present the results of the analyses we performed as we sought answers to the questions we wanted to answer about temporal depth, organizational age, and these variables' relationships with each other, with capital expenditures, and with the four indicators of financial performance (EPS, ROA, ROE, and ROS).

## Temporal Depths

We were particularly interested in learning what the data from the responding companies would reveal about the temporal depths respondents believed were actually used in their firms. These data were of particular interest because to the best of our knowledge they were the first such data ever collected concerning temporal depth, and can be used to get answers to the following two questions: (1) What time spans were used by people in these companies to define the short-term, mid-term, and long-term future? (2) What time spans were used by people in these companies to define the three counterparts of these time spans when they thought about things in the past? To provide precise answers to these questions, we converted each of the modified Temporal Depth Index's (TDI's) fifteen response categories to days and calculated the statistics presented in table 5.1.

In table 5.1 the statistics are presented in units of both days and years to make them easier to interpret, and we have presented both the means and the medians for each temporal-depth region because a few extremely long depths in each region could significantly skew the data. Fortunately, the general *pattern* was the same regardless of whether we examined the means or the medians. The short-term future had, on average, about the same depth as the recent past (both had means of about a third of a year). Likewise, the mid-term future and the middling past were about the same, with means a little over one and a half years. And the long-term future and the long-ago past were similarly close, with means in the general vicinity of five years. These results indicate a fair approximation

TABLE 5.1  **Temporal-Depth Statistics for a Random Sample of 193 Publicly Traded American Companies, Presented in Days and Years**

| Temporal Depth | Descriptive Statistics | | | | |
|---|---|---|---|---|---|
| | Mean | Median | Standard Deviation | Low | High |
| Future depths | | | | | |
| Short-term future | 148.78 | 91.0 | 167.27 | 1 | 1,825 |
| | (.41) | (.25) | (.46) | (.003) | (5) |
| Midterm future | 532.82 | 365.0 | 561.11 | 14 | 5,475 |
| | (1.46) | (1) | (1.54) | (.04) | (15) |
| Long-term future | 1,534.39 | 1,095 | 1,217.78 | 30 | 10,950 |
| | (4.20) | (3) | (3.34) | (.08) | (30) |
| Past depths | | | | | |
| Recent past | 116.81 | 91 | 181.24 | 1 | 1,825 |
| | (.32) | (.25) | (.50) | (.003) | (5) |
| Middling past | 575.59 | 365 | 1,140.39 | 1 | 10,950 |
| | (1.58) | (1) | (3.12) | (.003) | (30) |
| Long-ago past | 1,984.21 | 1,095 | 2,130.94 | 91 | 10,950 |
| | (5.44) | (3) | (5.84) | (.25) | (30) |

*Source:* Authors' compilation.
*Notes:* One missing value reduced the N for the long-ago-past statistics to 192 companies. Years in parentheses.

to the temporal parameters used in the financial investment tradition to define comparable temporal depths, which suggests that these normative depths for financial matters may have affected organizations' temporal depths in general.

The similarities between corresponding past and future depths reveal a symmetry that anticipates the relationships we found between past and future temporal depths. Empirical results had consistently revealed that for individuals (see the preceding discussions), past and future temporal depths were positively correlated. So the question was, would a positive correlation exist at the organizational level? As the regression results presented in table 5.2 reveal, the two temporal depths were positively correlated in our sample of organizations ($r = .29$, $p \leq .001$, two-tailed test) and this positive relationship persisted after controlling for organizational age and size, and for environmental complexity, dynamism, and munifi-

TABLE 5.2 **Multiple Regression Analyses for Temporal Depth, Organizational Age, Environmental Dynamism, and Capital Expenditures**

| Independent Variable | Standardized Regression Coefficients (Betas) | | | |
| --- | --- | --- | --- | --- |
| | Future Temporal Depth | Past Temporal Depth | Total Temporal Depth | Capital Expenditures |
| Total temporal depth | NA | NA | NA | .12* (.37***) |
| Past temporal depth | .19* (.29***) | NA | NA | |
| Organizational age | .23* (.35***) | .38*** (.40***) | .43*** (.46***) | .15** |
| Organizational size[a] | .04 | .04 | .05 | .74*** |
| Environmental complexity | .09 | −.13 | −.05 | .10* |
| Environmental dynamism | −.11 | −.12 | −.16+ (−.23**) | −.02 |
| Environmental munificence | .04 | −.03 | .00 | .01 |
| R-squared | .18 | .18 | .24 | .75 |
| F for overall equation | 5.22*** | 6.43*** | 9.07*** | 60.61*** |

*Source:* Authors' compilation.
*Note:* The listwise N was 153 for the multiple regressions for future temporal depth, past temporal depth, and total temporal depth. For capital expenditures the listwise N was 131. The coefficients in parentheses are the zero-order correlations between the independent and dependent variables.
NA = not applicable.
[a]Natural logarithm.
+$p \leq .10$, two-tailed test *$p \leq .05$, two-tailed test **$p \leq .01$, two-tailed test ***$p \leq .001$, two-tailed test

cence. Thus, the positive correlation between past and future temporal depths that had been found at the individual level in several studies is also revealed as existing at the organizational level. So for the organizational level of analysis we can now be more confident that the longer an organization's past temporal depth, the longer its future temporal depth will likely be. And given the symmetries between past and future temporal depths reported in table 5.1, it seems there is a general tendency for organizations to look about as far into the future as they do into the past, even perhaps, at the extremes (that is, the long-term future and long-ago past—see the medians in table 5.1).

## Organizational Age

We anticipated that organizational age would be positively related to past, future, and total temporal depths. However, the paucity of previous research on this question left us with a plausible rationale and only a few scraps of theory as the basis for our expectations about these relationships. Nevertheless, our expectations proved correct, as is revealed by the regression analyses in table 5.2. The zero-order correlations between organizational age and each of the three temporal depths were all positive (.40, .35, and .46), and all statistically significant. These positive relationships changed very little after we controlled for organizational size and environmental complexity, dynamism, and munificence—indicating that these relationships are quite robust.

## Temporal Depth and Environmental Dynamism

Previous research generally indicated a negative correlation between environmental dynamism and future temporal depth. But our interest was in dynamism's relationship with total temporal depth. The same logic used to explain future temporal depth's negative correlation with environmental dynamism seemed to apply to temporal depth as a whole, so we anticipated that if we found a relationship, we would find that relationship to be a negative correlation. We did indeed find a negative correlation. The results of the multiple regression analysis test of this relationship are presented in table 5.2, which shows that the zero-order correlation between temporal depth and environmental dynamism was $r = -.23$ (p $\leq$ .01, two-tailed test). After adding organizational age, size, and the two other environmental dimensions, the relationship was reduced to a marginally significant $-.16$ (p $\leq$ .06, two-tailed test). Thus there was a negative correlation between environmental dynamism and total temporal depth, but the relationship does diminish after other organizational and environmental variables have been controlled for.

## Temporal Depth and Organizational Investments

The specific organizational investment we investigated was capital investments, which we described earlier as explicitly infused with temporal characteristics (for example, "long-term approach"). And given their explicit focus on the long term, it seems reasonable to anticipate a positive correlation between capital investments and total temporal depth, if any relationship were to be found between the two variables. And as seemed so plausible, we found a positive relationship between them, as the results of the multiple regression test of this relationship reveals in table 5.2. However, the zero-order correlation between temporal depth and capital expenditures, which was .37 ($p \leq .001$, two-tailed test), diminishes to a materially smaller standardized regression coefficient, though a still statistically significant .12 ($p \leq .03$, two-tailed test), after controlling for organizational age, size, and the three environmental dimensions. As the results in table 5.2 indicate, most of this reduction is due to the effects of organizational size, which, as one would expect, is strongly related to capital expenditures (a standardized regression coefficient of .74, $p \leq .001$, two-tailed test). Thus the larger the company, the more resources the company devoted to capital expenditures. Nevertheless, despite the nearly determinant impact of organizational size, temporal depth still maintains a statistically significant positive relationship with capital expenditures.

## Temporal Depth, Organizational Age, and Financial Performance

From a strategic management perspective, any variable that is related to an organization's overall financial performance is noteworthy. But such questions also have a long history of research in organization theory as they reveal important characteristics about organizational functioning. Thus we were interested in seeing whether temporal depth, organizational age, or both could be added to the list of correlates related to organizational performance. The answer in our sample appears to be a qualified yes. The results of the hierarchical regression analyses that tested these relationships are presented in table 5.3. For the relationships between financial per-

TABLE 5.3 **Hierarchical Regression Analyses for Temporal Depth, Organizational Age, and Financial Performance**

| | Standardized Regression Coefficients (Betas) | | | | | |
|---|---|---|---|---|---|---|
| | Earnings per Share (EPS) | | | Return on Assets (ROA) | | |
| Independent Variable | Step 1 | Step 2 | Step 3 | Step 1 | Step 2 | Step 3 |
| Temporal depth | .30*** | .20* | .20* | .19* | .07 | .07 |
| Organizational age | | .14 | .13 | | .11 | .10 |
| Organizational size[a] | | .19* | .19* | | .37*** | .38*** |
| Environmental complexity | | | .04 | | | −.10 |
| Environmental dynamism | | | .03 | | | .01 |
| Environmental munificence | | | −.03 | | | −.12 |
| R-squared at each step | .09 | .15 | .15 | .04 | .19 | .22 |
| Change in R-squared | | .06* | .00 | | .16*** | .03 |
| F for overall equation | 13.42*** | 7.81*** | 3.88*** | 5.10* | 10.73*** | 6.14*** |

| | Return on Equity (ROE) | | | Return on Sales (ROS) | | |
|---|---|---|---|---|---|---|
| Temporal depth | .16+ | .13 | .13 | .19* | .09 | .10 |
| Organizational age | | −.04 | −.09 | | .15 | .12 |
| Organizational size[a] | | .26** | .27** | | .18* | .19* |
| Environmental complexity | | | .12 | | | .06 |
| Environmental dynamism | | | .00 | | | .01 |
| Environmental munificence | | | −.16+ | | | −.11 |
| R-squared at each step | .03 | .09 | .12 | .04 | .10 | .11 |
| Change in R-squared | | .06* | .04 | | .06* | .01 |
| F for overall equation | 3.71+ | 4.41** | 3.15** | 5.19* | 4.80** | 2.69* |

Source: Authors' compilation.
Note: The listwise Ns for the hierarchical regressions were 136 for earnings per share, 139 for return on assets, 140 for return on equity, and 135 for return on sales.
[a]Natural logarithm.
$^+$p $\leq$ .10, two-tailed test $^*$p $\leq$ .05, two-tailed test $^{**}$p $\leq$ .01, two-tailed test $^{***}$p $\leq$ .001, two-tailed test

formance and temporal depth, three of the four zero-order correlations were positive and statistically significant—for EPS, .30 (p ≤ .001, two-tailed test); for ROA, .19 (p ≤ .03, two-tailed test); and for ROS, .19 (p ≤ .03, two-tailed test)—and for the fourth, ROE, was marginally significant, .16 (p ≤ .06, two-tailed test). However, after we controlled for organizational size and age and the three environmental dimensions, the results became mixed. The relationships between temporal depth and ROA, ROE, and ROS all became statistically insignificant, but the positive relationship between EPS and temporal depth remained statistically significant: .20 (p ≤ .04, two-tailed test).

A similar pattern occurs for organizational age. Though not reported in table 5.3, the zero-order correlations between organizational age and the financial performance ratios were all positive, three statistically significant: for EPS, .29 (p ≤ .001, two-tailed test); for ROA, .26 (p ≤ .002, two-tailed test); for ROE, .11 (ns, two-tailed test); and for ROS, .25 (p ≤ .004, two-tailed test). But after controlling for organizational size and the three environmental dimensions, all four relationships were reduced in magnitude to statistically insignificant levels (see table 5.3). Thus at the zero-order level, both temporal depth and organizational age were consistently and positively correlated with several financial performance ratios. But after control variables were entered into the equations, all of the relationships became statistically insignificant, except for the positive relationship between temporal depth and EPS (the greater the temporal depth, the higher the EPS). Overall these findings reveal some associations with financial performance, but not consistently enough to claim anything like a temporal imperative to describe them.

## Interactions Between Organizational Age and Temporal Depth

By far the most exploratory question we examined concerned the possibility that organizational age interacts with temporal depth to moderate the relationship between temporal depth and both capital expenditures and financial performance. Far from being able to make a strong prediction as to what such a relationship would be, we were not even certain that there would be such a statistical

TABLE 5.4  **Hierarchical Regression Analyses for the Temporal Depth–Age Interaction**

|  | Standardized Regression Coefficients (Betas) | | | |
| --- | --- | --- | --- | --- |
|  | Capital Expenditures[a] | | Earnings per Share | |
| Independent Variable | Step 1 | Step 2 | Step 1 | Step 2 |
| Temporal depth | .16[+] | .33* | .19* | .40*** |
| Organizational age | .39*** | 1.59*** | .22** | 1.68** |
| Temporal depth multiplied by organizational age |  | −1.31* |  | −1.58** |
| R-squared at each step | .23 | .27 | .12 | .17 |
| Change in R-squared |  | .04* |  | .05** |
| F for overall equation | 19.85*** | 16.02*** | 10.03*** | 10.14*** |

*Source:* Authors' compilation.
*Note:* The listwise Ns were 135 for the hierarchical regressions for capital expenditures and 156 for the hierarchical regressions for earnings per share.
[a]Natural logarithm.
[+]$p \le .10$, two-tailed test *$p \le .05$, two-tailed test **$p \le .01$, two-tailed test ***$p \le .001$, two-tailed test

interaction. Thus our investigation of this question was purely exploratory, but even so, we believe the results we obtained are some of our more interesting ones. We employed moderator regression analysis (see table 5.4) to determine whether organizational age moderated the relationship between temporal depth and both capital expenditures and financial performance. These interactions were tested hierarchically by adding a (temporal depth) × (age) term to regression equations containing age and temporal depth as main effect terms (Cohen and Cohen 1983). Two of the six tests revealed significant interactions.

Subgroup analyses performed by splitting the sample at the median age (27.5 years) revealed similar interaction patterns for both capital expenditures and EPS. There was essentially no relationship between longer temporal depth and either EPS or capital expenditures in the group of older organizations, but there were significant positive relationships between temporal depth and both capital expenditures and EPS in the group of younger organizations. This pattern is illustrated in Figure 5.1.

FIGURE 5.1 **Earnings per Share by Temporal Depth for Younger and Older Organizations (Regression Lines)**

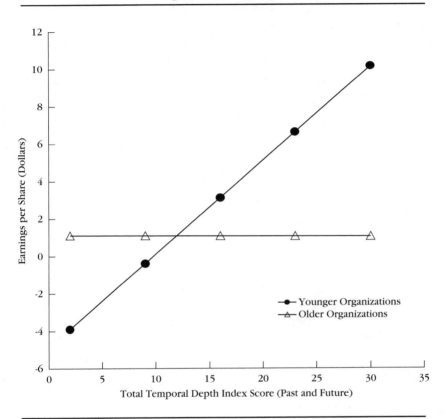

*Source:* Authors' compilation.

## RETHINKING TIME IN ORGANIZATIONS

As a whole, our analyses produced an interesting set of results. Past and future temporal depths were positively correlated, as was age with both depths as well as overall temporal depth. Further, temporal depth was negatively related to environmental dynamism. Notably, all of these relationships persisted after we controlled for organizational size, age, and the dimensions of the organizational environment. After controls were introduced, organizational age was not significantly related to firms' financial performance. Nevertheless, after we controlled for organizational size, age, and the dimensions of the organizational environment, temporal depth was significantly related to capital expenditures and one financial performance ratio, EPS. Finally, two significant interactions were identified: for younger companies but not for older firms, temporal depth was positively related to both capital expenditures and EPS. Several of these findings have important implications for rethinking a number of major yet taken-for-granted beliefs about time and its impact on organizations.

As noted earlier, most of the work that has been conducted on temporal depth in organizations has been conducted on future temporal depth; past temporal depth has been generally ignored. Thus discussions and research about time and planning horizons is normally all about future horizons. Yet the data presented in this chapter reveal that past temporal depth is an important component of overall temporal depth and must be considered when research is conducted on how far ahead and back in time individuals and organizations look when they make plans and decisions. So it is reasonable to ask, why has a concern with the future direction nearly monopolized such concern? Charlotte Perkins Gilman (1903, 51) once asked, "Does eternity only stretch one way?" An examination of the treatment of time horizons in contemporary organizational thought would seem to indicate that for theorists and researchers time does "only stretch one way." The results presented in this chapter clearly indicate that such a view is no longer tenable and must be not only rethought but rejected. And because such a rejection involves fundamental views that are often held unconsciously, doing so requires major rethinking indeed.

Almost as fundamental is the truism that greater temporal depth is always better than short temporal depth. But here, too, our results indicate that some major rethinking is in order. Out of four tests of main effects for temporal depth on organizational financial performance, temporal depth was related to only one measure—EPS—after several control variables were entered into the regression equations. These findings alone, based as they are on a representative sample of all publicly traded American companies, argue against anything like a long-term imperative. In fact, they suggest a better wisdom may be to look for the contexts in which greater temporal depth is better as well as to identify the contexts when it is not.

Along these lines our findings identified two such contexts. The findings are the significant statistical interactions between temporal depth and organizational age for capital expenditures and EPS, and they indicate a relatively longer temporal depth appears to benefit younger companies—but not older ones. And once the contingent nature of this relationship is known, other questions come to mind. One question is, why were relatively longer temporal depths beneficial for young firms but not for older ones? Given the median split at 27.5 years used to define young and old firms, why does about a quarter-century seem to be the point beyond which variance in temporal depth is unrelated to organizational capital expenditures or financial performance? Perhaps the marginal impact of modest increases in temporal depth have greater impacts for young than for old organizations, which suggests that even relatively small increases in temporal depth could confer material competitive advantages to young organizations.

If this is the case, how can younger organizations deliberately develop these longer horizons, since they lack the greater age that seems related to longer horizons? El Sawy's (1983) work suggests that individual future time horizons can be lengthened if individuals deliberately think about events longer into the past, leading to the question of how the people in an organization could collectively be led to do so. One possibility might be to focus on a known peer organization that has existed longer. Focusing on the long temporal shadow cast by such an "other" might allow the organization to adopt that history as a *shadow identity* to help produce the desired depth lengthening, especially if only modest changes, perhaps one or two years, are all that are required. Clearly these questions and issues indicate a need for new thinking that goes far beyond the simple truism that the long term is always best.

Even an anticipated finding leads to new questions, hence to new thinking. It was anticipated that capital expenditures and temporal depth were positively correlated, and this relationship persisted after we controlled for organizational size, age, and the environmental dimensions. The question is, why? A plausible explanation is that firms with longer past horizons can identify previous capital projects that paid off over a long period—say, twenty to thirty years—which can serve as models for current situations in which managers are considering similar types of decisions. Such models could bolster managers' confidence in making comparable expenditures as well as provide organizational learning about how to make them. Moreover, capital expenditures are inherently long-term, in terms of both the time required to complete the construction of facilities and the time required to recover and profit from the stream of benefits the facilities are expected to generate. Thus the inherent long-term nature of capital expenditures almost requires a long temporal depth for firms' decision-making processes about such expenditures. When decision makers operate within the context of a short temporal depth, the potential benefits of events and activities that occur beyond that depth are highly discounted. Indeed, decision makers are likely to discount such potential benefits to a present value of zero when they seem to accrue beyond the forward edge of the firm's temporal depth.

The rethinking of time in organizations that our findings mandate may even extend beyond academic theorists and researchers. For example, industry and company analysts in capital markets might now ask for information about temporal depth as they collect data about the companies and industries they study. Such information would not be definitive, but it could, when combined with the other information collected, enhance analysts' abilities to assess management's attitudes and decision processes, its attitudes toward and likely responses to matters such as product quality and recalls, repeat business, and litigation over a wide variety of issues. Thus these findings carry implications for the actions of professionals who observe managers—financial analysts, underwriters, auditors, and bankers—as well as for managers themselves.

Further, the descriptive statistics we found that define the depth of short-, intermediate-, and long-term futures and pasts should be useful to financial analysts and researchers in general as they interpret such parameters in specific companies. Thus for the average firm in a very representative sample of publicly traded American companies, the typical short-term future for planning and decision making is between a quarter- and a half-year ahead of the present, whereas the typical long-term future is four to five years ahead of the present. These statistics and others presented in table 5.1 provide relatively precise guidance for someone trying to decide whether a particular temporal depth is relatively long or short. And since such judgments will be based on data collected from a representative sample, they represent an advance over general impressions or rules-of-thumb based on traditional investment time horizons. This is clearly a straightforward form of rethinking.

But as we have already intimated, the rethinking prompted by our findings leads to many new questions. And even the questions our results seem to answer may not be resolved definitively. For example, we do not know whether our results, based on a representative sample of publicly traded companies in the United States, generalize to either privately held American companies and firms, the various forms of not-for-profit and government organizations, or to firms based in other countries. Since national cultures certainly have a great deal to do with developing the temporal depths of populations (Bluedorn 2000), an important extension of this research would be to attempt to replicate it in countries such as Japan that seem to emphasize different temporal depths than the United States.

A related question is whether these relationships are stable over major periods of one country's or culture's history. For example, would we have obtained the same results in the United States of fifty years ago? Reasons to suspect that we might have obtained different results include the rate and extent of technological development during the last half century, which might make less of the past seem relevant to today's managers, hence shortening their past temporal depths compared to past depths used by managers in earlier eras. Similarly, the increasing tempo of life over the last fifty years (Gleick 1999) could likely shorten today's managers' future temporal depths as well. Though plausible, these suggestions are speculations. No one knows how far into the past or the present managers in the past planned. In fact, to study such questions will require planning in terms of a long future temporal depth, one that allows for repeated data collection over a period of fifty years or more. Though rare and not necessarily planned at their inception to take so long, such projects have occasionally been undertaken— and, most important, completed successfully. A sterling example is *The Oxford English Dictionary,* which took seventy years to complete (Winchester 1998). But regardless of whether such an ambitious research program is ever undertaken, ample opportunities exist for extending temporal-depth research to different types of organizations and to different national cultures, and so not require research designs with daunting temporal depth.

Although the temporal variables we considered in the research reported in this chapter—temporal depth and organizational age—

are far from being all of the important temporal variables involved in organizations (see Bluedorn 2002), they are important temporal variables, and our findings led to major rethinking about them and their organizational contexts. But a more important direction for rethinking may be the recognition that time and temporal variables have received far too little attention in organizational research, and that their inclusion in organizational theory and research is not only an improvement, but a necessity. This chapter, indeed this book, should promote such rethinking.

## APPENDIX

In this appendix we present a detailed description of our sample and sampling procedure as well as the measures used in this study.

## SAMPLE

In this section we discuss the origin and makeup of the sample and the development and administration of the questionnaire.

### Description of Sample

Our sample consisted of 193 publicly traded firms, all of them incorporated and located in the United States. The population from which we obtained this sample consisted of all firms on the 1999 Compustat annual database that listed a specific individual as the chief executive officer (CEO) or president and a different person as the chief operating officer (COO) or executive vice president. We then sent a questionnaire to both the president or the CEO and to the COO or executive vice president of all 348 firms in Standard Industrial Classification (SIC) codes 4800 to 4999 and to 1,010 randomly selected companies from all other SIC codes. (SIC codes 4800 to 4999, which are the electric, gas, sanitary services, and communications industries, were oversampled as a result of the interest in these industries expressed by the principal funding source for this research.) Thus, questionnaires were sent to two people at 1,358 companies altogether. However, the U.S.

Postal Service returned the questionnaires sent to 80 of these companies as undeliverable and unforwardable, resulting in an effective mailing population of 1,278.

We received completed questionnaires from 193 companies (15.1 percent), which is a response rate consistent with the typical response rates from top executives in similar studies (Hambrick, Geletkanycz, and Fredrickson 1993, 407). We asked these top executives to complete the questionnaire because we felt that only very senior executives in most organizations would have the firm-wide knowledge and perspective necessary to provide the desired information. Technically we were tapping the "prevailing temporal agenda" of each of these top managers, a prevailing temporal agenda being "the individual actor's perception and construal of the organization's temporal structure from his or her particular vantage point within the firm" (Blount and Janicik 2001, 570). Nevertheless, our approach follows the common practice in organizational research of using the perceptions of individual leaders "as surrogate measures for organizational perceptions" (Ancona, Okhuysen, and Perlow 2001, 518). And as we demonstrate later in our discussion of interrrater reliability, the perceptions we obtained seemed to be shared by others in the executives' companies.

## Representativeness of the Sample

We compared responding with nonresponding firms on six variables: total assets, sales, book value of equity, number of employees, return on assets, and return on sales. Using a difference in means test (t-test), the only statistically significant difference between the two groups for this set of variables was for total assets, with the nonresponding firms having the larger mean. However, a difference-in-medians test revealed no statistically significant differences for any of the six variables. These results indicate few if any differences between responding and nonresponding firms. Further, the differing results for the mean and median tests for total assets indicates that the difference in means was likely produced by a few extremely large firms in the nonresponding group. Overall, we found no differences between the responding and nonresponding groups that seemed likely to bias the results, and this indicates our sample of responding firms can be regarded as representative of the pool of Compustat companies from which we drew them in terms of the variables tested. We also compared the proportions of sample firms in the ten major SIC codes with the proportions of firms in these categories listed on the 1999 Compustat Annual database. This generated a statistically significant chi-square, indicating a difference between proportions in the population of organizations and the proportions in our sample. However, this was to be expected, since we deliberately oversampled *part* of one of the ten major SIC codes (SIC codes 4800 to 4999). So we repeated this analysis after deleting the major SIC code containing the oversampled industries, producing a statistically nonsignificant chi-square, hence indicating no statistically significant differences between the proportions of companies in the sample and the corresponding proportions in the entire Compustat listing for the remaining nine major SIC codes. Thus, with the exception of the oversampled industries, the sample appears to be representative of the larger population of companies.

## Questionnaire Development and Administration

The questionnaire asked for information about temporal depth and organizational age, and was pilot-tested on a set of MBA students and managers. The actual questionnaire administration followed a modified Don Dillman (1978) procedure. The initial mailing (first-class postage) contained a cover letter and a professionally printed questionnaire. In the cover letter we requested the potential respondent's participation, explained that only a few top executives could possess the needed information, summarized the study's purpose, assured confidentiality regarding both the individual respondent and his or her company, and offered a report of the study's results if the questionnaire was completed and returned. A code number in the upper-right-hand corner of the questionnaire's first page identified the company and the respondent, which allowed us to maintain an accurate tracking of responders and nonresponders (the code number was identified and explained to each potential respondent in the cover letter). The code number also made it possible for us to match each questionnaire with the firm's investment and performance data contained on the 1999 Compustat database.

Two weeks after the initial questionnaire mailing, and after some responses had arrived, a second questionnaire was sent to nonresponding executives. It was identical to the first, except for an additional digit added to the code number to distinguish second- from first-mailing questionnaires. Also, the cover letter was modified to emphasize the importance of responding and the follow-up nature of the correspondence.

## MEASURES

Temporal-depth and organizational-age data were obtained from the questionnaire, and the measurement of temporal depth was described in the text. Data about all of the other variables were obtained from the 1999 Compustat database.

### Temporal Depth

Because we had adapted and modified the original Temporal Depth Index (TDI), we conducted principal-components analyses with orthogonal (varimax) rotations on the responses. We found the same basic factor structure that Bluedorn (2002) found for the original TDI, in which individuals' perceptions of their own temporal depths were measured. That is, we found only two factors with eigenvalues greater than one (2.78 and 1.79) that explained 76.13 percent of the variance, and the factor structure was clean (that is, no cross-loadings). The six loadings for the first factor were .88, .94, .87, −.03, .21, and .08, with the three loadings above .80 being for the three future-depth items. The loadings for the second factor were .04, .06, .16, .80, .85, and .84, with the three loadings at or above .80 being for the three past-depth items. We conducted another analysis and found only one statistically significant correlation among the six modified TDI items and parallel questions about the importance of each temporal distance. This was the correlation for the long-term temporal depth of future questions ($r = .25$, $p \leq .001$, two-tailed test). None of the other five correlations was larger than .10 or approached statistical significance at the .05 level. This pattern of correlations indicates that the modified TDI and the items about importance are measures of different variables, which demonstrates discriminant validity for the modified TDI. We also found an alpha coefficient (Cronbach 1951) for the modified and adapted version of the TDI of .79. The alpha coefficients for the modified TDI's two components, temporal depth of past and temporal depth of future, were .84 and .88, respectively. These alpha coefficients are consistent with those recommended by Jum Nunnally (1978, 245) for basic research.

## Organizational Age

Organizational age was measured by subtracting from 1999 the answer to the question "In what year was your firm founded?" This procedure provided a straightforward measure of age as well as an authoritative answer to how the firm defined its date of origin. The age of the responding companies ranged from 2 to 183 years.

Because sixteen of the responding firms returned two questionnaires, we were able to use these data to assess the interrater reliability of the temporal-depth and organizational- age measures, the variables that were measured by data obtained from the questionnaires. The small N involved in this examination led us to use the Wilcoxon signed-ranks test (Siegel 1956) to examine the sixteen pairs of responses for the temporal-depth and organizational-age measures. Doing so revealed no statistically significant differences ($p \leq .05$, two-tailed tests) between the respondent pairs for any of the temporal-depth and organizational-age measures. (Repeating these comparisons with paired-sample t-tests provided the same results). These results are supportive of sufficient interrater reliability. The higher-ranking respondent's questionnaire from each pair was the questionnaire included in the larger data set used to investigate the questions of interest.

## Organizational Size

Organizational size was measured as the natural logarithm of the total number of employees in 1998, the most recent year for which data were reported on the 1999 Compustat database. The organizations in the sample represented the full size range of publicly traded American firms, since the smallest firm employed 3 people while the largest employed 140,000.

## Organizational Investing

Capital investments data were those reported in the 1999 Compustat database as capital expenditures. We then calculated the mean for capital expenditures over the four most recent years contained on the 1999 Compustat database, 1995 to 1998. (For a more complete discussion of why this was done, see the discussion of financial performance measures later in this appendix.) However, because of significant skewing, we transformed these capital-expenditure means by calculating their natural logarithms, which reduced the skewness index for capital expenditures from 8.79 to 0.06. Thus the natural logarithms of the four-year capital-expenditure means were used for all analyses of capital investments.

## Environmental Variables

All three environmental dimensions were measured with data from the 1999 Compustat database, but as components in formulas developed in previous research to measure these dimensions. For each four-digit SIC code represented in the sample, environmental dynamism was measured by the standard error of the regression slope coefficient (annual sales regressed on year) divided by the mean of the sales in that SIC code for the number of years covered in the regression. This measure was developed by Gregory Dess and Donald Beard (1984) and has been used in several previous studies (for example, Bergh and Lawless 1998; Keats and Hitt 1988). In this analysis, the separate regressions for each SIC code were performed by regressing annual sales on calendar year for the period 1994 to 1998. We selected this period since it was the most recent five-year period on the 1999 Compustat tapes and thus will be comparable to the previous research just cited. This period also allows us to balance the dual needs of a measure representative of environmental conditions current at the time respondents completed their questionnaires, but with sufficient data points that would reasonably reflect environmental conditions.

For each four-digit SIC code represented in the sample, the measure of environmental complexity was 1 minus the four-firm concentration ratio. The four-firm concentration ratio is the sum of the sales of the four largest firms in an industry (four-digit SIC code) divided by the total sales of all firms in that industry (Scherer 1980, 56–57). The sales data required to calculate these ratios were from 1998, the most recent year reported on the 1999 Compustat database. The four-firm concentration ratio was subtracted from 1 so a higher score would indicate a greater amount of complexity.

For each four-digit SIC code, environmental munificence was measured by the regression slope coefficient (annual sales regressed on year) divided by the mean of sales over the most recent five-year period reported in the 1999 Compustat database. This approach was developed by Dess and Beard (1984) and has been used in other research (for example, Keats and Hitt 1988). In this analysis, the separate regressions for each SIC code were performed by regressing annual sales on calendar year for 1994 to 1998.

## Organizational Financial Performance

Firm financial performance was measured by four standard financial ratios: earnings per share (EPS), return on assets (ROA), return on equity (ROE), and return on sales (ROS). These ratios were calculated for each year from 1995 through 1998 as follows: EPS, as contained in the Compustat database; ROA as earnings before interest and taxes divided by total assets; ROE as earnings before interest and taxes divided by book equity; and ROS as earnings before income and taxes divided by net sales. The means of each of these ratios were then calculated for each firm in our sample over this four-year period. We chose a four-year period to provide stability in these indicators of the firms' recent financial performance and to avoid extending backward too far. We required stable indicators for recent performance, but wanted to avoid the problem of missing values, which increases with each year added to the mean calculations (thus, a two-year-old company would not have any of these data from three years before and would become a missing value in the analyses). In our judgment, a four-year period struck a reasonable balance between preserving most of the sample for analysis while providing a reasonably stable estimate of firms' recent financial performance. Further, we employed four ratios to provide a wide range of tests for possible relationships between both age and temporal depth with traditional measures of corporate financial performance.

Table 5.5 presents the means, standard deviations, and intercorrelations of all variables in the study.

**TABLE 5.5 Means, Standard Deviations, and Correlations of Study Variables**

| Variable | Mean | Standard Deviation | 1 | 2 | 3 | 4 | 5 | 6 | 7 | 8 | 9 | 10 | 11 | 12 |
|---|---|---|---|---|---|---|---|---|---|---|---|---|---|---|
| 1. Age of organization (years) | 44.57 | 42.33 | | | | | | | | | | | | |
| 2. Capital expenditures (dollars in millions) | 2.27 | 2.38 | 46*** | | | | | | | | | | | |
| 3. Earnings per shares[a] (dollars) | .23 | 2.25 | 29*** | 29*** | | | | | | | | | | |
| 4. Environmental complexity | .37 | .21 | 24*** | 24** | 11 | | | | | | | | | |
| 5. Environmental dynamism | .04 | .03 | −25*** | −11 | −08 | −43*** | | | | | | | | |
| 6. Environmental munificence | .11 | .10 | −18* | 01 | −08 | 03 | 15* | | | | | | | |
| 7. Future temporal depth | 7.40 | 1.31 | 30*** | 34*** | 26*** | 16* | −20** | −09 | | | | | | |
| 8. Past temporal depth | 7.13 | 1.55 | 33*** | 23** | 16* | 05 | −18* | −11 | 28*** | | | | | |
| 9. Return on assets | .01 | .24 | 25** | 41*** | 42*** | −03 | 00 | −14+ | 06 | 19* | | | | |
| 10. Return on equity | .16 | .63 | 10 | 30*** | 22** | 15* | −09 | −13+ | 09 | 14+ | 46*** | | | |
| 11. Return on sales | −.01 | .55 | 25** | 22* | 32*** | 14+ | −11 | −08 | 04 | 19* | 72*** | 50*** | | |
| 12. Size of organization[a] | 6.46 | 2.05 | 29*** | 82*** | 27*** | 11 | −02 | −03 | 13+ | 11 | 42*** | 29*** | 27*** | |
| 13. Temporal depth | 14.53 | 2.29 | 40*** | 34*** | 27*** | 13+ | −25*** | −13+ | 76*** | 84*** | 17* | 15+ | 16* | 14+ |

*Source:* Authors' compilation.
*Note:* The Ns for all correlations range from 135 to 193. Decimal points have been removed from the correlations.
[a]Natural logarithm.
+p ≤ .10, two-tailed test *p ≤ .05, two-tailed test **p ≤ .01, two-tailed test ***p ≤ .001, two-tailed test

An earlier version of this chapter was presented in the Strategic Management Seminar Series, INSEAD, Fontainebleau, France, October 13, 2000; and preliminary results of this research were presented at the Eighth Annual Research Symposium of the Financial Research Institute, College of Business, University of Missouri–Columbia, November 5, 1999. Primary funding for this research was provided by a grant from the Financial Research Institute at the College of Business, University of Missouri, Columbia, Missouri. Supplementary funding was provided by Summer Research Fellowships from the College of Business at the University of Missouri–Columbia and grants from the College of Business, University of Missouri, the Research Council of the University of Missouri, and the University of Missouri's Alumni Association. We are grateful for the valuable assistance provided by Nicholas Bluedorn, Ron Howren, Felissa Lee, Shin-Hua Liu, Lisa Smith, Rhetta Standifer, and Jared Wilmes in the collection of the data reported in this paper. We thank Richard A. Johnson for his helpful advice throughout the research and Yu Ha Cheung, James Mattingly, Michael S. Proctor, Terry Schroepfer, and Rhetta L. Standifer for their helpful comments on earlier drafts of this chapter.

## REFERENCES

Ancona, Deborah, Gerardo A. Okhuysen, and Leslie A. Perlow. 2001. "Taking Time to Integrate Temporal Research." *Academy of Management Review* 26(4): 512–29.

Barney, Jay B. 2001. "Resource-Based Theories of Competitive Advantage: A Ten-Year Retrospective on the Resource-Based View." *Journal of Management* 27(6): 643–50.

Barringer, Bruce R., and Allen C. Bluedorn. 1999. "The Relationship Between Corporate Entrepreneurship and Strategic Management." *Strategic Management Journal* 20(5): 421–44.

Baum, Joel A. C. 1996. "Organizational Ecology." In *Handbook of Organization Studies,* edited by Stewart R. Clegg, Cynthia Hardy, and Walter R. Nord. London: Sage Publications.

Bergh, Donald D., and Michael W. Lawless. 1998. "Portfolio Restructuring and Limits to Hierarchical Governance: The Effects of Environmental Uncertainty and Diversification Strategy." *Organization Science* 9(1): 87–102.

Blount, Sally, and Gregory A. Janicik. 2001. "When Plans Change: Examining How People Evaluate Timing Changes in Work Organizations." *Academy of Management Review* 26(4): 566–85.

Bluedorn, Allen C. 1993. "Pilgrim's Progress: Trends and Convergence in Research on Organizational Size and Environments." *Journal of Management* 19(2): 163–91.

———. 2000. "Time and Organizational Culture." In *Handbook of Organizational Culture and Climate,* edited by Neal M. Ashkanasy, Celeste P. M. Wilderom, and Mark F. Peterson. Thousand Oaks, Calif.: Sage Publications.

———. 2002. *The Human Organizational of Time: Temporal Realities and Experience.* Stanford, Calif.: Stanford University Press.

Burns, Tom, and G. M. Stalker. 1961. *The Management of Innovation.* London: Tavistock.

Carroll, Glenn R., and Michael T. Hannan. 2000. *The Demography of Corporations and Industries.* Princeton: Princeton University Press.

Cohen, Jacob, and Patricia Cohen. 1983. *Applied Multiple Regression/ Correlation Analysis for the Behavioral Sciences.* 2nd ed. Hillsdale, N.J.: Lawrence Erlbaum.

Collins, James C., and Jerry I. Porras. 1997. *Built to Last: Successful Habits of Visionary Companies.* New York: HarperBusiness.

Cronbach, Lee J. 1951. "Coefficient Alpha and the Internal Structure of Tests." *Psychometrika* 16(3): 297–334.

Das, T. K. 1986. *The Subjective Side of Strategy Making.* New York: Praeger.

———. 1987. "Strategic Planning and Individual Temporal Orientation." *Strategic Management Journal* 8(2): 203–9.

Deal, Terrence E., and Allan A. Kennedy. 1999. *The New Corporate Cultures: Revitalizing the Workplace after Downsizing, Mergers, and Reengineering.* Reading, Mass.: Perseus Books.

Dess, Gregory G., and Donald W. Beard. 1984. "Dimensions of Organizational Task Environments." *Administrative Science Quarterly* 29(1): 52–73.

Dillman, Don A. 1978. *Mail and Telephone Surveys: The Total Design Method.* New York: John Wiley.

Donaldson, Lex. 2001. *The Contingency Theory of Organizations.* Thousand Oaks, Calif.: Sage Publications.

Ebert, Ronald J., and DeWayne Piehl. 1973. "Time Horizon: A Concept for Management." *California Management Review* 15(4): 35–41.

El Sawy, Omar A. 1983. "Temporal Perspective and Managerial Attention: A Study of Chief Executive Strategic Behavior." Ph.D. diss., Stanford University.

Gilman, Charlotte P. 1903. *The Home: Its Work and Influence.* New York: McClure, Phillips.

Gleick, James. 1999. *Faster: The Acceleration of Just about Everything.* New York: Pantheon Books.

Hambrick, Donald C., Marta A. Geletkanycz, and James W. Fredrickson. 1993. "Top Executive Commitment to the Status Quo: Some Tests of Its Determinants." *Strategic Management Journal* 14(6): 401–18.

Hay Michael, and Jean-Claude Usunier. 1993. "Time and Strategic Action: A Cross-Cultural View." *Time & Society* 2(3): 313–33.

Javidan, Mansour. 1984. "The Impact of Environmental Uncertainty on Long-Range Planning Practices of the U.S. Savings and Loan Industry." *Strategic Management Journal* 5(4): 381–92.

Judge, William Q., and Mark Spitzfaden. 1995. "The Management of Strategic Time Horizons Within Biotechnology Firms: The Impact of Cognitive Complexity on Time Horizon Diversity." *Journal of Management Inquiry* 4(2): 179–96.

Keats, Barbara W., and Michael A. Hitt. 1988. "A Causal Model of Linkages Among Environmental Dimensions, Macro Organizational Characteristics, and Performance." *Academy of Management Journal* 31(3): 570–98.

Kerlinger, Fred N. 1973. *Foundations of Behavioral Research.* 2nd ed. New York: Holt, Rinehart & Winston.

Khandwalla, Pradip N. 1977. *The Design of Organizations.* New York: Harcourt Brace Jovanovich.

Kimberly, John R., and Robert H. Miles. 1980. *The Organizational Life Cycle.* San Francisco: Jossey-Bass.

Kotter, John P., and James L. Heskett. 1992. *Corporate Culture and Performance.* New York: Free Press.

Larwood, Laurie, Cecilia M. Falbe, Mark P. Kriger, and Paul Miesing. 1995. "Structure and Meaning of Organizational Vision." *Academy of Management Journal* 38(3): 740–69.

Laverty, Kevin J. 1996. "Economic Short-Termism: The Debate, the Unresolved Issues, and the Implications for Management Practice and Research." *Academy of Management Review* 21(3): 825–60.

Lawrence, Paul R., and Jay W. Lorsch. 1967. *Organization and Environment: Managing Differentiation and Integration.* Boston: Harvard University, Graduate School of Business Administration.

Lindsay, William M., and Leslie W. Rue. 1980. "Impact of the Organization Environment on the Long-Range Planning Process: A Contingency View." *Academy of Management Journal* 23(3): 385–404.

London, Barbara, and John Upton. 1994. *Photography.* 5th ed. New York: HarperCollins College Publishers.

March, James G. 1999. "Research on Organizations: Hopes for the Past and Lessons from the Future." *Norkiske Organiisasjonsstudier* 1(1): 69–83.

May, Ruth C., Wayne H. Stewart, and Robert Sweo. 2000. "Environmental Scanning Behavior in a Transitional Economy: Evidence from Russia." *Academy of Management Journal* 43(3): 403–27.

Nunnally, Jum C. 1978. *Psychometric Theory*. 2nd ed. New York: McGraw-Hill.

Ouchi, William G. 1981. *Theory Z: How American Business Can Meet the Japanese Challenge*. New York: Avon Books.

Quinn, Robert E., and Kim Cameron. 1983. "Organizational Life Cycles and Shifting Criteria of Effectiveness: Some Preliminary Evidence." *Management Science* 29(1): 33–51.

Robinson, W. S. 1950. "Ecological Correlations and the Behavior of Individuals." *American Sociological Review* 15(3): 351–57.

Scherer, F. M. 1980. *Industrial Market Structure and Economic Performance*. 2nd ed. Chicago: Rand-McNally College Publishing.

Siegel, Sidney. 1956. *Nonparametric Statistics for the Behavioral Sciences*. New York: McGraw-Hill.

Siehl, Caren, and Joanne Martin. 1990. "Organizational Culture: A Key to Financial Performance?" In *Organizational Climate and Culture*, edited by Benjamin Schneider. San Francisco: Jossey-Bass.

Thompson, James D. 1967. *Organizations in Action: Social Science Bases of Administrative Theory*. New York: McGraw-Hill.

Tung, Rosalie L. 1979. "Dimensions of Organizational Environments: An Exploratory Study of Their Impact on Organization Structure." *Academy of Management Journal* 22(4): 672–93.

Webber, Ross A. 1972. *Time and Management*. New York: Van Nostrand Reinhold.

Weick, Karl E. 1979. *The Social Psychology of Organizing*. 2nd ed. Reading, Mass.: Addison-Wesley.

Winchester, Simon. 1998. *The Professor and the Madman: A Tale of Murder, Insanity, and the Making of the Oxford English Dictionary*. New York: HarperPerennial.

—— Chapter 6 ——

# Bicycle Messengers and the Dialectics of Speed

## Benjamin Stewart

B ICYCLE MESSENGERS PROVIDE a valuable on-demand service to urban businesses that require same-day delivery of time-sensitive material. This chapter analyzes the spatial and organizational contradictions that enable and disrupt the urban bicycle messenger industry's production of speed. It begins with the industry's general context, describing the congestion that makes the "low-tech" bicycle the city's fastest mode of delivery. It then moves to explore two sides of the messenger's labor situation, the stress that arises conjointly out of that enabling congestion and the industry's demands for speed, and the stress-mitigating enjoyment that arises out of those aspects of the labor similar to athletic competition. This potential identity between labor and sport is evident in the phenomenon of messenger races: messenger-produced events that appropriate the labor's structures in the interests of extending its pleasures. Further, as messenger races have evolved, the organizational foundations undergirding those events have evolved as well, resulting in messenger associations; messengers have begun to take political advantage of these organizations: not only in the interests of decreasing obstructions to their labor's production of speed, but also of limiting the speed the industry can demand of that labor.

December 12, 2001. I'm at a party talking with Hermes—Hermes, who has been a messenger in San Francisco, Berlin, and New York. We're discussing one of the informal aspects of the job, the traffic rules bicycle messengers tend to break, and he suggests that such illegality is an important aspect of

150

the service our industry offers. At this point, Mike Dee, another messenger who has apparently caught parts of our conversation, jumps down from the steps above us, proclaiming, "The commodity we sell is speed."

## THE MESSENGER WITHIN ROLE THEORY: NEGOTIATING SPEED AND SPACE

Bicycle messengers, though a ubiquitous element of many urban streetscapes, are an underresearched group: apart from Jack Dennerlein and John Meeker's (2002) paper on injury rates (which concluded that messengers' occupation puts them at serious physical risk while often not providing health benefits), there has been little formal study of either the labor of bicycle messengers or the subculture those laborers have created. Dennerlein and Meeker's (2002) conclusion is in agreement with the more general assertion of Arne Kalleberg (2000) and Arne Kalleberg, Barbara Reskin, and Ken Hudson (2000) that nonstandard jobs tend to offer fewer benefits and lower pay than standard ones.[1] Given the complexities of the messenger's labor context—he or she is caught in the middle of poor compensation, the industry's demands for speed, and the immediate demands of the urban spatial context—the occupation offers valuable insights on the relationships between social structures, emotions, and social spaces.

Robert K. Merton's (1957) notion of a "role set" refers to the multiple roles involved in the constitution of a single subject position. Several other concepts within role theory—"role conflict" (Katz and Kahn 1966) and "role overload" (Heiss 1990)—are important to an understanding of the different kinds of demands placed on messengers. "Role conflict" refers to conflicts between roles and "role overload" refers to a lack of resources needed to fulfill a role. Because of the complexity of the messenger's role system and role context, I propose four additional terms to help clarify the messenger's situation— *role mise-en-scènew, role constellation, role destabilization,* and *role monolithism.* These terms account for the effects of multiple sites' simultaneously pressing conflicting demands on the messenger. (The relationships between the terms will become clearer in the context of the chapter.)

Some of these demands may be for emotional labor (Hochschild 1983; McCammon and Griffin 2000), however, the messenger seems to be among interactive workers whose customers care more about speed than about emotional production (Sutton and Rafaeli 1988). Messenger companies' regulation of emotional labor also appears haphazard, a situation that may result from messengers' positions at the endpoints of a distributive structure, thus making authority more difficult to enforce. Greta Paules (1991) has shown similar dynamics in restaurant work.

On the other hand, the industry itself may not have any investment in emotional labor, a possibility clarified by comparing Robin Leidner's (1993) description of the components necessary for job routinization with aspects of the messenger industry that seem to negate such possibilities. One such aspect is the blockage that exists within urban space itself, here understood through reference to geography (Harvey 1990; Jameson 1991; Lefebvre 1974/1991); additionally, Greg Downey's (2001, 2002) concept of "boundary work" helps clarify the connection between roles and space. The tensions surrounding that nexus also suggest that the messenger performs a complex form of what Everett Hughes (1956/1994) labels "dirty work" (that labor performed by the low at the behest of the high). But for messengers there is simultaneous pleasure in that work, a paradox explained by Michael Burawoy's (1979) suggestion that games can be used to support laborers' self-motivated productivity through individual competition against the self. Such isolated auto-competition can be alienating, a possibility messengers combat through communal "alley cat" races, which borrow the structures of work to extend their pleasure. Although Jeremy Bentham's (1802/1931) notion of deep play condemns the kinds of risk involved in messenger races, those events' appropriation of labor structures is consonant with Michel Foucault's (1979) understanding of power as fundamentally productive. Indeed, the races facilitate organization within the messenger community.

## METHODS AND DATA

I have worked as a messenger for approximately three years: two of them in Washington, D.C., from 1993 to 1995, and the remainder in New York City, where I have done this work on and off since moving there in 1995, the last time being in the summer of 2001. I continue to attend messenger races and other messenger-community events. The material for this paper comes from field notes accumulated during my participant observation within those settings, documentation produced by other messengers, and documentation by people outside the culture. The messenger-produced material includes two messenger memoirs, a book of photography, messenger zines, and material from the international (public) messenger list-serv. Nonmessenger documentation includes two recent documentaries, *Pedal* and *Red Light Go*.

My use of theory works along the lines of Burawoy's (2000) "theory reconstruction," the goal of which is to find theories that explain aspects of the phenomena under study, and to return to those phenomena to find aspects that the theory does not cover. Subsequently, one must look for ways to extend the theory, thus making it capable of more rigorous explanation in the future.

## SPEED AND ECONOMICS

In the early 1990s, a few years after the fax machine had become commonplace, the *New York Times* proclaimed that bicycle messengers in New York City were "becoming extinct" (Robert E. Tomasson, "Fax Displacing Manhattan Bike Couriers," *New York Times,* March 19, 1991, B3). Although the fax machine did undeniably undercut demand, the outcomes for the occupation have been less dire than the *Times* predicted. As the economy improved in the 1990s, demand for messengers increased as a side-effect of the dot-com boom (paradoxical considering the sophistication of the communications infrastructure on which that boom was based); of course, given the dot-com bust, the industry once again finds itself in difficult times. Indeed, the messenger industries of New York and Washington, D.C., have been especially hard-hit in the wake of September 11: New York City's because of that event's effects on the financial district, and Washington, D.C.'s, because increased security measures in government buildings are a new obstacle to messengers.[2]

Apart from these difficulties, if we judge the health of the industry by its geographic proliferation, it is doing quite well: the website of the International Federation of Bicycle Messenger Associations

(IFBMA) currently lists twenty-nine U.S. cities with bicycle messenger services. A new service not listed is the one in Buffalo, which was the subject of a recent *New York Times* article (Metz 2002; Michelle York, "Buffalo's Bicycle Messenger Industry: Two Wheels, One Man," *New York Times*, August 17, 2003, p. A1, 25). The industry's spread to smaller cities such as Buffalo—as well as its continued presence in larger cities—may be explained by increases in urban congestion in the last ten years. Certainly congestion provides the environment in which the bicycle becomes an information technology without parallel within the niche of same-day deliveries.[3] Messengers use the bicycle's small size to produce speed by taking advantage of spatial gaps or accesses that larger vehicles cannot use: splitting lanes of gridlocked traffic, attending more intently to traffic flows than traffic laws, locking up to whatever sign, post, or fence happens to be handy. In addition, a rider who carries the proper tools can fix minor problems (such as flats or broken spokes) on the spot.

Despite the bicycle's advantages within the compressed spaces of urban cores, the general labor conditions of messenger work present most, if not all, of the qualities Kalleberg, Reskin, and Hudson (2000) use to describe what they call "bad jobs" (low pay, lack of health insurance, lack of pension).[4] Messengers are paid on commission, which can be a positive or negative factor: as we will see, the informality of the means by which the industry generally assigns work has the potential to create "bad jobs" for some and "good jobs" for others.

Most messengers work for companies that employ some combination of bicyclists, motorcyclists, drivers of cars, vans, and trucks, clerical staff, and dispatchers. Messenger companies vary widely in size: some employ only one or two people while others employ hundreds. They exist to provide on-demand service for their clients: most companies offer regular delivery within two hours and rush delivery within an hour.[5] In *Pedal*, a documentary on New York City's messenger culture that was released in 2002, Steve, the owner of Mother's Messengers, explains that his company would charge seven dollars for a run within Midtown; a rush within Midtown would probably cost eleven to twelve dollars. But these rates are high: the average price of a regular run in Manhattan is probably closer to six dollars, of which the messenger gets between 40 and 60 percent. Thus, as Steve makes clear in the film, "To make decent money you have to make twenty-five runs a day, which is a lot of hustling, and that'll guarantee you at least a hundred dollars a day" (Sutherland 2002). Such "hustling" might lead us to believe that a messenger's production of speed is purely the result of a combination of physical capacity, motivation, and knowledge of the city, factors that are undeniably components of an individual's productivity (or lack of it). But the labor structure is more complex, incorporating a mode of organization that frames messengers' competition among each other in specific, and often unequal, ways.

Most companies use dispatchers to organize and regulate this competition by distributing groups of runs—often referred to as rows[6]—to individual messengers.[7] Some form of radio device (radio, pager, or cell phone) facilitates this distribution system, and messengers record pickup and delivery information, and collect signatures, on manifests. This system allows dispatchers to allocate work on-the-fly, either by assigning an individual run to a messenger already working on a row, or by creating new rows out of emergent patterns within a group of unassigned runs. In the case of an individual run, this means assigning it to the messenger who is closest to the pickup and already headed in the right direction.

Starting a new row means organizing runs such that a messenger can pick up several packages from the same general area (on a good day anywhere from six to ten at a time) before heading to more remote delivery points. This system is more efficient for both the individual messenger and the company; on a busy day, no dispatcher wants to have to reroute a messenger to pick up something from an area another messenger has just left. Of course, not all rows are equal: not all runs make geographical sense in relation to others, and not all buildings are equally receptive to messenger traffic. In principle, messengers tolerate bad rows with the understanding that the work has to be done and that taking care of the "trash" is a favor to the dispatcher, one that will be returned in the form of better work in the future.

This potential for good and bad rows helps us to see that the unit over which messengers compete is the row, not the run, for although some runs are worth more than others (rushes often pay 150 percent what regulars pay), even the most lucrative of these are worth comparatively little in isolation. We have to look at the spatial relations among a group of assigned runs—of a row—to begin to see that group's value, which arises from the amount of riding time implied in the distances between the nodes of its geographic cluster. Thus, without knowing how far apart those pick-ups and deliveries are or whether or not those runs' buildings facilitate quick entry and exit, we can't begin to speculate on how much money a messenger will make because we need to know how much time the group of runs will take.[8] By understanding the importance of the relationships among a given group of runs, we can more clearly see the character of messengers' competition over rows. This competition is not over who will do the most rows, but rather over who will be offered the best rows.

Such a system suggests two different categories of speed, un-mediated,[9] or "raw speed," the travel-time between two points, and mediated, or "delivery speed," the time it takes to complete a given number of runs.[10] In order to be able to better produce mediated speed, messengers compete for access to geographic relationships,[11] ideally those that offer greater probabilities of completing more runs in less time, for such synergy increases pay. This ideal situation results in the completion of fewer rows; these take longer because they have more work in them. Nevertheless, completing more rows is not necessarily something the messenger wants to avoid; indeed, the more often he or she calls in "clear," the greater the chance that the dispatcher will offer better work in the future.

Here we see an aspect of the work-assignment system that allows for dispatcher bias or, perhaps more accurately, that exposes an aspect of the system which makes such bias difficult to avoid. In other words, dispatcher partiality is not generally the result of a transgression of the system's rules (such as giving a messenger a new row out of turn would be), but generally results from an important aspect of that system's normal functioning. The particular mechanism we're interested in here is the row-construction process, and more specifically, its informal character—the fact that the dispatcher's organization of runs is itself an emergent process. It is no less emergent than the continuously unfolding relations among the runs themselves: clients call in more runs all the time. In fact there are not only more runs but more relations among runs, the latter becoming exponentially more complicated as the number of the former increases.

Because the most efficient row groupings are not always clear, dispatchers have a great deal of subjective leeway as to how they organize runs into rows. As we shall see, that leeway marks the complexity every dispatcher must face. But the bias that can arise out of that leeway is one of the means by which stratification enters the workplace.

Informal conversations with messengers and evidence from the messenger list-serv both suggest that the industry's labor force is highly stratified (see also Reilly 2000).[12] The messenger's place in the employment structure is constructed of nothing but the work offered by the dispatcher and his or her ability to complete it.[13] Thus, the dispatcher's acts—whether flowing from the dispatcher's or the manager's or the company owner's will—are partly responsible for the stratification that the company creates. In other words, while such "bias" can be the means by which companies value (or fail to value) workers in terms of things like raw speed or seniority,[14] it can also lead to stratification. Indeed, many messengers feel that the latter tendency is especially strong at larger companies (Reilly 2000). Not all messengers feel this way, however, as illustrated by a discussion from the messenger list-serv. In response to a complaint about the low rates of "big messenger companies" (D. C. Courier, "Messenger Mailing List Index," http://www.dccourier. com/messengers/messenger_archives_1994_1999/messengers 199609.txt), Greg Austin (somewhat inadvertently) raises the stratification issue:

> I still believe that with the larger firms there lie opportunities for high end earnings. If I am riding for a company with 20 riders, I know I will be in the top 2 in terms of earnings. I think that those in the top 10% will have excellent earnings potential. . . . The larger workforce allows the dedicated/high performance riders a consistent pool of work. Obviously for every high end rider there is a low end rider who ain't makin no money!

When Austin says, "The larger workforce allows the dedicated/high performance riders a consistent pool of work," he can only mean that the larger client base (which requires a larger workforce to service) creates consistent demand, thus maintaining the income of the "high end rider." In effect, Austin is implying that larger companies tend to overhire, a condition that inevitably produces stratification. Since pay is on a commission basis, there is no incentive for messenger companies *not* to overhire (as they only pay for completed runs). Indeed, there is much anecdotal evidence to suggest that overhiring is standard practice at many companies, especially the larger ones.

Shawn Bega, the owner of a messenger company, D. C. Courier, who testified at a Washington, D.C., city council roundtable, "Bicycle and Pedestrian Safety," addressed himself to this issue through his description of the changes he had seen in his sixteen years as a bicycle messenger (Bega 2001):

> Many years ago, a new courier company came to D.C. and as part of their corporate structure, brought with them a pre-designed dispatch system that contained in it a 15-minute rush delivery originally designed for Melbourne, Australia. Having no knowledge of downtown D.C., the safety issues surrounding a 15-minute run in our city was [*sic*] never considered by this company, and they began advertising this faster service at lower prices. . . . Established companies had to find ways to compete with this faster, cheaper service. . . . Companies admittedly hired more bikers than they needed, forcing their bicycle couriers into a cut-throat war against each other competing for work. Truthfully, few of them won, and companies continued with this high-turn-over system.

Such competition is an example of a situation in which an individual company's interest serves to undermine the general interest (lower rates being detrimental to companies and messengers): that is, the price war resulting from a messenger company's attempt to acquire clients produces a net loss for the industry.[15] The fact that this loss occurred in an industry whose "nonstandard" jobs lack traditional employment and salary protections makes it likely that the industry passed more of that loss on to the messenger than would have been the case in an industry with "standard" jobs (Kalleberg 2000). To avoid that outcome, a company would have to raise commissions while cutting rates, which seems highly unlikely. The above scenario also clarifies the potential implications of the industry's stratification, namely that the unproductivity of a "bad job" helps to maintain the high-end rider's "consistent pool of work." Thus, by regulating access to work in particular ways, dispatchers can create various configurations of good and bad jobs.[16]

Of course, such an informal system need not produce stratification, though the employee-demand equation can be difficult to balance to the workers' benefit. Indeed, given demand's variability, it may be difficult for a company to determine their optimum number of employees. If, for instance, a worker quits or is injured, the work that must be redistributed can strain the company's system to its limits, thus increasing client dissatisfaction. Companies care most about speed in the aggregate—whether or not their individual producers can collectively met all of the clients' demands. Stated another way, it doesn't matter how fast *most* of the packages are delivered if a messenger fails to deliver an important one by its deadline. Because a client might cancel its account in such a situation, the temptation to hire extra messengers is strong; the pressure exerted by this temptation (as well as the more general industry forces that keep rates low) makes nonstratified messenger companies rare.[17] The possible outcomes of this dilemma suggest a distinction between "efficient speed" companies, those with fewer messengers doing less work per run, and "inefficient speed" companies, those with more messengers riding further per run. The latter type of company creates a glut of low-end riders stuck in "bad jobs."

Since messengers are responsible for their bicycles, any tools they might need, and their bags and clothing, those with bad jobs are less likely to have the equipment necessary to do the job properly, for such gear is expensive: "a basic no-frills messenger bike could cost $175" (Downey 2002, 203). Actually, this understates the case: three hundred dollars is probably a minimum, at least for a new bicycle. Maintenance may cost even more—year-round, all-weather riding takes a toll—and components are far more expensive when purchased apart from a complete bike, even with the 10 percent discount most bike shops offer messengers.[18]

Maintenance involves more than the cost of replacement parts though, and those who do not have the knowledge or the tools to do their own repairs are at a disadvantage.[19] Consequently, though being a bicycle messenger may generally be perceived as an entry-level, low-startup-cost type of work, it certainly favors those who have the money to buy the proper gear for the job, and are skilled bicycle mechanics. "Inefficient speed" companies give their workers less disposable income, and so they also prevent many of those workers from having the means to buy and maintain the kind of gear that makes the job easier. Even here, the distinction between those who have capital to invest and those who do not, and between those who have bike mechanic's skills and those who do not, creates the terrain on which stratification can begin to take hold.

However, not all aspects of the job favor previous skills or monetary investment, especially since few messengers begin their careers knowing the city's geography to the extent the occupation demands. Generally, a messenger learns the city through experiencing it: consciously learning street locations and clients' addresses, carefully memorizing particular traffic light patterns, unconsciously mapping potholes, and occasionally getting lost. Dispatchers are also an important source of geographic knowledge and training, and it is not surprising that many dispatchers are former messengers. Indeed, *Pedal* follows Evil E, who, though he struggles to continue riding as injuries take their toll, ultimately resolves that becoming a dispatcher is his only viable career path: "in the future—oh god do I hate to say it—I see myself dispatching. I see myself sitting on a computer, with the whole city inside of my brain, with maybe 20 riders, sending them around, and hooking them up" (Sutherland 2001). If "hooking them up" means arranging the conditions under which riders might produce what I have called efficient speed, then Evil E's imagining also refers to the years of *having been sent around* necessary to produce a rider whose mental conditions are themselves maps of spatial arrangements. Such "cognitive mapping" (Jameson 1991) primarily concerns the social aspects of space (Lefebvre 1974/1991). Messengers and dispatchers are far less interested in "dead" physical relationships than in the aspects of their environment that enable efficient flows of traffic. Space here is a dialectical mediation between the physical and the social. For example, the relationship of a building— say, 601 West Twenty-sixth—to different but equidistant spaces in the city, such as the financial district (downtown) and Bloomingdale's (across town at Lexington and Fifty-ninth), would carry vastly different implications for the messenger assigned them (the former acceptable, the latter deflating).[20] Not all such distinctions in this realm are so obvious, and understandings of the most nuanced ones are acquired through years of riding, years of working to increase the efficiency of one's flow through the city's various spatial configurations.

Good dispatchers pass on knowledge of such social flows at a range of levels. Such transfers are not formal, but are oral histories, one generation of messengers passing knowledge on to the next, an informal progression that depends on individuals capable of, and committed to, making it happen. Consequently, there is not even any assurance that "hooking them up" is a given dispatcher's goal. The lack of formal structures designed to facilitate knowledge transfers also points to the difficulty of rationalizing the market the industry covers. Indeed, the industry's nonstandard structures have been constructed in relation to situations and spaces that serve as barriers to entry for the larger, express, delivery services such as UPS or Federal Express. Consequently, the structural limitations of those larger companies, which are strengths in the market they do serve, leave open the niche in which bicycle messengers remain one of the pillars of same-day delivery.

## THE LAST MILE:
## THE SPATIAL-EMOTIONAL DIALECTIC

May 25, 2001. It's the end of the day: the Friday of my first week of work in three years. I'm on the ninth floor of a downtown building with one last drop, but the addressee's office is closed. Since it's my first week, I've only been given a pager, so I have no way to contact the office other than to go downstairs to a pay phone. I'm tired, and I'm close to the bridge I take home to Brooklyn: I definitely don't want to have to take the envelope back to base (which I will have to do if I can't drop it). I decide to gamble, sliding it through the door's mail slot. Back down on the sidewalk—on the pay phone I should have used in the first place—my dispatcher is enraged: I don't know how many times he asks me "Did I tell you to drop it!?" or says "It's not going to be my ass—this is on you." I assure him that, whatever happens, I'll take full responsibility. Back upstairs, my arm doesn't fit though the mail slot; back downstairs, I head to a hardware store where I buy a mechanical arm. I retrieve the letter and take it back to base.

In Downey's recent work on telegraph messengers, focusing on the period between 1850 and 1950, he suggests (2001, 224) that telegraph "messenger boys" served as "boundary workers" in what he calls an "analog internetwork":

The telephone, telegraph, and Post Office networks were interconnected only through the constant labor of workers who used all three in their daily tasks—telephone operators accepting phoned-in telegrams for the telegraph company, Post Office letter carriers delivering duplicate telegrams through the mail, or telegraph messengers running urgent letters to and from the Post Office.

Bicycle messengers are also boundary workers, who "smooth connections" among business and government networks, networks that are far less clearly defined and more diffuse than the three on which Downey focuses. Indeed, we might think of the messenger industry's boundary work in relation to the telecommunications industry's last-mile problem, the difficulty and expense of bridging the approximately mile-long gap between the fiber-optic infrastructure and the majority of homes and businesses. In the case of package delivery, the analogous problem is the temporal expansion of the time it takes to get from one place to another as a result of urban spatial congestion.[21] As has been implied, such congestion is the result of the complex of forces arising out of multiple vectors and regulations: traffic densities, traffic lights, building policies, and so forth. For Downey (2001), effective traffic flow demands "protocols"—one of which we have already seen in the dispatch system structured around the row.[22] But as part of the process of creating more speed, protocols also constrain those workers, and necessarily so: failure to follow protocol would result in chaos.

Protocols are an effort to alleviate problems that arise out of what Robert Merton (1957) calls the "role-set": the multiple roles that constitute a single subject position. There are two categories of problem here. The first is "role conflict" (Katz and Kahn 1966; Merton 1957): a situation in which a social actor is presented with mutually exclusive, and equally compelling demands, such as between obeying traffic laws and safety rules, and meeting client and dispatcher demands. The second is "role overload," labeled and defined by Jerold Heiss (1990) as a situation in which the actor lacks the material and social resources—physical stamina, sufficient sustenance, knowledge of the city, correct package information—to support his or her role. In light of the variety of situations and demands that are the very definition of boundary work, protocols are indispensable to such labor.

In addition to the potentially conflictual factors listed above, the messenger must also negotiate with and through building policies, elevator flow, delayed packages, mailroom protocols, and receptionists' temperaments, not to mention the possibility that a package's recipient may have left the office early. Consequently, messengers' role conflicts tend to arise out of complex, systemic interactions: how many jobs the messenger has at a given moment; his or her location in the city in relation to those jobs; the priorities of those jobs relative to each other; the level of risk (both legal and physical) he or she is willing to shoulder with regard to getting a package there on time; the police presence along the route to that destination; the temperament of the drivers encountered along that route.[23] While "role-set" describes this potential for multiple inter-actions among roles, it does not necessarily convey the potentially differential weights of those roles; for this reason I will use *role constellation* in place of role-set.[24] Further, because spatial relations are such important aspects of so many of the messenger's roles, I will use *role mise-en-scène* to refer to those of that figure's roles that become visible *primarily* via spatial dynamics.

Beyond this terminology, we must keep in mind that, at a more general level, messengers are stand-ins for roles the client cannot fulfill; indeed, it is because of clients' need to outsource inconve-nient roles that messengers' labor becomes necessary at all. Thus, for clients, the purpose of boundary work is to prevent those inconveniences from leaking back into their spaces. Consequently, smoothing over inconveniences is primarily a task of what Erving Goffman (1959) refers to as "impression management," and the boundary worker, while in the client's space, must carefully main-tain the external world of the street as a "back region" (1959, 112). This is a space about which the messenger company's clients are ambivalent—they need to receive traffic through it but simultane-ously want to keep it at a distance. The nexus of this ambivalence is also the point at which the messenger must perform "emotional labor" (Hochschild 1983). However, despite the interactive service messengers enact for their companies, few of them are "trained to manage their own emotions to produce a particular emotional response in the service recipients" (McCammon and Griffin 2000, 280, 281). Indeed, messenger companies' general lack of formal behavioral requirements or rigid dress codes are in sharp contrast to the highly regimented scripts that structure much service work. Such informality is also a world away from the training and disci-pline to which telegraph messengers were subjected: company rule books, company schools, military-style uniforms, and attempts "to precisely script the way deliveries were handled" (Downey 2002, 26–67). Thus, it may seem strange that the bicycle messenger is subjected to so little formal training, especially when one considers that well-staged emotional labor can be a means of differentiating a company in a competitive market.

It may be that messenger companies wish to implement emotional labor norms for their employees but are prevented from doing so, either because of their own role conflicts, or because their workers would resist such demands (which would make this problem into a resource, or role overload, issue). The fragmentation of what Goffman (1959) calls the "teamwork" aspects of the labor situation make the latter possibility seem likely. Greta Paules (1991) has shown how waitresses were able to reduce their managers' control over them by taking advantage of a similarly decentralized structure to give food to customers and thus maximize their tips. Messengers work at an even farther remove from the source of discipline, so their companies may see attempts at control as being too costly. Thus, messengers' freedom from having to perform in scripted ways could be a de facto tradeoff that maintains the stability of the industry's nonstandard employment structures (Kalleberg, Reskin, and Hudson 2000). On the other hand, even if messengers were amenable to being trained to produce more scripted roles, such investments might not return the desired competitive advantage. For instance, Robert Sutton and Anat Rafaeli's (1988) study of convenience stores offers the possibility that where speed is the customer's main goal, emotional labor may get in the way of efficient service: "Managers and clerks . . . often contended that friendliness and warmth were unnecessary because 'our customers just want to get in and out quickly' " (473–74). Messengers, in an inverted form of the service relationship, also want to "get in and out quickly," and what little testimony the messenger list-serv offers in this regard runs along similar lines: "You know how it is— you get love at the MONADNOC building and then you get shit upon in the PYRAMID. As a messenger, you just want to get the signature and move on. If the receptionist smiles at you, give her a wink back, right? If she sneers, give her the gas-face. Either way, the job is done" (D. C. Courier, "Messenger Mailing List Index," http://www.dccourier.com/messengers/messenger_archives_1994 _1999/messengers199704.txt).

It's not that messengers don't perform emotional labor, it's that they do so on their own terms, tending either to offer few emotions other than the ones at hand or returning those they are offered in kind (though, like many emotional exchanges, I'm sure that some of the latter variety have the tendency to escalate).

It is also possible that the industry's general lack of "trained" emotional labor is the result of deeper structures and processes at the heart of the industry itself. We will be able to more clearly understand such possibilities by thinking about the problems of routinization. Leidner, in her 1993 book, *Fast Food, Fast Talk,* suggests, "For routinization to succeed, . . . interactive service organizations must work on people—both their workers and their customers or clients—to bring their attitudes and behavior into line with organizational needs" (25). Such goals are not possible within the current system of same-day delivery: clients negate those possibilities because, for them, the industry's ability to service nonstandard jobs is one of its *advantages* over the larger, overnight, couriers; laborers negate those possibilities, first, because those nonstandard jobs require more individual judgment (routing, estimation of package weight, decisions about when to ask the dispatcher for help, and so forth) and second, because, as we've seen, messengers are responsible for their gear: their bikes and, usually, their clothing (which should not be underestimated as a factor in whether or not they perform their jobs well or poorly). But clients and workers do not present the only intractable challenges to routinization. When client demands overload a company's ability to respond, the company itself has to resort to nonstandard demands: *No cars available to take a rush job from Newsweek out to the airport?—call in a biker; no cars available to deliver a heavy box?— call in a biker; you've already picked up more fashion portfolios and garment bags than you can safely handle?—well, do the best you can.* In such edge situations, the industry's protocols may be looser than messengers would like; consequently they must often solve their company's role conflicts and overloads in addition to their clients', a situation that exacerbates the complexity of the emotional terrain they face, even as they must continue to produce.

Of course, from the messenger's perspective it doesn't much matter whose conflict it is, since in the end the main goal is to please the clients: to smooth over the potential inconsistencies that come packaged with every run; to hide any conflicts neatly away backstage. The formal economy needs this service and it is willing to look the other way with regard to the methods by which it is accomplished. In this mutually beneficial but often uneasy relationship between messengers and their clients, we have a formation that is akin to one described by Hughes (1956/1994) in his discussion of "dirty work": "Law and medicine . . . have always required some sort of alliance, or, at least, some sort of terms with the lowliest and most despised of human occupations" (52). It would be far too simple to paint messengers as lowly and despised (and the complex valences of what we might call the occupation's "outlaw prestige" will become clearer below), yet messengers are undeniably caught in a division of labor in which their lot is the dirty work. But if this is so, and if the job commonly produces the blunt realities of unresolved role conflicts, not to mention "staggering" occupational injury rates (Dennerlein and Meeker 2002),[25] then why do people continue to perform the labor? As we shall see, the most immediate reason is probably the pleasure produced by the occupation's gamelike structure. But there may be another reason: a more abstract motivation related to the messenger's privileged access to the public sphere. For one could see the messenger's experience of the contrasts and contradictions of social space as an experience of the elements that constitute the public itself: from the polluted caverns of the street to the rarefied halls of congress; from wait-time spent in corporate offices to standby time spent at Tompkins Square Park or Farragut Square. In many of these spaces, the messenger is witness to and a subject of the conflicts that can arise out of the relations among those variegated social spaces. Consequently, it would seem that those social relations provide the messenger with what we might call an *emotional topography of the public* (which we should also see as the mental structure that could enable one to be a skilled dispatcher). Thus, the experience of the spatial creates emotional states; those states, in turn, become a psychic topography, creating one's spatial sense, one's "cognitive map" (Jameson 1991).

## AMBIVALENCE ABOUT UNCERTAINTY

March 27, 2003. An exchange took place on the messenger list-serv between a prospective messenger and an experienced one. Such exchanges happen several times a year, and this one is particularly relevant to our concerns here. Eric, the prospective messenger, wanted advice on how to become a messenger. Having "repeatedly" watched messenger films, he had decided that "those guys look pretty cool flyin through traffic" (D. C. Courier, "Messenger Mailing List," http://www.dccourier.com/messengers/messenger_archives_2003/msg00628.html). There was only one reply to Eric's post, from a messenger who goes by the name seventyseven: "i think, first you should get rid of any prejudices or ideas you have about bike messengers, especially those . . . learned by tv or newspapers. in my opinion bike messengers neither are heroes, nor asphalt-cowboys or whatever they are described as" (D. C. Courier, "Messenger Mailing List," http://www.dccourier.com/messengers/messenger_archives_2003/msg00628.html). Seventyseven went on to warn of the danger involved in trying to live up to such fantasies, but then added: "In the first place it is a service and it is sport."[26]

The latter statement both is and is not an about-face. If seventyseven consciously meant it as *not* an about-face, it still points toward a paradoxical aspect of messenger labor—a point at which the sport in it is simultaneously a site of measured discipline and something that goes beyond most labor identifications: as play.

Seventyseven and I are certainly not the first to theorize sport as an aspect of labor or even to examine the complexity of the valences that arise out of the relationships between those two terms. The most useful of such theories to the current discussion is found in Burawoy's *Manufacturing Consent* (1979), a participant-observation ethnography that documents the mise-en-scène of post-Taylorist capitalist production; his site is Allied Corporation, a unionized machine shop. The main formation that draws Burawoy's attention is a structure in which the workers are given a certain amount of freedom to play games: to make games out of work, to compete against themselves in order to enjoy their work. "Workers are sucked into the game as a way of reducing the level of deprivation" (1979, 199). We might extrapolate from this structure a suggestion that the game—and the pleasure of competition that comes with it—serves as partial payment to the worker for increased production. But payment or no, Burawoy suggests that such game playing is the structure through which Allied Corporation "secures and obscures" the continued production of surplus value. Things are similar but slightly different in the case of messenger work: the fantasies and pleasure that pulse around that labor not only obscure the extraction of surplus value, they also serve as a buffer against the more conflict-prone aspects of the job. As Austin asserts, "To get paid (some handsomely) for doing something that is so very much fun is a good thing for us" (D. C. Courier, "Messenger Mailing List," http://www.dccourier.com/messengers/ messenger_archives_1994_1999/messengers199609.txt). Here, then, we have another feature of the job that helps the industry retain its workforce despite the less desirous aspects of the labor that arise out of its nonstandard character (Kalleberg, Reskin, and Hudson 2000).

Burawoy's exploration of the power of the game can also help us make more sense of why so many messengers choose to ride a track bike. Originally made for riding on a velodrome, this minimalist, one-speed machine has no brakes and its gear is fixed such that, once in motion the rear wheel's momentum will continue to drive the chain (and therefore the crank and pedals), making coasting impossible. The rider stops by locking his or her legs, causing the crank and the rear wheel to lock, producing a skid. In the documentary *Red Light Go,* a messenger named Gandi demonstrates a track skid, after which he offers a curt "It's fun as shit" in response to the question of why someone would want to ride such a machine. His answer fits neatly within Burawoy's game thesis. Learning to ride a track bike provides a pleasurable challenge—something to keep the job interesting. Such skill development is in line with Burawoy's (1979) tentative conclusion that Allied's younger workers, rather than stick with one type of machine on which they were assured of being paid well, were more likely to "attempt to accumulate skill on as wide a variety of machines as possible" (152). So, too, many messengers ride a range of machines in order to develop their riding techniques, but riding the track bike develops a more general riding skill that other bicycles do not. The messenger Mike Dee states, "You really have to be able to look at the road in front of you and predict when fucked up things are going to happen" (Barraud, Kivowitz, and Barraud 2002). Thus, the track bike forces the messenger who rides it to think about traffic in a different way, to give more attention to the various possibilities of what *might* happen on the basis of the ever-changing conditions of the road ahead. The limits of the track bike as a technology provide an occasion for the development of new skills, producing the ground for new kinds of pleasure; these pleasures in turn support the rider caught in an otherwise conflictual labor process. Such pleasure is a vital part of the "production of consent" (Burawoy 1979)—an especially important asset for messenger companies given their decentralized labor structures. Skill and pleasure produce consent, which supports the production of speed.

Of course, the production of pleasure is not all or always about skill. Certainly, if my company's client had wanted me to drop that package in the mail slot, it's likely I would have congratulated myself for having made a wise, time-saving decision (never bothering to consider that such luck has nothing whatsoever to do with good judgment). And I don't suggest this possibility to point to my own irrationality (though it does) but rather to highlight such irrationality as a normal mode of functioning. We should also note that such a delusion is similar to one that our high-end rider might have if he imagines that his success is due solely to his own ability to produce speed. That rider may well be fast, but simultaneously the system, that "form itself," has a "mystifying" effect on those who labor within its structures (Marx 1867/1967, 71).[27] There is pleasure in delivering a heap of packages and in taking personal credit for systemic effects of one's speed. But perhaps just as much pleasure arises out of a lucky choice, out of the successful outcome of the risky gambit. Here we are close to Jeremy Bentham's (1802/1931) concept of "deep play": those forms of play in which the risks irrationally outweigh the potential benefits. Clifford Geertz (1973) helps us see that the pleasure of risk itself might need to be accounted for as a potential benefit. Geertz's belief was that the irrationality at the heart of "deep play" is the force that "increases the meaningfulness" (434) of the Balinese cockfight. The irrationality of the risk is counterbalanced, both by the possibility of future pleasure (from beating the odds) and the present-tense enjoyment of that imagining (savoring the idea) of pleasure to come. Such dynamics are no less present in messenger work, and they are often magnified by the gaze of the outsider—for what else is Eric's "those guys look pretty cool" but the desire to be one of those messengers, beating the odds (and, perhaps he also hopes, being admired by another outsider).

Burawoy (1979) is revealing here, for it is mainly through his careful analysis of the conscious and unconscious deployment of uncertainty by management and workers that he is able to understand the means through which that labor's individualizing game structure functions to produce surplus value. Certainly the individual stakes for the laborer are lower on Allied's shop floor than they are in the entirety-of-urban-space-*cum*-shop-floor that is the messenger's domain, but similar processes undergird both situations. Burawoy notes, "A game looses its ability to absorb players" when the uncertainty is either "too great" or "too slight" (1979, 87). Messengers rarely face too little uncertainty; indeed, role conflicts and role overloads can easily spin their uncertainty levels out of control. On the other hand, this volatility is one of the generative forces of the messenger labor game, a force that simultaneously threatens to destroy the very structure it enables. Among the more important situations through which this force flows are those that require messengers to make routing decisions, for even when the dispatcher offers well-organized rows, it is a rare dispatcher that has time to help them through every step of the process (nor do I imagine many messengers would enjoy such remote oversight).

Consequently, the variety of possible choices presents a compelling challenge to messengers left to route themselves. In the most complex of such situations, taking the time to systematically determine the most efficient order, would be a far more inefficient method than would relying on a well-informed guess. This is precisely the kind of uncertainty that can make the job feel like a game, the possibility of making a bad choice being the thing that supports the pleasure of, and adds value to, a good one. Lisa, a San Francisco messenger, affirms such pleasure: "It's like an alley cat [a messenger race]. I love it when a dispatcher gives me seven tags and says, 'Use your best judgment'" (Reilly 2000, 177). On the other hand, the complexity this flexibility is designed to manage can easily lead to chaos if, for example, one forgets to drop off a package and then finds it in one's bag half-a-city later. This is the kind of situation in which the role conflict (between the errant package's destination and the direction one is or was headed) immediately produces role overloads (the extra physical effort necessary to cover that lost space, not to mention the organizational problem of how best to cover that space in relation to whatever other runs one must do).

The worst of such situations do not allow for the possibility of making up for lost time, for that lone, errant run violates the prime rule of efficient speed: *runs,* not *a run,* are necessary to speed's production. Thus, that backtracking cuts the messenger out of the spatial structure of the rows set up by the dispatcher, making his or her progress within it exponentially slower. In Washington, D.C., where the general flow of work moves back and forth between downtown and the Hill, one might be able to negotiate such a situation without too much productivity loss; but in New York City, where the work is more dispersed, such a mistake could easily lead to an hour or more of inefficient work. The nonlinear scaling of such productivity loss makes it hard to quantify or even to approximate—a state of affairs that often adds to the laborer's frustrations. Further, if such a circumstance arises as part of a larger constellation of role conflicts and overloads, it could easily lead to what I call *role destabilization*, a moment in which the subject's relation to the formerly stable role constellation collapses, thus causing him or her to abandon some or all of those roles.

Relating this concept to Bentham's thinking, we might also consider such destabilizations, or collapses, more or less deep, a quantity to be measured by the extent of what is at stake for that subject with regard to identification with his or her role structure.[28] Clearly, it is important to have the city readily accessible inside one's head: the more of the city's spatial matrix one can recall without effort, the more easily one can deal with the intricate elements of the work as manageable variables in a game, thus decreasing the likelihood of deeper, productivity-stunting mistakes.

However, excess complexity is not the only danger to productivity: there is also excess speed itself. As AZ (1994) states in *Rush*, "How many times have I seen The Highest Chris fly by me, his head down, going well over the speed limit, chasing an invisible Greg LeMond or something, only to look up and realize he's a block and a half past his drop? I'm not sure, but more than once." This phenomenon may be the result of momentary forgetfulness, but not always. Reilly (2000, 321) describes Elite Courier's frustration with Felipe, one of their fastest riders: "Kevin says Felipe could easily make a thousand a week, 'but he'll come all the way to the office from uptown when he clears out instead of calling!' . . . We'll say, 'Why didn't you call, we had work up there for you.' Felipe tells them, 'I'm not in it for the money, I'm in it for the glory.'"

Thus, as Burawoy (1979) points out, while the game supports production, it also has the potential to undermine it. Felipe is an interesting case in this regard in that he seems to care more about raw speed than his delivery speed, which is unusual for a messenger. This desire for raw speed (and the glory that may come with it) points to something *Manufacturing Consent* does not consider: the potential for the labor structures to spill out beyond the borders of work to produce something else entirely.

In order to understand the drive behind this something else, we need only realize that Felipe may not achieve the glory he desires if his audience is limited to his dispatchers. Messenger work's solitary character means that its labor is also likely to be alienating and thus in need of some form of social venue through which to make (or at least attempt to make) some sense of it. Perhaps this explains the genesis of the alley cat race: as a form of such communal sense making. Sometime in the late eighties or early nineties messengers invented these races, which are held in live traffic and generally require racers to visit various checkpoints around the city. Amy, a messenger, describes the variety of motivations riders bring to messenger races: "I think racing is a way . . . for the people who want to be known as the fastest, for them to prove themselves. . . . Some people take it way more seriously than others; some people go out and have a good time and drink a beer along the way; and some people race to win" (Barraud, Kivowitz, and Barraud 2002).

Thus, alley cat races provide an opportunity for some messengers to measure themselves against, and build social capital in relation to, each other. As Carlos says, "If you're good in the races, people respect you" (Barraud, Kivowitz, and Barraud 2002). In addition, for those not as interested in competition, the races provide an environment that transforms the laborer's isolation into communality.

Alley cats borrow the work's demand for multiple stops (and thereby the need for riders to make their own routing decisions). These races also come in a variety of forms: all have manifests, some of which provide space for a stamp or signature at each checkpoint, others of which contain scavenger-hunt-type questions that racers have to answer at each step. Sometimes the course has been made public in advance; in others, each leg of the race unfolds as checkpoint personnel give riders new destinations. In some, riders can choose to do the checkpoints in any order; in others, they must stick to a preset route. Some races involve tasks or deliveries while others involve elaborate, choose-your-own-adventure-style stories or scenarios. A few races have involved using dispatchers and also required entry into buildings—including waiting for elevators and interacting with secretaries. One race, an all-night ride from the Bronx to Coney Island, reenacted the film *The Warriors,* replete with gangs in full regalia.

Such a proliferation of alley cat events, which has taken place mostly over the last ten years, might lead us to exaggerate a bit and suggest that the creation of that form invented messenger culture as we know it. But the informal institution of the alley cat is by no means the limit of the culture's productions—indeed, 2004 marks the twelfth year of the Cycle Messenger World Championships (CMWC), generally a three-day event that takes place in a different city every year.[29] But many messengers cannot afford the travel costs necessary to participate in the CMWC, and so the alley cat is the structure through which local communities thrive—a site at which to establish and maintain contacts with both local messengers and those who have come from other cities; a site at which to perform skills, thus exchanging cultural knowledge that might be lost in the more individualized patterns of the work.

As a result of understanding the alley cats as sites of labor catharsis, as well as of more general social exchange, we no longer need to ask why messengers would want to spend so much of their leisure time trying to re-create the mode of production in which they labor all week. Additionally though, the alley cat has an important relationship to Burawoy's (1979) claim that the ideological operations within the workplace are "relatively autonomous" (156) from those of external social situations. For Burawoy, a worker's "imported consciousness" (156) affects the workplace, but it is a force secondary to—and only expressed through—the structures of work: "Variations in the character and consciousness that workers bring with them to the workplace explain little about the variations in the activities that take place on the shop floor" (202).[30] Burawoy's analysis might not seem to apply to messenger work at all, especially in light of Lisa's comment, "It's like an alleycat. I love it when a dispatcher gives me seven tags and says, 'Use your best judgment.' "[31] Work is like an alley cat: experiences gleaned from association with the messenger community are imported to make sense of the labor.

What we have to bear in mind though—and this point will extend Burawoy's (1979) argument—is that most alley cats are themselves dependent upon structures originally borrowed from work. The conditions of messenger labor are much different from those at Allied. Within the rigid structures and bounds of a factory, Burawoy (1979) has no reason to consider the possibility of the work culture leaking out to influence people's external lives. The line between industry and culture is likely far more porous in the messenger world than at Burawoy's site, and so it might seem dubious to compare the two situations at all. However, the alley cat phenomenon does support Burawoy's assertion that labor structures influence behavior. Not only do the structures of messenger work dominate the character of that labor—its game structure explains much about why messengers continue to do the work in the first place[32]—but also those structures have been exported in such a way that they've played a large role in the creation of the messenger community. Thus, although messenger culture and messenger labor are not "relatively autonomous" (Burawoy 1979, 206) the reasons behind that condition, the power of the ideologies and social forms inscribed in the labor, are the very ones that support autonomy in most other cases. The alley cat reminds us that *messenger culture would not exist without messenger labor,* not just because that labor brings people together, but also because it offers subjects new social ways of being. There is no need for the absolutism of Foucault's (1979) assertion: "We must cease once and for all to describe the effects of power in negative terms: it 'excludes,' it 'represses,' it 'censors,' it 'abstracts,' it 'masks,' it 'conceals.' In fact, power produces; it produces reality" (194). An assertion that power is often productive in ways we might not expect is adequate to our situation.

The alley cat borrows vital aspects of the production system under which messengers labor, an appropriation that retools that system toward the production of community in addition to speed. Having pointed out that the community borrows from the industry, we also have to consider the possibility that the industry benefits from the community: that culture and industry are mutually engaged. I don't wish to put forth an overly functionalist argument here: training is obviously not the reason behind the races or anywhere near their primary outcome. Nevertheless, much of what goes on in those venues undoubtedly provides training in how to be a better messenger: the most durable kinds of clothing to wear, the most utilitarian bags, the most efficient kinds of bikes, as well as the proficiency necessary to ride them. Indeed, messenger races are the primary means by which the track bike and its attendant techniques have spread around the world.[33] Prizes generally consist of bags, clothing, or bicycles—ritualized distributions of the tools of the occupation. Furthermore, the races' benefits to the industry are not limited to their economies' of appropriation and exchange of techniques and technologies; those events also train riders to deal with situations that are simultaneously complex and physically stressful. As Lisa's comment above points out, alley cats prepare one to deal with complexity, for they mimic not the work's periods of lull, but its intensities, its excesses: times when both body and brain are overloaded. The body's exhaustion taxes the brain's ability to continue to make decisions on problems of spatial organization, its desire to quit limiting the body's ability to continue despite exhaustion. As such, alley cats might be seen as a training site for the extremes of what the labor demands.

Obviously, such informal pedagogy benefits the industry, but I am more interested in the messenger community's potential to disrupt what have become the industry's normative modes of functioning; to disrupt them in the interest of producing structures that offer the laborer more security. Intercompany competition has the potential to negatively affect the industry as a whole; consequently, the larger messenger community—not just the one that happens to have been strengthened and developed by the races—has an interest in seeing the industry develop in different ways.

## NEGOTIATING CONTROL

We have seen that the messenger industry has no formal structures in place to maintain the stability of the value of its product. Unfortunately, labor can do little to maintain prices, even via unionization: collective bargaining only enables negotiation over worker compensation. Under federal law, workers have no right to bargain over the prices companies charge their clients. As long as companies are in direct competition for clients, low prices will be a basic aspect of their competition. Of course, if several of a city's companies were to unionize, owners might be forced to raise rates, but so far that goal has been elusive.[34] There is also "the option of having the city regulate delivery prices, much like the city already regulate[s] taxi fees" (D. C. Courier, "Messenger Mailing List," http://dccourier.com/messengers/messengerarchives2002/msg00463.html). In 2001, the District of Columbia Bicycle Messenger Association (DCBCA) proposed such a structure in its "Minimum Industry Standards Proposal," which Shawn Bega presented to the city council. In his words, the proposal was "specifically designed by the [DCBCA] to address safety issues in the local bicycle messenger industry by focusing on the underlying situations that allow and encourage unsafe riding practices by bicycle couriers" (Bega 2001). The proposal includes the sections "Bicycle Courier Company Licensing," "Company Liability," "Safe Dispatching," "Proper Pay," and "Client Responsibilities" (DCBCA 2001). The proposal's suggestions would force messenger companies to work toward efficient speed rather than inefficient speed and would also limit the kinds of things messengers could be asked to do. For instance, the "Safe Dispatching" section of the proposal includes the proposed rule "No run shall be guaranteed by the courier company to the client for an amount of time less than half of an hour, regardless of distance or other considerations" (DCBCA 2001).

Compare these suggestions to those at the heart of Rudolph Giuliani's 1998 civility campaign, one of whose main targets was the bicycle messenger (Norimitsu Onishi, "Be Polite or Else, Giuliani Warns in Announcing Civility Campaign," *New York Times,* February 26, 1998, p. A1, B4). A version of "broken windows theory" (Kelling and Coles 1996), an approach to public order in which minor violations are intensely policed, this campaign as it related to messengers depended on the political disavowal of the formal economy's need for messengers to break traffic laws—labeled incivility by Giuliani. Many of Giuliani's proposals for messengers were not implemented (mainly licensing), but some were: police checkpoints were regularly set up to target traffic violations by messengers. It is unlikely that these efforts had much effect on the service clients received, other than delays of the amount of time necessary for a police officer to write a ticket. But they had a definite effect on messengers. Once the ticket has been written, the biker can only hope the officer will not show up in court. In New York, the charge for the rider's first red-light infraction is one hundred dollars; for the second, two hundred. It is doubtful that a company, let alone the clients who outsourced the dirty work in the first place—a ridiculous thought!—would take financial responsibility for a messenger's actions (the messenger being the only one in that chain whose actions are public).[35] Giuliani's denial of the existence of such tensions at the boundary between the public and the private also leads to his avoiding the difficult political work necessary to engage the roots of the very problems he bemoaned (even as he gained political advantage from the performance of addressing those problems).[36]

Certainly there is no guarantee that regulations along the lines of the DCBCA's proposal would do away with "uncivil" messengers, but at the very least they would eliminate the reason for the most dangerous, desperate practices—the need for speed. It should also be noted that the DCBCA's minimum-standards proposal suggests further regulations at the company level, which is where competition determines rates and demands speed and thus structures messenger labor's role mise-en-scene. Efforts at regulation constructed along the lines of Giuliani's civility campaign, by contrast, are more likely to exacerbate the desperation of messengers who are already in low-paying situations and whose only option to make more is to go faster, to break more traffic rules more recklessly. In fact, such citations may push some messengers to pay more attention to the police than to being careful. Those role demands are not only not the same thing, they are often mutually exclusive: the tension between them marks a role conflict that could have severe consequences. For example, if the messenger's normative operating mode runs along the lines of "Forget the traffic light. Look All ways, Always"[37] (Squid, "Track Bikes," *Animal* 1, May 2003, p. 68), a mode of excessive police awareness probably comes down to something like "Forget safety. Lookout for, but don't look at, the police Always" (where the loss of Squid's wordplay in the latter version is symptomatic of the exhaustion-produced decay of that messenger-brain's rational functioning).[38] This is not to suggest that messengers should continue to flout the law in the wake of a citation. Rather, it is a speculation on the likely outcomes of city-supported role destabilizations of subjects already enmeshed in excessive role demands—in other words, already exhausted and performing at the limits of their mental and physical capacities.[39] Given the potential of such situations to produce negative interactions with negative outcomes (something along the lines of an "overload feedback loop"), we have to question the wisdom of such expressions of the desire for "civility."

If we accept the validity of Burawoy's assertion concerning the power of workplace structures, we must assume that such expressions are not wise, for the companies will continue to demand speed and the individual laborers will either persevere or quit. Unfortunately, either outcome maintains the continuation of a system that has a high probability of producing deep role destabilizations. In sharp contrast to the superficiality of the New York City civility campaign, the DCBCA proposal is an attempt to mediate the power of the industry's structures, an engagement with the question of how to manage economies in a way that retains their positive, productive uncertainties but jettisons the negative, destructive ones.

The organization of bicycle messengers is not just an exercise in self-interest, a potential bulwark against forces that, in an unregulated labor market, can let companies too easily profit at the expense of their workers. It also has the potential to make the industry as a whole more efficient and thus more valuable in both senses of its value: its invested (monetary and emotional) capital, and its use value to its clients (Marx 1867/1967).[40] We should do more to recognize the value of the energy invested by the messenger community to further their industry's interests. Without the kind of intervention proposed by the DCBCA, the intense competition that thrives as a result of regulative lacks produces a tendency for an industry slide toward value-deflation; such a situation is a "tragedy of the commons" (Hardin 1968): a situation in which the messenger industry devalues the worth of its common asset, the value of its ability to produce speed.

It is not, however, inevitable that the industry will have to continue down that path: companies can do more to recognize and work to alleviate the excesses of the labor conditions. They can collaborate with messenger associations to attempt to reform the current lack of regulation that is a detriment to the industry as a whole. Indeed, such possibilities would begin to test the extent to which industry and labor might be mutually beneficial to each other—

messenger races being inversions of the potential for the industry to appropriate the culture's knowledge forms and mechanisms. Such collaboration will not come about from superficial efforts, but rather from groups of companies attending more carefully to the more general implications of the knowledge the messenger culture possesses about the character of its labor. As it is now, most companies are satisfied to route that knowledge into and through the industry in such a way that the incumbent structures within its current operations are largely maintained.

What is it, then, that messengers know about their labor? Here I want to return to the races—to trouble Burawoy's belief that "one cannot both play and at the same time question the rules" (1979, 81). There are many ways of questioning, and some of them might come in the form of apparently unproductive appropriations of the game.[41] Certainly not all that is unproductive can be thought of as a question, but doesn't the appropriation of the game for oneself open up the space where one *might* question? In which one might use the game to imagine other possibilities? Along these lines, it is interesting to note that only a handful of messenger races have ever appropriated the industry's dispatch-row structure, and of those that have, none have given the dispatcher the leeway to assign completely different rows to different racers. We can easily see the reasons why: if organizers were to introduce such disparity-producing (or stratification-producing) structures, the ensuing uncertainty would destroy the race's competitiveness, its "ability to absorb players" (87). In races that do employ dispatchers, unfair racer stratification still arises as a result of dispatcher mistakes. The expressions of frustration that result are fascinating, both to watch and experience, for racers find themselves caught in the same situations as those of work, but in this case their relation to other messengers is on the line, not their relation to their company. The observable affective expressions of this difference suggest that an average moment in a race tends to be more intense than an average moment at work, but that the extreme moments of a race tend to be less intense than those of work.[42] Thus, though race participants may exhibit momentary bursts of pleasure or anger, it is far less likely that they will experience the deeper role destabilizations possible at work, precisely because the role mise-en-scene of the races is less complexly layered. Nevertheless, the alley cat's potential to produce an ecology of emotions so similar to that experienced within the labor process is fascinating.

I believe that the structural register is an important aspect of a culture's unconscious expression of itself. To the extent that this is true, could we not read the alley cat as a staging of the limits to which messengers feel their labor should subject their bodies and emotions? Could the curtailment of the power of the row structure in the races be the beginning of a critique of an economy whose employees see their position within it as too tenuous, too uncertain—an inchoate call for more stable employment relations? If this reading of the races is true—if messengers' pleasure in them is more than pure "lumpen" pleasure—then this critique should not be understood as a desire for older, hierarchical arrangements, despite the benefits of their more stable structures, but rather as a desire for structures that provide them with stability in more flexible ways. Messengers do not long for "the efficiencies associated with organizing work in standard, hierarchical employment relations and internal labor markets" (Kalleberg 2000). But there may be another possibility implied in Kalleberg's (2000) suggestion that those hierarchical post–World War II forms "may have been more of an historical irregularity than is the use of nonstandard employment relations" (342). If standard employment is a "historical irregularity," the next question concerns the possibilities for *standardizing flexibility,* for mediating nonstandard employment relations in ways that would provide the "flexible worker" with protections similar to those offered by standard employment.

Indeed, the DCBCA proposal seems to suggest that, far from wanting to do away with the structures under which they labor, messengers would rather add stabilizing mechanisms to those structures. Some of these mechanisms, such as base pay, would offer individual protections, while others, such as the ban on contracts for half-hour deliveries, would buttress the value of the service the industry offers by slowing it down. These demands raise two questions: (1) How might nonstandard laborers work to have such demands met? (2) What forms of social organization would best facilitate such a process? Certainly not all nonstandard jobs are bad (Kalleberg, Reskin, and Hudson 2000), which raises the question of how the benefits offered by certain forms of nonstandard employment might be extended to others. What kinds of new employment relations would such extension require? Is it possible that the very flexible and, in the case of the messenger, distributive forms of organization that undergird the labor could be (and are being) appropriated to produce new labor movements? To produce new modes of organizing that could construct more stable (yet still flexible) employment relations? My hope is that messengers have only just begun the work of questioning what exists now and imagining the possible; that they are at the initial stages of creating—indeed, have already initiated—a movement based on such an ethic.

## NOTES

1.  Kalleberg (2000) defines nonstandard work arrangements as those "that depart from standard work arrangements in which it was generally expected that work was done full-time, would continue indefinitely, and was performed at the employer's place of business under the employer's direction" (341).
2.  In post–September 11 Washington, D.C., the "multiple"—a delivery in which the messenger distributes the same letter, trinket, or T-shirt to every House and Senate office—has been banned from the Hill; such jobs were once the cream of the D.C. messenger industry.
3.  Average crosstown traffic speed in the late 1990s in Manhattan decreased to four miles per hour. However, the Bloomberg administration has recently increased the average speed of crosstown traffic "from 4.0 to 6.1 mph" on select streets via its "thru streets" initiative (New York City Department of Transportation 2003), an exception to the more general trend toward increased congestion.
4.  Arne Kalleberg, Barbara F. Reskin, and Ken Hudson (2000) suggest: "To the extent that nonstandard jobs pay poorly, lack health insurance and pension benefits, are of uncertain duration, and lack the protections that unions and labor laws afford, they are problematic for workers" (257).
5.  Most companies also offer double- and triple-rush service (thirty and fifteen minutes, respectively), though there is some variability in these time limits among companies, as well as in the maximum distance possible for these super-rush services.
6.  "Row" might sound like an agricultural allusion, but I think the term probably originates from the rows of jobs on the dispatcher's board. However, the agricultural reference is not merely fortuitous: "row" refers to an underlying homology whose site structures the character of piecework itself. The divergence of the row structures in agriculture

and in messenger work (linear and nonlinear, respectively) points to differences in the character of piecework under modern and postmodern labor. The telegraph messenger, as described by Greg Downey (2002), supports this point, not only because Downey situates that figure within the modern period (1850 to 1950), but also because that figure only delivered one message at a time. Thus, in modern piecework there is either no reason to deviate from one's prescribed row (as with the agricultural harvest), or no such possibility of such a deviation (as with telegraph messengers, who, once they left their offices, only deviated from their route by deviating from work itself). That messenger work began to take hold in the United States in the late sixties and early seventies fits well with the period described by David Harvey (1990) as the beginnings of postmodernism. The bicycle messenger also helps us see, in addition to the tidiness of this structural evolution, the limits of conceptions of the postmodern condition in which it is characterized as "fragmented" or "de-centered," for these could also be described as aspects of the modern condition. Postmodern structures are distributive (along the lines of distributive computing) and flexible, although their frameworks may still retain highly centralized aspects.

7.   There is one other work-distribution system, free call, in which all riders on a radio channel have access to the same free market. As runs are called in by clients, they are broadcast to messengers; a run is assigned to the first messenger who claims it. Free call does have several important implications in relation to aspects of this chapter, but it is not used as widely as dispatcher systems, and for this and other reasons (a role conflict for the writer), the suggested implications could not be coherently dealt with in this general context (though see note 22).

8.   The point here is that the positive aspect of a well-paying rush job is decreased if that run is assigned in isolation. Completing a single out-of-the-way run is generally one of the favors messengers do for the dispatcher.

9.   Obviously, one's ability to ride a bike is a highly mediated skill, meaning that multiple factors have led to the extent of that skill within an urban context; however, when messenger work is considered synchronically, as an isolated, structural moment, "raw speed" is the unmediated term in relation to delivery speed, raw speed being one of the mediators of time-per-run.

10.   Given the previous note, it should be clear that both classes of speed are necessary to be a successful messenger. That said, delivery speed is what most people care about (although, as we'll see, there are

exceptions), and the number of runs one completed today or yesterday is an inevitable topic of conversation at any messenger office. That daily number and the money associated with it are the symbolic and material sites at which messengers iteratively measure their worth to the company and the economy. It is the index whereby they compare themselves to each other and to their previous efforts.

11. "Geographic" in this chapter refers to a simultaneity of physical and social geographies. An example of such mutual embeddedness is the geography created by the building regulations that shape a messenger's access to that space (Lefebvre 1974/1991). See also note 21.

12. The few messenger companies that are not highly stratified are the exceptions that prove the rule. They have achieved this by attracting high-paying, often environmentally conscious clients. See also note 17.

13. Even within the stratification that seems to arise as a result of individual riders' lack of motivation—their lack of drive to produce "unmediated speed"—I would want to know something about that lack's relation to the ways those riders are, or *perceive* they are, treated by their company.

14. For example, a dispatcher once complained to me about the owner's demand that he give more runs to a senior employee he did not like.

15. Burawoy (1979, 86) uses game theory's prisoner's dilemma to illustrate the means by which workers' overproduction can undermine their self-interest. Since the supply of jobs is limited, messengers themselves cannot overproduce; however, the dynamics of intercompany competition are similar to those of the dilemma Burawoy describes.

16. It is likely that pay is the only aspect of this job that is good under Kalleberg, Reskin, and Hudson's (2000) definition. Messengers who are classified as independent contractors are not covered under workman's compensation; very few messengers have health insurance or other benefits, let alone pensions.

17. Shawn Bega's company, D. C. Courier, is one that seems to provide the majority of its employees with stable, high-paying jobs; it also recently became a unionized company (D. C. Courier 2001).

18. Consider tires, which have to be replaced every two months (on some bikes that period is shorter); if a sturdy Kevlar tire costs, at a minimum, twenty dollars, then a messenger could spend two hundred forty dollars (twenty times two times six) per year on tires alone. Making similar calculations for chains, cassettes (gears), and brake pads, a rider could easily spend four hundred dollars per year on maintenance, and many in fact spend thousands per year on their bicycles. All bike parts are cheaper through mail order, though many messengers do not have credit cards.

19. Most messenger companies have accounts at a bike shop so that their employees can make purchases there; the shop charges the company, which then docks the amount from employee's paycheck.

20. The run from West Twenty-sixth Street to Bloomingdale's is an example of what many New York messengers refer to as "getting east-wested," a problem in relation to the heavy traffic flows that run along the north-south axis of Manhattan's avenues. See Edward Tufte (1997), in which a case of actual rather than cognitive mapping is described: Tufte analyzes the careful mapping that led John Snow to discover the pathway taken by a spreading disease, cholera. Snow was able to correlate death locations with the traces of social flows connected to one of the city's wells (the source of the cholera). Looking at that map, it is clear that many of those relationships are not about physical proximity; instead they mark the routes of the most efficient social traffic.

21. Such temporal expansion is a countervailing phenomenon to David Harvey's (1990) concept of "time-space compression." The messenger points us toward (and is an attempt to alleviate) this systemic underside.

22. Since in the free call system there are no dispatchers to construct rows (see note 7), they are instead constructed by the riders themselves via a more inductive process. Thus, free call is more of a distributive system, that is, it distributes more of the organizational labor to its messengers, than the dispatcher-centered model we've been looking at.

23. The limit case here is road-rage-induced murder, a fate that befell a Chicago messenger, Tom McBride (Culley 2001). The driver who killed him was sentenced to forty-five years in prison.

24. My notion of the constellation is borrowed from Theodor Adorno (1973).

25. Dennerlein and Meeker's (2002) pilot study suggested that the messenger industry's "national average lost workday" rate may be higher than any other industry's (522), but they also note that the rates of messenger injury are similar to those of recreational riders (524).

26. The epigraph underneath seventyseven's message: "Run head first into traffic—a mindset of annihilation."

27. Jacques Lacan's (1977) concept of the "split subject" offers a compelling explanation for such subjective "delusions": such splits are the means by which subjects are (more or less seamlessly) sutured into capitalism.

28. A situation in which a subject had no desire to maintain his or her role constellation could therefore not be considered role destabi-

lization, though depending on how it was expressed, it might be considered a performance of such, by which I mean the second of the two following classes of performance: (1) performances in which I believe I am self-identical (my everyday, bound-up-with-myself self), and (2) performances in which I act like someone else, whether self-impelled, externally compelled, or externally forced. I intend for this distinction to be read not as a complex theoretical one but as one we easily understand in normal everyday life. True, the borders between the two classes are often blurred, but this does not negate the distinction's accurate description of an aspect of the structure of our subjectivities.

29. The first CMWC took place in Berlin in 1993; subsequent host cities were London, Toronto, San Francisco, Barcelona, Washington, D.C., Zurich, Philadelphia, Budapest, Copenhagen, and Seattle. In 2004 the race will take place in Edmonton, Alberta, and in 2005, in New York City.

30. Aihwa Ong (1987) insists that Burawoy's assertion of relative autonomy did not apply to the Malaysian factories she studied (8). However, while the mixture of work and nonwork realms at her site is undeniable, her examples of the importation of religious beliefs into the factory setting can be read to support Burawoy's underlying (and to my mind more important) assertion of the power of labor structures. My suggestion here is that the spirits of resistance among the Malaysians Ong studied were assertions of traditional culture in the face of, and as a response to, the potential effects and power of those workplace structures. It should also be noted that Burawoy's claims refer to a post-Taylorist factory setting, whereas the situation Ong presents is bluntly Taylorist. I think it is likely that those assertions of traditional culture were largely motivated by the coercion that characterizes Taylorist employment relations (especially in light of Ong's descriptions of the spirits' connection to exhaustion, that is, role overload).

31. Both "alleycat" and "alley cat" are used by the messenger community. Two Google searches, for "alleycat messenger" and "alley cat" messenger, produced nearly identical results: 1,990 and 1,970 sites, respectively.

32. It is tempting to claim that Burawoy's point wouldn't apply if it could be proved that the labor's game structures attract people whose ideologies are predisposed to enacting the kinds of transgressions the labor framework demands. However, even if all messengers were so ideologically inclined, Burawoy's point would stand. He is not concerned with whether particular jobs attract people with particular

ideological tendencies; rather, the blunt version of the point is that *all* labor behaviors are determined to a greater extent by the labor frameworks than they are by any other factor. Therefore, the prediction is that people with different ideological positions will behave in much the same way under similar structures of labor. Thus, if I were opposed to breaking the law in all situations, I would probably have to make some exceptions if I wanted to make any money as a messenger; and if I decide to quit because I don't want to break the law, I am still bowing to the power of those structures.

33.  It is important to note here that the messenger track bike is both a British colonial artifact and a legacy of what Paul Gilroy (1993) calls the Black Atlantic. The fixed gear migrated from London to the Caribbean and then from the Caribbean back to the metropolis that had been its source, but also from the Caribbean to New York. Its purpose in both spaces was transformed from velodrome racing to helping business networks overcome the barrier of the city's space. Over the course of the 1990s the track bike spread around the Anglo messenger world (the United States, Canada, Britain); the process was gradual at first but recently its metastasis has increased as it has made its way to messenger cultures as far-flung as Tokyo and Warsaw and has also become popular with non-messengers.

34.  There have been several unionization attempts in the industry in the last ten years, but most of these failed. In San Francisco, however, two companies (out of approximately thirty) have successfully unionized.

35.  Through this outsourcing of legal responsibility (clients to companies, companies to messengers) we can see the kinds of negative possibilities enabled by distributive structures (see also note 6).

36.  Such troubling of the public-versus-private distinction is a hint that boundary work may have a tendency to blur the boundary between those realms, a hunch also supported by Downey (2002).

37.  "Forget the traffic light. Look All ways, Always" (Squid, "Track Bikes," *Animal* 1, May 2003, p. 68). It should be noted that the operations "forget" and "look" mitigate (or more accurately negate) the role conflict between traffic laws and safe riding in traffic. Focusing on only one of those two realms (especially when you consider all the other things the messenger must keep track of) makes the rider more functional.

38.  In August 2000, New York City held Metropoloco, an international alley cat that was a CMWC pre-event. Metropoloco's (2000) race program warned riders: "Do not make eye contact with officers when you go through red lights!!!"—a non-act we might refer to, via Louis

Althusser's (1971) notion of interpellation, as an avoidance of the interpellative call.

39.  I am interested here in the tendency for subjects, as a result of deep role destabilizations (or even in intensified conflict or overload situations), to prioritize one role demand to the exclusion of others. This is to suggest the possibility that exhausted subjects may, as a defense mechanism, prioritize one role demand over others (most of the energy that had maintained the relative stability of roles having been transferred to that one). Such an outcome should be termed "role monolithism," a state that is to be strictly distinguished from a situation whose normative state contains only one role.

40.  The point here being that, by increasing the commodity's price by mandating increased rates, the exchange value of speed would increase, thus progressively increasing the industry's value as a whole—if the price did not produce an exchange-value-deflating drop in demand. The problem is that there may be no monetary incentive for companies to change. It is possible that even under much "healthier" industry conditions, companies would profit at approximately the same rates as they do now. Furthermore, owners would have to invest energy or, at the very least, time in order to change the system, and there would be no guarantee of success. Inertia being the powerful force that it is and morality being, in many cases, a poor motivator, there is a long way to go.

41.  "Unproductive" here refers to the industry perspective; obviously the races are a community-building force.

42.  Two examples of ordinary alley cat tensions, witnessed in races that took place in New York City in late summer and early fall in 2003, are interesting here. I worked at a checkpoint in both, handing out packages to racers who presented their manifests. The chaos of a group of riders arriving simultaneously at my checkpoint created the first tension: a rider handed me his manifest and I handed it to the manifest stamper, intending to help him get out of the checkpoint more quickly. Amidst all the confusion, however, manifests were mixed up and the rider I had tried to help couldn't seem to get his back, at which point he got mad and started yelling at people (mostly me). Later, at the finish line, he apologized to me and expressed surprise at how angry he had become: "I just got caught up in the race." The second tension arose out of a race that involved dispatchers (the first did not). Several riders who came to the checkpoint complained about their dispatcher: one had instructed a rider to head uptown only to tell him later, by which time he was in the high fifties, three miles away, that he needed to be way downtown, on Houston Street.

He was enraged. My checkpoint partner kept saying, "Just like work. It's just like work." Certainly the emotions we saw were amplified by the racers' physical exertion, but again, that exhaustion, while more intense in the moment, dissipated much faster than the exhaustion of work, which is a slower, much more persistent drain that builds over weeks, months, years.

## REFERENCES

Adorno, Theodor W. 1973. *Negative Dialectics,* translated by E. B. Ashton. New York: Continuum.

Althusser, Louis. 1971. "Ideology and the Ideological State Apparatuses." In *Lenin and Philosophy.* London: New Left Books.

AZ. 1994. *Rush* 1: entire issue. Washington, D.C.: AZ.

Barraud, Ben, Manny Kivowitz, and Tony Barraud, directors. 2002. *Red Light Go.* New York: KSK Studios.

Bega, Shawn. 2001. "Testimony of Shawn Bega." Available at http://www.dccourier.com/dcbca/testimony2001bega.htm. Accessed on November 15, 2003.

Bentham, Jeremy. 1802/1931. *The Theory of Legislation.* New York: Harcourt, Brace, and Company.

Burawoy, Michael. 1979. *Manufacturing Consent: Changes in the Labor Process Under Monopoly Capitalism.* Chicago: University of Chicago Press.

———. 2000. *Global Ethnography.* Berkeley: University of California Press.

Carlsson, Chris. 2002. *Critical Mass.* Oakland, Calif.: AK Press.

Culley, Travis Hugh. 2001. *The Immortal Class.* New York: Villard.

Dennerlein, Jack, and John D. Meeker. 2002. "Occupational Injuries Among Boston Bicycle Messengers." *American Journal of Industrial Medicine* 42(6): 519–25.

District of Columbia Bike Couriers Association. 2001. "Minimum Industry Standards Proposal." Available at http://www.dccourier.com/dcbca/standards.htm. Accessed on November 15, 2003.

Downey, Greg. 2001. "Virtual Webs, Physical Technologies, and Hidden Workers: The Spaces of Labor in Information Internetworks." *Technology and Culture* 42(2): 209–35.

———. 2002. *Telegraph Messenger Boys: Labor, Technology, and Geography 1850–1950.* New York: Routledge.

Foucault, Michel. 1979. *Discipline and Punish.* New York: Vintage.

Geertz, Clifford. 1973. *The Interpretation of Cultures.* New York: Basic Books.

Gilroy, Paul. 1993. *The Black Atlantic*. Cambridge, Mass.: Harvard University Press.

Goffman, Erving. 1959. *The Presentation of Self in Everyday Life*. New York: Anchor.

Hardin, Garrett. 1968. "The Tragedy of the Commons." *Science* 162 (December 13): 1243–48.

Harvey, David. 1990. *The Condition of Postmodernity*. Cambridge: Blackwell.

Heiss, Jerold. 1990. "Social Roles." In *Social Psychology: Sociological Perspectives*, edited by Morris Rosenberg and Ralph H. Turner. New Brunswick, N.J.: Transaction.

Hochschild, Arlie. 1983. *The Managed Heart: Commercialization of Human Feeling*. Berkeley: University of California Press.

Hughes, Everett. 1956/1994. *On Work, Race, and the Sociological Imagination*. Chicago: University of Chicago Press.

Jameson, Fredric. 1991. *Postmodernism, or the Cultural Logic of Late Capitalism*. Durham: Duke University Press.

Kalleberg, Arne L. 2000. "Nonstandard Employment Relations: Part-Time, Temporary and Contract Work." *Annual Review of Sociology* 26(1): 341–65.

Kalleberg, Arne L., Barbara F. Reskin, and Ken Hudson. 2000. "Bad Jobs in America: Standard and Nonstandard Employment Relations and Job Quality in the United States." *American Sociological Review* 65(2): 256–78.

Katz, Daniel, and Robert L. Kahn. 1966. *The Social Psychology of Organizations*. New York: Wiley.

Kelling, George, and Catherine Coles. 1996. *Fixing Broken Windows*. New York: Free Press.

Lacan, Jacques. 1977. *Écrits: A Selection*. New York: W.W. Norton.

Lefebvre, Henri. 1974/1991. *The Production of Space*. Malden, Mass.: Blackwell.

Leidner, Robin. 1993. *Fast Food, Fast Talk: Service Work and the Routinization of Everyday Life*. Berkeley: University of California Press.

Marx, Karl. 1867/1967. *Capital*. Volume 1. Reprint, New York: International Publishers.

McCammon, Holly J., and Larry J. Griffin. 2000. "Workers and Their Customers and Clients." *Work and Occupations* 27(3): 278–93.

Merton, Robert K. 1957. "The Role-Set: Problems in Sociological Theory." *British Journal of Sociology* 8(2): 106–20.

Metropoloco. 2000. Race Program. New York: New York Bicycle Messenger Association (in author's collection).

Metz, Joel. 2002. "Travel." San Francisco: International Federation of Bike Messenger Associations. Available at IFBMA website, http://www.messengers.org/travel.

Ong, Aihwa. 1987. *Spirits of Resistance and Capitalist Discipline: Factory Women in Malaysia*. Albany: State University of New York Press.

Paules, Greta. 1991. *Dishing It Out*. Philadelphia: Temple University Press.

Reilly, Rebecca. 2000. *Nerves of Steel*. Kenmore, N.Y.: Spoke & Word.

Sutherland, Peter, director. 2001. *Pedal*. Documentary film. New York: Fractured Media Inc. and Cinema Capital.

Sutton, Robert, and Anat Rafaeli. 1988. "Untangling the Relationship Between Displayed Emotions and Organizational Sales: The Case of Convenience Stores." *Academy of Management Journal* 31(3): 461–87.

Tufte, Edward. 1997. *Visual Explanations: Images and Quantities, Evidence and Narrative*. Cheshire, Conn.: Graphics Press.

U.S. Department of Transportation. 2003. "Executive Summary: Summary of Program." Available at http://www.nyc.gov/html/dot/pdf/thrustreets.pdf.

— Chapter 7 —

# Engineering Overwork: Bell-Curve Management at a High-Tech Firm

## Ofer Sharone

A FTER STEADILY DECREASING throughout the first half of the twentieth century, in the late 1960s the number of hours Americans work made a sudden U-turn and began to rise (Schor 1991).[1] In 1999, American workers surpassed the Japanese to earn the dubious distinction of working the longest hours in the industrialized world (International Labour Organization 1999). Among American workers, it is the relatively well-off professional, managerial, and technical workers who are putting in the longest work hours (Jacobs and Gerson 1998).[2] This paper explores the causes underlying long work hours among a group of workers on the front line of this trend, software engineers working at a large American high-tech firm which I call "MegaTech."

Given the severe consequences of increasing work hours on families (Hochschild 1997), communities (Putnam 2000), and worker health (Golden and Jorgensen 2002), surprisingly little research has been done on the causes of this phenomenon. Economists focus on material motivations such as consumption desires (Schor 1991) or, more directly, the pursuit of high incomes (Reich 2000). Sociologists point to management strategies that seduce workers to put in long hours with a cozy, family-like work atmosphere (Hochschild 1997), or encourage workers to identify with their company (Kunda 1992). Popular books portray high-tech engineers' long work hours as flowing from enjoyment of their exciting work (Kidder 1981). However, my in-depth interviews and direct observations (described further in the appendix) suggest that none of these theories adequately accounts for the work hours of MegaTech's engineers.

Although my findings support the sociologists' focus on management strategies, the particular strategy deployed at MegaTech is different from those described by Arlie Hochschild and Gideon Kunda. MegaTech is not a cozy comfortable workplace, and its management does not expend much energy to foster employee loyalty. Instead, MegaTech's management's strategy is to engender intense anxiety among its engineers regarding their professional competence, which leads them to self-impose long work hours. This strategy, which I call "competitive self-management," combines two practices: the periodic grading of employees' relative performances, distributed along a rigid bell-shaped curve, which requires that 70 percent of the engineers receive an average or below average score, and the dictate that employees actively participate in their own management. Although neither of these practices is new, this paper describes how they work in tandem to produce long work hours. I draw on Michael Burawoy's (1979) theory of "work games" to show that the combination of worker discretion and uncertain performance grades generates a high-stakes competition over recognition of professional competence. Specifically, the engineers' anxiety regarding their uncertain performance grades propels them to exercise their discretion to "choose" to work nights and weekends in an effort to preserve their identity as competent and valued professionals.

## CAUSAL EXPLANATIONS
## OF LONG WORK HOURS

MegaTech engineers work on average sixty-seven hours per week. A few work over eighty hours per week, but no one averages less than fifty hours per week. During long stretches they frequently work from 9:00 A.M. to midnight, and some do not take a single day off for weeks in a row. These work hours persist despite tensions with spouses, guilt about children, and concerns about personal health. Before examining the causes of these work hours, I will first describe their rhythms.

MegaTech engineers' day-to-day work revolves around the three phases of the "product cycle." During the first phase, called "milestone zero," the specifications of the software features to be included in the product are determined. This is the shortest phase, normally making up only 5 percent of each year. During this period the engineers spend most of their time performing preliminary coding tasks and calculating time estimates for the completion of different coding projects. At this stage, the engineers are recovering from the "crunch mode" that accompanied the last phase of the previous product cycle, and their work hours are at their lowest level, on average forty-eight hours per week. One engineer described this phase as a "chance to breathe" and a time for the "batteries to get recharged."

During the second phase of the product cycle the bulk of the coding work is performed. This period is divided into several "milestones," about ten weeks apart, each milestone representing a deadline for the completion of specific "deliverables." During this period, engineers spend most of their time coding and emailing or meeting informally with other members of their "team" (usually four to six other engineers) to solve problems. This is the longest phase of the product cycle, taking up roughly 55 percent of each year. Work hours increase to routine levels of sixty-three hours per week, on average.

The third and final phase of the product cycle (as well as the last two or three weeks before each milestone deadline in the second phase) are known as the "crunch mode" or the "march of death," making up approximately 40 percent of each year. During this phase, the engineers are no longer writing new code, but focus on fixing the bugs in the software they developed in the second phase. In this final phase, engineers work an average of seventy-five hours per week in order to meet the sacrosanct "product shipment date." Finally, when the crunch period is over and the product is shipped, there is a big celebration with champagne and strawberries. Then the next cycle begins. One engineer used a driving metaphor to describe the cycle: In the first phase, you are "coasting." In the second, you "go fast but are not killing yourself." And finally "it's pedal to the metal" and "total crisis." A full cycle usually takes one to two years. The work hours of the engineers I interviewed at each phase of the product cycle are detailed in table 7A.1 in the appendix.

What explains these extraordinary work hours? In *The Time Bind,* Hochschild (1997) claims that the company she studied successfully seduced employees to work long hours by creating a supportive work atmosphere that made them feel more comfortable and relaxed at work than at home. At first glance MegaTech seems to fit this theory. It presents itself as a "fun" company, and a natural extension of college for its predominantly young engineers. Its low-rise office buildings are scattered across a large "campus" of well-manicured lawns and athletic fields. Hallways contain Ping-Pong tables and arcade games, and each floor has several refrigerators where employees can get free sodas. The engineers' offices are usually equipped with stereo systems, CD racks, and college-dorm-like posters and decorations.[3] The engineers are casually dressed in jeans and T-shirts, and suits appear to be strictly taboo.

Yet the Ping-Pong tables are conspicuously unused, and there is little socializing in the hallways. Most engineers describe spending their typical workday secluded in their office with little time or opportunity for social interaction. The most frequent mode of communication is email, even with colleagues a few doors down the hall.[4] The need to talk to a colleague about a work issue that cannot be dealt with by email arises only once or twice a day, and such conversations generally focus on the work issue at hand. In addition to being unsocial, the engineers described their work environment as "aggressive" and "competitive."[5] The isolated and aggressive reality of daily work contrasts starkly with the haven of collegiate fun that MegaTech tries to create (or at least portray), as well as with the cozy and familial workplace reported by Hochschild (1997). Contrary to the workers observed by Hochschild (1997), who lingered at their pleasant workplace to escape their chaotic homes, MegaTech engineers frequently went home to escape their tense workplace, and to continue working from their home computers.

MegaTech's work environment also differed from the high-tech firm researched by Kunda (1992). In *Engineering Culture,* Kunda (1992) studied a high-tech firm that "engineered" employee loyalty and identification with the firm through techniques of "normative control." Kunda's firm systematically attempted to instill a "culture" in which the company was portrayed as one large family. The engineers Kunda studied were encouraged, through an array of trainings, seminars, and company rituals, to embrace a "member role" in which they viewed themselves as part of a collectivity to which they felt loyalty. In contrast to this attempt to blur the boundaries between the self and the organization, MegaTech's competitive self-management, and the competitive work culture that flowed from it, highlighted the boundaries between individuals. MegaTech's engineers did not express any particular loyalty to MegaTech but articulated a variety of utilitarian reasons for staying at MegaTech, such as the opportunity to do interesting work or the acquisition of valuable skills. The engineers' lack of emotional commitment matched MegaTech's lack of effort to instill this sort of connection.[6]

If MegaTech is not a seductively pleasant workplace and the engineers do not feel particular loyalty to it, what explains their long work hours? The work hours of technical and professional workers are commonly explained by their supposedly insatiable appetite for higher incomes (Reich 2000). Along these lines, Juliet Schor (1991) theorizes that workers are motivated by a desire to consume the goods necessary to keep up in the competition for relative status with their neighbors. My interviews, however, revealed that income was not a significant factor behind the engineers' long work hours. No engineer mentioned money or the desire to consume goods as a motivator to work long hours.[7] When I asked the engineers what it meant to them to receive a pay raise or bonus, most often they replied that these were gratifying as expressions of their professional achievements. The engineers emphasized the symbolic meaning of the money as validating their professional worth and value, rather than conferring the ability to consume more goods. My findings suggest that although Schor (1991) is correct to emphasize the importance of relative status competition, she misplaces its locus. The status competition that motivated MegaTech's engineers concerned professional competence and not consumption, and the relevant arena for status maintenance was not the neighborhood but the place where the engineers spent most of their time: the workplace.[8]

Another common explanation for the long work hours of high-tech engineers is enjoyment. Popular books frequently portray the writing of software code as a uniquely absorbing activity.[9] MegaTech's engineers indeed reported enjoying aspects of their work, including the "intellectual challenge," the creativity, and the immense gratification when "your code works." Such enjoyment may account for their decision to become software engineers, but cannot explain their long working hours. Almost all of the engineers reported feeling that they were working too many hours.[10] If long work hours were merely the result of enjoyment, one would not expect the engineers to be unhappy about them. Even more telling was the fact that the engineers described the creation of new code as the most enjoyable part of their work, but they put in the longest hours during the final crunch phase of the product cycle, when they spent their time fixing bugs. In contrast to the creative process of generating new code, the engineers described fixing bugs as the dullest aspect of their work and equivalent to proofreading and editing. The fact that the engineers worked their longest hours while performing the least enjoyable work strongly suggests that enjoyment cannot account for their work hours.

In sum, MegaTech engineers' long work hours are not primarily motivated by a pleasant work environment, loyal identification with their company, consumption desires, or the joy of coding. Long work hours are also not officially required by MegaTech, which proudly boasts of its flexibility. What then accounts for the engineers' hours?

My findings point to MegaTech's management system of competitive self-management, which turns work into an anxiety-laden competitive game. It combines two complementary practices. First, the practice of supervised self-management grants the engineers considerable autonomy to manage numerous aspects of their work lives, including their work hours, though managers retain ultimate authority to alter any of the self-imposed deadlines, plans, or objectives. Second, the practice of competitive peer ranking involves the period assignment of performance "scores" distributed on a bell curve, which compare the engineers' performance against their peers'. This bell-curve distribution renders professional recognition competitive, uncertain, and scarce, and generates continuous uncertainty and anxiety among the engineers about their relative professional status. The anxiety drives the engineers to engage in austere self-management and to exercise their autonomy to self-impose long work hours. The engineers become anxiously absorbed in the game of trying to obtain good scores because these scores address their core identity as competent and valued professionals.

To explain the workings of this management strategy I depart from the work-hours literature and draw on Burawoy's (1979) observations of factory workers. In his ethnographic study of machinists, Burawoy found that work effort can be intensified through the organization of work into a suspenseful game. Workers become absorbed in the "work game" if they have a realm of autonomy in which they exercise discretion over decisions that significantly affect their chances of attaining some uncertain but important outcome. In the factory that Burawoy studied, and in Jeffrey Sallaz's recent application of Burawoy's theory to casino workers (Sallaz 2002), the area of autonomy was carved out by the workers themselves, in tension with official management policies (though with the cooperation of lower-level supervisors). In these cases management conceded some worker autonomy in an implicit bargain for worker consent and effort.[11] At MegaTech, by contrast, worker autonomy is an essential element of management's strategy.

Conscious managerial attempts to establish control over workers through the granting of discretion or by using competitive performance rankings are not new.[12] MegaTech's management strategy in fact reflects the continuation of well-documented trends toward greater employee involvement in decision making and increased individuation and competition among workers (Osterman 1999; Smith 1997). This study sheds new light on how these practices operate in powerful synergy to turn work into an absorbing and anxious game over professional status, and how this status competition in turn accounts for long work hours. The remainder of this paper will describe how competitive self-management succeeded in driving MegaTech's engineers to work long hours and why—in a sharp contrast with the fierce worker resistance described by Vicki Smith (1990) against the application of a similar management strategy[13]—MegaTech's engineers accepted competitive self-management as a legitimate practice.

## COMPETITIVE SELF-MANAGEMENT AND PERFORMANCE REVIEWS

MegaTech's confidential management manual, which is made available only to employees with supervisory roles, spells out the vision behind competitive self-management:

> MegaTech has found a way to sustain a culture of high personal achievement [utilizing] a performance management system that *creates and drives*

*competitiveness* and achievement. This system helps sustain a level of internal performance excellence that operates almost independently of external market realities. It keeps our people *on the edge,* constantly driving, seeking new ways to excel [emphasis added].

To keep the engineers "on the edge," the manual further explains that at the heart of MegaTech's "performance management system" are frequent performance reviews that "focus on individual results." The performance reviews deploy a "challenging normative rating curve" that ranks individual performances "across relevant peer groups." The manual acknowledges that "this may seem to be an aggressive approach to evaluate performance," but reassures supervisors that this "ensures" that the "most outstanding, driven, passionate . . . performers of that term are setting the standards against which all will be compared."

The performance of all MegaTech employees—including managers—is formally reviewed twice a year. During "review meetings" with their immediate supervisor, employees receive oral and written feedback on their performance over the past six months, as well as numeric scores ranging from 4 to 10 that quantify their supervisor's assessments. The requirement that scores be distributed along a bell-shaped curve means that, regardless of the quality of an individual's actual overall performance, an equal number of engineers must receive scores that fall above and below the average, which is 7. Forty percent of the engineers get this score, representing the peak of the curve; 30 percent receive a 6 or below, and 30 percent receive an 8 or above.

Very few engineers receive a 4 or 5, and receipt of either such score means that "you are on probation and are having real problems." It is "a hint" that you should leave MegaTech.[14] The meaning of a 6 was contested. "D-leaders," who, in addition to writing code, also supervise and review the performance of three to five engineers, insisted that a 6 means the engineer is "meeting expectations," which "is not bad, but just relatively not as good as others" and suggests the engineer may not be "growing." The engineers, by contrast, interpreted a 6 as "a slap on the wrist," a message that "you should be working a little harder." There was even less consensus on the meaning of the average score of 7. D-leaders explained that, when they give a 7, it means the engineer is doing a "pretty good job" or "doing well." The engineers, however, referred to a 7 as merely "keeping up with the pack," and most were not satisfied with it. Since D-leaders both gave and received scores, at different points during the interview I asked them to interpret the meanings of these scores from both perspectives. Strikingly, D-leaders who interpreted a 7 as "doing well" when giving scores stated that, when they receive a 7, they are disappointed and interpret is as a sign that they need "to improve." One D-leader, for example, explained that, when he gives a 7, it means "a very good job," but when he receives a 7, it means "I didn't meet my goals"; and "I still have a lot of room for improvement." There was greater consensus regarding the meaning of higher scores. An 8 means "great job"; 9s are rare and are interpreted to mean that "everybody is flabbergasted at how much you can get done." None of my interviewees knew anyone who received a 10, but there are "legends."

The employee handbook explains that performance review scores are determined by reference to two standards: (1) Did you "meet your objectives?" and (2) did your work make "an important contribution" to the product? Although no mention is made in these official criteria of the number of hours worked as a factor in scores, pressures to work long hours are firmly embedded within both.

The first review criterion of meeting your objectives illustrates the workings of supervised self-management. The very wording of this criterion, meeting your, as opposed to management's, objectives implies self-determination. During each biannual review meeting, the engineers are asked to "set their objectives" for the next six-month period. The employee handbook encourages employees to "demonstrate an enthusiastic commitment to excellence as you set your performance goals." The setting of "objectives" at the review meeting is actually a reinforcement ritual for a prior moment of self-management. The engineers' work inevitably revolves around two central objectives—completing their coding assignments within the milestone deadlines and fixing all their bugs by the "shipment date." The crucial moment of self-management occurs during the initial "milestone zero" phase of the project, when the various deadlines are set for the completion of coding projects and the "shipping date" is carved in stone.

During the milestone zero phase, managers ask engineers to estimate how many weeks of coding work each particular feature will require. Although seeming to provide the engineers with control over their schedule, the engineers' descriptions of the estimating process reveal a far more complex reality. To produce these estimates, I had assumed that the engineers would first calculate the total number of hours they expect a coding task to require and then estimate the required number of weeks by reference to the number of hours they plan to work each week. However, none of the engineers calculated estimates in this manner because, as they repeatedly explained, accurately guessing the total required hours is nearly impossible. Each coding project is unique, and all the different subtasks that will be necessary to make a certain feature work cannot be foreseen prior to actually doing the coding work. It's a bit like giving a time estimate for a hike without knowing the topography of the terrain.

Because precise estimates cannot be provided and there is no "objective" way to justify a longer than "usual" estimate, engineers' time estimates depend on their sense of how many weeks it should take for a competent and diligent engineer to complete the given type of coding job. The estimates are influenced by the engineers' perceptions of their managers' expectations. One engineer explained, "Even though the managers ask you how long it's going to take, they have something in their mind as well. So if they think it will take shorter than your estimate, you will have to negotiate." Providing a longer-than-expected estimate is an invitation for a supervisor to say, "I think there may be quicker ways to do this." By contrast, a short time estimate brings "kudos." One engineer suggested that anticipating what time frame a manager may have in mind leads him to provide time estimates that are shorter than the manager would have dared suggest. He explained: "If someone asks, 'When will you have this done?' I always tend to say earlier than when my boss would say I should have it done. He doesn't want to seem like a brute; self-imposition is stricter." The engineers' provision of the initial time estimates and the subsequent writing of their commitment to meeting these estimates as one of "*their* objectives" during the six-month review meeting lead the engineers to anticipate, and declare as their own, management's expectations regarding reasonable time estimates.

The second criterion by which engineers are reviewed is the importance of their contribution to the product or, as the engineers often call it, the "visibility" of their work. It was widely understood that, independent of the quality of their performance, "the more critical an assignment is to the product, the more recognition you are going to get." The coding tasks that are deemed important are invariably the most complex and time-consuming, and come with the greatest pressure that they be completed within tight deadlines. In another instance of supervised self-management, engineers are encouraged to proactively negotiate their assignments with their supervisors, and given this review criterion, the engineers predictably lobby for the most "visible" assignment they can receive. To receive such assignments, engineers must "earn the trust" of their manager by demonstrating that they have the ability, drive, and stamina to perform well under strict time pressures. Thus, during any given project, the engineers who are not working on "high-visibility" tasks are working hard to prove themselves capable of handling such assignments in the future. As a result, although on the surface the "importance to the project" criterion appears unrelated to work time, in practice, it pushes all engineers to work long hours. In addition, it also renders the hardest jobs most desirable and prestigious. Those receiving "important" assignments have lobbied for them and feel honored and trusted to have received them. This reinforces their sense of self-determination even as they work long hours to complete such assignments.

When I asked MegaTech engineers to explain their long work hours, a common response was that such hours were necessary "to get their work done on time." At first I found this answer puzzling because I had also been told by the engineers that hours are "up to the individual" and that they had meaningful say over which projects they received and the deadlines for completing them. The apparent tension in the engineers' responses vanished once their discretion over which assignments to request, and what time estimates to provide, was placed in the context of the ever-looming bell-curved performance review system.

## Bell-Curved Scores and Uncertainty

The review structure ensures that all engineers—even experienced veterans who provide short estimates and receive important assignments—are never secure that their performances will be judged as above average or even as a competent 7 ("keeping up with the pack"). There are two structural reasons for the engineers' ever-present uncertainty. First, individual scores are strictly relative to the performances of other engineers, which for any particular engineer in the midst of a coding project is difficult to gauge. The management manual reveals that uncertainty about the scores is an intended consequence of the system. It advises managers to clarify to their engineers that "performing as well as the last review period in no way guarantees an equivalent rating this term." The manual also warns managers to "take caution when an employee asks 'Tell me what I need to do to get' a [high rating]" because the relative ranking system provides no absolute standard for good performance. As one engineer described it, "It's not like, if you do this, you get a good score. It's you do this and then you are compared to others." Although the engineers set forth "objectives" for each review period, merely "meeting your objectives"—doing everything that "you" set forth at the prior six-month review session—is not enough to assure even an average score. Another engineer explained, "In reality, everyone is trying to exceed their objectives. Meeting your objectives, that's like doing satisfactory work, so you try to do extra." Yet it is never clear how much "exceeding" of objectives will be necessary to get the above-average score of 8 or even the average 7.

Uncertainty regarding performance scores is further sustained by the continuous escalation of competition and expectations as engineers acquire greater skill and experience. Each engineer is located within a hierarchy of experience levels. Each of these levels has its own compensation curve and expectations about the engineer's ability. When engineers are graded during the review process, their performance is not compared to that of all engineers performing similar tasks, but only against engineers at their experience level. Engineers who receive an 8 or a few consecutive 7s are promoted to the next level. The promotion in levels does not change the kind of work performed, but heightens the level of competition. After each such promotion, as one engineer lamented, "chances are you won't do as well 'cause you are being compared to a better set of people." The upshot is that there are no resting points in a MegTech engineer's career. "It's this treadmill where you are blowing out your expectations by doing more, then they get reset, and then you have to do even more." The system is designed so that no one can "coast," secure in the feeling that he or she is doing a great or competent job.

I have explained how the performance review criteria indirectly link long work hours to performance scores and the structures that keep engineers perpetually uncertain about their scores. Yet uncertainty alone is not enough to generate an engrossing and anxiety-inducing work game. Competitive self-management succeeds only because the engineers deeply care about their review scores.

## The Significance of Review Scores

The review scores are profoundly meaningful to the engineers because they are the primary way by which they come to feel that they are professionally competent and valued. In discussing their work lives, the engineers do not present themselves as simply "making a living," but as the proud possessors of skills and abilities that they believe meaningfully contribute to the creation of socially valuable products. Central to their self-image is a sense of competence, if not mastery, and usefulness, if not indispensability, to their product teams. Every six months MegaTech's review process puts the engineers' self-image on the line, when they find out in unambiguous terms whether they are good, average, or below average and whether their contributions are considered "important."[15] As one engineer put it, a good review score means that "my work has been noticed and I have gotten some confirmation of my abilities."

The bell-curve distribution means that in order for MegaTech engineers to be validated in their belief that they are "good" in their work, they must perform better than 70 percent of their peers, and to avoid the humiliating slap of a "below-average" ranking, they must perform better than at least 30 percent of their colleagues. In this context, MegaTech engineers "choose" to self-impose long work hours. Long hours are the price of, a prerequisite to—being "good" and "valuable."

MegaTech's review process was significant not only for the engineers' self-image, but equally so for their social standing. Although the scores remained confidential, the engineers could roughly determine who is doing relatively well depending on the importance of the assignments each received. Some engineers sought to prove that they were the "go-to guy" (Cooper 2000), but for many others the central concern was to avoid appearing like a "slacker" and to "keep up with the pack." One engineer expressed this anxiety as follows:

> I always find myself working that much because I feel that I am going to fall behind the curve if I don't. I think it's something that probably a lot of MegaTech people feel, and it could be a pressure put upon myself, and I guess the problem is they hire a lot of bright people at MegaTech, and everybody is used to being really good at school or whatever and it's hard to give that up. I guess it kind of scares me when I think that I could be using this time to better myself at work but instead I'm sleeping or instead I'm just goofing around. If I am not using my time wisely, then, you know, relatively I may not do as well when I am compared to my peers. I don't want to fall behind the curve, right. It's important because career-wise you want, I think, at least I can say for myself, I want to be valued as a member of the team, right, and just self-esteem [nervous laugh]. If I were at another company, I probably wouldn't work as hard because I wouldn't have the competition that I have here.

## COMPETITIVE SELF-MANAGEMENT'S EFFECTS ON INDIVIDUAL WORKERS

Although competitive self-management powerfully drives the engineers to work long hours, each engineer's subjective response to this management system was to some extent unique. An important dimension of variation was the degree to which the pressure created by competitive peer ranking was experienced as negative anxiety or as an exciting positive stimulus. Many engineers reported feeling a combination of both, with negative anxiety being the more salient response.

To illustrate the different ways in which the system motivates long work hours, I compare its effects on two engineers. Charlie and Tom are both married white males in their early thirties from middle-class backgrounds. Although they work in different product divisions, as D-leaders Charlie and Tom occupy parallel locations within the organizational hierarchy of MegaTech. Both work long hours and are deeply affected by competitive peer ranking. However, how the ranking affects each of them is different.

Charlie typically works from 9:00 A.M. to 9:00 P.M. on weekdays and usually does not work weekends. He enjoys "certain aspects of his work," particularly "solving tangible problems" and "building things." He explains that, for him, writing code is like "woodworking or building houses," and it gives him a "sense of accomplishment." In discussing his long work hours, Charlie initially explained that he really enjoys his work, comparing himself to a dedicated "craftsman" working long hours out of choice. However, as typically occurred in the course of my interviews, at a later stage when I again asked Charlie about his present work hours, his answer revealed a more complex picture:

OS: How do you feel about your current work hours?

Charlie: Um, I think it's too much. I'd love to work forty hours a week, but it's not going to happen.

OS: So forty hours is not possible?

Charlie: Yes, it's not practical. I couldn't get what I need to get done.

OS: What if you lessened your load?

Charlie: Well, if I lessened my load, I would have less responsibility. I wouldn't get a good review score, that'd be OK, I guess. [Long pause] These questions that you ask spawn a certain amount of introspection, I guess you'd call it. I find that I am contradicting myself in some of my answers here. It's making me think about it. . . . I hear stories of in Germany everybody takes two months off, and I think wow, great, but I couldn't do that. I'd feel guilty about it. I don't know if that's self-imposed or imposed by MegaTech culture or what.

By "MegaTech culture," Charlie explained that he meant the atmosphere of competition he feels in his work group regarding review scores:

OS: That competition, how does it play out? How do you feel that there is competition?

Charlie: It's not necessarily competition with one another because you don't share your review score. It's not like you go to lunch and say, "Hey show me what you got. Right. Oh you suck." It's not like that at all. When you get a good review score, you know you are doing a good job. It's competition with yourself and implicit competition with your peers. Because if you get an eight you did better than x percent. It's really covert, I'd say, that if there is any, I [long pause], I'm having a really difficult time answering your question actually, um. I think part of it is, I am having a hard time articulating what my motivating factors are. Why do I work hard, why am I here so often, what keeps me here. I'm having a difficult time articulating, and I think the reason is that most of the factors, most of the motivation is really a covert kind of subtle thing. If I am not working many hours it's not like someone comes in and says, "Hey you are not working enough hours." Right, there are subtle sort[s] of pressures that I feel, and I don't know if it's self-imposed or it's external.

Charlie's confusion and his reference to "covert" and "subtle" pressures suggest that the review scores play an ordinarily unacknowledged role in motivating him to work the hours that he does. Charlie usually imagines his long work hours to arise from enjoyment or dedication to his craft. However, in the course of the interview, he painfully acknowledged the "covert" pressure exerted by the review scores and the "implicit competition" generated by the review system.

By contrast to Charlie, Tom provides the clearest example of an engineer positively driven by this competition. Like Charlie, Tom averages twelve hours of work per weekday, but he typically works an additional four to five hours on weekends. He enjoys the "technical challenges" presented by his work and describes his work hours as largely self-imposed because of his "really wanting to code particular features." But as the interview progressed further layers of motivation became apparent. When I asked Tom, "What does your work mean to you?" after a long pause and a deep breath, Tom responded, "Work is the place I feel most empowered" and "competent." He continued, "It's just a place where I've been recognized as a star, you know, from previous performance evaluations and all that, and that means a lot to me. That actually really motivates me, which is interesting from an organizational standpoint. I think that this is what MegaTech has in mind."

He then elaborated on the meaning of the review scores, and how he is made to feel like a "star":

My running average is actually more than an eight [laughing] which I am cognizant of. And while that's something that's not public at all, it's just between me and my manager, it's something that I personally take a great deal of pride in and a great deal of satisfaction cause I know that I am at a company that's doing some amazing things, and I am right up there with some of the best people in a group of really smart people. So I feel like I'm pretty smart, but sometimes I have to work hard to make up the difference between me and these real genius people [laugh]. So that's part of what motivates me to work hard.

Tom explained that when he first arrived at MegaTech he wanted to "prove that [he] belonged" and then "at some point it was kind of trying to prove that I am not just on the Olympic Team but I am going to get a medal to boot, I am going to be one of the best achievers here."

The competitive review system drives both Charlie and Tom to work long hours, but this common pattern of behavior masks a significant subjective difference in how the system affects them. Charlie sees himself as a devoted craftsman choosing to work long hours, and only with great difficulty acknowledges that he is pushed by subtle pressures arising from the review system. By contrast, Tom sees himself as a "star," basking in his high review scores. Unlike Charlie, Tom does not seem haunted by "subtle" pressures, but openly acknowledges the fact that the review scores motivate him. While Charlie's experience was more typical than Tom's, and Tom was the only engineer reporting predominantly positive effects, several engineers did express some degree of positive stimulation.

## CONSENT AND LEGITIMACY

Despite causing intense anxiety for most engineers, competitive peer ranking was largely accepted by them without resistance or resentment. Although the engineers acknowledged that in some unusual cases the review scores are based on "political" calculations and not merit, by and large the ranking system was viewed as fair and as a source of pride and social status.[16] Even an engineer who received a low score was not critical of the competitive peer-ranking system per se, but only of how it was applied in his case.[17]

My findings suggest that the principal reason for the absence of resistance to competitive peer ranking and its rigid bell-shaped distribution curve is MegaTech's extensive use of supervised self-management. By formally granting the engineers discretion over various aspects of their work, MegaTech appeared to respect their autonomy, which is something MegaTech engineers, like most American workers, highly value (Freeman and Rogers 1999, 40–41). Self-management also encouraged the engineers to attribute their performance scores to their individual abilities and efforts, which diffused any feelings of resentment toward MegaTech.[18] At a more specific level, the engineers' consent to their individual scores was fostered by a more particular deployment of supervised self-management. Prior to being reviewed by their supervisors, engineers were required to evaluate their own performance and assign themselves a score. The engineers described this self-evaluation as "a chance to enumerate and explain your accomplishments" and "reflect on how you can improve." As with previously discussed instances of supervised self-management, such as "setting your own goals," this practice compelled the engineers to actively participate in their own management and to take the perspective of their supervisors—often resulting in the engineers being their own harshest critics. For example, one engineer explained that he gave himself a mediocre score despite feeling that he did a "stellar" job because, during the previous six-month period, "I didn't ship anything." Even though shipment was out of his control and did not reflect anything about his performance, he nonetheless felt that he didn't accomplish anything "tangible" that "made MegaTech money," and therefore he did not deserve a high score.[19]

The legitimacy of the competitive ranking system among the engineers may also be attributable to the fact that most of them had experienced, and perhaps grown accustomed to, similar grading practices in college. The striking resemblance between the twice-a-year reviews and the familiar end-of-semester report card was not lost on the engineers. As one engineer stated in discussing the review system, "I think the review model is actually really valuable in the same way that grades are really valuable. People may disagree; some like schools where there are no grades. Personally, I wouldn't like that at all." Several engineers explicitly equated their review scores to letter grades at school, comparing a 6 to a C, a 7 to a B, and an 8 to an A. One engineer likened getting a good review score to "being the smartest guy in class." Another stated, "Everybody likes to get an A."

## CONCLUSION: IMPLICATIONS FOR THEORY, RESEARCH, AND SOCIAL CHANGE

This paper explores the causes driving high-tech engineers to work long hours. Although a qualitative case study of a single firm cannot purport to provide a general explanation, it can generate new hypotheses, and suggest directions for future research.

The central finding of this paper is that long work hours can result from management strategies that generate worker anxiety and competition over professional status. Whereas the work-hours literature has focused on the role of consumption (Schor 1991), income (Reich 2000), pleasant, homelike workplaces (Hochschild 1997), and loyal identification with the employer (Kunda 1992), my findings point to management strategies that absorb workers in an anxious competition that lead them to self-impose long hours. To explain the dynamics of this management strategy I draw on Burawoy's (1979) factory observations that consent-producing games can be generated wherever workers have discretion over decisions that affect an uncertain but important outcome. The MegaTech practices explored in this paper are by no means limited to high-tech workers, and in fact are part of a general trend toward greater employee involvement and individuation. As Taylorist routinization becomes increasingly ineffective in more and more sectors of the economy, employers everywhere face the challenge of simultaneously giving employees greater discretion while maintaining the intensity of their work effort. MegaTech's practices of involving workers in traditionally managerial realms and individuating worker's performance assessment reflect two essential features of what has been called the "new economy" workplace (Osterman 1999). Thus, MegaTech's competitive self-management, as described in this paper, can be seen as a paradigmatic "new economy" strategy of control that is likely to be widely replicated.

At a more specific level, this paper points to the need for further research on competitive self-management or similar practices using curved grading to review employees' performances. Further research could investigate the diffusion of curved grading and its effects,[20] and could also attempt to explore the gendered nature of the engineers' response to competitive self-management. If the intense anxiety exhibited by the engineers about their relative professional competence is partly a function of internalized notions of masculinity, then we would expect cross-gender comparisons to reveal different patterns of responses to practices such as competitive self-management.

The findings of this paper also have important implications for the possibility of social change. For those concerned about the effects of rising work-hours on families and communities, it is critical to understand the causes underlying this phenomenon. The analysis in this paper suggests that merely pushing firms to change their formal flexibility regarding work hours may not be enough. Official flexibility can be rendered meaningless by other organizational structures that create anxious competition over professional status. In MegaTech's case, it can "safely" offer various "programs" promoting work-family balance, earning it a prestigious spot in the top half of *Fortune* magazine's list of the "100 Best Companies to Work For," because regardless of official work-hour flexibility, competitive self-management drives workers to self-impose long hours.[21] Change requires a holistic examination of all the interacting elements of work organization, in particular the mechanism for determining professional competence and status. Although profit-seeking employers who perceive a benefit from spiraling and anxious competition among workers can be expected to make the recognition of professional competence scarce, standards of competence do not have to be monopolized by employers. Professional associations or other worker-controlled institutions can reclaim from corporate management the standards for competence and define these in a manner that allows for useful economic production while also preserving the well-being of the communities and families currently under assault by rising work hours.

## APPENDIX: METHODS AND DATA

I conducted a total of fourteen interviews with MegaTech employees, directly observed the workplace, and reviewed company materials such as the confidential management manual, the human resources web page, and the employee handbook. I used two un-related personal contacts to find my initial interview subjects at MegaTech, and then relied on snowball technique to find the remainder of the interviewees. Ten of the fourteen interviews were open-ended and lasted approximately two hours each. I conducted these interviews in the employees' offices, which enabled me to observe their work environment, from their office decorations to the social atmosphere in the hallways. After the interviews, I occa-sionally lingered around the workplace, shadowing the engineers as they went about their work. Subsequent to completing these ten interviews at the work site I decided to interview four more engi-neers to obtain further data regarding the specific practices that I describe in this paper. These interviews were conducted by tele-phone. Aside from the interviews, direct observations, and docu-ments, I gathered additional data by walking around the MegaTech campus, having lunch at the employee-only cafeterias, and touring the employee-only MegaTech "museum."

My sample consisted of thirteen men and one woman, nine of whom were married. Their ages ranged from twenty-five to thirty-eight; the average age was thirty. Their tenure at MegaTech ranged from two and a half to ten years, five years on average. Eight of the fourteen interviewees had held at least one job prior to MegaTech. Twelve of the fourteen interviewees were software engineers, including six "developers" and six "D-leaders." Developers are engi-neers exclusively engaged in writing software code, and D-leaders are one rung up the managerial hierarchy and are involved in both writing code (40 percent of their time) and supervising three to five developers (60 percent of their time). The twelve engineers were dispersed among various product divisions at MegaTech. The two nonengineers that I interviewed provided a unique perspec-tive on their engineer colleagues from their position internal to the company but external to the engineers' work teams and culture. Both nonengineers were marketing researchers who work together with engineers in designing products. Because this paper focuses on engineers, my interviews of the nonengineers did not deal with their work experiences per se but with their perceptions of the work lives and motivations of the engineers with whom they work.

TABLE 7A.1  **Breakdown of Work Hours**

| Engineers | Phase I "Milestone Zero" Hours 5 Percent per Year | Phase II "Regular" Hours 55 Percent per Year | Phase III "Crunch" Hours 40 Percent per Year | Weighted Annual Average |
|---|---|---|---|---|
| Frank | 48% | 67% | 82% | 72% |
| Sean | 45 | 63 | 78 | 68 |
| Ernest | 55 | 80 | 95 | 85 |
| Bob | 42 | 55 | 65 | 58 |
| Barry | 50 | 84 | 88 | 84 |
| Doug | 45 | 47 | 54 | 50 |
| Charlie | 48 | 60 | 75 | 65 |
| Albert | 45 | 54 | 60 | 56 |
| Tom | 48 | 64 | 76 | 68 |
| Dan | 46 | 52 | 57 | 54 |
| Howard | 56 | 71 | 99 | 81 |
| Nick | 42 | 57 | 67 | 60 |
| Average | 48 | 63 | 75 | 67 |

*Source:* Author's compilation.

I wish to thank the Institute for Labor and Employment and the Society for the Study of Social Problems for their financial support during the research of this paper (the latter through its Harry Braverman Award). I am deeply grateful for all the helpful comments from colleagues and friends, especially Michael Burawoy, Nancy Chodorow, Liz Drogin, Malcolm Fairbrother, Arlie Hochschild, Tom Medvetz, Gretchen Purser, Marjorie B. Schaafsma, Kim Voss, and Ana Villa-Lobos.

## NOTES

1.  In *The Overworked American,* Juliet Schor (1991) established that from 1969 to 1987 the average number of annual hours worked by Americans increased by 163 hours. Confirming that this trend has continued, the International Labour Organization (1999) found that during the 1990s, average annual American work hours increased by 36 hours. Robert Reich's (2000) analysis of 1999 data from the U.S. Department of Labor's *Report on the American Workforce* provides further empirical support. Reich found that, depending on the

method of calculation, average annual work hours increased from 1979 to 1999 by either 71 hours or 142 hours. Finally, using 1999 data from the Organisation of Economic Co-operation and Development, Lawrence Mishel, Jared Bernstein, and John Schmidt (2001) found that American work hours increased by 61 hours between 1979 and 1998. Pointing in the other direction, John Robinson and Geoffrey Godbey (1997) claim in their time-diary study that free time actually increased between 1965 and 1985. However, these findings have been criticized by numerous researchers who point out that Robinson and Godbey's sample was small and unrepresentative, consisting only of individuals with enough time on their hands to keep such diaries (Hochschild 2001; Reich 2000). Moreover, even if one is convinced by Robinson and Godbey's claims regarding overall average work hours up through the mid-1980s, this does not contradict the findings regarding the general increase in American work hours during the 1990s of Mishel, Bernstein, and Schmidt; Reich; and the International Labour Organization. Robinson and Godbey's findings also do not dispute the fact that work hours of professional, technical, and managerial workers, on which this paper focuses, have increased over the past thirty years.

2.  Among men, 35 percent of professional, managerial, and technical employees work more than fifty hours a week, whereas only 20 percent of men in other occupations work such hours. For women, 17 percent of professional, managerial, and technical employees work more than fifty hours per week, as compared to 7 percent for women in other occupations (Jacobs and Gerson 1998). Also supporting this trend are CPS data showing that the percentage of employees working more than fifty hours per week increases with income (Rones, Ilg, and Gardner 1997).

3.  The fun collegiate image is further cultivated at the "MegaTech museum," a private facility used for official company events, including the orientation of new recruits. Although the museum displays focus mostly on MegaTech's technological achievements, several panels provide quotes and video clips from employees who emphasize MegaTech's playful social atmosphere. A movie that repeats every five minutes asserts that "people have fun here. It's like being in college; the office is like the dorm room."

4.  As one employee described it, "Everything happens through email; it's hard to take it out of email and talk personally." Email is preferred to face-to-face contact because it allows the other person to respond when he or she has time. According to several engineers, another purported advantage of email is that "you can be more terse and direct, and in giving criticism, there is less need to soften the blow."

5.   One engineer described the environment as follows:

> You definitely need to have thick skin to work here because it can be kind of a hard working environment; it's not unusual to be at a meeting where people are yelling at each other; it happens all the time. . . . Someone who used to work here wrote an article about how refreshing it was at her new job that people chat at the water cooler while here people go to their office and immediately close their door. She also wrote about how on her first day at MegaTech she introduced herself to someone in the kitchen who responded with the question, "Do I need to know you?"

6.   Unlike at the firm studied by Kunda, at MegaTech there was no systematic dissemination of cultural messages, whether through seminars, speeches, or bulletin boards. MegaTech's most conscious attempt at self-presentation and cultural dissemination, the MegaTech museum, tried to convey the image of MegaTech as "fun," but contained no references to or metaphors about MegaTech being a family or a caring community.

7.   One might suspect that this finding reflects the engineers' hesitation to reveal potentially embarrassing "shallow" monetary desires, but this does not appear to have been the case, because in other contexts the engineers did openly cast themselves in an unflattering light by discussing feelings such as envy, anxiety, and fear.

8.   Given the hype surrounding "stock options" in the late 1990s, my interviews also included questions about their motivating role, which I expected to be significant. In fact, although stock options played an important role in some engineers' decision to join MegaTech, and for some it remains an important reason to stay (at least until their options "vest," that is, become available for cashing out), the engineers consistently stated that the options do not affect their day-to-day work lives.

9.   The classic book on the passion for coding is Tracy Kidder's *The Soul of a New Machine,* which depicts work at a large high-tech company in the early 1980s. Engineers are described as deeply absorbed in programming, which for them is "like a drug," and programming is compared to playing in a "jungle gym" (Kidder 1981, 96–102).

10.  This sentiment appears to be shared by most Americans who work more than fifty hours a week. Basing its findings on 3,381 phone interviews of working-age adults, the National Study of the Changing Workforce found that 80 percent of those working over fifty hours a per week preferred working shorter hours (Jacobs and Gerson 1998).

11.  In Sallaz's (2002) study, the casino management largely acquiesced to the dealers' ignoring of official management schema requiring equal service to all customers, and permitted the dealers' orientation toward maximizing tips, because the tip earnings facilitated the dealers' con-

sent to low wages. I note that the tip-maximizing games of the casino dealers, in sharp contrast to the game at MegaTech, was cooperative and not competitive, since all tips were shared.

12. For example, Leslie Perlow (1996, 40) alludes to the existence of annual performance reviews that appear similar to MegaTech's, noting that each year managers "rank the software engineers." Self-management practices are even more widespread. Surveying the literature, Smith (1997) estimated that 35 percent of large firms deploy some form of "flexible work organization" that involves employee participation in traditional managerial realms.

13. In her case study of a large bank, Vicki Smith developed the concept of "coercive autonomy" to describe the simultaneous increase of middle managers' discretion and heightened monitoring of the managers' performance by use of normative curves (Smith 1990). However, unlike the present case, "coercive autonomy" generated considerable resistance on the part of the middle-manager bankers to upper management's goals. Smith's bankers were encouraged to exercise their autonomy to eliminate jobs among their subordinates, and to use ranking procedures to "identify poor performers" and manage them "out" (Smith 1990, 93). The bankers resisted upper management's policies because they believed weakening job security among their subordinates would undercut their efforts to encourage hard work and commitment, and as a consequence undermine their success and professional status. By contrast, MegaTech's engineers' professional status was enhanced by exercising discretion to increase work hours. Thus, whereas in Smith's case workers faced a trade-off between upper management's goals and their own status, at MegaTech the trade-off was between professional status and the quantity of time left for life outside work.

14. However, even engineers who receive a 4 or 5 are rarely fired. The consensus was that "to get fired, you have to really screw up," and not in terms of performance, but by committing an "HR violation [like sexual harassment] or leaking private information." Much more common than being fired, engineers quit after receiving bad performance reviews because they feel that they are not wanted or appreciated. This system allows MegaTech to promise job security to new recruits while pressuring low performers to quit.

15. The review scores also have financial implications. Higher scores entail larger pay raises, bonuses, and stock options. For example, engineers obtaining a 6 or less do not receive any stock options. Yet, as previously discussed, the scores were not significant to the engineers because of money per se; on the contrary, money was signif-

icant as another kind of score, providing validation to the engineers of their competence and worth.

16. Two non-merit-related or "political" factors were acknowledged. First, following a promotion to a new level it is an unwritten convention that managers give the newly promoted engineer a lower score regardless of his or her relative performance. By giving "newcomers" a lower score, managers are able to boost the score of others who have been at their level for a while and nudge them toward moving up a level. The other nonmerit basis involved the ranking of employees who were in the process of transferring to another product division. The transferring engineer's last score in the old division is bound to be low regardless of actual performance. The engineers explained that managers have no incentive to give departing engineers a high or even average score, which, given the bell-shaped distribution of scores, necessitates giving someone else who will continue to work in the unit a potentially demoralizing low score. Instead, managers give departing engineers low scores and save the scarce high scores for engineers who stay in their division.

17. Nick was the only engineer I interviewed who explicitly criticized the review system. Perhaps not surprisingly, he had received a low score. Nick was openly bitter and was seriously considering interviewing with other companies. He attributed his low review score to having "an extremely poor manager," who "did not give me good feedback and therefore I wasn't giving him what he wanted, though I thought I was." He also thought that managers are not telling him "the truth about the review criteria." Although Nick was clearly demoralized and appeared to be on his way out, he did not question the fairness of the system, but only its unfair application by an incompetent and perhaps less than honest supervisor. Moreover, Nick's departure would not necessarily be a bad result from MegaTech's perspective because the review system aims to motivate the "good" engineers and to nudge out those who are deemed to be relatively low performers.

18. The lack of resistance at MegaTech may also be attributable to the fact that internal competition leads to individualization and dispersion of conflict from vertical to lateral antagonisms (Burawoy 1979, 81).

19. The engineers had a further incentive to give themselves a low score. Engineers who gave themselves scores higher than the manager thought appropriate were advised by their manager not to give themselves such high scores because this requires the manager to "defend" the lower score that he gave the engineer and emphasize the engineer's weak points when he writes up his review. To avoid such a

negative emphasis, it is safer for engineers to give themselves a modest or average review score. Even so, it rarely happens that engineers get a higher score than they give themselves. Thus, on the one hand, engineers are encouraged not to give themselves a high score because this may lead to a more negative review, but on the other hand, by keeping their own scores low, they are foreclosing any future objections for receiving a mediocre or low score.

20.    On March 19, 2001, a front-page story in the *New York Times* described the technique of grading employees on a bell curve as increasingly popular and cited several large American corporations, including Ford Motor Company and General Electric, that have adopted this practice.

21.    This finding is supported by the existing literature. Hochschild's (1997, 8, 25) "Amerco" also provided a wide range of options for "flexibility" in work hours, including part-time, flextime, and job sharing, but almost no one cut back. The company researched by Perlow (1996, 104) was likewise one of *Fortune* magazine's "100 Best Companies to Work For," and it offered "a wide array of flexible options, including flextime, flexplace, job sharing, and part-time work." Yet, as at MegaTech, most engineers did not take advantage of such options.

## REFERENCES

Burawoy, Michael. 1979. *Manufacturing Consent: Changes in the Labor Process Under Monopoly Capitalism*. Chicago: University of Chicago Press.

Cooper, Marianne. 2000. "Being the 'Go-To Guy': Fatherhood, Masculinity, and the Organization of Work in Silicon Valley." *Qualitative Sociology* 23(4): 379–405.

Freeman, Richard, and Joel Rogers. 1999. *What Workers Want*. New York: Russell Sage Foundation.

Golden, Lonnie, and Helene Jorgensen. 2002. "Time After Time: Mandatory Overtime in the U.S. Economy." Economic Policy Institute Briefing Paper. Washington, D.C.: Economic Policy Institute.

Hochschild, Arlie. 1997. *The Time Bind*. New York: Metropolitan Books.

———. 2001. "Overwork: Causes and Consequences of Rising Work Hours. A Roundtable Discussion with Arlie Hochschild, Neil Fligstein, Kim Voss and Juliet Schor, Moderated by Michael Burawoy." *Berkeley Journal of Sociology* 45(1): 180–96.

International Labour Organization. 1999. *Key Indicators of the Labour Market, 1999*. Geneva: International Labour Organization.

Jacobs, Jerry, and Kathleen Gerson. 1998. "Who Are the Overworked Americans?" *Review of Social Economy* 56(4): 442–59.

Kidder, Tracy. 1981. *The Soul of a New Machine*. Boston: Little, Brown.

Kunda, Gideon. 1992. *Engineering Culture: Control and Commitment in a High-Tech Corporation*. Philadelphia: Temple University Press.

Mishel, Lawrence, Jared Bernstein, and John Schmidt. 2001. *The State of Working America: 2000–2001*. Washington, D.C.: Economic Policy Institute.

Osterman, Paul. 1999. *Securing Prosperity*. Princeton: Princeton University Press.

Perlow, Leslie. 1996. *Finding Time: How Corporations, Individuals and Families Can Benefit from New Work Practices*. Ithaca, N.Y.: Cornell University Press.

Putnam, Robert. 2000. *Bowling Alone: The Collapse and Renewal of American Community*. New York: Simon & Schuster.

Reich, Robert. 2000. *The Future of Success*. New York: Knopf.

Robinson, John, and Geoffrey Godbey. 1997. *Time for Life: The Surprising Ways Americans Use Their Time*. State College: Pennsylvania State University Press.

Rones, Philip L., Randy E. Ilg, and Jennifer M. Gardner. 1997. "Trends in Hours of Work Since the Mid-1970s." *Monthly Labor Review* 120(4): 3–14.

Sallaz, Jeffrey. 2002. "The Hours Rules: Autonomy and Interests Among Service Workers in the Contemporary Casino Industry." *Work and Occupations* 29(4): 394–427.

Schor, Juliet. 1991. *The Overworked American: The Unexpected Decline of Leisure*. New York: Basic Books.

Smith, Vicki. 1990. *Managing in the Corporate Interest: Control and Resistance in an American Bank*. Berkeley: University of California Press.

———. 1997. "New Forms of Work Organization." *Annual Review of Sociology* 23(1): 315–39.

# Chapter 8

# The Power of Time: Leadership, Management, and Gender

## David L. Collinson and Margaret Collinson

T HE ANALYTICAL SIGNIFICANCE of time has long been recognized in the natural science writings of Galileo, Newton, and Einstein and in the philosophical tracts of Heidegger, Kierkegaard, and Nietzsche, among others. Indeed an awareness of a past, a present, and a future, and of the finiteness of life are central features of human existence (Berger and Luckmann 1967). Human beings find meaning and identity in the temporal character of existence (Urry 1991, Collinson 2003). Yet it is only relatively recently that the importance of time has been acknowledged in theories of society (Giddens 1979, 1984, 1987; Adam 1990; Harvey 1990; Nowotny 1992), organization (Clark 1990; Hassard 2000; Epstein and Kalleberg 2001; Fagan 2001; *Organization Studies* 2002; Cunha 2004), or management (Ancona et al. 2001; Huy 2001; Mainemelis 2001; Whip, Adam, and Sabelis 2004). This chapter explores the significance of time in the workplace and examines corporate leaders' strategies for utilizing time as a resource for exercising power, control, and discipline.

In what follows we explore how time may operate as a form of workplace discipline and in particular, how temporal transformations in the workplace can be a means to discipline middle managers, an issue that has tended to be neglected in the literature. The chapter begins by reviewing some of the relevant literature, particularly that which considers how time can operate as an organizing principle, shaping the division of labor in the workplace and at home. It then draws on empirical data from the U.K. insurance industry to examine leaders' disciplinary impact on managers through three key time-related change strategies: age restructuring, work intensification, and the erosion of "free" time. We also examine surviving managers' coping strategies and the significant gender-specific effects of these processes.

## TIME AND POWER

Edward Thompson's (1967) landmark study revealed how time and power are often inextricably linked within capitalist society and how the control of time is a key feature of organizational life. Exploring the conceptions of temporality forged during the industrial revolution, he described how the mechanistic, controlled, and more coercive logic of the clock replaced feudalistic working patterns based on nature's changes, cycles, and seasons. In contrast with the rhythms and vagaries of nature, the clock enabled time to be standardized and divided into infinitely small and universal units. Workers' performance was increasingly measured by the hour, day, week, and month. Highlighting the historical interconnections within capitalist societies between time, money, and religion, Thompson's ideas were influenced by those of Karl Marx and Max Weber. For Marx (1867/1971), the measurement of time as an exchangeable commodity was central to the commodification of labor, a process in which labor power is treated as an object that can be purchased, sold, and rendered disposable (Braverman 1974). The capitalist's control over labor time was a key source of power that facilitated capital accumulation. For Weber (1930/1958), the puritanical influence of the Protestant work ethic encouraged workers to display a compulsive commitment to ceaseless toil, sacrifice of self, and frugality with time in the hope of achieving economic success that in turn would ensure their salvation in the afterlife.

Building on Thompson's ideas, labor-process writers argue that time discipline is central to managers' control over manual workers in production contexts (for example, Burawoy 1979; Beynon 1980) and service workers, for example, in fast-food restaurants (Leidner 1993; Ritzer 1996) and call centers (Fleming 2002; Callaghan and

Thompson 2002). Empirical studies describe how workers frequently create strategies to "manage" the monotony of work time (Roy 1958) and how time is often highly contested and negotiated (for example, Palm 1979; Theriault 1995). As a central feature of "the effort bargain" (Baldamus 1961), disputes regarding time can occur over the length, pace, intervals, and sequencing of work (Adam 1990; Collinson 1992, 2000). Jason Heyes (1997) describes how the introduction of new working-time arrangements of annualized hours in a U.K. chemical plant reinforced managerial control, reduced earnings, and also generated considerable worker resistance (see also Bell 2001).

Contemporary practices in "post-bureaucratic" organizations that utilize new technologies to render work more flexible, contract-based, and "nomadic" are currently restructuring working time in ways that reinforce its disciplinarity. Richard Sennett (1998) observes that the labor process has become increasingly flexible, and this has resulted in more disjointed and fragmented notions of time, which in turn have led to a corrosion of moral character. He contends that the growing emphasis on flatter hierarchies, project and team work, and performance monitoring has promoted employee preoccupation with short-term thinking, chameleonlike strategies of impression management, and adapting and acquiescing to change. For Sennett, this shift away from linear conceptions of time has led to the erosion of more long-term social bonds and of deeper values of loyalty, mutual trust, community, and caring. He concludes that, in this context of fleeting workplace associations, employees are unable to form coherent stable identities that provide meaning and continuity for their lives. This experience of disjointed, fragmented, and flexible time threatens individuals' ability to form their characters into sustained, long-term narratives.

Extending this focus on contemporary forms of workplace temporality and their disciplinary consequences, other writers highlight the interconnections between time and space. David Harvey (1990) argues that the history of capitalism has always been characterized by continuous speedup in the pace of life combined with the inexorable overcoming of spatial barriers that has "largely been organized in ways that favor capital rather than labour" (231). Observing that this "time-space compression" has become particularly intense over the last two decades, Harvey argues that individuals are now forced to cope with dramatic increases in disposability, ephemerality, and instant obsolescence. Anthony Giddens (1979, 1984, 1987) observes that workplace discipline has always depended upon the calculative division of time (and space), highlighting the monastery as the precursor of modern forms of regulated "time-space zoning." Modern organizations, he contends, involve the intensification of surveillance as a means of accumulating, collating, and retrieving information so as to maximize control over time-space.

Both Giddens and Harvey point to the distinction between "work" and "home" that emerges within bureaucratic and industrial capitalist organizational forms. Giddens suggests that in contemporary society capitalist commodification processes create temporal and spatial separations between the "public" sphere of work and the "private" arena of family and leisure (see also Berger, Berger, and Kellner [1973] on pluralized and segmented life worlds). Harvey asserts that the home can become "a private museum to guard against the ravages of time-space compression" (Harvey 1990, 292). According to Harvey, the significance of the home may be intensified precisely because of the growing turbulence and impermanence around it. The domestic sphere may facilitate the search for secure identity and "for secure moorings in a shifting world" (Harvey 1990, 302).

For Giddens, time never becomes fully commodified. Emphasizing the importance to employees of "free time," when they are free of the control of capitalist organizations, he argues that the ability to control the temporal organization of one's everyday life, as well as one's projects and aspirations, acts to counterbalance the commodified nature of time. Following Weber, Giddens argues that administrative discipline is likely to be most effective when other aspects of employees' lives are separated out from it. Individuals will be willing to submit to discipline for parts of the day, he suggests, "usually as a trade-off for rewards that derive from being freed from such discipline at other times" (1984, 154). This view leads him to problematize Michel Foucault's (1979) conception of time and space and his generalization of the very tight discipline of incarcerating institutions to other forms of organization. Giddens insists that control in less all-embracing organizations is more subtle, utilizing methods to produce collaboration and compliance rather than the coercive, tight control of the "total institution" (Goffman 1968).

Gibson Burrell (1988) questions Giddens's critique of Foucault. Pointing to the considerable influence of organizations on our "personal" time, he contends that "the real point is . . . that, as individuals, we are incarcerated within an organizational world. Thus, whilst we may not live in total institutions, the institutional organization of our lives is total" (232). Similarly, Chris Grey (1994) suggests that the concern with career for aspiring U.K. accountants "links home and work, leisure, . . . and . . . past, present and future through the vector of the self." Nonwork lives can become totally subordinated to the notion of career as "an organising principle of existence" (492) with friends redefined as "contacts" and social life reduced to the instrumental activity of "networking." One respondent's acknowledgment that it was "important to have a well-packaged wife" (493) illustrates how even marriage can become an extension of career.

An important issue frequently neglected, but central to the foregoing debates, is that of gender. Feminist studies reveal how gendered assumptions about time and space are historically embedded in the traditional sexual division of labor that emerged with the onset of the industrial revolution (Adam 1990). The "Fordist" model of time described by Thompson presupposed a male breadwinner working standard hours in full-time life-time employment for the "family wage," while women managed home and family, performing the primary tasks of housework, child rearing, and servicing the male breadwinner (Davies 1990). Organized male labor reinforced the gendered nature of workplace discipline through exclusionary labor market practices (Cockburn 1983; Walby 1986). Feminist studies demonstrate that domestic work often constitutes unfree time for women and a source of power for men. Eli Zaretsky (1976), for example, shows how the historical shift from feudalism to industrial capitalism removed production from the home and created a view of the family as a "private" area entirely separate from the economy.

Such deeply embedded gendered assumptions about the temporal organization of home and work continue to be influential. Typically, women still take primary responsibility for domestic matters. The growing "flexibilization" of work (part-time, temporary, and outsourced employment) has reduced the number of male manual workers and increased the number of female breadwinners. It has also increased the tension between paid work and family commitments (Hochschild 1997). Carol Buswell and Sarah Jenkins (1994) argue that time is used to segregate women in the workplace—they are more likely to work part-time—and that the current speeding up of workplace processes is primarily accomplished by men who are "using the fuel of women's time" (90) both at work and at home. David Collinson (1998) highlights various ways that offshore employment had negative "spillover" effects for North Sea oil-rig workers' "personal" lives. This research found that the economic pressures (job insecurity, fixed-term contracts, lack of sick pay) and "time-space pressures" (managing home and work, marital relations, commuting to the North Sea) of offshore work spilled over into workers' domestic lives, significantly eroding the quantity and quality of their "free" time and intensifying the pressure on family relations.

Paul Glennie and Nigel Thrift (1996) argue that women's lives have fundamentally and radically different temporal structures than men's, featuring less linear temporal structures, ones associated with birth and beginnings, mothering, and the care of others. Arguing that time is more relational for women, they link "the body" to the experience and understanding of time. Similarly, Mary O'Brien (1981) suggests that because men do not give birth, they do not have the intimate connection to past and future that women have. Anne Marie Cunningham (1986) contends that menstruation reminds women of "the biological deadline," which in turn prompts them to think more about the future than men. Judith Lorber (1994) argues that women's experience of time may be primarily cyclical, whereas men's is more linear. Jeff Hearn (1992) observes that time and space, travel and movement, speed and image are central to men's sexualities. For men, speed is often erotic and sexy as is the distanced gaze on the objectified female body; as he elaborates, "the more distant, the more erotic, the more erotic, the better" (198).

In some of the feminist literature there is a tendency to talk of "men's time" and "women's time," as if they were fundamentally different, biologically-based categories. Such an approach tends to romanticize women's bodies and neglects the extent to which difference is socially constructed. Equally, a one-dimensional focus on gender distinctions in relation to time can neglect differences between men and between women, for example, according to class, ethnicity, nationality, age, and so on. Hence, while acknowledging (socially constructed) gender differences in relation to time and space, we would question the use of essentialist statements regarding the very nature of time discipline and gender. Universalizing assertions, that exclusively emphasize differences between men and women may well reinforce the very distinctions and stereotypes they seek to critique.

Most studies of time discipline in the workplace address the temporal monitoring of manual labour. There has been very little consideration of temporality in relation to management.[1] This chapter explores how managers, like workers, may also be subject to temporal controls introduced by corporate leaders. The case-study material explores the impact of time discipline on managers and their survival strategies within a major U.K. insurance company. Before outlining our empirical findings, we now discuss the background to this research project.

## THE TIME-DISCIPLINE OF MANAGERS

Our empirical analysis is based on a three-year (1993 to 1996) research project designed to address the impact of corporate restructuring on managerial careers. The case-study company illustrates wider patterns of restructuring that occurred during the 1990s. In both the United Kingdom and the United States, (middle) managerial labor became highly disposable (Cascio 1993). This represents a dramatic change, since throughout the twentieth century it had always been manual workers who were most vulnerable to layoffs.[2] Widespread restructuring saw high levels of "corporate liposuction," in which senior executives sought to "slim down" the "bulky" middle layers of their organizations. In 1991 alone, nearly one million U.S. managers earning over forty thousand dollars lost their jobs (Cascio 1993). The paternalistic exchange relationship of undivided managerial loyalty in return for a lifetime career had disappeared (Heckscher 1995; Hallier and Lyon 1996). In many ways these were indeed "hard times for the salariat" (Burrell 1996).

At the beginning of the project, the case-study organization employed over 8,500 people, including approximately 500 managers. The study combined a questionnaire survey of 50 managerial respondents (30 women and 20 men) in both the general insurance and life insurance divisions of the company with semistructured in-depth follow-up interviews. Our initial intention was to survey and interview a similar number of men and women, but 10 male managers did not complete the questionnaire and were therefore not interviewed. It was a condition of research access that the Personnel Department compiled the names of the cross section of middle managers who participated in the research. All the respondents or interviewees were either currently employed in the life and general insurance divisions or had recently been made redundant.

Research interviews were conducted after the "delayering"—that is, layoffs of middle managers—exercises commenced and repeat sessions were undertaken with all respondents (to explore subsequent changes). All interviewees were assured that their comments would be treated confidentially. The main topics covered in the survey and in all the interviews were career histories and progression; management style and culture; relations between managers and between managers and subordinates; gender relations in management; and the impact, if any, of corporate restructuring on all these processes. Extensive information was also collected from interviews with the two full-time staff union officials and two elected representatives, all of whom were interviewed on several occasions over the course of the research.

This chapter emphasizes the importance of time discipline for the critical examination of leadership. While leadership has been the focus of considerable research (such as trait, styles, contingency, and situational leadership, "new leadership," action-centered leadership), studies have tended to concentrate on "charismatic," "inspirational," and "transformational" leaders. This literature has also been rather leader-centric, failing to recognize that the leadership process involves a relationship between leaders and led. Few studies critically examine leadership, leaders' strategies of power and control, or the potentially detrimental effects of their policies and practices on the complex dynamics that characterize leader-led relations. In our case study, successive company CEOs were concerned to reduce costs and exercise power by restructuring workplace temporality. In particular, they utilized three interrelated strategies of time discipline that had a significant impact on middle management: age restructuring, work intensification, and the erosion of "free" time, as we now elaborate.

## WORKPLACE CHANGE AND
## AGE RESTRUCTURING

During the 1990s the U.K. insurance industry experienced unprecedented technological, economic, and structural changes. Like the vast majority of its competitors, our case-study company had been undergoing "major reorganization." In many ways simply a euphemism for branch closures and large-scale redundancies, these "reorganizations" were designed to cut costs. Within an eight-year period, five different CEOs were appointed, creating considerable upheaval in leadership styles, strategic vision, and corporate culture. All appointed on three-to-five-year rolling contracts, even CEOs were now subject to increasing time discipline. These changes had the effect of eroding trust and reinforcing a division between middle and senior managers. Since even highly productive employees had been laid off, middle managers no longer knew what they had to do to survive in the organization. They no longer trusted those in leadership positions.

At a "managers' conference" in November 1992, a new American CEO in the life sales division announced the closure of eleven (several of which were profitable) of the one hundred branches across the country. This meeting became notorious throughout the company as "the survivors' conference"—a watershed symbolizing the shift toward a more competitive and aggressive organizational culture. Informed only that the conference would explain the reorganization, all senior managers were required to attend. On arrival, they were individually interviewed by more senior managers and informed whether they had retained a place in the restructured company. Those who had were instructed to attend the conference, while the rest, who had lost their jobs, were told to leave immediately. The conference was held on a Friday. Those who had lost their jobs were told to return their company cars on Saturday morning and bring their car keys to reception, where any personal belongings cleared out of their offices would be waiting for them.

For middle managers job loss was a fundamental shock to their entire sense of personal identity as well as financial security. As discussed earlier, time crucially shapes notions of career, identity, and a sense of personal linear progression. When this is undermined by company practices, individuals can feel betrayed. One manager stated, "It was the biggest culture shock since I started working for the company twenty years ago." Another long-serving manager employed with the company for over fifteen years questioned the procedure, only to be told, "If you can't take the pace then you had better leave; we have to cut costs and this is the quickest way." There appeared to be no consistent, rational or work-related basis to explain the survival or departure of particular individuals. A language of death began to permeate research interviews, replete with talk of "survivors," those who "hadn't made it" and even jokes about human resources being renamed "human remains."

Eighteen months later, in 1994, a second restructuring exercise was initiated. Although senior managers guaranteed no compulsory redundancies, many middle managers' jobs were downgraded and the vast majority were reevaluated and their responsibilities increased. In some cases managerial workloads doubled. A third wave of restructuring occurred in 1995, when another five hundred redundancies at all levels were announced, and the after-effects of this exercise were compounded in the spring of 1996 when a further five hundred redundancies were implemented. Within this four-year period over 25 percent of the managerial-level employees lost their jobs. Restructuring had particularly detrimental effects on women managers. For example, the first two women life assurance sales managers in the company, promoted to manager grade in the 1980s, were made redundant despite outstanding performance records. This reestablished an all-male sales-management team (see Collinson and Collinson 1996).

These processes reflected an increasing leadership preoccupation with cost reduction through intensified time discipline. Central to this cost-cutting agenda was the restructuring of the age profile of middle management.[3] Unlike in the United States, there is currently no legislation in the United Kingdom outlawing age discrimination, although this may soon be changing as a result of forthcoming European legislation. Older managers with long service records seemed to be especially vulnerable to being laid off. After restructuring, the average age of the management team went down considerably. Indeed, in the life insurance division, the average age of the entire workforce dropped to twenty-five. As one manager commented, "Why do they want someone at forty-seven when they can pay a lot less for someone who is twenty-seven? The company thinks it's better to get younger people in on shorter contracts."

These time-disciplinary processes were exemplified by several cases of managerial layoffs. A number of branch managers were offered lower-status sales jobs in other parts of the company network. In some cases they had already moved several times in reaching managerial status and their families were now settled in one particular locality. Yet they had to move house, uprooting their families, to go to a lower-status position with a drop in salary and other benefits. In effect they were being offered a demotion, and in a different part of the country. By making such offers to long-serving managers that they hoped would be refused, corporate leaders encouraged these more experienced managers to resign. This would save the company considerable sums in statutory redundancy payments.

This deliberate targeting of older managers was informed by the leadership's concern to reduce the average age of its managerial team, not least because they believed that managers over forty were much more vulnerable to heart attack and other serious illnesses that could be costly to the organization. As this was an insurance company, it is hardly surprising that such life-course data were available to the company leadership. Another consideration was that younger managers, those seeking to develop a career in the company, were perceived to be more flexible, malleable, and willing to sacrifice their personal time for the good of the company. These age-related practices illustrate the extent to which leaders' concerns to restructure workplace time significantly shaped the layoff process. They utilized the restructuring processes to transform the age profile of middle management.[4] These findings suggest that age may be an increasingly important facilitator of time discipline in the context of managerial work.

## WORK INTENSIFICATION

Work intensification was a second key feature of leaders' time discipline of middle managers. Flatter hierarchies and slimmer management numbers resulted in managerial survivors' working longer hours. In his opening address at the aforementioned "survivors' conference," the new CEO emphasized the need to refocus on more stringent company targets and the need for almost unlimited employee commitment. His evangelical corporate message described the restructuring as a "major reorganization intended to strengthen the company's sales and distribution network." He stated that the reorganization was "a good exercise in motivation"; remaining managers should recognize that they had been successful in a very competitive process, with "only the best people" being selected as part of the restructured "leaner" and "healthier" company. No mention was made of the managers who had lost their jobs.

Surviving managers were now expected to operate with fewer subordinates. Once one manager made a significant cut in staff numbers, others felt pressured to do likewise. Any managers who refused to "downsize" their departments or branches were immediately under scrutiny. With fewer managers, those who survived the cuts had to work longer hours in order to process the increased amounts of information and data now on their desks. The CEO also made it abundantly clear that he did not expect any managers to "Arrive home in time to bathe the baby." This was a key statement defining the new culture of long working hours. Senior managers echoed the CEO's message, making explicit statements about the need for managers in particular to "set an example" and work longer hours, especially in the evening.

Although some managers, especially those in more junior positions, questioned these increased time pressures, many responded by working longer hours during the week and at weekends and by minimizing holiday entitlement and sickness absence. Working long hours was not only the leadership's stated policy, and necessary to cope with the expanded managerial workloads, but for some managers it also was central to the construction of workplace identity. They embraced the leaders' intensified time discipline. Some male respondents viewed staying late as a way of constructing a heroic reputation as a highly committed manager. Evening work especially was used as a means of defining those with commitment, endurance, and toughness. Where managers who arrived early to work might not be seen by colleagues, those working late could be conspicuously displayed within the managerial pecking order. Time sacrifice was viewed as confirmation of masculine and hierarchical identity. Hence, though working long hours was primarily an explicit leadership policy it was also reinforced by managerial identity strategies.

Middle managers also became increasingly competitive with one another. Some managers developed reputations for starting meetings late in the day. One interviewee explained how, once a senior manager began working late on a regular basis, middle managers felt obliged to do the same. "Politically it's now more important to be seen working late rather than starting early. People are beginning to compete with each other on how long they work in the evenings." It was common for most managers' cars to be still parked in the company car park at eight o'clock every night. Research respondents repeatedly commented on the growing need to "stand out" and "be noticed" by their superiors. They observed how managers were vying with each other to be thought of as effective. One manager stated that in formal meetings colleagues seemed to be primarily concerned with finding ways of criticizing one another.

In the context of this highly politicized, competitive, and insecure working environment, middle managers also learned new survival strategies designed to create the impression of continuous workplace presence. Within the open-plan offices the most common strategy was to leave jackets on chairs during the day and overnight. One manager kept two jackets at work, one that he wore and the other that he left on the back of his chair during absences. In other cases managers left car keys on their desk and traveled home either by public transport or by using their spare car keys. Managers who had their own private office left their door open with both the light and the computer switched on after they had left for the day. All these strategies were intended to give the impression that managers were still working. When they actually did leave the building some managers made it abundantly clear that they were taking work home to process in the evening. Hence, in the context of leaders' intensified time discipline, many middle managers believed that impression management was the key underlying criterion for organizational survival.

Junior managers were less likely to accept corporate demands for increased hours and availability in the office. They criticized their senior counterparts for adopting highly aggressive management styles, for sacrificing ever greater amounts of personal time and for expecting them to do the same. One junior woman manager stated, "We need to get rid of the view that the more hours you work, the better manager you are and that this is necessary for promotion." A junior male manager commented, "I don't see why a career in management should involve long hours. I would not want to pursue this route if it impacted even further on my social and family life." He observed that he could not remember the last time he had a meal with his partner. Another manager acknowledged that his wife was complaining that she never saw him during the week.

The leadership's policy of work intensification had destructive consequences, not only for relations between managers but also for managers and their families. Under this enormous pressure, some managers became ill and had to have time off work. However, they also felt unable to disclose the reasons for this, fearing that it would be seen as a sign of "weakness." One woman manager observed, "People are scared to ask for help because no help is available. Most managers are scared." Managers therefore had to engage in further impression-management survival strategies. Absenteeism was now subject to much tighter scrutiny. Managers on long-term sickness absence were required to undergo a medical examination by the company's own doctor. The general secretary of the staff union confirmed that "stress levels in management are going through the roof." He added, "Managers fear if they admit to stress it's the kiss of death certainly for their careers and possibly even for their jobs. So if they have to have time off work for stress they'll say they had flu for two weeks. If a manager complains he is under stress, the company says, 'You can't manage.' In the old days if managers got burnt-out, the company would give them the time off but now managers know if they are taken ill, the company will be looking to get rid of them."

New technology also facilitated work intensification. Managers and salespeople were required to use cell phones, carphones, answerphones, email, and pagers and were expected to be contactable at all times via at least one of these media. As one manager observed sardonically, "I never thought there would come a time when my boss would expect to talk to me when I was on the toilet." In new premises built to house the general insurance division, clocks were banned from all office walls and desks as part of a managerial policy encouraging people to work hard and avoid clock watching.

## THE EROSION OF "FREE" TIME

For surviving managers, time sacrifice and workplace visibility were not only primary measures of managerial commitment but also were major sources of tension and stress. Work intensification undermined the possibility of achieving any kind of balance between work and life. To differing degrees all interviewees talked about the problems of managing home and work. Temporal pressures reinforced the dominant masculine culture of management in which employment and domestic life are kept largely separate with the latter subordinated to the former. In terms of "free" time, these relatively senior-level employees were indeed impoverished.

Believing that "presenteeism" and constant availability may be effective survival strategies, most managers prioritized paid work commitments above all other "personal" concerns. When describing the significant pressures of his work, one manager joked that he simply made "guest appearances at home." Another male manager outlined how, after informing his immediate superior that he intended to take the final week of his annual vacation as intermittent single days to fit in with domestic commitments, the former replied, "Oh, so you don't really need these holidays, then?"[5] The pressure to be present at work became particularly acute for managers who could not comply with its requirements. One manager described how his wife had recently recovered from a severe bout of postnatal depression after the birth of their second child, as he elaborated: "The strain has been awful, what with the long hours and the weekend working. I didn't feel that I could tell anyone at work as it might be seen as weakness on my part that I was feeling the strain." In certain cases the corporate demands to be present at work had even resulted in the breakdown of marriages.

The most senior woman manager in the company had a reputation for working very long hours. One of the other senior women managers confirmed that she herself sometimes worked up to nineteen consecutive days until ten o'clock in the evening, also working two weekends a quarter. "Without a very supportive husband

I would find it hard to combine career and marriage," she added. Another senior woman manager believed there was no alternative but to comply with the long-hours culture: "There is a very macho culture of long hours now established in the company. If you resist it you won't get on. The rules are set and everyone knows them. It must be a problem for women with children."

Women managers were under particular pressure to minimize their use of statutory maternity leave.[6] Their "commitment" was judged by how long they worked during pregnancy and how soon they returned after having their baby. The pressure on women managers was so intense that after childbirth they found themselves returning to work and working long hours much sooner than anticipated. One commented that the commitment of women in senior positions was judged by how long they worked during pregnancy and how soon they returned after having their baby, adding, "One woman was actually in work the day her baby was due. She seemed to think we would be impressed!" Another woman manager complained, "There is an informal culture which states that if women in management are going to insist on having children, then they must do so with the minimum impact on the smooth running of management. This culture is stronger than any formal entitlements which women may have." Women managers were placed under enormous pressure to prioritize the interests of the organization above the welfare of themselves and their child. Working in this highly competitive, adversarial managerial culture, women managers felt an added pressure to be present, believing that absence for long periods could leave them vulnerable either to criticism or to missing out on recognition that was rightfully theirs. Wanting to ensure that projects were not reallocated and taken out of their control, all the senior women managers tried to protect themselves by maximizing their workplace presence and by not taking full maternity leave.

Junior women managers criticized their more senior female counterparts for reinforcing the informal culture that was undermining statutory maternity provision. One junior woman manager complained about the considerable pressure she was placed under by her female senior manager to relinquish statutory maternity leave. She described how, after she had worked until three weeks before giving birth, "There was a lot of pressure to return. She would ring and ask when I was thinking of returning. I managed to hold out for four months." Junior women managers pointed to the fact that the only woman senior manager in the personnel department had not taken full maternity leave; one stated: "Senior male managers hold her up as an example for women in management. What chance is there for us to take full maternity leave with this example held over us?"

In order to comply with work intensification, the senior women managers with children relied on extensive child-care support. In pursuing their managerial careers, these women had to employ other women to look after their children. Yet all of them had concerns about the child care they purchased. One senior woman manager who had two children stated that many nannies did not want to work for the extended periods necessary to support her employment patterns. Rather than question the long-hours requirement, however, this manager criticized the attitudes of nannies. She discussed in some detail the problem of "finding suitable nannies" who would be willing to respond flexibly to the long hours she worked. Emphasizing the "real problems in choosing someone to bring up your children," she added, "I have a career. We have to work around the long hours. I have just hired my fifth nanny this year. The others just weren't suitable."[7]

Junior managers were particularly frustrated about the lack of balance between "work" and "home." One complained, "I would like to spend more time at home. The long hours are a real problem." Another junior male manager resisted the work patterns expected of managerial-level employees. Preferring to start work at 7:45 A.M. and leave at 5:30 P.M., he experienced the disciplinary sarcasm of (male) colleagues. His work schedule was not only compatible with domestic responsibilities, but, in his view, was also more productive because there were fewer office distractions early in the morning. However, evening work for managers had now become so pervasive that his departure was quickly noticed by many late-working colleagues, as he explained: "Every evening I get comments like 'set your watches everyone, Dean's leaving' and 'We'll book you in for a half day's holiday.' It seems someone always draws attention to the fact. Nobody acknowledges that I am in before everyone else. You see the boss always leaves late so everyone else does too." These comments illustrate the difficulties for managers seeking to balance the responsibilities of paid work with those of their personal lives.

In sum, the leadership's explicit policy of intensified time discipline had a particularly adverse effect on the ability of men and women managers to retain any kind of balance between home and work. By continuing to erode "free time," corporate leaders were breaking down the time-space differentiation between office and domicile. However, although domestic life was increasingly circumscribed, it remained crucially important to many employees as a back region of private time, a means of perceived escape, respite, and refuge from the demands of the workplace. These findings provide some support for Giddens's (1987) contention that time can never be fully commodified. Yet the impact of delayering processes also graphically illustrates that "private" time is interdependent with the "public" sphere of paid work. By attempting to sustain a complete separation between home and work, individuals may try to deny an inescapable interdependence between these two spheres. It may be that the home is rarely the "free" space it is often assumed to be.

## POSTSCRIPT

At the end of our research project we presented a preliminary verbal report outlining the contradictions of delayering and work intensification. When the project commenced, senior managers requested that a written report of the findings be presented. Yet following the presentation and having agreed with the foregoing description of these dynamics, a company director stated, "There is no going back. We intend to have a flexible and cost-effective management structure. This is how we want the company run. So there is no need to put your report in writing." His reaction demonstrates the extent to which those in leadership positions were aware of the effects of their policies. Leaders acknowledged that work intensification and delayering reinforced divisions and internal competition within the managerial structure. This is turn produced a highly politicized and defensive managerial culture of insecurity, individualism, and mistrust. Yet in their determination to change the culture, the company's leaders remained indifferent to these consequences or their policies' impact on employees.

## DISCUSSION

The foregoing research findings suggest that managerial work in contemporary organizations, like manual labor since the industrial revolution, is increasingly subject to temporal discipline. Twenty five years ago Rosabeth Moss Kanter (1977) observed that managers' contribution to production is usually indirect, and thus what they do and how well they do it are frequently contentious issues. She suggested that because of the difficulties in assessing and quantifying their contribution, social credentials and gender considerations often become "substitutes for ability measures in management positions" (61). In recent times, corporate leaders have increasingly been concerned to evaluate middle managerial performance. As Kanter might argue, working long hours and increased workplace visibility, like social credentials and gender, may constitute important substitutes for ability measures in contemporary organizations.

A small number of studies suggest that leaders in other organizations increasingly see work intensification and time surveillance as an effective measure of managerial performance, providing a more tangible means of calculating managerial commitment than previously used measures. In the United States both Vicki Smith (1990) and Robert Jackall (1988) document how the corporate emphasis on working long hours and achieving stringent output targets intensified after large-scale redundancies. Cynthia Epstein et al. (1995) found that some male lawyers in New York City wasted time during the day and instead worked late into the evening. Whereas women tried to use their working time more efficiently, many men only started working in the late afternoons in the hope that senior partners would notice them as especially industrious. Similarly, in the United Kingdom, Tony Watson (2000) reveals how corporate expectations of working long hours, especially in the evening, were central to notions of managerial "commitment." Male managers in particular deliberately stayed at work late into the evening, wasted time, artificially extended meetings, and criticized managers who left at, say, 7:15 P.M. Ray Pahl (1995) describes the neurotic, compulsive characteristics of "successful" businessmen who, in their obsession with work and the "search for glory," displayed consistent patterns of working long hours, taking few holidays, and being detached from the home. Angela Coyle (1995) argues that managers' working long hours was a key feature in all five U.K. organizations in which she conducted research. Similarly, Judy Marshall (1995) found that, having experienced male-dominated cultures in management, the women managers she interviewed decided to move on, in many cases to build a life more balanced between home and work.

Increased temporal demands may intensify workplace stress, which in turn can lead to greater inefficiency, sickness, and absenteeism (Bartle et al. 1995). In 1996 a Japanese advertising agency was ordered to pay £790,000 compensation to the family of a junior manager, Ichiro Oshima, who killed himself after working seventeen months without taking a day off, getting as little as half an hour's sleep per night (Michie and Cockroft 1996). In Japan, suicide through overwork has been given a specific name, "Karoshi," a reflection of its prevalence in that country. In U.K. tribunal cases, workplace stress is now treated like any other health hazard. Employers have a legal duty to ensure that employees' health is not put at risk through excessive stress. The *British Medical Journal* has argued that long working hours can endanger physical as well as mental health and safety in the workplace (Michie and Cockroft 1996).[8] Research also suggests that those working long hours are more likely to die from coronary heart disease (Cartwright and Cooper 1997). In a landmark case in the United Kingdom (*Walker v. Northumberland County Council,* 1995) an industrial tribunal awarded damages of £175,000 to a social services manager who had two nervous breakdowns as a result of continual work intensification. In sum, a growing number of studies suggest that increased time surveillance and intensification in the workplace may have detrimental physiological, psychological, and personal as well as cultural and organizational consequences.

## CONCLUSION

This chapter has examined the impact of increasing time discipline on middle managers. It has described the extension of time discipline to relatively senior grades of the organization previously immune from close surveillance. The foregoing analysis suggests that in post-restructuring cultures unprecedented levels of time-surveillance are now being applied to middle managers—traditionally the very function required to supervise and control labor through "time and motion" studies and other forms of scientific management. In particular, the chapter has explored the age restructuring of management through delayering, the increasing demands on surviving managers to work longer hours, and the erosion of their "free" time. We have also discussed surviving managers' responses to these time disciplines and the gendered dynamics embedded in the discursive practices of post-restructuring cultures. Surviving managers were increasingly subject to temporal discipline. Managerial selves were "saturated" (Gergen 1991) with increased workloads, information, and time-space pressures within a workplace culture where reputation and image were prioritized and increasingly insecure (see also Collinson 2003). Middle managers had no time to stand back and reflect upon their everyday practices. They were too busy surviving the next restructuring exercise and its ensuing intensified time discipline.

It might be objected that managers have always been expected to work more flexibly and longer than other employees. Certainly corporate leaders have sought to sustain the temporal flexibility of managers, usually by leaving open-ended the contractual length of a manager's working day. While there is no doubt that the politics of time, presence, and availability in the workplace has a long and somewhat neglected history, our argument concentrates on the relatively unique workplace events of restructuring and demotions over the past decade and their specific effects on the informal dynamics of managerial cultures. It is in this unprecedented climate, where managerial job insecurity appears to be greater than ever before (LaNuez and Jermier 1994) and where managers may have fewer options to take positions elsewhere, that leaders' time discipline of managers has reached new levels of intensity.

In conclusion, we wish to highlight two particularly important organizational consequences of this intensified time surveillance. One is the tendency for these developments to reinforce significant inequalities and insecurities within managerial structures and between managerial levels. A division appears to be growing between "corporate leaders," who concentrate on broad-ranging strategic issues, and middle and junior managers, who supervise and are increasingly responsible for the complex and frequently contradictory task of policy implementation in localized contexts and practices. At the same time as the work of many middle managers has been intensified and they are increasingly monitored and rendered insecure, those in corporate leadership positions typically retain job security and in many widely reported cases have received substantial salary increases.[9] Corporate leaders exercise power and control by defining the strategy of the organization and by then monitoring how well middle managers are able to implement these "strategic visions" through particular localized practices. The foregoing research findings highlight the concern of corporate leaders to increase their control of middle managers through age restructuring, the monitoring of long hours working, and their giving up of "free time" such as holidays and flexdays.

The second important implication of this analysis is the gendered consequences of leaders' time discipline in terms of intensified work demands, the difficulties of managing home and work, and the erosion of statutory maternity leave. Women managers in particular experienced enormous pressure as they tried to manage home, family, career, and paid work in their nonstop schedules. The interpretation of working long hours as a heroic expression of masculinity reflected and reinforced the continued male domination of managerial positions. Most important, the informal erosion of statutory maternity leave had particularly crucial consequences for workplace gender equality. This provision, part of the U.K. Sex Discrimination Act, introduced in 1975, was designed to assist women in combining career and family. Hence, despite women's inroads into managerial grades, our analysis suggests that prevailing managerial structures, cultures, and practices may actually reinforce, as well as be shaped by, the norms defining masculinity that historically have dominated management and leadership (Roper 1994; Collinson and Hearn 1996). Although restructuring and time discipline might undermine men's managerial power in one sense, in other they could also bolster it, by reinforcing a culture of "masculinity" within management. Time discipline may contribute to a "remasculinization" of management in which women managers at all hierarchical levels will only survive if they follow the example of most of their male counterparts and subordinate home and family to company and career.

## NOTES

1. One exception here is Gibson Burrell's (1992) critical examination of the management-of-change literature, where he questions taken-for-granted conceptions of temporal linearity. A small number of other exceptional studies are discussed later in this chapter.

2. In the United Kingdom the term "redundancy" refers to the loss of employment through no fault of one's own. In the United States the term "layoff" is more commonly used.

3. Historically, hierarchical progression has been closely related to age, especially for male employees. Yet recently this connection between age and status has been eroded, especially in managerial hierarchies. The "delayering" of management has impacted particularly those aged forty and over. The 1990s may be seen as a period during which many "middle managers" ceased to be "middle-aged." Increasingly, during the 1990s, there has been a growing awareness that in, for example, banking, accounting, or sales, managers are seldom over fifty years of age (Industrial Relations Services 1997). This privileging of the younger manager reflects a "culture of youthism," or valorization of youthful attributes, which is increasingly apparent in many aspects of society. Typically, the younger managers are held to be more dynamic and flexible than their older counterparts, who are caricatured as cynical and resistant to change (Hallier and Lyon 1996).

4. The loss of work available to the older, in particular the older male, worker over the last 25 years has been well documented. Age and work have primarily been addressed in terms of ageism and age discrimination, coupled with theories of retirement and early exit. In recent times within the U.K. economy the older worker has increasingly become a core member of the "reserve army of labour"; targeted by industry-led initiatives as candidates suitable primarily for insecure or "secondary" work, typically within the service sector.

5. Two other male managers described how, as they prepared to leave on the first morning of their vacation, they received telephone calls from superiors requiring them to come into work and to postpone holiday arrangements for a few days. When they arrived at the office, it was evident to them that there was no pressing need to be at work. These managers believed that disrupting their vacations was a test of their willingness to prioritize the organization above and beyond personal and family interests.

6. In the United Kingdom all pregnant women in paid employment in private- and public-sector organizations have the right to fourteen

weeks' maternity leave and to decide when maternity leave begins, provided that this is not before the eleventh week prior to the birth of the baby. In addition, women with a minimum of two years' service at the beginning of the eleventh week before their baby is due are entitled to delay their return to paid work for up to twenty-nine weeks after their baby's birth. Women who have twenty-six weeks' service at the fifteenth week before their baby is due also qualify for statutory maternity leave, which is payable at two rates: 90 percent of average weekly earnings for the first six weeks and a specific amount for the following twelve weeks. Women who take fourteen weeks' general maternity leave have the right to return to exactly the same job as before, while those who return from extended maternity absence are entitled to return to work of the same nature, in the same capacity, and in the same place as their former position.

7.    The employment of women by women illustrates the analytical importance of class differences between women generally and the pay differentials between women managers and the nannies they hire more particularly. Indeed, in the case of nannies these power and identity differences may also be ethnic, cultural, and national and may take economic or symbolic forms.

8.    British employees work by far the longest and most unsocial hours in the European Union. The United Kingdom is the only member state where the length of the workweek has increased over the past decade. A quarter of British men employed in industry and services worked more than forty-eight hours per week and this was three times the proportions in Germany, France, Italy, the Benelux, and Denmark (Bartle et al. 1995). In October 1998 the European Union Working Time Directive limited the working week to forty-eight hours unless employees signed away their rights. Yet since that date, numerous surveys continue to highlight the long hours worked in the United Kingdom and the detrimental impact this has on all aspects of family and private time.

9.    In some instances CEOs have also benefited financially from downsizing because share prices tend to increase when layoffs are announced and senior managers and executives usually own company shares as part of their remuneration package. Indeed according to *Business Week's* 2003 salary survey, companies with the largest layoff program also had the highest-paid CEOs. The survey found that in 2003 CEOs earn more than 280 times their average employee, compared with forty-two times in 1982. Equally, when CEOs are fired or are forced to resign, they typically receive enormous "golden handshakes" (Collinson and Hearn 1996).

# REFERENCES

Adam, Barbara. 1990. *Time and Social Theory*. Cambridge: Polity Press.

Ancona, Deborah G., Paul S. Goodman, Barbara S. Lawrence, and Michael L. Tushman. 2001. "Time: A New Research Lens." *Academy of Management Review*. 26(4): 645–63.

Baldamus, Wilhelm. 1961. *Efficiency and Effort*. London: Tavistock.

Bartle, Martin, Ivan Briscoe, Geoff Mulgan, Zina Sar-Wiwa, Joanna Wade, and Helen Wilkinson. 1995. *The Time Squeeze*. London: Demos.

Bell, Emma. 2001. "The Social Time of Organizational Payment Systems." *Time and Society* 10(1): 45–62.

Berger, Peter L., Brigitte Berger, and Hansfried Kellner. 1973. *The Homeless Mind*. London: Penguin.

Berger, Peter L., and Thomas Luckmann. 1967. *The Social Construction of Reality*. Harmondsworth: Penguin.

Beynon, Huw. 1980. *Working for Ford*. Harmondsworth: Penguin.

Braverman, Harry. 1974. *Labor and Monopoly Capital: The Degradation of Work in the Twentieth Century*. New York: Monthly Review Press.

Burawoy, Michael. 1979. *Manufacturing Consent*. Chicago: University of Chicago Press.

Burrell, Gibson. 1988. "Modernism, Postmodernism and Organizational Analysis. Part 2: The Contribution of Michel Foucault." *Organization Studies* 9(2): 221–35.

———. 1992. "Back to the Future: Time and Organisation." In *Rethinking Organization,* edited by Michael Reed and Michael Hughes. London: Sage.

———. 1996. "Hard Times for the Salariat?" In *The Management of Expertise,* edited by Harry Scarbrough. London: Macmillan.

Buswell, Carol, and Sarah Jenkins. 1994. "Equal Opportunity Policies, Employment and Patriarchy." *Gender, Work and Organization* 1(2): 83–93.

Callaghan, George, and Paul Thompson. 2002. "We Recruit Attitude: The Selection and Shaping of Routine Call Centre Labor." *Journal of Management Studies* 39(2): 233–54.

Cartwright, Sue, and Carey Cooper. 1997. *Managing Workplace Stress*. London: Sage.

Cascio, Wayne F. 1993. "Downsizing: What Do We Know? What Have We Learned?" *Academy of Management Executive* 7(1): 95–104.

Clark, Peter. 1990. "Chronological Codes and Organisational Analysis." In *The Theory and Philosophy of Organisations,* edited by John Hassard and Dennis Pym. London: Routledge.

Cockburn, Cynthia. 1983. *Brothers*. London: Pluto Press.

Collinson, David L. 1992. *Managing the Shopfloor: Subjectivity, Masculinity and Workplace Culture*. Berlin: Walter de Gruyter.

———. 1998. "Shifting Lives: Work-Home Pressures in the North Sea Oil Industry." *Canadian Review of Sociology and Anthropology* 35(3): 301–24.

———. 2000 "Strategies of Resistance: Power, Knowledge and Subjectivity in the Workplace." In *Work and Society,* edited by Keith Grint. Cambridge: Polity Press.

———. 2003 "Identities and Insecurities: Selves at Work." *Organization* 10(3): 527–47.

Collinson, David L., and Jeff Hearn, eds. 1996. *Men as Managers, Managers as Men*. London: Sage.

Collinson, Margaret, and David L. Collinson. 1996. "It's Only Dick: The Sexual Harassment of Women Managers in Insurance Sales." *Work, Employment and Society* 10(1): 29–56.

Coyle, Angela. 1995. "Women and Organisational Change." Research Discussion Series paper no. 14. Manchester, U.K.: Equal Opportunities Commission.

Cunha, Miguel Pina. 2004. "Organizational Time: A Dialectical View." *Organization* 11(20): 271–96.

Cunningham, Anne Marie. 1986. "The Time Pressured Life." In *Organizational Reality: Reports from the Firing Line,* edited by Peter Frost, Vance F. Mitchell, and Walter R. Nord. Glenview, Ill.: Scott, Foresman.

Davies, Karen. 1990. *Women and Time: Weaving the Strands of Everyday Life*. Aldershot, U.K.: Avebury.

Epstein, Cynthia Fuchs, and Arne L. Kalleberg, 2001. "Time and the Sociology of Work." *Work and Occupations* 28(1): 5–17.

Epstein, Cynthia Fuchs, Robert Sauté, Bonnie Oglensky, and Martha Gever. 1995. "Glass Ceiling and Open Doors: Women's Advancement in the Legal Profession." *Fordham Law Review* 64(2): 291–449.

Fagan, Collete. 2001. "The Temporal Reorganization of Employment and the Household Rhythm of Work Schedules." *American Behavioral Scientist* 44(7): 1199–1213.

Fleming, Peter. 2002. "Diogenes Goes to Work: Culture, Cynicism, and Resistance in the Contemporary Workplace." Unpublished doctoral thesis. Department of Management, University of Melbourne, Australia.

Foucault, Michel. 1979. *Discipline and Punish*. Harmondsworth: Penguin.

Gergen, Kenneth. J. 1991. *The Saturated Self*. New York: Basic Books.

Giddens, Anthony. 1979. *Central Problems in Social Theory*. London: Macmillan.

———. 1984. *The Constitution of Society*. Cambridge: Polity Press.

————. 1987 *Social Theory and Modern Sociology*. Cambridge: Polity Press.

Glennie, Paul, and Nigel Thrift. 1996. "Re-working E. P. Thompson's 'Time, Work-Discipline and Industrial Capitalism.' " *Time and Society* 5(3): 275–300.

Goffman, Erving. 1968. *Asylums*. Harmondsworth: Penguin.

Grey, Chris. 1994. "Career as a Project of the Self and Labour Process Discipline." *Sociology* 28(2): 479–97.

Hallier, Jerry, and Phil Lyon. 1996. "Job Insecurity and Employee Commitment: Managers' Reactions to the Threat and Outcomes of Redundancy Selection." *British Journal of Management* 7(1): 107–23.

Harvey, David. 1990. *The Condition of Postmodernity*. Oxford: Blackwell.

Hassard, John. 2000. "Images of Time in Work and Organization." In *Work and Society*, edited by Keith Grint. Cambridge: Polity Press.

Hearn, Jeff. 1992. *Men in the Public Eye*. London: Routledge.

Heckscher, Walter. 1995. *White Collar Blues: Management Loyalties in an Age of Corporate Restructuring*. New York: Basic Books.

Heyes, Jason. 1997. "Annualised Hours and the 'Knock': The Organization of Working Time in a Chemical Plant." *Work, Employment and Society* 11(1): 65–81.

Hochschild, Arlie R. 1997. *The Time Bind: When Work Becomes Home and Home Becomes Work*. New York: Henry Holt.

Huy, Quy Nguyan. 2001 "Time, Temporal Capability and Planned Change." *Academy of Management Review* 26(4): 601–23.

Industrial Relations Services. 1997. "Barclays Removing Older Staff, Claims Unifi." *Industrial Relations Services Employment Trends* (February 1997): 5.

Jackall, Robert. 1988. *Moral Mazes: The World of Corporate Managers*. Oxford: Oxford University Press.

Kanter, Rosabeth Moss. 1977. *Men and Women of the Corporation*. New York: Basic Books.

LaNuez, Danny, and John Jermier. 1994. "Sabotage by Managers and Technocrats: Neglected Patterns of Resistance at Work." In *Resistance and Power in Organizations*, edited by John Jermier, David Knights, and Walter R. Nord. London: Routledge.

Leidner, Robin. 1993. *Fast Food, Fast Talk: Service Work and the Routinization of Everyday Life*. Berkeley: University of California Press.

Lorber, Judith. 1994. *Paradoxes of Gender*. New Haven: Yale University Press.

Mainemelis, Charalampos. 2001. "When the Muse Takes It All: A Model for the Experience of Timelessness in Organizations." *Academy of Management Review* 26(4): 548–65.

Marshall, Judy. 1995. *Women Managers Moving On*. London: Routledge.

Marx, Karl. 1971. *Capital*. Vol. 1. Reprint: London: Allen & Unwin.

Michie, Susan, and Anne Cockroft. 1996 "Overwork Can Kill." *British Medical Journal* 312: 921–22.

Nowotny, Helga. 1992. "Time and Social Theory: Towards a Theory of Time." *Time and Society* 3: 431–55.

O'Brien, Mary. 1981. *The Politics of Reproduction*. London: Routledge & Kegan Paul.

*Organization Studies*. 2002. Special issue on time and reflexivity. *Organization Studies* 23(6): entire issue.

Pahl, Ray. 1995. *After Success: Fin-de-Siècle Anxiety and Identity*. Cambridge: Polity Press.

Palm, Goran. 1979. *The Flight from Work*. Cambridge: Cambridge University Press.

Ritzer, George. 1996. *The McDonaldization of Society*. Thousand Oaks, Calif.: Pine Forge Press.

Roper, Michael. 1994. *Masculinity and the British Organization Man Since 1945*. Oxford: Oxford University Press.

Roy, Donald. 1958. "Banana Time: Job Satisfaction and Informal Interaction." *Human Organisation* 18: 158–68.

Sennett, Richard. 1998. *The Corrosion of Character: The Personal Consequences of Work in the New Capitalism*. New York: Norton.

Smith, Vicki. 1990. *Managing in the Corporate Interest: Control and Resistance in an American Bank*. Berkeley: University of California Press.

Theriault, Reg. 1995. *How to Tell When You Are Tired*. New York: Norton.

Thompson, Edward P. 1967. "Time, Work-Discipline and Industrial Capitalism." *Past and Present* 38: 56–97.

Urry, John. 1991. "Time and Space in Giddens' Social Theory." In *Giddens' Theory of Structuration*, edited by Chris Bryant and David Jary. London: Routledge.

Walby, Sylvia. 1986. *Patriarchy at Work*. Cambridge: Polity Press.

Watson, Tony. 2000. *In Search of Management*. London: Thomson.

Weber, Max. 1930/1958. *The Protestant Ethic and the Spirit of Capitalism*. London: Allen & Unwin.

Whip, Richard, Barbara Adam, and Ida Sabelis, eds. 2004. *Making Time: Time and Management in Modern Organizations*. Oxford: Blackwell.

Zaretsky, Eli. 1976. *Capitalism, the Family, and Personal Life*. London: Pluto Press.

— PART III —

# TIME NORMS, GENDER, AND WORK

— Chapter 9 —

# Gender, Work, and Time: Gender at Work and at Play in Futures Trading

## Peter Levin

URING A LULL following an extremely busy morning of futures trading on the floor of the American Commodities Exchange (ACE),[1] Nancy, a woman clerk at a large international bank, approached the trading pit and, angrily but matter-of-factly, told Carl, a broker, that he'd "better watch out if you're going to pick off my orders." This was a suggestion that Carl had been watching the woman use hand signals to relay her orders into the trading pit, and then, knowing what the bank intended to do, had traded ahead of those orders. It is an unethical and potentially illegal practice.

Carl, surprised by both her presence and her rather public warning, was indignant about being accused of shady trading. He was also being egged on by other men in the all-male trading pit: while a few snickered, one trader goaded him on, suggesting that it was "quite an accusation. Quite—an—accusation—indeed." Finally, Scott, another male trader in the pit, said to Carl, "What a bitch. What a fucking bitch." Scott then turned to me and said, "No stupid bitches allowed on the floor. They can't handle this. Put THAT in your thesis."

This incident conveys two key insights. First, this event elicited a particular gendered response—gendered in a temporal fashion. The context for this confrontation came during a lull, after a hectic morning of trading. Other men in the pit noticed and commented on this confrontation, which would not have occurred during a busier time, when attention would be on the market itself. The temporal discontinuities of the market—the market pace that oscillates between busy and slow—provide a key frame through which gender on the trading floor operates. This incident shows in situ what I intend to disentangle: that gender is sometimes invoked as *competence* and other times as *sexualized difference*. Gender in this context consists of the social relations that create and sustain differences between men and women. "Bitch," along with a handful of other offensive terms, refers explicitly to women. But it wasn't just that Nancy was a bitch. It was that she was a bitch who could not "handle this," referring to the work of making futures markets. Saying that she couldn't handle it, Scott made an argument about her (in)ability to get trades done in a fast market. Her performance was linked to her gender, and in key ways both were found wanting.

The second insight this incident conveys is that gender actually matters more in markets than the neoclassical vision of rational markets might lead us to believe. After all, the woman in question was a customer, a woman whose stream of market orders provided the livelihood for brokers in the trading pits. Scott, actually one of the main beneficiaries of Nancy's business, displayed an odd disjunction between his belief that women—or at least certain kinds of women—were not suitable for work on the trading floor and his own economic self-interest. If "ongoing social relations" (Granovetter 1985) are one of the bedrock foundations of how markets work, these are ongoing relations that are heavily marked by the social identity of gender.

My argument in this chapter is that participants on the ACE trading floor mobilize two distinct repertoires, or clusters, of meanings, beliefs, and practices to understand and articulate gender difference. When the market was moving and the emphasis of the floor was on work, people rarely referenced gender directly. They spoke instead about whether a trader or clerk was competent. When the market was slow, participants idled—standing around, making small talk, joking, waiting for something to happen. In this context, gender reemerged as sexualized differences between men and women. As clusters of meanings and practices, "competence" and "sexualized difference" were neither mutually exclusive nor temporally segregated. Sexuality did not fully become submerged during work times, nor did a person's skills and abilities somehow disappear when the market slowed down. Competence and sexualized differences nevertheless formed the basis for explaining who was a "good" market participant, who should or should not be part of the workplace community, and what kinds of success and failure people might expect to have.

The chapter further extends my earlier work on gender and temporality (Levin 2001) by explicitly connecting it to ways that gender becomes *contestable* on the ACE trading floor. To the extent that both gendered difference and competence were used both to refer to women and to designate women as less able *as a group* to compete on the floor with men *as a group,* these different gender repertoires extract a different toll. When gender is understood as sexualized difference, it is visible, invoked as an overt category of attention. Although this kind of gendering is overtly hostile and was often interpreted as fatiguing and relentless, it is also more visible and thus easier to deal with. Basing decisions about promotions, employment, and pay based on more overt forms of gender— to claim that a worker is unsuccessful simply because she is a woman—is illegitimate. But when gender is couched in language of "competence" it is more insidious and more difficult to contest. There is power in being able to claim that a worker is unsuccessful because he or she is inefficient, or incompetent. Paying attention to the ways gender gets folded into such gender-neutral concepts as competence, and how these processes are themselves folded into temporal patterns, forms the basis for understanding the ACE as a "gendered organization" (Acker 1990).

The distinction between these two gender repertoires map onto what Jean Comaroff and John Comaroff (1991) call "non-agentive" and "agentive" forms of power. Drawing on the work of Antonio Gramsci (1971), they argue that power operates on multiple levels. Some forms of power (non-agentive) are taken for granted as part of how the world works, whereas others (agentive) are overt and identifiable. The key distinction between non-agentive and agentive forms of power is that the former is "non-negotiable and therefore beyond direct argument." The latter is "more susceptible to being perceived as a matter of . . . interest and therefore is open to contestation" (Comaroff and Comaroff 1991, 24). Non-agentive power is hegemonic and difficult to see; agentive power is more visible.

At the ACE, nobody contests that competence, efficiency, and ability are crucial determinants of success. These features are taken for granted, built into the workplace, and heightened by the market assumption of economic individualism. By contrast, sexualized jokes and overt references to women's (and men's) bodies' gender *are* contestable, if at a minimum by legal statute. As I will argue, different gender repertoires have different consequences for how gender can be challenged on the ACE floor.

That gender has multiple meanings is not a surprising finding. There is a growing consensus among feminist scholars who have concluded on the basis of empirical examination across a range of settings that gender, rather than being a static, biological given, is a set of socially produced, hierarchically organized relations between men and women (Stacey and Thorne 1985; West and Zimmerman 1987; Connell 1987, 1995). Men and women face differential conditions in the context of organizations, and in labor markets more broadly (Kanter 1977; Hartmann 1976; Epstein 1970). Furthermore, a number of scholars have documented how processes of bureaucracies, at the macro level, as well as workplaces, at the micro level, are also "gendered" (Ferguson 1984; Pringle 1989; Acker 1990; Leidner 1991, 1994; Hall 1993; Britton 1997; Salzinger 1997).

Not surprisingly, understandings of gender vary across work locales. Gendered meanings change across factory settings and management strategies, so that they "take place within the framework of local, managerial subjectivities and strategies" (Salzinger 1997, 550). Studying three different factory settings, Leslie Salzinger found that managerial labor practices—at factories all doing the same work, with roughly the same mix of men and women—influenced the meaning of gender, highlighting it in one context and downplaying it in others. With variations in factory-level labor processes, gender takes on different subjective meanings and varies in its distributional effects.

What is surprising is that gender on the trading floor is temporally ordered. Whereas previous research has focused on gender in the context of the life course (Rossi 1984; Krüger and Baldus 1999), empirical work on the variations of gendered meaning *within* the ebb and flow of work itself are more scarce, and have focused primarily on gender distinctions in how people negotiate careers (Reskin and Padavic 1994) and work-family balances (Thompson and Bunderson 2001; Jacobs and Gerson 2001; Hochschild 1997).

For many occupations and in many organizations, the pacing of work significantly affects both the subjective understanding of gender and the way gender is arranged structurally. Temporality complements studies of gender variation across both spatial locales and the life course. The ACE is not a continuous or homogeneous work environment. Rather, the temporal shifts in market activity shape the ways men and women understand gender and the ways they behave.

In addition to contributing to research on gender, this work contests arguments whose authors perceive market rationality as historically coming to predominate over non-economic considerations (Hirschman 1977; Carruthers 1996). Research on the ACE floor—a global, financial market where we might expect economic rationality to be at its strongest—shows instead an easy coexistence between more rationalized, market-oriented behavior and behavior explicitly oriented toward asserting a strong masculinity. Examination of gender relations in what is perhaps the closest real-life example of an ideal-typical "marketplace" contributes to research on gender and work by identifying the ways organizations mediate gender relations even in an environment where market rationality is presumed to take precedence most decisively.

Rather than conceiving of rationality—understood locally on the ACE floor as competence—as a form of subjectivity that trumps or subsumes gender in economic markets, I argue that competence for ACE traders is itself understood in distinctly masculine terms. As Joan Acker (1990) points out, the operating logics of organizations that appear gender-neutral are in fact deeply inscribed by gendered processes. One challenge for economic sociologists and feminist scholars alike is to understand the circumstances under which different gender repertoires are more or less salient. Gender should not be narrowly conceived of in overtly sexualized terms of "difference." Likewise, the language and action of competence should not be considered gender-neutral.

## GENDER, WORK, AND TIME

Temporality pervades organizational life (Epstein and Kalleberg 2001; Fine 1990; Hassard 1996; Maines 1987; Roy 1960; Zerubavel 1981), yet remains an only recently emergent area of research. To be sure, the study of time as a key variable of social life has come into its own. Recent special volumes and monographs attest to time's importance both in the study of substantive areas of social life and in the development of theory and methods in the social sciences themselves (Abbott 2001; see Epstein and Kalleberg 2001).

Micro-level examinations of time focus on organizations and workplace situations themselves. External temporal constraints such as rush hours, high-volume periods, deadlines, and slow days all influence the subjective experiences of work. Studies of hospitals (Zerubavel 1979) and police work (Martin 1980; Manning and van Maanen 1978) illustrate the significance of temporal routines to both the constitution and experience of work. Gary Alan Fine (1990), for example, shows how cooks prefer "smooth" days that are busy enough so that cooks are able to show off their competence but not too busy as to make them feel rushed. The argument made in these accounts is that organizational time alters the subjective experiences of workers.

This concern with time differs from the traditionally Marxist and neo-Marxist concern with the extraction of surplus value through piece rates and other capitalistic controls over time (Braverman 1974; Burawoy 1979; Hochschild 1983). In the present case, commodities exchanges are membership organizations, owned by the approximately 2,700 members themselves. Instead of evidencing a centralized division between management and workers, exchanges are a vast assembly of individual traders and employees who gather each day to buy and sell commodity futures. Even though piece rates, speedups, and other features of capitalist workplaces may be central to the subjective experiences of these workers, the Marxist and neo-Marxist lines of research tend to focus on the exploitative nature of capital rather than the temporal variation in social identity.

In work on temporality attention is seldom directed to the salience of social identities such as gender. Workplaces constitute and mediate the gender identities of individual members, ordering as part of the organization of occupations what it means to be a "real" man or woman (Pringle 1989; Leidner 1991; Cockburn 1985, 1991). Work sites are also important places where hierarchical relations between men and women are maintained and legitimated (Acker 1990; Connell 1987; McDowell and Court 1994). Managers manipulate definitions of femininity and masculinity in order to extract surplus labor from workers (Hossfeld 1990; Milkman 1987), as well as to create conditions under which workers will do particularly dangerous jobs. This is not always done *by* managers *to* workers: workers themselves are often active participants in the "gendering" of their occupations (Leidner 1994; Gray 1987).

Previous studies of floor traders document a type of dominant, or "hegemonic," masculinity (see Connell 1987), which is highly heterosexual, hyperrational, and based on ideals of domination, aggressiveness, and competition (McDowell 1995; Lewis 1989; McDowell and Court 1994). As Linda McDowell and Gillian Court (1994) put it, in their comparison of the bond markets of the United States with merchant banking in the United Kingdom, the trading floor is part boys' private school and part street gang (241). Men and women on the floor are confronted with work practices that "play a crucial part in the construction of a gendered subjectivity in the workplace" (238).

The intersection between these two literatures—one on temporality, the other on the construction of gender at work—illustrates the limitations of both. Work that foregrounds organizational time does an excellent job of describing workers' subjective experiences, but it largely misses the importance of time to the construction and maintenance of social identities other than class, such as race, gender, and sexuality. At the ACE, gender can literally have a different meaning during the hectic opening bell than it has at noon. Similarly, research on gender convincingly shows the ways in which work is gender-typed and the ways masculinity and femininity are malleable across managerial and occupational contexts (Salzinger 1997; Lee 1995). However, this literature assumes that gender within individual organizations is temporally static. On the trading floor, this is not the case.

## INTO THE TRADING PITS—
## METHODS AND DATA

In this paper I show how gender is reconstructed and sustained at the organizational level, in the context of a premier national commodities exchange, the American Commodities Exchange. This analysis is based on over six months of participant observation and fieldwork conducted between 1995 and 2000. My participation took the form of working for an extended period of time as a clerk in one of the trading pits, going to training sessions offered by the exchange, and participating in the work life of the ACE. This amounted to over 720 hours spent observing on the trading floor. Each day I took notes on trading cards in order to capture as much information as possible about events and the many informal discussions, arguments, and interactions I observed. During my train ride home each day I elaborated further while transferring my notes to note cards, and then I entered the contents of these note cards into a log by the end of each day. In addition to working and observing on the trading floor, I conducted twenty-five formal interviews and over seventy-five informal interviews with a variety of floor participants, across five trading pits. Of the formal interviews, which lasted one to three hours, twenty-three were taped, transcribed, and coded.[2] Interviewees came primarily from the middle to upper range of occupations on the trading floor. In all, eighteen men and seven women were interviewed. Ages ranged from twenty-four to fifty-four. Eight of the participants had worked for five or fewer years on the floor, while seventeen participants worked for ten years or longer.

## THE FINANCIAL SECTOR AND THE AMERICAN COMMODITIES EXCHANGE

The popular image of workplaces in the financial sector is that they are highly sophisticated, cerebral or technical environments, whereas in fact, futures exchanges in the United States remain largely anachronisms harking back to mid-nineteenth century. The first formal exchanges opened in the mid-nineteenth century in the United States, and nearly 20 percent of the world's seventy-one futures exchanges were founded before 1900. Even these early exchanges drew on a tradition of trading futures dating back to the rice markets of Osaka, Japan, in the mid-1600s. The practice of "open outcry"—making bids and offers in an open auction of commodities prices—characterized the earliest of the exchanges. Although since 1998 the emergence of electronic trading has led to dramatic changes in the futures trading industry, on exchanges in the United States, face-to-face interaction continues to be the dominant method of trading.[3]

Although their importance has grown to an unparalleled degree in the late 20th century, the operations of the futures exchanges themselves remain rooted in traditions over a century old.

The actual work done on the American Commodities Exchange's trading floor is apparently simple. Traders buy and sell contracts on commodity futures—fixed quantities of a commodity at a fixed future date—by "bidding" and "offering" in open auction within the designated trading areas. Members trade using a combination of shouting and hand signals that correspond to price and quantity indicators. When the price of an offer to sell "matches" a bid to buy, the trade is completed. This happens with exceptional rapidity. Often the trade occurs verbally, with the contracts written up only afterward, and oral agreements between traders are understood to be binding.

Clerks working for brokers in the pits and for trading firms whose employees sit at the vast banks of telephones around the trading areas report what happens in the trading pits. When bids and offers occur within the trading pits, pit clerks relay that information to clerks on the telephones, who relay that information to off-floor traders working in brokerage offices of the ACE itself, or to brokerage offices around the world. Clerks are also responsible for taking orders from the ultimate buyers and sellers of the futures contracts and transmitting them into the trading pit for execution.

The floor itself is a large open space separated into "pits" by railings, walls, and steps indicating where different commodities—pork bellies, Swiss francs, Treasury bonds, soybeans—trade. Each pit is octagonal; around each pit is a rim two steps higher than the trading area. Trading-pit size varies roughly by the volume of trades conducted in that particular market. The exchange determines the size of each pit when a new market or "contract" begins trading. In addition, a number of trading pits have expanded and contracted over time, depending in part upon changes in their trading popularity. Thus, a brief glance at the pits can tell an onlooker about the prominence of that market. The number of traders operating in a pit depends on the volume of the commodity traded as well and the level of activity connected to the trading. The smallest pits at the ACE have ten to twenty traders in a space the size of a small conference table; the largest pits have over four hundred traders in a space almost seventy yards long by twenty yards wide.

The ACE trading floor is a relatively young, male-dominated workplace. Men make up over 90 percent of the over four thousand members and employees working on the Exchange floor. Particularly at the upper levels of clerks and traders, the number of women employed is a small percentage of the total labor force; in many pits the number of women traders can be counted on one hand. Women are more prominently represented at the lower ends of the occupational hierarchy, including runners and trade checkers, where the work tends to be more tedious and resembles clerical work. Similarly, although it varies by trading pit, traders and their employees tend to be young. The physical wear and tear of standing, pushing, and shooting all day, the high stress of the job, and the possibility of making (or losing) fortunes in a short career span, make for early career exits from the trading floor for both men and women.

## GENDER AT WORK AND AT PLAY
## ON THE TRADING FLOOR

My work confirms Wayne Baker's (1984) analysis of trading patterns at a U.S. stock options market; he identifies the market as diurnally curvilinear, with heightened activities in the morning and afternoon and a slow midday period. Investor orders build up overnight and are released as the market opens, providing a spurt of trading in the early part of the morning. Also, economic data are often released within the first hour of trading, providing additional impetus for speculative market activity. This was readily apparent while I was working as a clerk during the market's opening. As the clock ticks toward the opening bell, an almost palpable sense of expectation and excitement emerges. Cordiality and muted greetings to colleagues and competitors turn to intermittent shouts about "the call," the anticipated opening range, which is based on overnight market activity. In the moments before the bell rings to announce the opening of trading, the volume can climb to a loud, continuous shout. Many respondents call the atmosphere electric, as did this thirty-nine-year-old male pit clerk:

> I could have gotten three hours of sleep the night before, come in on a train, deadbeat tired, I step on the floor . . . the lights and the noise and . . . just zip, my adrenaline kicks in immediately. . . . I just call it electric. If you don't feel that when you walk in that place, you hate that place then.

I noticed early on that the tone of the floor ratcheted up as the time advanced to the trading bell, which was reflected in my field notes. This feeling of excitement was indeed palpable but difficult to explain. It came from the intuitive feeling that the floor was broadly a part of the global economy combined with the more proximate sense that money was actively, and visibly, changing hands at a rapid clip.

At the end of the day, activity picks up again as traders make their final trades of the day. There are categories of trades made explicitly during the market's closing range. For instance, an order for an "MOC," or "market on close," requires that the trade be executed within the closing range of a contract, which is determined within the last moments of a trading session. Clients watching their orders throughout the day try to "fill or kill" these contracts at the end of the day. And individual traders often trade out of orders to end up "flat," not carrying a buy or sell order into the next day's trading. Heightening the sense of urgency, a bell sounds for the last minute, the last ten seconds, and the end of trading. Taken together, these activities produce a sense of excitement and anticipation as the trading day ends.

Participants anticipate other busy times as well—the release of economic data, meetings of the Federal Reserve Board, and announced political speeches. During these spells, lasting anywhere from moments to hours, traders and employees adopt a "triage" mentality. When the boards posting market prices "go fast market," indicating an inability of the electronic boards to keep up with the pace of changes in trading prices, the most important thing to do is minimize errors, stay controlled, and remain alert for unanticipated market movements and customer responses. Breaks for lunch or coffee are shortened or canceled. Because it is impossible to predict what will happen when the market starts to move, all participants remain in a state of high readiness.

Despite these "predictable" times when the market moves, there is a constant uncertainty about the market's movements. Activity often occurs for no apparent reason and with no warning. Those leaving the floor are routinely queried by those traveling in the opposite direction concerning how fast or slow the market is moving— identifying "triage" moments is in everyone's interest: "Is it busy?" "How's it going up there?" "Is it dead?" "Are you swamped?" On the floor, participants keep one eye on the market at all times, ready to reengage with trading activity almost instantly even when they are taking a break. "When it's quiet you see guys up there reading the paper, talking and stuff like that," said a thirty-four-year-old phone clerk. "And something will come out that wasn't scheduled, you know, something, somebody says something, and boom they're turned, they're right into the market." Occasionally a conversation will stop in midsentence while the market reacts to some piece of news, and then pick right up again when the market has slowed back down.

The market does slow down, particularly in the middle of the day. When trading activity diminishes, a different set of rules apply. The pace and intensity of actual working time changes from day to day. As a twenty-four-year-old male pit clerk said, "You could be for twenty minutes under an unbearable amount of stress, and then once that twenty minutes is over, you could have two hours of doing nothing." During slow periods, traders leave the pits or stand around waiting for something to happen. People on the floor amuse themselves by telling jokes, goofing around, doing crossword puzzles, reading newspapers, or standing around engaging in idle conversation.

Field observations that the ACE operated under two distinct modalities, depending on the amount of market activity, were confirmed in focused interviews. Respondents routinely distinguished between the exchange's fast and slow periods. A twenty-eight-year-old female trade checker described her work in the following manner:

> When it's fast, it's all about business, it's like you're in an accounting firm during tax time, and it is all business, nobody smiling . . . you might not be pleasant, some of them are fighting, as you know, they get upset. And then when it's slow, it's laid-back, people are smuggling in food, they're doing the stupid little sharking,[4] which I think is so, it's hilarious . . . and then, the wrestling between the boys. . . . It's like kindergarten, when it's slow, and you're looking for something to do.

This awareness of two modes was typical of my respondents' accounts. Interviewees talked about the adrenaline rush that comes from a busy market, which was then contrasted with the extreme boredom of the down periods. Another phone clerk, a twenty-seven-year-old woman, spoke about the necessity, in a fast market, of doing many tasks simultaneously, quickly, and accurately:

> Mentally if you're in a fast market, you've got like ten different orders working in ten different markets, you know, three of them are spreads, and all different spreads, you're working for back months, you're working a strip here, you're working individual back month, you know, you're working front four, bids and offers, that kind of gets mentally taxing, and you have to just stop and think, or just write everything down. And you need to keep everything, just all the balls juggling at all at the same time.

However, when I asked her "So what do you do when the market's slow," she expressed a rather different view:

> "Read. Try to. Um, do some paperwork, usually that's done in five minutes. Read. Sometimes trade, not that I trade. Talk, yak. Call Eddie [a colleague], bug him on the phone. What are you doing? Nothing. What are you doing? Nothing. It's boring, I want to go home."

Time seemed to stand still for floor participants during these broad swaths of time for them to do nothing, talk with others, and wait around for the market to pick up again.

## At Work—Gender as Competence

These fast and slow periods provide the temporal context for distinguishing the two gender repertoires operating on the ACE floor. The "constituting narratives" (Salzinger 1997) of gender as a set of social relations between men and women vary widely between these two contexts. These temporal shifts and the different gender repertoires operating during work and play reveal the localized content of gender on the trading floor. During work, men on the floor rarely noted women *as women*. Instead, men gauged women's success and failure in the pits with seemingly gender-neutral criteria. Although women were somewhat more likely to see the different application of these criteria to men and women (for example, in the different meanings of aggressiveness assigned to men and women), they too were as likely as men to accept competence as gender-neutral.

Thus, men and women insisted that gender itself was not the cause of success or failure on the trading floor. Instead of pointing to gender, participants would talk about competence as being able to "get the job done," particularly under the heavy stress of a fast market. Gender did not, however, disappear during work times. Competence, though imbued with a gender-neutral veneer, smuggled in a distinctively "gendered logic" (Acker 1990; Smith 1987). Rather than being subsumed or displaced by competence, gender operated through it, for the components of competence were interpreted as masculine. This gender repertoire was manifested in three key facets of competence on the trading floor: handling stress; being aggressive; and being physical. Thus, competence and masculinity coincided considerably. Enacting a hegemonic masculinity coincided with proving oneself to be an aggressive, assertive participant in the market. Women were often put in positions where they were forced to compromise between being competent and distancing themselves from conventional ideals of femininity.

One element of competence at the ACE is the ability to handle stress under fast market conditions. The fact that the markets potentially change very quickly creates specific challenges for working on the floor. For example, at the height of trading in 1994, contracts traded hands at an average rate of fifty per second. Incremental changes in the price of a contract, known as a tick, range between $12.50 and $32 per tick. For a hundred contract order, a single tick is often worth over two thousand dollars; a thousand contract order can be worth twenty-five thousand dollars. Given these high stakes, participants often sought to reassure themselves of their trading partners' abilities to work quickly and efficiently, avoid mistakes, and effectively "handle" the stress of the job.

Handling pressure was presented by some participants as being nongender-specific. For example, when I asked, "Are there successful brokers, traders, that are women that you know?" a longtime male broker, speaking about the qualities that make a successful trader, made no distinctions between men and women:

> Everybody . . . possesses one real capability, and that's to turn it on, or to turn it up, when they have to. When they're under pressure, to really work quick and fast and accurately, and everybody shows stress and pressure in different ways. You know, it's tough to hide yourself under that kind of condition. So, yeah, they all are able to turn it up, and that's the quality there, I think that everybody pretty much is themselves . . . it's basically the ability to turn it up when the market starts to move, be able to move with it.

The qualities this respondent pointed to were available to everybody, and were not limited to men or women. In this respect, his response was quite gender-neutral. Later in the interview, he made a point of saying that there are no barriers for women to be successful on the floor.

But despite this seeming gender-neutrality, he did nevertheless recognize that only a few women were on the floor. By way of explanation he went on to say, "The socialization process, the gender process doesn't prepare a woman to handle that kind of in-your-face aggression." This reference to the "socialization process" smuggles gender back into a seemingly gender-neutral conception of ability. Unable to account for women's absence in any other way—overt exclusion, for example—this respondent reaffirms the essential universality of qualities that lead to being a successful trader. *Anyone* who is able to handle the stress of the ACE floor can succeed; the low number of women on the floor is attributed to lack of ability (the fault of a generalized gender socialization process) rather than any overtly gendered elements of the ACE environment.

Other responses were less nuanced than the previous account. Participants often simultaneously talked about handling stress as a universal activity, while directly linking stress management to distinctly masculine attributes. For instance, clerks and traders coped with stressful, mistake-laden days by trying to deliberately forget about errors made under pressure. A twenty-four-year-old pit clerk said:

> It's like when you make an error when you're playing baseball, I played sports my whole life, and whenever you made an error, you sat there and moped about it, chances were the next time . . . the ball was hit to you, you're going to make an error again. So you, it's like, so key to just forget about it. And how weird is that, that you say to yourself, OK, forget about the fact that I just lost twelve thousand dollars for that guy, let's go back to work. That's challenging.

Sports metaphors are a significant and often pervasive component of accounts of trading, and in fact a number of former athletes actually work on the floor. Linking competence to sports allowed men to interpret their experiences in the context of a competitive masculinity unavailable to women (Messner 1992, 17–19; Hearn and Parkin 1983). Metaphors such as sports and battle were often used to describe the pressures of a fast-moving market. Women do participate in both athletics and armed service; however, for men the metaphor of sports denoted manliness as much as masculinity. Without making explicit references to gender, these narratives nevertheless linked masculinity and the ability to handle pressure.

Because handling pressure acts explicitly as a gender-neutral concept but was implicitly constituted as a masculine ideal, the success of women who do excel under pressure must be explained—they are "held to account" for their abilities (West and Zimmerman 1987). Under these circumstances, men grudgingly acknowledged successful women as competent, but not also as women. That is, women traders could be respected as a trader or treated as a woman, but rarely both. A handful of female brokers, traders, and clerks on the floor were identified as competent in this manner, as this fifty-four-year-old trader made clear:

> Take Susan, that's a perfect example. Now there's a person. There's a player, there's a market maker, and so for her, you have to respect her. Forget about the fact that she's a woman. You have to respect her as a person, because she was in there, was constantly in the market. I think you just know that there's a person that I can go to with a fifty [contract order] and know that it's going to clear the next day at that price.

This account by a successful woman who could handle the pressure downplayed gender as a constituent element of this woman's competence, focusing rather on the importance of being reliable under pressure. But later in the same interview, he remarked that her ability to compete "maybe makes her less of a woman." Despite the rhetoric of gender-neutrality, women who enjoyed high status for their abilities often were viewed as having compromised their femininity. Successful male traders, by contrast, were held in higher esteem through their abilities to "step up" in fast markets.

The second element in the gender repertoire of competence is the ability to be aggressive. In an active market, clerks compete with each other to get orders from customers, and traders compete with each other to buy and sell contracts at the best possible prices. Almost 85 percent of my respondents (twenty-one of twenty-five) explicitly listed aggressiveness as an important element of competence. The imagery respondents used to describe aggressiveness was vivid, often sexual or violent, and revealed its gendered character: "You have to want to cut someone's balls off" (fifty-four-year-old male); "From seven-twenty to two, I turn it on" (thirty-five-year-old male); "I'm trying to buy a thousand at a better price, we're not going to sit there and discuss it over a cup of tea" (twenty-five-year-old female); "It's survival of the fittest. It's a war" (twenty-six-year-old male).

Participants linked aggressiveness to masculinity in a way that often excluded women directly from positions of authority on the trading floor. Especially during busy times, women were constantly held to a higher level of scrutiny than their male counterparts as whether they could be aggressive enough. I had the following exchange with a twenty-seven-year-old female phone clerk:

Respondent: There's customers that will not speak to females.

PL: Customers, like phone customers?

Respondent: Yeah, there's one I remember . . . they did not want women on the opening and numbers.

PL: Why was that?

Respondent: They didn't think that women could handle it, and they trusted a man more than a woman. And I know some pretty shitty male phone clerks that shouldn't be phone clerks. You know, so that was pretty ridiculous. But, uh, oh yeah . . .

PL: [Joking] What if you were a woman and you were six foot five?

Respondent: You'd have definitely, you could probably go down into the pit, but you'd have to prove that, you'd have to kind of look, this sounds bad, but you kind of have to look kind of Amazon-ish, kind of she-male. You know what I mean? A guy will look at you, especially with that floor mentality, kind of women are kind of [a] genteel thing, I know a lot of guys who think that women do not belong in the business. Um, they'll look at you, sure you're six foot five, but can you be aggressive? They'll look at that.

Here, the joke was that the usual manner in which women were excluded was on the basis of physical size. But given a hypothetically tall woman, the issue of aggressiveness was heightened rather than reduced. Even a tall woman would have to be "Amazon-ish, kind of she-male." And even *then,* she would be questioned over whether she could be aggressive enough.

Although both women and men considered themselves aggressive traders, gender once again operated through rather than instead of competence. Most women on the floor did describe themselves as aggressive, a quality heightened by the work environment. A twenty-five-year-old female pit clerk, proud of her ability to "hold her own" in a male-dominated environment, conceptualized aggressiveness as universally practiced and at the same time highly defeminizing:

> Everything about the pit goes against what would be, I think, considered feminine. You're yelling, you're screaming, you're spitting, the guys fart and burp all day long, the place smells, it's sweaty, the language is foul, it's aggressive, you're competing aggressively for business. Whether you're a clerk or if you're in the pit as a broker, you're competing aggressively to get your order filled ahead of the next guy. I don't think it's a very feminine environment.

With respect to the actual practices of being aggressive, women were virtually indistinguishable from their male counterparts in their ability and willingness to "get in the face" of a recalcitrant clerk or trader who was not allowing them to get their orders filled.

Nevertheless, aggressiveness continued to be coded as an eminently masculine characteristic. Women on the floor were often considered "bitchy," a term applied widely to women in men's worlds (see also Williams 1989; Kanter 1977). For instance, this same woman, when I asked if people called her Deborah or Debbie, replied that "they mostly just call me bitch." By contrast, men were often criticized for not being aggressive enough. Nonaggressive men were considered ineffective; they did not command enough attention, fill their orders, or get good trades.

Being physically strong, tough, and if possible physically imposing is the third element of competency on the floor. In one respect the job is in fact physically demanding. The exchange requires all floor participants to remain standing while on the floor, which often means that people stand on their feet for hours at a time. Yelling is an integral part of the labor process, and some traders go to voice therapists in order to strengthen their voices to be heard. Finally, particularly during busier times on the floor, there is quite a bit of physical jostling as traders struggle to execute their orders and clerks attempt to get the attention of both traders and their customers.

Working on the ACE floor highlights the importance of physical size and space. Depending upon the day, there were anywhere from four hundred to a thousand people standing in the trading area where I worked. Clerks often observed that the amount of space that was "theirs" during the day is roughly the space of their body. A twenty-four-year-old male pit clerk had control of "the space of my body, pretty much. I mean, I stand, I just stand there, and that's my office. You know, I just stand in a little spot, like the area of a floor tile, all day long." The press of bodies on the floor emphasizes physical size and floor presence, especially height. Large physical size—being not only tall but also big—is an advantage in this environment.

Being physical is the component of competence that most closely dovetails with connotations of gender as a reference to male and female bodies. Not surprisingly, physical differences became a locus for discussion about women on the floor. Respondents assumed that most women were at a disadvantage owing to the physical nature of the floor. Women's voices are "not as heavy" and seemingly not able to carry as well as men's. Women are also seen as less physically able to hold their own. One forty-year-old male trader argued:

> Just the physical size of these people and their strength, and just stand there all these hours every day, and scream and be seen and be heard and resist the pushing, hold your ground. It's hard for a guy, it's hard for little guys, short guys, skinny guys or weak guys, it's tough for them. It's got to be tough for a woman. Not that women aren't capable, I just think it's a tough environment for them. There's a lot of jobs that are more suited for men than women, and it's not on an intellectual level that I'm talking about. Maybe it's on a more physical level.

In addition, many of the respondents pointed out that even for the women who could "hack it," the floor would not be a desirable work environment. A thirty-nine-year-old clerk said:

> With girls, and being in the pits, you're like this [claps his hands together]. You're pancaked, man. Some women don't feel comfortable with that, probably. You know, having a guy pressed right up, you know, you're pressed up against a guy, and having a guy pressed up against you from behind. All day long. I would think that'd be uncomfortable for a woman.

The forty-year-old trader's response stresses that the work environment is physically demanding. Like handling pressure and being aggressive, physical toughness was considered to be a universal attribute of successful traders. But behind this neutral assessment lies the conviction that the strength demanded by the floor also effectively defines the job as more suitable for men. The thirty-nine-year-old clerk's comment takes a different tack, noting that the environment—normally just a physically demanding one—becomes sexualized with the addition of women. The structure of floor trading makes it necessary for participants to squeeze into the pits, sometimes to press their bodies against others' bodies. Invoking women's perceived inability to be as physical as necessary to "hold their own" in the pits used gender language of competence but attributed this difficulty to the "fact" of women's bodies.

The definition of competency that emerges from the discussion of "work" is a gender repertoire that maintains a veneer of gender neutrality while actually constructing in masculine, and often sexual, terms. Sexualized language was likely to be used in speaking of the market itself rather than of women. Traders often spoke in quite a coarse manner about getting "fucked" by the market or accidentally "screwing" a customer, but these constituting discourses were captured in competence rather than in sexualized difference. In periods of "work," gender is not made less salient; instead, masculinity is codified in ways that give shape to putatively gender-neutral work activities.

## At Play—Gender as Sexualized Difference

Whereas gender is interpreted as a form of competence during "work," during "play," gender becomes much more directly tied to sex and heterosexual imagery. Here women's bodies became objects for heterosexual masculinity. I focus on joking and getting along as important mechanisms through which the informal social structure of the floor is maintained in gender-dichotomous ways. When the market is less active, a dominant part of the exchange's "atmosphere," or cultural context, consists of risqué storytelling, practical-joke playing, and joke telling. Masculinity becomes more explicitly sexualized and women are more fully excluded from the men's world of trading.

On the ACE floor, humor and joking act as a primary language through which group solidarity is formed and maintained (Hughes 1958, 109; Lyman 1987; Norman 1994). As such, jokes acted as a key element of the constituting discourse of gender. Rosabeth Moss Kanter's (1977) study of a large male-dominated corporation treats joking as a part of corporate culture where men would use off-color or sexual jokes to emphasize women's differences from their male counterparts (1977, 225–26). On the ACE trading floor, many women did attempt to participate in the joking culture. They spoke about "playing the game" or being able to joke without being offended by the men's apparently juvenile and sexualized behavior. Many women on the floor stress their thick skins and their aptitude for "taking a joke." Despite the efforts of these women to assume the role of "honorary men"—women who could be expected to laugh at jokes and listen to ongoing banter without reacting negatively— the repertoire of sexual joking during times of play highlighted rather than minimized the differences between men and women and created visible in-groups and out-groups.

The sexual content of the trading floor corresponds to other accounts, of merchant bankers (McDowell and Court 1994) and bond traders (Lewis 1989). I observed that joking often had very explicit sexual connotations. In one typical example, after an altercation between two male clerks, one said to the other, "You weigh one hundred pounds more than me, you could probably beat up my sister too." The second clerk's response, both to the clerk and laughing onlookers, was "Yeah, I could, but I'd fuck her first. Up the ass!" Violent and sexually aggressive jokes in particular facilitate the identification of the ACE trading floor as a man's world. These jokes are ubiquitous. They include reworking comic strips in sexually suggestive ways, alluding to the sexual practices of co-workers (and their relatives), putting sexual spins on current events, and making jokes about individual women on the floor.

The heterosexualization of jokes in this male bonding precludes women from being able to be "honorary big swinging dicks" during these periods of play, as McDowell (1995) put it in her study of British merchant bankers (see also Acker 1990 regarding "honorary men" in organizations). Although many of the women on the floor did swear and occasionally behave in a sexually coarse manner with men, their status as women made it difficult for them to joke with men on equal footing. Men continued to see women *as a group* as sexual objects. For instance, although some women considered themselves "one of the guys," this did not preclude them from being sexually objectified. Women on the floor who told dirty jokes were seen as having their femininity "eroded," and participants spoke of this erosion as "not very delicate," "unladylike," or like "talking like a truck driver." The contradiction lies in the fact that for a woman to be "one of guys," she has to stop being feminine. For men on the floor, discursively constructing even "unladylike" women as potential sexual objects maintains their ability to assert themselves as masculine men.

At play, joking on the trading floor explicitly linked market ideologies and gender. A twenty-eight-year-old female clerk discussed the ways in which sexual joking occurred among men and was implicitly directed at women, all in the context of the "market" metaphor:

> They had a shirt on the floor circulating that said Wall Street on the front and it said, "You've got to know when to pull out" on the back. And it was a bull and a bear, you know, on the back, the bull was in the back and the bear was bent over. And I'm sitting there, and they'd flash these shirts and I'm like, they're buying them up like water on a hundred-degree day. And they're like "Did you see this?" Everybody was buying this shirt. So I mean, they know, they know we're not going to appreciate that, I don't. Some of the girls don't care.

With some exceptions—there was one female phone clerk who was jokingly sharing pictures of beefcake shots from *Playgirl* to an audience of men, who claimed to be disgusted by the photos—there is little opportunity for women to joke as sexual aggressors.

Men used joking and sexual banter about women as a way to reinforce a highly gendered group solidarity. This took place particularly during play periods. Talk about sexual exploits over the weekends was pervasive: graphic descriptions of receiving oral sex from a date; picking up women and taking them home from a bar; or paying for prostitutes to come to a party. One floor clerk summed up his feelings about women on the floor by suggesting that the ACE should operate "with no women at all, like a Turkish bath. We could sit around in our towels with drinks and cigars." When I asked whether some of the more competent women on the floor should be included, he laughingly replied, "Well, okay, some women. They can serve us drinks."

Comments and joking stories told throughout the less active moments of the trading day provided a way for the men on the floor to communicate their manliness to each other. Often, the objects of these jokes were women who had little experience or who worked in more subservient and low-status positions. In one trading pit, a male trader pointed out a large-breasted female runner; her job was to take trading cards in and out of the trading pit throughout the day, which made it necessary for her to enter and leave the pit ten to twenty times every day. This "trade-checking" work occurred as market activities slowed down and those double-checking the actual paperwork of trades were able to catch up with the fast pace of trading. The trader joked that each time she walked into the pit, a group of men would comment and joke to each other about her breasts. This ceaseless daily joking had continued unabated over the three months that she had worked there. As part of the overwhelmingly male landscape, then, women stand out, and they stand out in a particular manner: as sexual objects for the men. This is what it meant for women to be used for the purposes of male bonding.

However, these jokes were not limited to low-status women on the floor. I recorded numerous jokes and rather crass sexual discussions about a woman trader at a large trading desk, including one where a broker loudly announced that he'd like to "bend *her* over a rail," to the general agreement of the other men in the pit. These jokes were not limited to comments about a woman (rather than *to* her). A senior-level woman phone clerk recounted:

> I'm down here so long, and I'm forty-three years old. But I, I remember going over, stepping on one of the steps and stretching my Achilles out one day, and someone made some sexual comment to me, and I just turned to him, and that's when I said, "Geez I hope somebody's talking to your wife like you're talking to me now. God, wouldn't it be cool? Wouldn't you just love it? I hope it's a big grizzly guy, you know, talking to your little girl, and frightening her." You know, and he's like "Woah." It does happen.

The point here is not the degree to which senior women were included or exempted from the sexualized forms of humor on the floor but, rather, the difference in the response—a theme I discuss more explicitly in the following section.

## GENDER AND FORMS OF POWER

If this account of the importance of incorporating a temporal dimension into analyses of work and gender is to be useful for analyses
of gender meanings, it is not enough to say that there are multiple
gender repertoires without examining the effects of this attribution
process. The construction and maintenance of gendered meanings
should be linked more explicitly to the question of power. The main
problem is that when gender is visible, it is more overt and most
able to be challenged. When gender "looks" neutral, it is less hostile but also more difficult to identify and challenge (see table 9.1).

When the market is fast and gender is articulated through the
supposedly gender-neutral language of competence, it creeps back
in by means of equating competence with three "masculine" qualities: handling stress, being aggressive, and being physical. Here, gendered views of the trader's work do not take the same overt, openly
hostile form as they take during play periods. Consequently, gendered attitudes are actually comparatively difficult to challenge.
Attitudes toward female coworkers may actually sound like a benign

TABLE 9.1 **Definition and Consequences of Gender Repertoires
by Temporality**

| Gender Repertoires | Temporality | |
| | Fast Market: Work | Slow Market: Play |
| --- | --- | --- |
| Content of repertoires | Competence: Handling stress under extreme conditions; being able to be aggressive in pursuit of trades; being able to hold one's own physically. | Sexualized difference: camaraderie and solidarity; sexually explicit jokes; getting along with people on the floor. |
| Effects of repertoires | More difficult to challenge because gender is asserted in gender-neutral language of efficiency and ability. | Easier to challenge because language and actions are explicit. More overtly hostile. |
| Form of power | Non-agentive; gender is hegemonic. | Agentive; gender is ideological. |

*Source:* Author's compilation.

form of seeming support, while still reaffirming gender differences. A thirty-nine-year-old male clerk pointed out how "chauvinistic" he thought the ACE floor is:

> You know, you'll get guys that will just say, I don't want Jamie [one of the women in his quadrant] there, she's not good enough. You know, I'll work with Paul [a coworker] and this guy's not even close as being as good as her but it's because she's a girl, she's out. She doesn't have a chance. Because you know a lot of times guys won't yell at a girl like they will yell at a guy, because you don't want to make them cry. And I've seen it happen. I mean, not all the time, I don't want to say, I'm not chauvinistic. I believe if a woman has earned her right to be there, so be it, hey, I want her to work.

Speaking about the unfairness of men treating women as de facto worse workers than men, the clerk seems to appeal to competence rather than sexualized difference as the dominant frame with which to evaluate this woman. He notes that women who "earn their rights" should be on the floor, and compares a "competent" woman favorably to his male coworker.

At the same time, gendered views of coworkers creep back in as their being unable to get yelled at without crying—and he notes his own reservations that women may in fact be less able to handle pressure than their male counterparts. When pressed as to whether women should be excluded from the trading floor and whether being able to get yelled at without crying actually was important, the clerk retreated:

> Aw, you hate to get bypassed . . . being chauvinistic, whatever, you know, I guess a guy, probably just like a woman would think, hey, I can do a better job than he can, or most of the guys, probably every guy'll say, I *know* I can do a better job than her. . . . Plus women's voices aren't as heavy as men's, and like in the [pit], unless, if you're by yourself, you can trade by yourself . . . but trying to be a filling broker, to me, it looks like a really tough.

Even as he argues that women should be treated as the equals of men ("I believe if a woman has earned her right to be there, so be it, hey, I want her to work"), this clerk illustrates how gendered notions become embedded in concepts of competence. Women's voices are not as heavy as men's voices, and women were less able to "handle" pressure on the floor. These responses were quite typical: men on the floor who "in theory" want women to be treated equitably also use criteria to judge competence that replicate the perceived strengths of men and that support gender differences without ever making overt claims about gender. The endpoint of this conception of gender is that women get passed over not because they are women per se but because they are less competent at their jobs than men.

The flip side of this process is that while women are seemingly "naturally" unsuited for many of the high-status jobs on the floor, they are also assumed to be "naturally" suited to more low-status positions such as trade checkers. Here, a thirty-one-year-old male pit clerk noted that women make excellent trade checkers:

> Notice you'll see, a bulk of the women, will be what you'd call deck holders. Why that is [is that] they're real good at it, I don't know what the thing is. I've seen a lot of guy deck-holders butcher orders. Guys would rather be in the pit, doing the yelling and shouting, and you'd rather have, it's like your girl deck holder is your secretary, because she's got all this clerical paperwork in front of her, and a guy doesn't want to get near it. Because I've handled a deck before, and when it gets busy, those things are a real pain in the ass.

Here gender is also subsumed under the language of competence and skill, but here the case is made for women being "better" at clerical work. This provides the other bookend for understanding how jobs are allocated. Not gender is set forth as the reason for women to work as trade checkers, a position very near the bottom of the ACE occupational hierarchy, but women's competence with this kind of work—"like your girl deck holder is your secretary."

In times of work, gender is submerged under the more universalistic conception of competence. Gender operates here as a form of non-agentive, or hegemonic, power. The local construction of competence—ability to handle stress and be aggressive and physical toughness—accepts implicitly that these elements are linked to practices that advantage men over women. One female respondent told me after an interview that she had been fired from her first job as a phone clerk because her clients were convinced she couldn't get the respect she needed from pit brokers. But at the time, she didn't know if this was because she was a bad clerk or if she was a woman. Only after becoming a successful phone clerk was she able to reinterpret the incident as being gendered.

When the market is "slow," gender awareness is manifested through joking and getting along. This dynamic is obvious to participants, both the men and women. For example, a forty-three-year-old white woman pointed out her own direct and confrontational response to overt and antagonistic jokes on the floor:

> The guys next to me, I mean, I've for years seen them dragging out the *Playboys* and doing the whole centerfold, and I just . . . and I never thought that, the other day, they did it next to me, and I just ignored it. You know, it happens every day, but they kept talking and talking, together as a group, and they're standing right next to me, and you know, all of a sudden it got into what they're going to do, Oh, wouldn't you like to see her, you know. Finally, I turned to the guy's boss and said, "Are you calling security or am I?" You know, kind of on the kid, and he goes, "Let's both call security," and I turned to the guys, and I said, "I want it put away now." They still weren't sure if I was kidding, and I reached for the phone, and they put it away.

In her response she was able to both note and deal with the behavior directed at her. More typically, women on the floor responded to jokes in one of the manners described by Kanter (1977, 228), by "letting it slide." It was itself a mark of this forty-three-year-old woman's seniority at the ACE (she had worked twelve years on the floor) that she was able to call those engaging in inappropriate behavior to account.

Responding to such comments, which are often pervasive and can be relentless, does, however, take a psychic toll. As she noted later regarding the incident:

> I felt funny all day, I felt, god, there she is, ruining the good time, party-pooper, oh, are you sexually uptight, all the things that connotes when a woman doesn't want to be an object, you know. You're a prude, you know, and that part of me that still wants to be so popular, you know, just had a big fight . . . I guess I get tired of parenting, you know, I get tired of parenting.

Gender that is articulated through sexualized difference may be visible, but it is nevertheless costly to confront. In this context, gender is agentive. It operates on a more overt level, which makes it more able to be seen as a form of power and thus confrontable, but there is still a toll.

## CONCLUSION

The primary claim I make is that attention to temporality on the ACE floor highlights competence and sexualized difference as two gender repertoires that serve as the constituting discourses of gender—that workers' gender actually operates differently to influence behavior according to the temporal rhythms of the market. When the market is active, gender is articulated through the language of competence. The components of competence—handling stress, being aggressive, being physical—are understood to be "gender-neutral" on their face but in fact obscure highly gendered logics of action. This explains why both men and women perceived women as having to "fit in" in a man's world by being getting in people's faces, shouting, pushing, and shoving. This construction of competence is hegemonic: it postures as gender-neutral but actually tilts the playing field in favor of men.

When the market is less active, gender is articulated through the language of sexualized difference. During these times, an emphasis on joking and getting along emerges. Men and women use jokes to pass time, fit in, and relieve tension, but a direct result of men's sexual banter is to facilitate group solidarity among men and the exclusion of women. Strong heterosexual joking is predicated on men's being the sexual agents of jokes and women being the objects. Although a few long-tenured women were able to joke with the men, for most this was not the case. Women could not easily participate in these jokes precisely because women-as-agents disrupts the "normal" pattern of female objectification. If both men and women were able to be agents of sexual banter, who would be left to be the objects?

This essay links these different gender repertoires to two distinct forms of power. Agentive power refers to the times when gender becomes visible and thus able to be contested. When men joke about women, they do so *as men,* and they talk about women *as women.* This moves gender to the foreground of attention. This overt behavior can be contested or challenged by men and women who find it objectionable, contrary to sexual harassment law, or personally distasteful. By contrast, when gender is articulated through the language of competence, it seems to disappear. Men and women are held to the same criteria for being successful members of the market community, even when these criteria result in dramatically differentiated outcomes for the two genders. In this repertoire, gender moves to the background of attention. It becomes dramatically more difficult to contest or challenge gender in this mode, because challenging gender here is tantamount to challenging the structure of trading itself.

Finally, the more general claim is that temporal rhythms are a key to understanding variations in gendered work practices. Salzinger (1997), for example, makes a convincing argument that the meaning of gender can vary greatly at the shop-floor level, depending upon local conditions such as management attitudes and labor processes. My argument is that even at the local level, how gender takes shape changes dramatically depending on the pace of work. Particularly in workplaces characterized by lots of temporal variation in the workday—hospital emergency rooms, police departments, restaurants—time and the intensity of work matters a great deal with regard to how gender is articulated. In most workplaces, there are lunch hours, coffee breaks, speed-ups, or slowdowns, all of which have important consequences for the study of gender. Not only time-of-day temporal variance but also temporal patterns in larger time frames need to be explored. Agricultural work is seasonal in nature. At the ACE, different contract pits have a "life course"—busy for weeks on end or slow for days or months at a time. We know little about how these longer-term shifts might affect localized conceptions of gender.

---

The author wishes to thank Carol Heimer, Marc Ventresca, Wendy Espeland, Bruce Carruthers, Barry Cohen, Lisa Amoroso, Leslie Salzinger, and the editors for reading this manuscript.

## NOTES

1. The American Commodities Exchange, and all names of participants, are pseudonyms.
2. The remaining two interviewees requested that they not be tape-recorded. Notes on those interviews were also coded as part of the analysis.

3. This may, finally, be changing as electronic exchanges increase their share of world futures markets.

4. "Shark fins" are trading cards ripped into the shape of a fin. These fins are then surreptitiously attached to an unaware person's jacket collar, and the "sharked" individual is then often sent on a bogus errand. As he or she passes along the lines of clerks and runners, people will scream out "Shark!" until the individual, often turning red in embarrassment or anger, notices he or she has been tagged.

## REFERENCES

Abbott, Andrew. 2001. *Time Matters: On Theory and Method.* Chicago: University of Chicago Press.

Acker, Joan. 1990. "Hierarchies, Jobs, Bodies: A Theory of Gendered Organization." *Gender and Society* 4(2): 139–58.

Baker, Wayne E. 1984. "The Social Structure of a National Securities Market." *American Journal of Sociology* 89(4): 775–811.

Braverman, Harry. 1974. *Labor and Monopoly Capital: The Degradation of Work in the Twentieth Century.* New York: Monthly Review Press.

Britton, Dana M. 1997. "Gendered Organizational Logic: Policy and Practice in Men's and Women's Prisons." *Gender and Society* 11(6): 796–818.

Burawoy, Michael. 1979. *Manufacturing Consent: Changes in the Labor Process Under Monopoly Capitalism.* Chicago: University of Chicago Press.

Carruthers, Bruce G. 1996. *City of Capital: Politics and Markets in the English Financial Revolution.* Princeton: Princeton University Press.

Cockburn, Cynthia. 1985. *Machinery of Dominance: Women, Men, and Technical Know-How.* London: Pluto Press.

———. 1991. *In the Way of Women: Men's Resistance to Sex Equality in Organizations.* Ithaca, N.Y.: ILR.

Comaroff, Jean, and John Comaroff. 1991. *Of Revelation and Revolution: Christianity, Colonialism, and Consciousness in South Africa.* Chicago: University of Chicago Press.

Connell, Robert W. 1987. *Gender and Power.* Cambridge: Polity Press.

———. 1995. *Masculinities.* Berkeley: University of California Press.

Epstein, Cynthia Fuchs. 1970. *Women's Place: Options and Limits in Professional Careers.* Berkeley: University of California Press.

Epstein, Cynthia Fuchs, and Arne L. Kalleberg. 2001. "Time and the Sociology of Work: Issues and Implications." *Work and Occupations* 28(1): 5–16.

Ferguson, Kathy. 1984. *The Feminist Case Against Bureaucracy.* Philadelphia: Temple University Press.

Fine, Gary Alan. 1990. "Organizational Time: Temporal Demands and the Experience of Work in Restaurant Kitchens." *Social Forces* 69(1): 95–114.

Gramsci, Antonio. 1971. *Selections from the Prison Notebooks*. Edited and translated by Quintin Hoare and Geoffrey Nowell Smith. New York: International Publishers.

Granovetter, Mark. 1985. "Economic Action and Social Structure: The Problem of Embeddedness." *American Journal of Sociology* 91(3): 481–510.

Gray, Stan. 1987. "Sharing the Shop Floor." In *Beyond Patriarchy: Essays by Men on Pleasure, Power, and Change,* edited by Michael Kaufman. Oxford: Oxford University Press.

Hall, Elaine J. 1993. "Waitering/Waitressing: Engendering the Work of Table Servers." *Gender and Society* 7(3): 329–46.

Hartmann, Heidi. 1976. "Capitalism, Patriarchy, and Job Segregation by Sex." In *Women and the Workplace: The Implications of Occupational Segregation,* edited by Martha Blaxall and Barbara Reagan. Chicago: University of Chicago Press.

Hassard, John. 1996. "Images of Time in Work and Organization." In *Handbook of Organization Studies,* edited by Stewart R. Clegg, Cynthia Hardy, and Walter Nord. Thousand Oaks, Calif.: Sage.

Hearn, Jeff, and P. Wendy Parkin. 1983. "Gender and Organizations: A Selective Review and Critique of a Neglected Area." *Organization Studies* 4(3): 219–42.

Hirschman, Albert O. 1977. *The Passions and the Interests: Political Arguments for Capitalism Before Its Triumph*. Princeton: Princeton University Press.

Hochschild, Arlie Russell. 1983. *The Managed Heart: Commercialization of Human Feeling.* Berkeley: University of California Press.

———. 1997. *The Time Bind: When Work Becomes Home and Home Becomes Work*. New York: Metropolitan Books.

Hossfeld, Karen. 1990. " 'Their Logic Against Them': Contradictions in Sex, Race, and Class in Silicon Valley." In *Women Workers and Global Restructuring,* edited by Katheryn Ward. Ithaca, N.Y.: ILR Press.

Hughes, Everett. 1958. *Men and Their Work*. Glencoe, Ill.: Free Press.

Jacobs, Jerry A., and Kathleen Gerson. 2001. "Overworked Individuals or Overworked Families: Explaining Trends in Work, Leisure, and Family Time." *Work and Occupations* 28(1): 40–63.

Kanter, Rosabeth Moss. 1977. *Men and Women of the Corporation*. New York: Basic Books.

Krüger, Helga, and Bernd Baldus. 1999. "Work, Gender and the Life Course: Social Construction and Individual Experience." *Canadian Journal of Sociology/Cahiers canadiens de sociologie* 24(3): 355–79.

Lee, Ching Kwan. 1995. "Engendering the Worlds of Labor: Women Workers, Labor Markets, and Production Politics in the South China Economic Miracle." *American Sociological Review* 60(3): 378–97.

Leidner, Robin. 1991. "Serving Hamburgers and Selling Insurance: Gender, Work, and Identity in Interactive Service Jobs." *Gender and Society* 5(2): 154–77.

———. 1994. *Fast Food, Fast Talk: Service Work and the Routinization of Everyday Life*. Berkeley: University of California Press.

Levin, Peter. 2001. "Gendering the Markets: Temporality, Work, and Gender on a National Futures Exchange." *Work and Occupations* 28(1): 112–30.

Lewis, Michael. 1989. *Liar's Poker: Two Cities, True Greed*. New York: Norton.

Lyman, Peter. 1987. "The Fraternal Bond as a Joking Relationship: A Case Study of the Role of Sexist Jokes in Male Group Bonding." In *Changing Men: New Directions in Research on Men and Masculinity*, edited by Michael Kimmel. Newbury Park, Calif.: Sage.

Maines, David R. 1987. "The Significance of Temporality for the Development of Sociological Theory." *Sociological Quarterly* 28(3): 303–11.

Manning, Peter K., and John van Maanen. 1978. *Policing: A View from the Street*. Santa Monica, Calif.: Goodyear.

Martin, Susan Ehrlich. 1980. *Breaking and Entering: Policewomen on Patrol*. Berkeley: University of California Press.

McDowell, Linda. 1995. "Body Work: Heterosexual Gender Performances in City Workplaces." In *Mapping Desire: Geographies of Sexualities*, edited by David Bell and Gill Valentine. New York: Routledge.

McDowell, Linda, and Gillian Court. 1994. "Missing Subjects: Gender, Power, and Sexuality in Merchant Banking." *Economic Geography* 70(3): 229–51.

Messner, Michael A. 1992. *Power at Play: Sports and the Problem of Masculinity*. Boston: Beacon Press.

Milkman, Ruth. 1987. *Gender at Work: The Dynamics of Job Segregation by Sex During World War II*. Urbana: University of Illinois Press.

Norman, Karin. 1994. "The Ironic Body: Obscene Joking Among Swedish Working-Class Women." *Ethnos* 59(3–4): 187–211.

Pringle, Rosemary. 1989. *Secretaries Talk: Sexuality, Power, and Work*. London: Verso.

Reskin, Barbara, and Irene Padavic. 1994. *Women and Men at Work*. Thousand Oaks, Calif.: Pine Forge Press.

Rossi, Alice S. 1984. "Gender and Parenthood." *American Sociological Review* 49(1): 1–19.

Roy, Donald. 1960. "Banana Time: Job Satisfaction and Informal Interaction." *Human Organization* 18(4): 156–68.

Salzinger, Leslie. 1997. "From High Heels to Swathed Bodies: Gendered Meanings Under Production in Mexico's Export-Processing Industry." *Feminist Studies* 28(3): 549–74.

Smith, Dorothy E. 1987. *The Everyday World as Problematic: A Feminist Sociology*. Boston: Northeastern University Press.

Stacey, Judith, and Barrie Thorne. 1985. "The Missing Feminist Revolution in Sociology." *Social Problems* 32(4): 301–16.

Thompson, Jeffrey A., and J. Stuart Bunderson. 2001. "Work-Nonwork Conflict and the Phenomenology of Time: Beyond the Balance Metaphor." *Work and Occupations* 28(1): 17–39.

West, Candace, and Sarah Fenstermaker. 1995. "Doing Difference." *Gender and Society* 9(1): 8–37.

West, Candace, and Don Zimmerman. 1987. "Doing Gender." *Gender and Society* 1(2): 125–51.

Williams, Christine L. 1989. *Gender Differences at Work: Women and Men in Nontraditional Occupations*. Berkeley: University of California Press.

Zerubavel, Eviatar. 1979. *Patterns of Time in Hospital Life: A Sociological Perspective*. Chicago: University of Chicago Press.

———. 1981. *Hidden Rhythms: Schedules and Calendars in Social Life*. Chicago: University of Chicago Press.

— Chapter 10 —

# Work Devotion
# and Work Time

## Mary Blair-Loy

S CHOLARS MAINTAIN THAT a major source of work-family conflict is
the lack of sufficient time in the day to meet work and family
obligations (see, for example, Hochschild 1997; Parcel 1999). This
time crunch is exacerbated by the increase in work hours over the
past thirty years, especially for professional and managerial workers
and for women (Jacobs and Gerson 2004). Work-family researchers
generally see long work hours as negative consequences of employer
demands or increased competition wrought by globalization and
industry consolidation (Schor 1992; Hochschild 1997; Jacobs and
Gerson 2004; Blair-Loy and Jacobs 2003; Fraser 2001). But to fully
comprehend why people maintain demanding careers in the first
place we also need to understand the normative and emotionally
charged cultural understandings that inspire, organize, and justify
work dedication. These schemas, the cultural facets of structure
(Sewell 1992), help define people's moral identities and their desires
about how to spend their waking hours.

In this chapter I delineate the cultural schema of work devotion
using the case of female finance executives. In so doing, I question
the common assumption among scholars that long work hours are
automatically associated with "overwork" and necessarily exacerbate work-life conflict.

"Ideal workers," those highly valued employees who can work
long hours without being burdened by family responsibilities, are
typically male (Williams 2000; Acker 1990). In this chapter, however, we study "ideal workers" who are women, specifically female

finance executives who have been generously rewarded for intense work commitment. My respondents are at the extreme end of the distribution of employed women, and are the only women or are among the very few women who have reached top positions in their firms. They are the "wrong" gender for these positions. Being outsiders has made them particularly self-conscious and articulate about the rewards and dilemmas of ideal-worker status. This extreme case helps reveal taken-for-granted assumptions about work devotion and allows us to understand work commitment from the perspective of these ideal workers themselves.[1]

## WORK HOURS, COMMITMENT, AND WORK DEVOTION

In this section I review some of the research on work hours and on organizational commitment.

### Long Work Hours

The work-family literature has documented increases in work hours for many employees, especially among highly educated managerial and professional workers (Jacobs and Gerson 2004; Galinsky and Swanberg 2000). In this literature it is generally argued that many employees work longer hours than they want to (Clarkberg and Moen 2001). Employees say they feel overworked for several reasons, including pressure from demanding supervisors, a high volume of tasks to accomplish, frequent interruptions, lack of flexibility, inadequate workplace support, and fear of curtailed mobility or unemployment (Galinsky and Galinsky 2001; Jacobs and Gerson 2004; Maume and Bellas 2001; Perlow 1997). Jill Fraser (2001) characterizes large American corporations as "white-collar sweatshops," coercively requiring long and stressful workdays and motivating their employees to put forth greater effort with the fear of job loss.[2]

Alongside other factors, researchers have begun to analyze how a corporate culture of long hours helps tie people to their desks. A "culture of overtime" (Fried 1998), the emphasis on "face time" over efficiency (Fried 1998; Hochschild 1997), a firm's "unwritten rule that employees can't take care of family needs on company time" (Maume and Bellas 2001, 1153), and the stigmatization of part-time work among professionals (Epstein et al. 1999) are all examples of coercive norms enforcing the lengthening workday.

In a similar vein, scholars have lamented how firms reserve the best jobs and opportunities for "ideal workers," who can give long hours to their employer without being encumbered by family responsibilities (Williams 2000; Acker 1990; Drago et al. 2001). These studies agree that "ideal worker norms" (Drago et al. 2001) bolster workplace discrimination against women, part-time professionals, and any employee involved in family care (Williams 2000, Acker 1990; Blair-Loy and Wharton 2002). Most of these studies advocate that employees should be able to spend less time at work in order to have less conflict and more balance between work and the rest of their lives.

Most work-family research on long hours tends to assume that long work hours are just the unfortunate byproduct of external forces rather than analyzing the culture of long hours or ideal-worker norms as important cultural phenomena per se. And when this literature does study these norms, researchers assume that the norms are just another set of external constraints on workers' actions rather than investigate the ways these norms may powerfully shape and be shaped by workers' own self-understandings. The literature generally neglects to consider how some workers may be "architects" as well as "prisoners" of the long-hours regime (Hochschild 1997).

Without an analysis of work-devotion norms as powerful and partially internalized components of social structure, we cannot fully understand why employees spend so much time at work. Our lack of understanding is most evident regarding senior managers and executives, who despite their relative autonomy and power within the firm often still feel compelled to devote long hours to their jobs (Hochschild 1997; Blair-Loy 2003; Kanter 1977; Wajcman 1996).

## Organizational Commitment

A literature on organizational commitment provides additional insights into the relationship between the hard-working employee and the firm. In contrast to the emphasis on coercion that characterizes research on work hours, studies of organizational commitment highlight the voluntary, or value-identification, aspect of commitment. For example, Paul Osterman (1995, 686) defines commitment as "the employees' willingness to engage themselves and offer their ideas and knowledge with a degree of authenticity that, by its very nature, is not enforceable and which therefore requires [a] substantial element of volunteerism on the part of the workforce."

James Lincoln and Arne Kalleberg (1990) argue that corporatist control practices such as social integration, internal job ladders, and decentralized decision making induce employees' commitment to their employers. These management practices "attempt to turn the employment relationship into an enveloping, communal and harmonious interdependence between the company and its workforce that generates loyalty and commitment to the firm" (Lincoln and Kalleberg 1990, 14). Furthermore, these structures "control labor, not through coercive or utilitarian methods but through the use of normative, social and symbolic inducements" that create this enveloping, communal interdependence (Wallace 1995a, 812).

Lincoln and Kalleberg (1990) implicitly view organizational commitment as a complex orientation with cognitive, normative, and affective dimensions:

> Organizational commitment implies *identification* with an organization and acceptance of its goals and values as one's own. . . . The committed employee's involvement in the organization takes on *moral* overtones and *his stake extends beyond the satisfaction of a merely personal interest* in employment, income, and intrinsically rewarding work. The employee becomes *conscious* of the needs of the organization and sensitive to how his or her actions contribute to the fulfillment of those needs. . . . The firm's performance is experienced as a personal success or failure as well. Moreover, committed employees are loyal to the organization, *feel* personally defensive when it is threatened, and *desire* to maintain the employment relationship even when presented with attractive alternatives. (22–23, emphasis added)

Cognitively, the committed employee becomes "conscious" of the employers' needs and sees them as linked to his or her own contributions. Normatively, one's work takes on "moral overtones" with implications beyond narrow self-interest. And affectively, employees feel loyalty and protectiveness toward the organization; they "desire" to remain connected to it.

Lincoln and Kalleberg (1990, 23) say further that this orientation envelops the committed employee in an identification and interdependence with the firm and demands a "sacrifice of allegiance to subgroups" within the organization. Note the normative and almost religious connotations of the phrase "sacrifice of allegiance." For the executive women I interviewed, careers require the sacrifice of almost all nonwork commitments (Blair-Loy 2003).

Lincoln and Kalleberg (1990) primarily study the effects of corporatist management practices on workers' organizational commitment and job satisfaction in manufacturing firms. Their approach has been used to study a variety of occupations outside the manufacturing company, including lawyers (Wallace 1995a, 1995b), ordained ministers (McDuff and Mueller 2000), and workers in small firms (Mueller et al. 1994). Following Lincoln and Kalleberg's lead, these applications have used survey data on large samples to examine whether particular structures and conditions of the workplace increase workers' commitment, attachment, or job satisfaction. Although these applications have taught us a great deal, they have ignored Lincoln and Kalleberg's insights into the normative, affective, and symbolic dimensions of work. Moreover, this literature has not examined employees and firms as potentially having an "enveloping, harmonious and communal interdependence" but instead treats workers as empirically autonomous from the firm and as simply reacting with narrow self-interest to inducements provided by management.

A related literature has examined organizational commitment in terms of organizational citizenship behavior. Employee citizenship behavior is workers' extra effort, cooperation, enthusiasm, and productivity—any effort beyond what is minimally required or can be enforced by the firm—to reach organizational goals (Organ 1988). Citizenship behavior on the part of management vis-à-vis workers entails managers' conforming to broad norms about providing sufficient resources so that the technical side of work runs smoothly and treating employees with fairness and respect. Management citizenship behavior can enhance employee citizenship (Hodson 2002). For example, Susan Lambert (2000) uses an exchange model to suggest that norms about reciprocity influence employee behavior. In her study, management's provision of work-family benefits that demonstrate respect for workers "may create a generalized sense of obligation to the workplace," leading employees to engage in a variety of behaviors helpful to their company (Lambert 2000, 811).

The organizational citizenship literature provides insights but does not push the notion of employees and managers as fellow citizens of a single workplace community far enough. Like much of the organizational-commitment literature, it tends to treat workers as distinct from the firm and reacting with narrow self-interest to the leadership, training and job benefits, and job security provided by management. Organizational-citizenship research generally and Lambert's exchange model specifically have not yet systematically analyzed the normative cultural structures potentially defining, linking, and transforming worker and management interests, identities, and emotional and moral commitments. This issue may be especially salient for elite employees, who have been entrusted with high levels of resources, autonomy, and responsibility.

In contrast to these earlier approaches, my research takes seriously the potential interdependence between firm and employee. This insight from Lincoln and Kalleberg will help us more fully understand the corporate culture of long work hours identified by work-family scholars. Although many employees undoubtedly feel coerced by their employer into putting in long hours, this is only part of the picture. Some employees may also be motivated by an allegiance to their employer born of a sense of interdependence between the mission of the firm and their own vocation.

## Schema of Work Devotion

I analyze work commitment as a schema, a cultural model that orients senior managers toward a preoccupation with their own advancement, defines their priorities, and evokes a passion for their careers. My analysis is informed by William Sewell's (1992, 27) formulation of structure as composed of "mutually sustaining cultural schemas and sets of resources that empower and constrain social action and tend to be reproduced by that action." Schemas are the virtual dimension of structure, resources are the material dimension. Resources are dependent upon schemas to define their meaning and use. At the same time, schemas require resources to validate and regenerate them.

In my usage, a cultural schema is an ordered, socially constructed, nonmaterial element of social structure, a framework for understanding and evaluating a particular dimension of society and ascertaining one's own relationship to it. Particular schemas are objective in the sense that they are shared, communicated, publicly available understandings. They are also subjective in that they are partially internalized and thus shape personal aspirations and identities.

In contrast to the psychological and neoinstutionalist use of the term "schema" to mean cognitive classifications (for example, Bem 1983; Powell and DiMaggio 1992), I argue that cultural schemas can also provide powerful normative evaluations and evoke intense emotions. These aspects of culture are highly salient in what I term *schemas of devotion:* particularly gripping cultural models that orient us toward where we devote our time, energy, and passion. In a historical time and place, they tell us what to care about and how to care about it. I use the term "devotion" rather than "commitment" or "interest" to emphasize that these schemas define more than just cognitive maps or rational interests. Like pseudo-religious articles of faith, they promise to provide meaning to life and a secure connection to something outside ourselves (Blair-Loy 2003).

This chapter delineates a cultural model of work commitment, which I call the *schema of devotion to work.* This schema defines and regulates everyday social processes in specific employer organizations. It is institutionalized into real career paths and influences employers' and spouses' expectations. It also shapes respondents' personal aspirations, desires, and normative beliefs.

Note that firms need not necessarily be "greedy institutions" (Coser 1974), demanding of immense amounts of time, energy, and passion. One may work in a firm in order to earn money to live, but biological survival does not require sixty-plus-hour work weeks, deal negotiating that can go on all night, extensive travel, and the willingness to use social connections for business ends. Even people who are preoccupied with their personal advancement or profit rely on a shared and communicated schema to tell them that these concerns are meaningful and worthwhile. The devotion to work articulates the "moral imperative" in U.S. society that orients managers toward preoccupation with their own advancement (Jackall 1988, 43) and helps motivate them to put in long work hours.

Empirically, devotion to work can take the form of dedication to one's job, one's employer, or one's profession or occupation. The object of devotion varies depending upon the case studied, the time period, and the conditions of employment.

Although a full analysis of the origins of the work-devotion schema is beyond the scope of this paper, I briefly sketch some aspects of that history. The work-devotion schema has been socially constructed by human beings over time. Its contemporary incarnation among U.S. managers and executives is rooted in both a religion-based work ethic and in the material incentives and constraints of twentieth-century capitalism.

Prior to the twentieth century this work ethic had been part of a larger perspective "that placed all work in context as a means" to a greater end (Hunnicut 1988, 313), the higher good of leading a biblically virtuous life of love for God and for one's neighbor (Wuthnow 1996, 63). This early ideal potentially sacralized almost any productive endeavor as a calling.

By the early twentieth century, "Work had become its own justification, . . . an end in itself . . . —a part of an older tradition broken off and worshipped for itself. Meaning, justification, purpose, and even salvation were now sought in work, without a necessary reference to any traditional philosophic or theological structure" (Hunnicut 1988, 313; see also Weber 1930/1958). People today continue to work to provide legitimate, moral accounts of themselves, but these moral accounts are today likely to be "supplied by the workplace itself" rather than by broader theological or philosophical traditions (Wuthnow 1996, 332). These accounts provided by the workplace tend to channel work devotion into dedication to a specific employer.

The work-devotion schema also has roots in the material incentives offered by the U.S. capitalist economic system to employers for demanding longer work hours. In the twentieth century these incentives include the fixed annual salary for white-collar workers, in which extra hours are worked at no extra charge to employers, and the rising cost of fringe benefits as a proportion of individual wages and salaries (Schor 1992).[3]

The development of internal labor markets in large firms (see Schor 1992; Althauser and Kalleberg 1990) was an overlapping process that also helped cultivate and channel managers' and executives' work devotion toward a specific employer. These firm structures helped create the reciprocal employment relationship characterizing white-collar workers in the mid- to late twentieth century, in which managers expected to receive firm-specific training, long-term tenure, and promotion in return for their commitment to their employer. This relationship has been characterized as a "psychological contract," in which "employee commitment to the organization" was exchanged "in return for employer offerings such as job security and other protections from the variability of employment associated with outside markets" (Cappelli et al. 1997, 10). These firm structures helped support the masculine, middle-class, twentieth-century, urban model of an upwardly mobile managerial career (Whyte 1956), in which commitment to and meaning and identity derived from dedication to a specific firm.

Lincoln and Kalleberg (1990) maintain that an individual's commitment to work in general is distinct from and causally antecedent to commitment to an employer. But with the increasing pace of restructuring and layoffs in the 1980s and 1990s, many employers have broken the psychological contract between worker and employer. There is some evidence that commitment to the employer is being supplemented or replaced by the more general commitment to one's work or occupation (Cappelli et al. 1997).

For the executives I study, dedication to their firms and absorption in the work itself overlap empirically.[4] My respondents develop their work commitment and a concern for personal advancement not in the abstract but within the context of commitment to a particular group of bosses, colleagues, and clients. These firm-specific relationships are so important to respondents that if ruptured, respondents may lose their faith in the work-devotion schema entirely.

As finance managers progress up the firm hierarchy, they may become partners or major investors in the firm and thus, in a sense, their own employer. In this instance, devotion to the firm and devotion to their own advancement are completely aligned.

Particularly for career-committed women, the work-devotion schema competes with the schema of family devotion. The family-devotion schema ordains women's commitment to and fulfillment in caring for family members (Blair-Loy 2003; Hays 1996).

## METHODS AND DATA

This qualitative, exploratory case study relies on a reciprocal process of inductive insights and deductive analysis. Although case-based approaches cannot yield general statements of empirical regularity about large populations, they can uncover and yield interpretations of constellations of forces that change or reproduce social processes (Ragin 1987).

In contrast to studies of representative or typical samples, I pursue the strategy of the extreme case. My respondents are on the extreme end of the distribution of employed women. They are unusually career-committed and successful. As members of a tiny minority of women in such senior and powerful positions, many are self-consciously aware of the benefits and problems of being ideal workers.

As a group of *unusually successful* women, this case allows the analyst to more clearly see the taken-for-granted assumptions about the meaning of work devotion. However, since the sample has little variation on the level of career success, it is limited in providing explanations for the relationship between career success and other variables, including the level of work devotion.

I collected life histories from female executives and then conducted in-depth interviews with them on their careers, family, triumphs, and adversities. I looked for patterns in work and family behavior and in respondents' interpretations of that behavior. This process led me to an inductively derived picture of the work-devotion schema, an understanding that was refined by the study of other research.

The present analysis is based upon interviews I conducted from 1994 to 1995 with fifty-six women in high-ranking finance-related jobs. Respondents belong to a professional and networking organization, based in a large U.S. city, that only admits women with senior-level finance-related jobs. Each respondent filled out a detailed life history questionnaire. I then interviewed each on her career, family, accomplishments, and regrets. Respondents work in financial services (including investment and commercial banks, real estate investment firms, and financial consulting firms), manufacturing and diversified service companies, and public accounting and law firms. They have all reached senior levels, and their job titles include vice president and treasurer, senior vice president, chief financial officer, managing director, partner, managing partner, and chief executive officer.

In 1994, respondents ranged in age from thirty-six to sixty. All have bachelor's degrees; 86 percent have graduate degrees. Twenty-one respondents (38 percent) are mothers. Forty-seven women had been married at least once. Twenty were divorced at least once; six have remarried. Annual compensation for for-profit employees in 1993 ranged from $125,000 to $1,000,000, with a median of $250,000.

Since the sample includes only *women* who enjoy unusual career success, it does not directly speak to gender differences in the experience of work devotion. Yet it is significant that these women have ignored or rejected the dominant feminine cultural expectation of middle- and upper-class white women, which is to be primarily devoted to family (Blair-Loy 2003). To understand them from the perspective of the life they have rejected, I supplemented these interviews with interviews from twenty-five women who had relinquished promising business careers after having children. I briefly consider implications from this comparison sample in the "Conclusion."

All the respondents are white except for one, an African American. The findings are thus limited in terms of racial generalizations. All names of firms and individuals have been changed.[5]

This case is theoretically important because it helps us understand work devotion from the perspective of ideal workers themselves. Moreover, my respondents have the power to enforce at least outward conformity to the work-devotion schema among their subordinates and thus potentially to exacerbate the conflict between work and family for their subordinates. More broadly, cultural models of white middle- and upper-class professionals and managers have a dominant role in shaping expectations around work and family generally in the United States (Garey 1999).

The work-devotion schema is a cultural model specifying a reciprocal relationship between elite employee and employer. My data are at the individual level of analysis. Thus, my findings emphasize the work-devotion schema from the perspective of managers and executives. Research focused on the employer qua employer, at the firm level of analysis, would more directly illuminate the presence, variation, and consequences of this model from the perspective of the firm.

## FINDINGS AND DISCUSSION

I now delineate the elements of the ideal-typical work-devotion schema. Next, I will consider variation in respondents' embrace of this world view.

## The Work-Devotion Schema

Empirically, devotion to work can take the form of dedication to one's job, one's employer, or one's profession or occupation. In these data, this work devotion is developed within the context of and channeled toward commitment to a particular employer. It begins as a reciprocal relationship between employer and manager, featuring an often unarticulated psychological contract that the employer will repay the talented and dedicated manager with learning opportunities, advancement, and loyalty. Work devotion is somewhat portable; it is possible for respondents to leave one employer on good terms and dedicate themselves to a new employer. As my respondents progressed up the firm hierarchy, many became part owners of the firm and thus, in a sense, their own employers.[6]

As an ideal type, the work-devotion schema creates normative expectations among managers and employers. It shapes respondents' objective job descriptions and opportunities at the same time it influences their ambitions and desires. It is assumed to operate until it is violated.

Dedication is induced early in a manager's career by the employer's demands for wholehearted allegiance. If the manager provides allegiance and proves her trustworthiness, the firm will reward her with salary raises and promotions. Promotion into senior levels ushers her into the organization's elite ranks and gives her responsibility for shepherding the organization toward its goals. As the senior manager continues to express fealty to the firm, she receives increasingly challenging and autonomous work. These responsibilities may require longer hours and closer involvement with colleagues and clients. Dedication becomes devotion as her work takes on a single-minded, emotional intensity that fuses personal and professional goals and inspires her to meet these goals. In some cases, this intensively devoted work and close integration with colleagues allow her to "lose herself" in her work and at the same time induce a powerful sense of transcendence.

The devotion to work schema serves the economic interests of the employer, which are more or less tightly linked with senior managers' economic interests through bonuses, stock options, or shares. Yet this chapter will show that the devotion schema has a power beyond legitimating economic rationality or veiling exploitation.[7]

About half of the respondents have seen their devotion to work grow over time. Their devotion has been amply rewarded, and their commitment remains firm. The schema gives meaning and direction to their lives. But the others have seen their faith in the devotion schema falter. Employers sometimes cavalierly break the schema's promises, such as by demoting or laying off an executive or by betraying her trust. Since the work-devotion schema is so central in organizing their worlds, these women can be devastated if it is broken.

## The Schema's Manifestation in Respondents' Lives

The central elements of the ideal typical devotion-to-work schema are the senior manager's allegiance to the firm, the senior manager's sense of intensity and single-mindedness about her responsibilities, and the evocation of a sense of transcendence. Financial rewards and promotions are the means through which executives connect with senior management and gain access to exciting work. Space permits me to consider only a few examples of each of these strands in respondents' lives.

*Allegiance*    Allegiance to employers entails long hours, hard work, emotional involvement, financial investment, and restrictions on geographical freedom. For example, the CFO of an investment bank expressed her allegiance to her firm with hard work, long hours, and fidelity: "I devoted my life to my career. Since I don't have any kids yet, I could work nights. I don't have any other commitments." At another investment bank, a senior vice president says that management is expected to signal allegiance by financially investing in the firm: "Now I'm a stockholder in the firm. Whenever you become a VP, you start owning stock. Owning it is supposed to be a good thing. You show your confidence in the firm."

Allegiance can also entail a loss of geographic freedom. Relocations are common among respondents, who often drag a spouse with them to the new location.

*Financial Security, Independence, and Status*    For senior executives, allegiance to employer and career promises a multiplicity of rewards. Generous financial rewards, including stock options, play a large part in respondents' decisions to enter and to stay in finance-related occupations. In past years, some respondents made millions with the sale of stock; others look forward to future wealth when they sell current stock holdings.

Yet money does far more than provide a comfortable life. It also provides security, cements one's membership within a high-status group, and bestows independence from male breadwinners. Many respondents cherish their incomes because they provide independence from men who might otherwise limit their autonomy.

There are few gender differences in preferences for particular attributes of jobs (Tolbert and Moen 1998). However, the desire to be recognized as an expert with her own achieved social status may have more salience for women, who traditionally have had to make do with the reflected social status of the men in their lives. For example, a former treasurer of a Fortune 500 company discussed how she had been motivated throughout her career by the desire for status and recognition.

> It seems that for an awful lot of my career, I was fighting to get recognition and fighting to get the promotions and fighting to get ahead. When I became treasurer of United Foods, it was great fun when people would say, "And what do you do?" And I would say, "Well, I'm the treasurer of United Foods." And they'd go, "*The* treasurer?"
>
> You know, it was an impressive position, and you could see that in the reaction people gave you. So, I think that I felt like I finally made it. . . . I felt like I had gotten to the point where people had to recognize that I was an important person like the guy next to me was important, a senior executive kind of thing.

Senior jobs in finance-related fields are accorded respect and an achieved status. This recognition was not based upon being a prominent man's wife or secretary but on being important oneself, "like the guy next to me was important, a senior executive."

Another respondent, Sarah Jacobs, contrasts her work as a mother in which "ultimately, the child's success is his own, not yours," with her work as a corporate lawyer, in which her achievements are her own. Her career represents her independent accomplishment. "It is my space. It is my alley. This career is mine and no one else can own it, only I can own it, and I needed that." Jacobs elaborates further on the importance of professional recognition:

> With all the therapy [I've been through, I realize that] you're supposed to feel terrific within yourself. But it helps that outside people sort of recognize your professional accomplishments. Pat you on the head and say you're really good. . . . In business, the gratification is much more constant [than one gets in motherhood]. The other lawyers think you're fabulous. The clients think you're fabulous. Fabulous deals have been brought into the city and you're the attorney chosen to do it.

A successful career constitutes a sphere in which respondents' identities are not defined by their relation to family members, a sphere in which the gratification is reliable and their triumphs are their own. Raises and promotions are not only valuable in and of themselves but as the means of access to an elite management corps and exciting work.

*Challenging Work and Exciting Opportunities*    Respondents frequently mention the interesting opportunities that their companies provide them. Their hard work is rewarded by more hard work, but it is work they find interesting and absorbing. For example, when I asked one respondent about her career pace, she answered:

> It's been terrific. It couldn't have been any faster. Virtually every opportunity is available. It's a meritocracy. By your own hard work you can prosper. . . . There's enough newness in this work that it keeps it intellectually challenging. You can't find in a book how to do this deal. Instead there are these personalities and these goals.

Autonomy and creativity also constitute valued rewards. For instance, a banker tells me what she likes most about her job: "I like the variety, the creativity, the independence. The fact that our work is discretionary. We self-determine the best way to meet our general objectives." Another respondent fantasized about quitting her job and living full-time at her lake-front vacation home. When I asked her what keeps her from doing that, she said: "When all is said and done, I like having an interesting and challenging job to go to every day." Similarly, the vice president and treasurer of a Fortune 500 company said, "I basically do my own thing. There's a lot of creativity on the job. I like the idea of being considered the authority in my area for this company."

*Collegiality and Community*    Several respondents reported valuing the time they spent with their coworkers. As one vice president in a Fortune 500 manufacturing company put it, organizations exist so that people can be in relationship with other people: "Emotional capital, relationships—that's why organizations exist. Otherwise, we'd all be at home with our faxes and our modems. That's why people want to work in organizations." Workplace relations were not always auspicious for respondents, but when they were positive, they were highly appreciated.

A banker glowingly described the colleagues she had had in her previous organization: "It was the best group of people I ever worked with: smart, aggressive, open-minded. It was great." Several respondents discussed becoming personally invested in clients and the success of their businesses. For example, one woman described her relationships with long-term clients as "the great satisfaction of this practice. Keeping involved with their businesses and getting to know them well. You form fun, gratifying relationships."

In sum, if the devotion-to-work schema is observed within particular firms, respondents enjoy a generous array of rewards. Respondents value raises and promotions because they promise financial security and also move them into the elite corps of senior management. They are also motivated by the status and recognition their jobs entail and by the challenging and autonomous nature of their work. Not all respondents have positive workplace relationships, but those who do described collegiality as one of the most fulfilling aspects of the job.

*Intensity and Transcendence*    There is more to the compelling nature and the emotional charge of the schema of devotion to work. Rather than simply appreciating the status that their job accords, some invest their entire subjectivity in the goal of promotion. More than just enjoying their challenging tasks, some respondents speak of being thrilled by their work. Rather than merely valuing their workplace colleagues, some feel urgently committed to those colleagues and strongly identify with them and with the success of the organization.

Intensity and transcendence are the key elements of the work-devotion schema. Intensity is the emotional quality, the life blood, that makes the rewards of status, challenge, and collegiality so compelling. Respondents describe the emotional charge in the long hours they give their employers. They speak of being "totally consumed by" their work; they cite their "drive" to be promoted. Intensity evokes the torch of excitement that fuses corporate and personal goals and the rush of adrenaline that rouses the energy to meet these goals. One hard-working head of an investment firm said, "I find the stock market absolutely thrilling. I really love it."

Amy Peterson, a public accountant, reported that her hard work was motivated by a "consuming drive" to make partner. She describes the workplace intensity as an "adrenaline flow" connected to the urgency and excitement of the broader corporate culture. She said, "And so you work really hard, and it's a cultural thing too. There's an adrenaline flow and there's a big deal going on. It's much more than a job and it demands much more than a job." The organizational culture consumed her but also held out the promise of a new, exalted identity, that of partner in the firm.

Another respondent emphasized the "rush of adrenaline" her job gave her each morning. The "positive feedback" she personally received was intimately connected to fulfilling the "mission of the organization." The fused goals of personal and corporate fulfillment were realized through her connection to her "team." Working together, she and her colleagues transcended limits and accomplished seemingly impossible tasks.

Similarly, Yvonne Smith describes her career as doing more than simply allowing her to garner the rewards of challenging work, promotions, and recognition. She characterizes her feelings about her work as euphoric. At midcareer she left a Fortune 500 company to become president of a small company.

> [When I joined the company], it was a two-hundred-thousand-dollar business in sales. I built it up to a three-and-a-half-million-dollar company in three years. . . . We had a really fun team. It was complete euphoria. I used all my skills. That's the most fun you can ever have, running your own small business. We were a cohesive group. . . . I worked with some very impressive women. It was a fun, great group.

Her job claimed all her talent, energy, and dedication. In return it gave her the euphoria of successfully working with like-minded devotees toward a common goal.

In sum, the schema of devotion to work contains within it a compelling normative force and a promise to bring the worker into a communion with like-minded believers in the firm. Respondents describe the emotional charge, the euphoria, and the sense of transcendence realized in a group of people intensely working toward a common end.

These reports are similar to Emile Durkheim's classic account of the religious ceremony of Australian native groups, in which "the very fact of the concentration [of people together] acts as an exceptionally powerful stimulant" and the participants are raised to a level of exaltation (Durkheim 1965, 246). My respondents credit the group dynamism and cohesiveness for their tremendous success. As one woman put it: "There were no barriers to what we accomplished . . . to forward the mission of the organization." In Durkheim's words, their association with their colleagues "raises [them] outside of [themselves]" into an "environment filled with exceptionally intense forces" that transform and empower them (465, 250).

Sarah Jacobs, who is a partner and board member of a large law firm and a celebrated "rainmaker" (business generator) in the city, explained her meteoric rise to partner status by citing her intense effort ("I busted my ass") and her sociable connection to business associates. The long hours she put in were as vital for cementing relations with colleagues and clients as for the number of deals she closed.

Her drive was based on more than personal ambition. In the law firm, she discovered a mentor to revere and new facets of an identity to cultivate.

> I really worshipped my mentor. . . . [When I made partner], it was thrilling. . . . This profession gives me, in a lot of ways, a real piece of me and the longer you do it, the more it gives you. . . . It's been enormously good for me and not just financially. I mean, in terms of who I think and know I am.

Jacobs admits that she thinks her work is "sometimes obsessive." Yet it is an obsession that makes sense in light of the schema of devotion to work. In immersing herself in the long hours and intense, sometimes worshipful relationships, Ms. Jacobs says she has been given "a real piece of me." In losing herself in her work, she has found herself. In Durkheim's words, Ms. Jacobs feels "dominated and carried away by some sort of external power which makes [her] think and act differently"; she believes she has become "a new being" (Durkheim 1965, 249).

*Single-Mindedness*   As "ideal workers" (Acker 1990; Williams 2000), my respondents find that work devotion stands in tension with other commitments. Allegiance to a job with extreme demands required respondents to maintain an almost single-minded focus on their professional responsibilities.[8]

Almost two-thirds of the sample did not have children; their work commitment remains undivided. Those who are mothers contract out child-care labor to others so that they can fulfill the demands of work devotion (Blair-Loy 2003). For example, a managing partner in a large law firm maintained, "I started from the premise that I had to have a full-time live-in child-care person. When Elizabeth was little, we had a live-in nanny, always." Another woman stated in a matter-of-fact tone: "I see my [eighteen-month-old] daughter for fifteen minutes before I leave. Her caregiver comes in, and I head for the train." A managing director of a real estate investment company said, "My husband and I go through some periods of intense work schedules. We are thinking about hiring someone to take over for the nanny when we can't get back in time."

The actions of the mother who sees her baby for fifteen minutes in the morning and the parents who hire a baby sitter to relieve their full-time nanny make sense in light of the devotion-to-work schema. In the past, managerial and professional men commonly justified their absence from the home by the social legitimacy of their breadwinning role and their vocational calling. Now some executive women are doing the same thing.

## Firms' Violation of the Work-Devotion Schema

My retrospective interview data suggest that all fifty-six executives *initially* shared some version of the devotion-to-work schema. For about half of these women, their fidelity has been generously rewarded and their commitment to their firms has grown over time. However, the others have seen one or more strands of the schema broken. Their dedication has turned to ambivalence or, for six women, completely soured.

Respondents who had grown disillusioned by the devotion-to-work schema explained it to me in terms of deteriorating rewards, disenchantment with top management's practical ethics, and negative implications of industry consolidation. As some have ascended the ranks of the corporation, they have become disenchanted with what they regard as the self-serving and sometimes unethical behavior of those running the firms. Others maintained that their businesses were becoming more grueling in an increasingly competitive and consolidated industry. The past twenty-five years have seen a high merger and acquisition rate among companies, a corporate real estate recession, a stock market crash, increased competition from globalization and technological advances, and continued industry consolidation. These developments reduce the client base of financial services firms and lower the fees surviving clients are willing to pay for their services. Most respondents are senior enough to enjoy some protection from layoffs, and very few had lost their jobs in their firms' restructuring efforts. Yet shrinking revenues in service firms can be devastating for younger and more vulnerable managers.[9]

A limitation on researchers' use of the term "psychological contract" is that it emphasizes the financial dimension of the employer-employee relationship (the promise of job security) while neglecting the social and moral covenant that this relationship also assumed. Disillusionment with work devotion was often not simply due to fewer material rewards but rather rooted in the rupture of workplace relationships and sense of social and moral betrayal. The real sting lay not in diminished financial rewards but in personal experiences of promises broken by human beings they were connected to.

To illustrate, Amy Peterson was a young rising star at a "big six" public accounting firm until she was demoted from partner to manager during the economically troubled early 1990s. She was among numerous new partners who were demoted during that time. She maintains that in a competitive environment, public accounting firms no longer make good on their implicit promise of financial rewards and secure partnership in exchange for intensive work.

> Public accounting firms really count on promises of big rewards, probably to middle-class people who had never dreamt of making that much money in their life. And so you work really hard. . . . When the recession hit, the social contract was clearly broken. . . . It was naïve of me to have thought that if I did a really good job and did everything the firm wanted, that they would take care of me. . . . I think the goal that all of us were willing to put in all those crazy hours for was joining the club [partnership] with the assumption that once you were in, it was a lifetime membership. . . . After working so hard to achieve a goal, you think you're entering this club and you realized that you've entered a pool of sharks.

Rather than accepting her fate as being due to an economically troubled industry, Amy Peterson blames the greed of the firm's senior partners. What stung most was her realization that she had sacrificed ten years of her life to join the elite ranks of an organization that turns out to be run by "sharks and cannibals" who did not value her. It was a painful discovery that the partners in charge, trying to make "more than they ever made before," deemed her expendable. The taken-for-granted link between her personal success and the firm's success was broken. Ms. Peterson condemns the "greed" that broke what she calls the "*social* contract," which suggests a broader moral critique than the term "psychological contract" implies.

In addition to general complaints about exhaustion, practical ethics, and industry consolidation, some women reported more particular and personal experiences of rejection or betrayal. These were executives who wholeheartedly devoted themselves to their organizations and found themselves repaid by being cheated, laid off, or subjected to discrimination or sexual harassment.

A few respondents reported being defrauded by employers or business partners. A more common story was of explicit or implicit gender discrimination. The most traumatic episodes occurred when women were faithfully serving their companies and then were blindsided by an unexpected rejection. For example, Jane Buckingham began working at a national public accounting firm in the late 1960s. She had worked hard, relocated to a new city upon request, and anticipated further promotions. Eleven years later, her career was derailed when she was denied consideration for partner. She explained:

> I'd been at the public accounting firm for eleven years and done exemplary work. My evaluations were always excellent. I would've been the first woman partner in my division. They weren't ready for it. After you'd been manager there for four to five years, they'd tell you whether you'd be partner material. One year before I would've been admitted, they took my name off the list. They said I "lacked interpersonal skills." In other words, I wore a skirt to work. I had no idea this was going to happen. I felt like I was kicked in the stomach.

If we generally accept Ms. Buckingham's interpretation of these events, the firm's discriminatory actions in the late 1970s are not particularly surprising. What is most striking about the story is Ms. Buckingham's behavior and emotions: her complete dedication to the firm, astonishment at being rejected because of her gender, and subsequent anguish. Her embitterment had less to do with the loss of a job than with the personal rejection and betrayal that the job loss signaled.

A decade later she took a job as the chief financial officer (CFO) of a bank known for its frequent reorganization of senior management. When she was fired from this position she was neither astonished nor anguished. She reported:

> One day the CEO got tired of me and fired me. This time I was not a victim. I called my lawyer, and we took him to the cleaner's. My experience at the public accounting firm taught me that you had to be in charge of your life. I used to think of the firm as a family. That's what they tell you. Baloney. They will take your twelve years and then you're out on the street. I learned that I would never be a helpless victim again, and I'd never expect a company to take care of me. Big companies are shit places to work, whether you are a man or a woman.

Ms. Buckingham had already learned to be skeptical of the devotion-to-work schema's promises. This time she responded to the firm's rejection not with gut-wrenching distress but with a counterattack. Since her gender seemed irrelevant to the loss of the CFO position, her critique of the devotion-to-work schema has broadened to a denouncement of all large firms as "shit places to work whether you are a man or a woman."

Four respondents discussed experiences of unwelcome sexual attention from male bosses. This recently happened to the only female senior colleague of an investment banker named Alice Witt. According to Ms. Witt, this colleague was even more devastated by her coworkers' lack of support for her afterward than by the harassment incident itself. The CEO gave the man who harassed her a medical leave of absence and asked the woman not to discuss the incident with anyone, and she said nothing. "But the guy [the harasser]," Ms. Witt continued,

> called everyone in the group and trashed her. So now, she said, many people in her group don't talk to her. Monday she told me she was going to resign today, after her horrible year. I felt so bad. She could have sued the hell out of the firm. She just wanted to do her job, and now she's the victim, and she has to leave. Either you report it and you have to leave, or you don't report it and you have to leave. I felt bad—angry, sick. She became aware of four others who had been harassed. . . . You go along and you think: "This is pretty good. I'm well liked by management." Well, don't kid yourself.

Sexual harassment is not uncommon.[10] What is striking are the actions and emotions of the harassment victim and the narrator. After experiencing the harassment and the CEO's lukewarm response, Ms. Witt's colleague reportedly continued to subscribe to the devotion-to-work schema. She wanted to be a "good corporate citizen," part of the team, and just do her work. It was not until well after the episode, when the other team members stopped speaking to her, that she resigned. The worst aspect of her "horrible year" was not the harassment incident but, rather, the experience of being rejected by her colleagues. Alice Witt's own response to the story is to feel "bad—angry, sick." Like Jane Buckingham's sense of being kicked in the stomach when she was denied partnership, Ms. Witt is sickened and surprised at the corporate community's disloyalty.

After relaying the story of her colleague's sexual harassment and rejection, Alice Witt talked about wanting to quit. A few moments later, I asked her what she wanted to be doing ten years from now. I hid my surprise when she said enthusiastically: "I'd like to be president of our firm. It's a very challenging job." Ms. Witt was shocked and sickened by the treatment of her female colleague precisely because it breached the schema's promises. At the same time, she continues to assert, and on some level to believe, that she wants to become president of the company, which is the required attitude of aspiring managers. Despite the evidence of her colleague's downfall, she continues to hope that her abiding fidelity will continue to be rewarded. Even for people accustomed to reading profit-and-loss statements, the commitment to work is more than a rational decision reached by calculating costs and benefits. Utility curves can only be drawn through the lens of the schema of devotion to work.

## Identifying Faithful Adherents and Skeptics

For fifty of the fifty-six respondents I was able to make a fairly clear judgment as to whether each respondent had embraced the devotion-to-work schema early in her career and whether she continued to embrace it or had rejected it at the time of the interview. Initially, all fifty seemed to incorporate some version of the schema. It remains basically intact for twenty-six respondents. Dedication has shifted to ambivalence for eighteen women, and for six more individuals, belief in the schema has been shattered.

As a heuristic tool, I used simple cross tabs to explore associations between faith in the work-devotion schema and several variables: the year in which respondents entered finance, promotion rate, turbulence in the firm or industry, and job level. (See Blair-Loy 1999 for a discussion of these variables.) Job level has the closest relationship to whether women retain faith in this schema. In my data, women who had reached the very highest levels in their organizations (chief executive officer, chief financial officer, managing partner) were more likely than women at relatively lower levels to continue to fully embrace the work-devotion schema, less likely to regard it with ambivalence, and less likely to have completely rejected it.[11] Promotion rate is weakly related to the intactness of the work-devotion schema.

These analyses are preliminary and heuristic for several reasons. The sample size is small, and the sample is truncated to include only women who have reached top levels. This design restricts the variation in career advancement and thus limits our ability to analyze the relationship between career advancement and work devotion. Moreover, the analysis is based upon retrospective data, which must be interpreted with caution. People's present accounts of their pasts may be shaped as much by the present as well as by what "really" happened in the past (Cohler 1982; Ricoeur 1984). Further research should more fully examine the correlates, causes, and consequences of work devotion, preferably using larger sample sizes and multivariate models. Nonetheless, I do find an association between career advancement and work devotion, and this result echoes other studies that have found correlations between work commitment and job hierarchy level (see the discussion in Lincoln and Kalleberg 1990, 80–81, 115, 120).

I am unable to determine the causal direction or directions of this association but expect that it is likely due to several processes. First, the most ardent believers may be most likely to devote the effort and loyalty necessary to succeed. In addition, the highest-ranking managers get to shape their firm's version of the schema to serve their own interests. Similarly, more powerful members of the firm can ensure that they receive the rewards promised by the schema. For example, they may be able to insulate themselves from layoffs related to industry consolidation. Finally, those who have moved ahead the furthest are more likely to consider the schema—

within which they have been very successful—to be a fair and accurate description of reality. In sum, the ideology of work devotion seems to get purer at the top of the firm.

## IMPLICATIONS AND CONCLUSION

This chapter has developed a fuller, more theoretically nuanced understanding of what others have studied as the "culture of overtime" or "ideal worker norms." Executive women's career attainment is incomprehensible without an understanding of the work schema that motivates their effort, determines how they allocate their time and energy, and elicits their passion. Among finance executives, the typical ideal work-devotion schema implies a relationship between employer and manager in which the manager's allegiance will be rewarded with financial security, a positive sense of identity and recognition from peers, challenging work, and collegiality.

Previous literature has pictured these employer-employee dynamics too thinly, characterizing employees as workers enjoying corporatist work rewards (Wallace 1995a; McDuff and Mueller 2000) or workers repaying the firm for the benefits they receive by being good organizational citizens (Lambert 2000). These characterizations are insufficient. In addition, employees can be defined and transformed by their relationships to the people they work for and with. Newly revealed here is the importance of an intense connection to and interdependence with one's colleagues and clients.

Furthermore, this finding questions the work-family literature's automatic equation of long work hours with "overwork" and with work-life conflict. My respondents do not experience long work hours as "overwork" as long as their faith in the work-devotion schema remains strong. Immersion in work allows female executives occasionally to transcend ordinary time and experience a heightened sense of purpose and meaning. Comments from two respondents illustrate this point:

> I was there Christmas Eve day until seven P.M. I was usually there until eleven P.M. I worked all the time. I was very challenged, stimulated. I had a lot of drive and ambition. . . . I got promoted very early. . . . I always found a lot of career success, a lot of attention and credibility.

[My husband and I] were in the office until nine or ten at night. All our friends were in the office. We had no other interests. We worked on Saturdays and were exhausted on Sundays. It was a totally stimulating and all encompassing job. . . . You have no casual clothes because you are never casual. You don't read. Holidays are a nuisance because you have to stop working. I remember being really annoyed when it was Thanksgiving. Damn, why did I have to stop working to go eat a turkey?

From the perspective of the work-devotion schema, holidays and hobbies become nuisances. Any nonwork activities are defined as mundane compared to the excitement, significance, and intensity of work. Some respondents admit that the long hours are exhausting, yet as long as the work-devotion schema remains strong, they wear this exhaustion as a badge of honor and a symbol of career commitment. To say that these women lack "work-life balance" is beside the point. For these women, work *is,* in large part, their life.

For about half the women in my sample, their fidelity has been generously rewarded and their commitment to their firms has grown over time. However, the other half of the sample has lost its faith in the schema owing to an experience of rejection or betrayal by the firm or their colleagues. This loss of faith was often precipitated by factors such as deteriorating rewards, disenchantment with top management's practical ethics, sexual discrimination or harassment, or fraud. This disenchantment was not caused solely or simply by the loss of material rewards or job security. Rather, the disenchantment was ultimately based on a sense that cherished social-professional ties and been severed and moral commitments had been betrayed. These women's anguish over seeing the schema's promises broken reveals the centrality of the schema in their lives. And once their faith in the work-devotion schema is shattered, they come to resent the long hours their careers demand. No longer providing "an adrenaline flow" of meaning, work becomes grueling.

The work-devotion ideology may become purer at the top of the firm. In addition to shaping subjective understandings, faith in the schema may be both cause and consequence of career achievement. My homogeneous sample of high-achieving women limits my ability to detect other correlates of work devotion. Future research on a more diverse sample should study if and how other factors, such as gender, family status, race, occupation, economic turbulence, and the presence of high-commitment work systems and family-friendly corporate policies, are associated with work devotion.

There is no consensus in the literature as to whether industry consolidation, restructuring, and downsizing will weaken commitment among elite managers (Grunberg, Anderson-Connolly and Greenberg 2000; Heckscher 1995; Cappelli 1999; Jacoby 1999; Cappelli et al. 1997; Osterman 1996; Kunda and Van Maanen 1999). The erosion of corporatist control practices, such as internal job ladders, may diminish employees' commitment to their employers (Lincoln and Kalleberg 1990). Furthermore, according to Osterman (1996, 9), top managers have been less vulnerable than middle managers or nonmanagerial workers to downsizing in the 1980s and early 1990s. Peter Cappelli et al. (1997) report that morale has dropped among middle managers, but top-level executives tend to maintain personal loyalty to the firm. Kevin Leicht and Mary Fennell (2001) argue that elite managers have increased their autonomy and authority in recent decades. And Gideon Kunda and John Van Maanen (1999) suggest that despite an erosion of loyalty between employers and many workers, core managerial and professional employees are still expected to display what I call work devotion:

> For employees still considered central or core, the relationship with their employer remains ostensibly the same. Employers may rely on a thinner, presumably more select cadre of managers and professionals, but they still expect an intense continuing relationship with them governed by the rules of exchanging emotional investment for corporate benefits. . . . Major corporate decisions such as restructuring, outsourcing, plant closings and downsizing . . . are choices made by people at the top of the corporate hierarchy. (74–75)

Respondents, like Amy Peterson, who lost jobs earlier in their careers did experience disillusionment with the work-devotion schema. But the senior executives studied here are, as a group, largely insulated from the threat of layoffs. The most powerful, protected, and ideologically pure executives remain in positions that reaffirm their own work devotion.

The embodiment of the work-devotion schema is enabled by ample support from spouses or paid caregivers at home and is rewarded by the accumulation of resources at work. These greater resources give the work-devotion schema the power to persist despite the pulls of schemas with competing moral and emotional claims, including the family-devotion schema (Blair-Loy 2003) and the ideology of work-life balance supported by many human resource professionals, policy makers, and academics.

Where the devotion to work is strong, female executives can sometimes ignore the family-devotion schema's mandate that a worthwhile life entails family caregiving and thereby sidestep what scholars call work-life conflict. My respondents either forgo having children (only 38 percent are mothers) or contract out most caregiving duties to full-time paid caregivers (Blair-Loy 2003).

This chapter has relied upon the analysis of fifty-six executive women who work full-time. Here I briefly add that my comparison sample of twenty-five mothers who left full-time jobs reveals patterned forces behind these women's relinquishment of their careers. The comparison group of twenty-five mothers had on average married younger and had less labor market experience than the primary sample and thereby had fewer ideological and material resources to demand the egalitarian marriages necessary for prioritizing their careers. Yet even the mothers who had earlier evidenced extremely high career dedication and enjoyed great success ran up against the powerful cultural model that mandates women's moral responsibility of family devotion. If negative contingencies or family tragedies required that their families receive more attention than paid caregivers could provide, it was these high-achieving women rather than their often lower-paid husbands who abandoned their careers in order to provide that care. This highlights the remarkably high levels of work devotion exhibited by executive women in the primary sample, despite the competing pressure of family obligations. (See Blair-Loy 2003 for a full discussion.)

Thus, the work-devotion ideology reinforces gender and class hierarchies in organizations. Employees who either have no young or school-age children or who have spouses or paid caregivers at home to care for them are more likely to display and to be rewarded for making work the center of their lives. The work-devotion mandate favors men over women, women without children over mothers, and those who can afford to hire full-time caregivers over those who lack those financial resources or who wish to be involved parents.

Despite the efforts of human resource managers and policy makers promoting work-life balance, the demand that executives and aspiring managers work extremely long hours remains a stable structural aspect of elite managerial work. This structure is maintained by a taken-for-granted understanding of this type of life as meaningful and worthy and by the resources that accrue to those expressing the most work devotion. Devoted executives in turn have the power to demand long hours from their subordinates. Thus, elite managers' voluntary commitment to and identification with the firm is translated into a coercive demand for long hours from their subordinates.

There are many ways in which the buying and selling of financial products and services could be organized. But work devotion helps define the institution of the financial services firm and determine which kinds of employees will be most successful.

For example, one respondent explains that she will not promote a talented subordinate who, because of her motherhood responsibilities, "only works forty-five hours a week and [can't] stay all night to finish a deal." Despite her competence, such a woman is unpromotable to the highest ranks because she lacks the "commitment and time" to embrace the long-work-hours regime mandated by the work-devotion schema. Another respondent complains about her female subordinates who want to drive in their children's carpool. Instead, she recommends that her subordinates send their children to school in a cab so that they themselves can get to the office earlier.

The work-devotion schema is a highly salient model of reality. Whether the women I interviewed ultimately hold fast to it or renounce it, they never regard it with indifference. More than simply providing a cognitive category of the successful worker, the work-devotion schema also organizes normative understandings of how executives ought to be spending their time, inspires intense emotional commitment to coworkers and clients, and potentially provides a meaningful and exalted identity that allows executives to transcend themselves to reach seemingly impossible goals.

The most general implication of this study is that human agency is shaped by cultural schemas such as the work-devotion schema that organize categories of thought, belief, and emotion. Work devotion, along with family devotion, defines a normative and emotional universe, the parameters within which female executives work out who they are as moral adults. Attempts to prescribe and enforce policies that address work-life conflict will likely be more effective if they take this into account.

---

Parts of this chapter appeared in Blair-Loy (2003).

## NOTES

1.  In the general population, men are more likely than women to work very long hours (Jacobs and Gerson 2004). In ongoing research, I am also investigating work devotion among male executives.
2.  Among managers, long work hours are further explained by two decades of mergers, acquisitions, downsizing, deregulation, and "investor capitalism" (Useem 1996), which have led to layoffs of white-collar workers and created longer work hours for the employees who survived the cuts (Powell 2001; DiMaggio 2001; Cappelli et al. 1997).
3.  Since World War II the labor movement has been unable to resist lengthening hours (Schor 1992). Furthermore, since the 1980s, competition and shareholder pressure have led to a rise in restructuring and layoffs among large companies, which often results in more work hours for the remaining employees (Cappelli et al. 1997; Useem 1996).
4.  Open for empirical investigation is whether other types of workers channel their devotion more toward their work per se (possibly writers, musicians, craftsmen) or toward the profession or occupation and its clients (possibly clergy [see McDuff and Mueller 2000], doctors, and some attorneys [see Wallace 1995b]).
5.  See Mary Blair-Loy (2003) for additional details on data and methods.
6.  Nine respondents (14 percent) have formed their own small firms. These entrepreneurs are strongly committed to their own success and to the success of their firms, which they see as inextricably linked. Senior managers in large companies tend to be committed both to their own advancement and to their colleagues and organizations. The schema of devotion to work makes the link between personal and corporate success, which is so clear to the entrepreneurs, compelling for the managers in larger firms.
7.  Gideon Kunda (1992) and Stephen Barley and Kunda (1992) argue that an employer's expectation of emotional commitment is a mechanism of normative control believed by employers and managers to enhance worker productivity. Michael Roper (1994) and Rosemary Pringle (1988) have also emphasized the emotional bonds and psychic rewards in business organizations that go beyond economic considerations.
8.  Several researchers have studied how the male ideal worker is supported by family members' labor (Hochschild 1989; Wajcman 1996; Williams 2000). For example, in a study of a large corporation,

Arlie Hochschild (1989, 255) found that among top executives, two-thirds of the men and none of the women were married to full-time homemakers.

9.    On competition, volatility, and consolidation in the finance industry, see Linda Stearns and Kenneth Allan (1996) and Robert Litan and Anthony Santomero (2000). On the negative effects of restructuring and layoffs on employee commitment and morale, see Peter Cappelli et al. (1997) and Jill Fraser (2001). Yet despite this potential disruption of the "psychological contract" in many companies, some studies show that executives are the occupational group maintaining the highest personal loyalty to their employer (Cappelli et al. 1997). My data were collected in 1994 and 1995, before the stock market bubble expanded in the late 1990s and burst in 2000. This more recent volatility, coupled with corporate scandals involving firms in which some respondents worked, likely created disillusionment among people like my respondents.

10.   Sexual harassment may be endemic to the financial services industry (Antilla 2002).

11.   The job-level analysis excludes seven long-term entrepreneurs, reducing the sample size to forty-three. In this group, twenty-three women still fully embraced the schema, fifteen felt ambivalently toward it, and five had rejected it completely. Among the eighteen women at the very highest levels, twelve (67 percent) had fully intact schema, five (28 percent) were ambivalent, and only one person had abandoned the schema. Compared to their highest-achieving colleagues, the twenty-five respondents who had not reached the very top levels were less likely to embrace the schema and more likely to view it with ambivalence or repudiation. Specifically, only eleven of them (44 percent) had fully embraced the schema, ten viewed it with ambivalence (40 percent), and four respondents (16 percent) rejected it entirely. Presenting the same cross-tab results from a different angle, among the twenty-three true believers in the schema, twelve (52 percent) were those who reached the very highest levels. In contrast, the twenty skeptics were in relatively lower positions. Specifically, among the fifteen ambivalent women, only five (33 percent) had reached the very highest levels, and among the five rejecters of the schema, only one (25 percent) had reached the very top level.

# REFERENCES

Acker, Joan. 1990. "Hierarchies, Jobs, Bodies: A Theory of Gender Organizations." *Gender and Society* 4(2): 139–58.

Althauser, Robert P., and Arne L. Kalleberg. 1990. "Identifying Career Lines and Internal Labor Markets Within Firms." In *Social Mobility and Social Structure,* edited by Ronald L. Breiger. Cambridge: Cambridge University Press.

Antilla, Susan. 2002. *Tales from the Boom-Boom Room: Women Vs. Wall Street.* New York: Bloomberg Press.

Barley, Stephen R., and Gideon Kunda. 1992. "Design and Devotion: Surges of Rational and Normative Ideologies of Control in Managerial Discourse." *Administrative Science Quarterly* 37(3): 363–99.

Bem, Sandra Lipsitz. 1983. "Gender Schema Theory and Its Implications for Child Development: Raising Gender-Aschematic Children in a Gender-Schematic Society." *Signs* 8(4): 598–616.

Blair-Loy, Mary. 1999. "Career Patterns of Executive Women in Finance: An Optimal Matching Analysis." *American Journal of Sociology* 104(5): 1346–97.

———. 2003. *Competing Devotions: Career and Family Among Women Financial Executives.* Cambridge, Mass.: Harvard University Press.

Blair-Loy, Mary, and Jerry A. Jacobs. 2003. "Globalization, Work Hours, and the Care Deficit Among Stockbrokers." *Gender and Society* 17(2): 230–49.

Blair-Loy, Mary, and Amy S. Wharton. 2002. "Employees' Use of Family-Responsive Policies and the Workplace Social Context." *Social Forces* 80(3): 813–45.

Cappelli, Peter. 1999. *The New Deal at Work.* Boston: Harvard Business School Press.

Cappelli, Peter, Laurie Bassi, Harry Katz, David Knoke, Paul Osterman, and Michael Useem. 1997. *Change at Work.* Oxford: Oxford University Press.

Clarkberg, Marin, and Phyllis Moen. 2001. "Understanding the Time Squeeze." *American Behavioral Scientist* 44(7): 1115–36.

Cohler, Bertram J. 1982. "Personal Narrative and Life Course." *Life-Span Development and Behavior* 4: 206–41.

Coser, Lewis A. 1974. *Greedy Institutions.* New York: Free Press.

DiMaggio, Paul. 2001. "Making Sense of the Contemporary Firm and Prefiguring Its Future." In *The Twenty-First-Century Firm: Changing Economic Organization in International Perspective.* Princeton: Princeton University Press.

Drago, Robert, Ann C. Crouter, Mark Wardell, and Billie S. Willits. 2001. "Faculty and Families Project: Final Report to the Alfred P. Sloan Foundation." State College, Pa.: Pennsylvania State University.

Durkheim, Emile. 1965. *The Elementary Forms of Religious Life.* New York: Free Press.

Epstein, Cynthia Fuchs, Carroll Seron, Bonnie Oglensky, and Robert Sauté. 1999. *The Part-Time Paradox.* New York: Routledge.

Fraser, Jill Andresky. 2001. *White Collar Sweatshop: The Deterioration of Work and Its Rewards in Corporate America*. New York: Norton.

Fried, Mindy. 1998. *Taking Time: Parental Leave Policy and Corporate Culture*. Philadelphia: Temple University Press.

Galinksy, Kim, and Bond Galinsky. 2001. *Feeling Overworked: When Work Becomes Too Much*. New York: Families and Work Institute.

Galinsky, Ellen, and Jennifer E. Swanberg. 2000. "Employed Mothers and Fathers in the United States." In *Organizational Change and Gender Equity*, edited by Linda L. Haas, Philip Hwang, and Graeme Russell. Thousand Oaks, Calif.: Sage.

Garey, Anita. 1999. *Weaving Work and Motherhood*. Philadelphia: Temple University Press.

Grunberg, Leon, Richard Anderson-Connolly, and Edward S. Greenberg. 2000. "Surviving Layoffs: The Effects on Organizational Commitment and Job Performance." *Work and Occupations* 27(1): 7–31.

Hays, Sharon. 1996. *The Cultural Contradictions of Motherhood*. New Haven: Yale University Press.

Heckscher, Charles. 1995. *White Collar Blues: Management Loyalties in an Age of Corporate Restructuring*. New York: Basic Books.

Hochschild, Arlie. 1989. *The Second Shift: Working Parents and the Revolution at Home*. New York: Viking.

———. 1997. *The Time Bind: When Work Becomes Home and Home Becomes Work*. New York: Metropolitan Books.

Hodson, Randy. 2002. "Management Citizenship Behavior and Its Consequences." *Work and Occupations* 29(1): 64–96.

Hunnicut, Benjamin Kline. 1988. *Work Without End: Abandoning Shorter Hours for the Right to Work*. Philadelphia: Temple University Press.

Jackall, Robert. 1988. *Moral Mazes: The World of Corporate Managers*. Oxford: Oxford University Press.

Jacobs, Jerry A., and Kathleen Gerson. 2004. *The Time Divide: Work, Family, and Gender Inequality*. Cambridge, Mass.: Harvard University Press.

Jacoby, Sanford M. 1999. "Are Career Jobs Headed for Extinction?" *California Management Review* 42(1): 123–45.

Kanter, Rosabeth Moss. 1977. *Men and Women of the Corporation*. New York: Basic Books.

Kunda, Gideon. 1992. *Engineering Culture: Control and Commitment in a High Tech Corporation*. Philadelphia: Temple University Press.

Kunda, Gideon, and John Van Maanen. 1999. "Changing Scripts at Work: Managers and Professionals." *Annals of the American Academy of Political and Social Science* 561(January): 64–80.

Lambert, Susan J. 2000. "Added Benefits: The Link between Work-Life Benefits and Organizational Citizenship Behavior." *Academy of Management Journal* 43(5): 801–15.

Leicht, Kevin T., and Mary L. Fennell. 2001. *Professional Work: A Sociological Approach*. Malden, Mass.: Blackwell Publishers.

Lincoln, James R., and Arne L. Kalleberg. 1990. *Culture, Control, and Commitment: A Study of Work Organization and Work Attitudes in the United States and Japan*. Cambridge: Cambridge University Press.

Litan, Robert E., and Anthony M. Santomero, eds. 2000. *Brookings-Wharton Papers on Financial Services*. Washington, D.C.: Brookings Institution.

Maume, David J., and Marcia L. Bellas. 2001. "The Overworked American or the Time Bind? Assessing Competing Explanations for Time Spent in Paid Labor." *American Behavioral Scientist* 44(7): 1137–56.

McDuff, Elaine M., and Charles W. Mueller. 2000. "The Ministry as an Occupational Labor Market: Intentions to Leave an Employer (Church) Versus Intentions to Leave a Profession (Ministry)." *Work and Occupations* 27(1): 89–116.

Mueller, Charles W., E. Marcia Boyer, James L. Price, and Roderick Iverson. 1994. "Employee Attachment and Noncoercive Conditions of Work." *Work and Occupations* 21(2): 179–212.

Organ, Dennis W. 1988. *Organizational Citizenship Behavior*. Lexington, Mass.: D. C. Heath.

Osterman, Paul. 1995. "Work/Family Programs and the Employment Relationship." *Administrative Science Quarterly* 40(4): 681–700.

———. 1996. Introduction to *Broken Ladders: Managerial Careers in the New Economy*, edited by Paul Osterman. Oxford: Oxford University Press.

Parcel, Toby. 1999. "Work and Family in the 21st Century: It's About Time." *Work and Occupations* 26(2): 264–74.

Perlow, Lesile A. 1997. *Finding Time: How Corporations, Individuals and Families Can Benefit from New Work Practices*. Ithaca, N.Y.: ILR Press.

Powell, Walter W. 2001. "The Capitalist Firm in the Twenty-First Century: Emerging Patterns in Western Enterprise." In *The Twenty-First-Century Firm: Changing Economic Organization in International Perspective*, edited by Paul DiMaggio. Princeton: Princeton University Press.

Powell, Walter W., and Paul J. DiMaggio, eds. 1992. *The New Institutionalism in Organizational Analysis*. Chicago: University of Chicago Press.

Pringle, Rosemary. 1988. *Secretaries Talk: Sexuality, Power and Work*. London: Verso.

Ragin, Charles C. 1987. *The Comparative Method: Moving Beyond Qualitative and Quantitative Strategies*. Berkeley and Los Angeles: University of California Press.

Ricoeur, Paul. 1984. *Time and Narrative*. Chicago: University of Chicago Press.

Roper, Michael. 1994. *Masculinity and the British Organization Man Since 1945*. New York: Oxford University Press.

Schor, Juliet. 1992. *The Overworked American: The Unexpected Decline of Leisure*. New York: Basic Books.

Sewell, William E. 1992. A Theory of Structure: Duality, Agency, and Transformation. *American Journal of Sociology* 98(1): 1–29.

Stearns, Linda Brewster, and Kenneth D. Allan. 1996. "Economic Behavior in Institutional Environments: The Corporate Merger Wave of the 1980s." *American Sociological Review* 61(4): 699–718.

Tolbert, Pamela S., and Phyllis Moen. 1998. "Men's and Women's Definitions of 'Good' Jobs: Similarities and Differences by Age and Across Time." *Work and Occupations* 25(2): 168–95.

Useem, Michael. 1996. *Investor Capitalism: How Money Managers are Changing the Face of Corporate America*. New York: Basic Books.

Wajcman, Judy. 1996. "Women and Men Managers: Careers and Equal Opportunities." In *Changing Forms of Employment: Organisations, Skills and Gender*, edited by Rosemary Crompton, Duncan Gallie, and Kate Purcell. London: Routledge.

Wallace, Jean E. 1995a. "Corporatist Control and Organizational Commitment Among Professionals: The Case of Lawyers Working in Law Firms." *Social Forces* (3)73: 811–39.

———. 1995b. "Organizational and Professional Commitment in Professional and Nonprofesional Organizations." *Administrative Science Quarterly* 49(2): 228–55.

Weber, Max. 1930/1958. *The Protestant Ethic and the Spirit of Capitalism*. New York: Charles Scribner's Sons.

Whyte, William H. 1956. *The Organization Man*. New York: Simon & Schuster.

Williams, Joan. 2000. *Unbending Gender: Why Family and Work Conflict and What to Do About It*. Oxford: Oxford University Press.

Wuthnow, Robert. 1996. *Poor Richard's Principle*. Princeton: Princeton University Press.

— Chapter 11 —

# Border Crossings: The Constraints of Time Norms in Transgressions of Gender and Professional Roles

## Cynthia Fuchs Epstein

How do we account for the constraints faced by women and men who wish to move beyond the boundaries of their traditional sex and gender roles in contemporary society? Despite the opportunities for change made possible by advocates for equality, liberating technological advances, and changes in the law, women find it difficult to move upward through glass ceilings and men find it difficult to moderate time commitments at work to take on child-care responsibilities in the home. Ideologies and institutionalized practices in the workplace and the community form obstacles to breaking down boundaries. Among them are time ideologies and the norms attached to work and sex roles.

This chapter will analyze how time ideologies integrate with gender and work ideologies to undermine the ability of individuals to move beyond the conventional and historic role prescriptions for men and women—to transgress the role boundaries that define the structure of their lives and their activities. We live in a time of rapid social change in which many women and men have defied stereotyping. Women have moved into male-dominated spheres of work such as the legal profession and police work and men are reconsidering their parental roles, performing more nurturing activities as fathers. Yet cultural boundaries continue to impose controls on free choice and often limit the possibilities promised by an ideology of equality between the sexes.

Cultural boundaries defining what men and women ought to do and be are a case in point of general processes of boundary creation and maintenance that I shall explore in this paper.

Further, I shall illustrate how time norms and time ideologies ensure the compliance of gender boundaries. I shall first describe the process of boundary creation and enforcement; I shall then discuss the ideology of time use and norms in the workplace generally; and then, how norms regarding time use differ by gender at work and in the home.

## BOUNDARY CREATION AND MAINTENANCE

People become invested in the borders or boundaries that define places, social groups, and social life. Although created by human imagination, people regard boundaries as real, and attribute to them origins in some divine or genetic order, historical precedent, or political or economic logic. Just as boundaries are devised to mark the physical arrangement of countries or cities, they also define classes and groups by conceptual markers such as labels, names, and behaviors. For example, racial boundaries are contrived to mark humans (however imperfectly and arbitrarily) by color and hair texture, and class boundaries divide those who work as craftsmen with their hands from those who work on abstract matters. Most ubiquitous are boundaries dividing men and women; they do so by assigning them social roles in the division of labor unrelated to physical or intellectual competence. Of course, societies vary in their assignment of social roles to men and women, but there is some consistency across cultures in the ways in which women have been delegated to homemaking and child care as a primary role and men have been given governing and other public roles. It is widely believed that these assignments are rationally determined by the particular attributes of each sex to perform them rather than to their differential political power (an alternative perspective). I have noted in previous analyses (Epstein 1988) that no society leaves sex role assignments to "nature" or to chance. Rather, the enforcement of sex and gender boundaries, like that of other boundaries (Lamont and Wuthnow 1990), is accomplished by both subtle and direct means: through the conscious agency of powerful religious, military, and political institutions and their leaders and through the institutionalized social practices of everyday life embedded in etiquette, social conventions, and the internalized beliefs of individuals. The controls that keep people "in their place" are lodged in everyday conventions, as Michel Foucault (1977) noted. Pierre Bourdieu (1984) called the process the symbolic violence of "habitus"—"the sets of dispositions shaped by former conditions of existence"—affirmed by political and managerial protocols. Many controls are internalized simply as the "right thing to do." And individuals who wish to change must confront identity issues that are linked to their gender, work, and family roles.

Further, boundaries often *create* characteristics in large groups and in individuals as well as marking them. For example, a boycott of a country may reduce it from a prosperous nation to a supplicant one; access to good nutrition and education may raise the intellectual level of a population. Social conventions that create a sex division of labor result in "women's and men's jobs," preventing women from developing managerial and technical competence and giving men public roles as managers, workers, and warriors that result in their selective availability or disability for roles as caretakers of children. Further, certain roles are difficult or easy to perform depending on whether a person has access to the social resources and human capital appropriate to them. For example, access to research assistants and good libraries make it easier for a scholar to be productive, and well-connected businessmen learn of investment opportunities not available to those more isolated.

Time is also marked by conceptual boundaries. Parts of the day and week are assigned to workplace activity, family engagement, leisure, and religious observance. Although these designations are generally socially prescribed, individuals have the ability to make some choices about time management and individuals from favored groups have more power to manage their own time. Typically these favored groups are men more than women; whites more than minority persons; and the affluent more than the poor (though privileged women may confront much the same restrictions on the use of their time as middle-class and working-class women).

The walls that define occupational and sexual groups in the Western world have no armed guards or physical barriers to separate and segregate them as they do in other parts of the world. In the West, many have broken through boundaries to take roles of those on the other side. In trying to follow, many more find they face constraints set by people who are acting out cultural scenarios. Of course, particular boundaries may invoke varying defenses, depending on the group, and some groups may be highly invested in keeping it strong. Yet individuals and groups develop competencies or may benefit from social and technological change in moving between regions marked by boundaries, as Christina Nippert-Eng (1996) has described. For example, today geographic boundaries and time zones are made less important by the use of email and faxes. Similarly, the use of computers and development of other technology makes work boundaries permeable between younger and older workers and men and women, because most work no longer requires great physical strength and the new technology gives many access to networks they might not otherwise have. Cell phones can make physical location irrelevant; they also, like other technologies, create permeability between what I shall call "role zones"—the categories of time and space allocated to the performance of particular roles. Individuals may retreat from role demands by enclosing themselves in automobiles during long commutes or may use tape recorders and videos to make themselves "available" to their children when they are not physically present.

## IDENTITY AND TIME ISSUES

One of the greatest problems facing women and men who wish to cross boundaries is the fact that social disapproval is often internalized and becomes an identity problem. Their very stake in the "who" of "who they are" is called into question.

Identity usually is thought to be derived from socialization and the other components of personality structure, but many scholars now argue that it is also situationally produced—for example, an individual might think of herself as a "star" when an audience applauds her performance on a stage, but not in home at the breakfast table. (Markus et al. 1982; Deaux and Major 1987; Epstein 1996). Jeffrey Thompson and J. Stuart Bunderson (2001) find that when individuals' identities are anchored in certain roles but they are forced to spend time in alternative roles they experience a sense of conflict, which they do not feel if their identity and activities match. Yet identity salience may be situationally triggered, as when a white person walks on a street in a black neighborhood and suddenly feels "white," they point out. Furthermore, when a person encounters disapproval for assuming a role not regarded as anchoring a proper identity, it can trigger guilt.

Furthermore, though borders create barriers that often seem impenetrable, even the most severe of them invite transgression. This may happen when the rewards for transgression are high enough, when identification with the other realm is strong, or when barriers have become lax. Thus even some East Germans found ways to pass the Berlin Wall and Mexicans defy border guards to get to the United States—but many people accept their situational boundaries and stay put. This is often as much a matter of collective acceptance of a boundary, the way it is rooted in one's identity, as it is of the reality of barbed-wire fences, guards, legal restrictions, and lack of money and other resources.

## TIME NORMS AND IDEOLOGIES AS MECHANISMS OF CONTROL

Controlling the ways in which individuals of various groups spend their time—in the workplace or the family, for example—can ensure or reinforce conformity. Controls may be harsh or lax depending on surveillance or the person's ability to insulate himself or herself against them or through collective action. In addition, controls may be internal when the rules for proper conduct are part of a person's identity. Thus the social and the personal are deeply intertwined.

Rose Laub Coser in her "defense of modernity" (1991) pointed out that in premodern society it was difficult to transgress boundaries because each individual's behavior was so highly visible to other members of the community. Of course, this surveillance extended to the ways in which people used their time. For example, strictures regarding the Sabbath prescribed only religion-related activities on that day; by engaging in commercial or playful activity on that day of the week, a violator risked severe punishment or social isolation. As Coser observed, in modern society, especially in urban life, what one chooses to do may be protected from visibility. Thus, one might be free to skip going to church and instead go to the movies on the Sabbath. Theoretically, urban life makes it possible for individuals to slip from role to role without attracting the notice and activating the accompanying strong arms of boundary keepers. But even in modern society, accountability is demanded for one's actions at specific times of the day or year, and although one's activity may not be visible to gatekeepers, time accountability has been made visible by means other than the human eye, and certain conventions of time use, as we shall see, persist in modern urban life.

Time ideologies are part of every major institution of society and they are a major element of control in each of them. Ideologies about appropriate roles and the time norms attached to them, as well as the meaning of such constructs as the week, the workday, and holidays (Zerubavel 1981), provide the context and values that order people's sense of what they as men or women or workers ought to be doing at any given time. Thus, time norms as well as gender norms place demands on them (Epstein 1996). Certain role combinations are complementary but others may cause strains and conflicts in the identities one develops from one's roles. However, conflict and consistency are products of social norms that prescribe "feeling rules" (Hochschild 1979) and "time rules" as well as expected behaviors in many roles. And of course, organizations create structures that help or hinder women in performing multiple roles (Epstein 1996).

Max Weber theorized that in the workplace, the Protestant ethic—that is, working hard—was regarded as the sign of God's favor. Modern versions of the Protestant ethic may be found in the ideologies demanding total commitment to such "greedy institutions" (Coser 1974) as the professions, the ranks of the managerial class, the army, religious orders, and other occupations that demand continual diligence. "Greedy institutions" demand that their members be on tap "all the time," subordinating other role demands to theirs. The modern family (Coser and Coser 1974) has been characterized as a greedy institution in that it asks mothers to give first priority to family demands and to be available on demand. Mothers who do not do this are prime candidates for feeling guilt.

There have been different ideologies about what constitutes a proper workweek. With industrialization work became separated from the home, creating a clear distinction between work time and leisure time. In American society, the forty-hour workweek—with time off for national holidays and paid periods designated as vacation time, was fought for and legislated over time. Although many women worked outside the home, national policy was based on an understanding that men worked outside the home for pay and women worked inside the home, presumably sharing the paycheck of husbands. But women had been recruited into the "outside-the-home" labor force during both World Wars, and they began moving into the workplace in growing numbers after World War II. The expectations of employers that workers on the job would give their entire devotion to the workplace clearly marked the boundary between and work and family, making it difficult for American women and men to have a role in caring for or supervising their children during work hours. The ideology of "work only" during the hours devoted to the employment setting has held fairly constant, although employers have offered to assist workers who have home-based obligations with part-time and flexible schedules, financial assistance with child care, child-care centers, and permission to make personal calls during the workday. But there are costs for workers who take "too much" advantage of some of these opportunities, particularly time off or reduced hours, because they are not regarded as connected to the workplace as those who ask for few concessions. In addition they are aware of other trends, such as the escalation of work output (Collinson and Collinson, chapter 8 in this volume; Jacobs and Gerson 2004; Epstein et al. 1995). For example, in recent times professionals such as lawyers and doctors have been expected to work long hours, their time now monitored by records of their "billable hours," and managers in corporations similarly are expected to work overtime. At lower levels, many workers are asked to put in "compulsory overtime" in the evenings and on the weekends. Not only are these expectations higher than before (Jacobs and Gerson 2004; Epstein et al. 1999) but "workaholism," whether by assignment or personal decision, is regarded as a virtue and a sign of commitment and excellence.

## TIME AND GENDER IDEOLOGIES:
## PERSISTENCE AND CHANGE

In a period of great social change, ideologies of gender have remained quite persistent. Both women and men are encouraged to feel good about conforming to gender roles and uncomfortable about transgressing the boundaries.

The women and men ideologically and economically motivated to transgress gender boundaries find themselves corralled and punished in ways that are both subtle and direct. Men who take on women's occupational roles are often regarded as effete, and this image keeps their numbers low in such women-dominated occupations as nursing, grade-school teaching, and clerical work. And women who become truck drivers, firefighters (Chetkovich 1997), coal miners (Yarrow 1987), factory workers (Reskin and Padavic 1988) or stock and bond traders (Lewis 1989; Levin, chapter 9 in this volume) find that they are subject to peer disapproval (Epstein 1992) and negative sanctions that may range from sarcasm and joking to sexual harassment.[1] Controls at all levels of the social system operate to keep men and women in their "place" even at a time when social change is providing opportunities to move beyond the conventional boundaries of work and family roles (Epstein 1988).

An escalation of time demands has occurred in the family as well as in the workplace. Parents once were expected to provide their children with physical care, discipline, and affection (loosely conceived). In the 1960s, care for the child's physical well-being was extended to include care for children's emotional well-being and, by the eighties and nineties, to include enrichment of their social life and building their future networks. Thus it is that today, mothers in particular are subjected to parenting conventions that require attention to children's psychological well-being and to acquisition of various forms of social capital. Supervision of homework, participation in numerous sports activities, most dramatically supported by the now institutionalized role of "soccer mom," as well as tutoring in subjects ranging from computer skills to music are demanding of parents' time (Lareau and Weininger 2003).

The ideology of "intensive mothering" identified by Sharon Hays (1996) may be regarded as an extreme, but it typifies a trend.

It defines proper motherhood as putting the child first and meeting the norms described above.

In my studies of women lawyers (Epstein 1981) I found that women who spent long hours at work when they were mothers of small children often were regarded as poor mothers by relatives, and particularly by younger women they knew who disapproved of their efforts to be "superwomen." Thus women lawyers were regarded as hardhearted, and as making sacrifices that were unusual and deviant. Often it was believed that they had bad marriages or that they were missing important markers of their children's development, such as seeing them take their first step or hearing them speak their first word.

The ideology of motherhood is formed and re-formed all the time. Fashions in child care have changed to fit it. In the past, when upper- and middle-class women were not in the paid labor force, the culture supported use of surrogates. Housekeepers and nannies took care of the home and children, freeing their mothers for charitable work, socializing, sports, shopping, or other activities. Working-class employed women depended on family members or on older children to take care of younger children while they worked.

After the World War II, women's steady movement into the paid labor force coincided with a blossoming emphasis on mothering. In the 1950s motherhood ideology turned to Freudian psychology and developmental psychology for insights into child rearing, particularly in the first years of life. Some child-care professionals urged women to perform mothering in an ordered, scheduled way. Presumably this left women the option to do other things in the time between feeding and tending to the child's other needs. But this arrangement didn't last long. Permissive, child-centered mothering arrived and generated new norms, such as on-demand feeding for infants. Today this has reached an extreme form in a movement called "attachment mothering" (Sears and Sears 1993).[2] The philosophy of the movement is that in the early years parents should bond with their children through breastfeeding, "wearing" their babies, and sleeping with them. Some advocates suggest that the child be breastfed into the toddler stage and beyond—sometimes as long as four or five years. Thus the "attachment mother" (obviously the father cannot participate in many of the crucial activities such as breastfeeding) may never be able to mesh work life with her home life and must fit all work into time left over—if there is any—from family roles.

The home-schooling movement represents another ideology requiring educated women (it is invariably the mother) to be confined to the household all day in order to educate their children in the values of their group—sometimes right-wing fundamentalist groups but increasingly professionals who believe public schools are incapable of meeting their expectations and hopes for their children. Here, too, the mother is to be tied to the home and to mothering tasks and not to be free to do other things.

These ideologies are profoundly subversive of the movement of women into important and fulfilling work.

Time and gender ideologies also specify marital roles. In the past, wives were supposed to be available for their husbands' needs. They were regarded as the supporting players in their husbands' careers and they were to provide the "haven in a heartless world" (Lasch 1977) that the man of the household depended upon. Indeed, until the 1980s, women who applied for jobs as lawyers encountered employers who asked how they could be good wives if they worked at a high-demand occupation. Women who pursued careers in the male-dominated professions were seen to be taking a job away from a man. "Go back to the kitchen," male law students would taunt the few (Epstein 1981) women who went to law schools before the 1970s, when they faced active discrimination both in training and employment. Women were not to seek demanding jobs that might place them higher in the status hierarchy than the men in their lives, lest they damage their egos, displace them as breadwinners, or have competing demands for their time. The appeal of jobs as schoolteachers in the fifties and sixties was that the school day ended at three and summers were "off," freeing a woman to be both a good homemaker and mother.

## IDEOLOGIES OF MULTIPLE ROLES

The culture's focus on work and family conflict make all working women sensitive to society's labeling of multiple work and family roles as problematic. The conflict rhetoric suggests that both women and men are under stress when they assume multiple roles *that are not regarded as mutually supportive.*

It is often believed that the stress women feel is due to over-load—too many responsibilities. Research shows, however, that the amount of responsibility is less important in creating stress than the inconsistency of the role demands on women and the extent to which a woman is supported in her choice of roles (Epstein 1987).

The conventions associated with time allocations and the ways in which they are integrated into the cultural fabric are an important factor in society's response to women who choose to assume multiple roles.

Several elements are intertwined in women's and men's opportunities to play both multiple and nontraditional roles. It may be assumed that multiple roles are limited by time constraints, but we know that higher-status individuals tend to have many more roles than do individuals in lower strata. Individuals from some groups are encouraged to take on many roles (for example, corporate executives are asked to become board members of charities, serve as heads of professional associations, join prestigious clubs), and members of other groups (such as mothers of small children) are discouraged from taking on additional roles, which restricts their choices and opportunities for expanded horizons.

It is important to understand how the privileged get to take on so many roles, given the fact that they have the same twenty-four hours in their day as a person with limited roles.

Some time ago I theorized (Epstein 1987) about the mechanisms available to individuals who wish to expand their number of roles, and to perform complex and demanding roles, including those not regarded as integrated or compatible. As Mary Blair-Loy points out (this volume, chapter 10), women who are both professionals and mothers are seen as having "competing devotions," not compatible devotions. Holding demanding roles in the home as well as the family is regarded in American culture as potentially or inevitably stressful, and individuals are persuaded to reduce the stress by casting off demanding roles. A woman who leaves a partnership track for a "mommy track" in a law firm is one example of this. Robert Merton (1957) and William J. Goode (1960) noted that role strain might be controlled by activating a number of mechanisms, including compartmentalizing, delegating, and protecting the time reserved for certain tasks, as well as casting off a problematic role. I suggested these mechanisms are available to some people and not others. (Epstein 1981). I pointed out that privileged men are most able to use such mechanisms and that women and minority groups are least able to use them. This is due partly to differential access to material and cultural resources such as symbolic capital; an example would be rank, which confers authority and legitimation. Women and minorities typically have not had the financial resources to delegate and find surrogates to perform some of their role obligations, or to protect them from intrusions while performing certain roles so they can turn to alternate activities. Furthermore, women live in cultural environments in which the use of such surrogates is disapproved. Men may use surrogates, as we shall see, as long as they do so conforming to traditional male roles. Yet women who have full-time nannies and household help and wish to work long hours face disapproval and often internalize guilt for doing it. The husband typically is not encouraged or permitted to take over more than a modest amount of child care. It's feared that if he does he may suffer career consequences, or it seems a better economic bet to invest the husband's time in a career. As one lawyer in our study of part-time lawyers put it, "We decided that the financial rewards of partnership versus the hours that I would have to work were not worth it . . . and that it was better for me to go part-time and take on the bigger role at home. . . . It was better to invest in *his* career [emphasis added]" (Epstein et al. 1999).

In this study, wives were supportive of their husbands' participation in child care when the activity with the child was gender-appropriate, such as coaching soccer, and did not interfere with the normal (male) workday.

As we have seen, women and minorities face more rules than more dominant groups about how they *use* time. For women, this stems from the role obligations society imposes on them in the sphere of the family, which undercuts their full commitment to professional demands. Furthermore, and most important, they face often subtle cultural prohibitions on fully exploiting the mechanisms for making time expand by using the privileges of authority and assertiveness attached to "male roles," which permit delegation, flexibility, and retreat from certain family obligations.

Of course, most women and minorities and many working-class men are lodged in occupations that do not offer the options of upper-rank male privilege. They are subject to a regime of accountable time in a workplace structured by time clocks and strict rules on the job. But even at the blue-collar level, men may be less subject to time surveillance than women. For example, I found in a study of telephone company workers in the mid-1980s that most women worked at easily monitored "inside" jobs and a sizable number of men worked at "outside," jobs where they were less likely to be in panopticon-like settings subject to the gaze of supervisors (Foucault 1977). As to men working in the professions, although they are under pressure to work long hours, those at the top of their professions often are masters of their schedules, free to take time off during the day and to decide when they will arrive or leave. Although they too, of course, are subject to performance norms set by professional peers, it is nevertheless the case that upper managers and doctors and lawyers may leave the workplace without being accountable to others (Epstein et al. 1995). This is true whether they are taking time off to go to conferences, to have extended lunches and dinners, to play golf or tennis, or to have assignations with lovers. Professionals and executives may exercise this freedom because they can delegate part of their role responsibilities to secretaries, junior associates, research assistants, or wives, and pass beyond the borders of the screen visible to others as they take time off from role duties. This freedom, of course, is not available to all, but it is a possibility, one that is workable within the normative structure with social approval from peers, and, most important, one not resulting in a sense of role conflict.

Thompson and Bunderson (2001) point out that "the experience of work-nonwork conflict may at least partially be explained by social-structural considerations" and that "meaning-based conflict is more relevant for individuals in certain occupations, certain industries, or at different levels of the hierarchy" (12).

Women do not have the flexibility that men may use in managerial and professional jobs and in many crafts positions. Just when they are achieving access to upper-level jobs—jobs that demand irregular hours and involve subjective evaluations based on markers of commitment such as demonstrations of "face time" in the office in the evening and on weekends (Epstein et al. 1995, 1999; Bailyn 1993)—they are put in a double bind. If they put in extra hours at work they are not fulfilling the time norms that specify their primary obligation to the home. If they don't put in the time, they cannot hope to fulfill the work norms that might lead to promotion and the freedom to delegate that comes with it. At every level they face severe constraints on their use of flexible time assignments and services that would support fulfillment of multiple work and family roles. Indeed, they are made to feel guilty about using the mechanisms long available to men to cope with time pressures at work and in the family. Furthermore, should their male partners wish to help them in any systematic way by performing family roles at times when their wives are expected to be at work, the men face negative sanctions as well. Of course, in some spheres we are seeing change, particularly in academic life. But not enough to solve the problems.

Not only the availability of surrogates but also the legitimation of their use is subject to gender ideology. Now that women have moved into occupations in which they can afford surrogates, at home and in the workplace, they face disapproval from the ideological left as well as the right: middle-class women are condemned for using the labor of immigrant women (Ehrenreich and Hochschild 2003; Flanagan 2004); the "family values" agenda supports women staying at home to care for children; motherhood ideology prescribes the mother's "hands-on" approach to child care (Hays 1996); some fear possible dangers to the child from immigrant or minority child-care workers (Glassner 1999; Wrigley 1995); others fear harm will be done to the psychological or physical development of the child from "part-time" mothering (Epstein et al. 1999); there is fear of harm to the woman from overwork, dual shifts, or denial of her "true" nature (Baruch and Barnett 1986); and the final pressure is that old refrain, that subordinates will resist taking orders from a woman.

The notion that women should take on many roles and can perform them competently and without stress or with stress of the positive kind (Selye 1974) is usually regarded as impossible, and it has generated a multitude of popular and scholarly works that define such activities as overburdening and problematic. Women who "stretch" time, using it efficiently and packing it heavily with activities, are regarded as deviants (Epstein 1987; Epstein et al. 1995, 1999). I found in my studies of women lawyers (1981; Epstein et al. 1995) that attorneys who do many things are regarded as "superwomen" and are labeled not "real women." They often face ridicule behind their backs or outright resistance from women whose role sets are narrow and from men who find them to be "ball busters" (Epstein 1981). Indeed, repeated references to concepts such as "role overload," "role strain," and "work-family conflict" suggest that taking on numerous activities *must* lead to stress and negative outcomes. I have noted elsewhere (Epstein 1985, 1987, 1996) that in the past, women's assumption of numerous roles did not elicit negative reactions because the women typically were engaged in gender-appropriate activities both in the home and at work. In agrarian society women worked on the farm, raised children, made clothes, and provided food for their families and hired hands without public concern or notice. Even women's working in sweatshops or doing piece work at home was viewed as problematic only when cast as a public health concern of the larger culture. However, when women began to move into occupational roles guarded jealously by men, a rhetoric of social and mental disorder linked to "role overload" began to proliferate, supported by an accompanying social science literature (Epstein 1985; Baruch and Barnett 1986). In the study of women attorneys who attempted to solve the family-work conflict by working part-time (Epstein et al. 1999), my colleagues and I found that when women assumed multiple roles, even on a limited basis, they encountered hostility. Coworkers resented the women's defiance of workaholic time norms by working limited schedules and viewed them as transgressing both work and family norms. One colleague, reflecting the views of many, said, "If you want to be a mother, be a mother; if you want to be a lawyer, be a lawyer." Some colleagues suspected they would have to assume the part-timers' obligations; others were jealous of the part-timers' attempt "to have it all."

More than two decades ago, Stephen Marks (1977) and Sam Sieber (1974) showed that individuals' accumulation of roles often engenders pleasure and increases energy rather than producing strain. Others have found that people with many roles often produce more than those with few roles. For example, in a study of large New York City law firms I found (Epstein 1981) that of forty-one women partners about three-quarters, or twenty-seven, were married and twenty-five of them had children. Jonathan Cole and Harriet Zuckerman (1991) also report in their study of scientists that the most successful women were married (74 percent had children) and published more than their single counterparts. The work of scholars, such as Rosalind Barnett and Caryl Rivers (1998) show that dual-earner families indicate more life satisfaction than families in which the man is the sole breadwinner. Yet, as they point out, no "Go for it!" ideology has developed to express this collective experience. Of course, the people who manage these complex and multiple roles must make different use of their time than others who work and play during the time periods conventionally set aside for these activities.

There is no doubt that many people today are overworked both at work and in the family owing to escalating time pressures (Epstein et al. 1999). But certainly the popular and scholarly focus on "crisis" seems aimed particularly at women and not at men. Where people are genuinely overworked, the source of the strains that they "feel" are to a great extent imposed by an unyielding cultural ideology about the time norms associated with gender. Women who work a conventional workday are performing within the realm of role acceptability. They are not unlike the women who in the past worked in conventional jobs as secretaries or teachers and were regarded as augmenting the family income but not as providing its basic bread. But women who work irregular hours are seen as working in the time and space that normatively are reserved for their performance of family roles. Women are not supposed to work during the dinner hour or on a weekend. Only if they are working at jobs sex-labeled as female, such as nurses or telephone operators, can they deviate from the conventional time norms with approval. Women who do so in jobs labeled as male are apt to encounter disapproval. If a woman news reporter has an assignment to cover a breaking story on a weekend, or a novelist feels the muse at the dinner hour, they are apt to face disapproval (often quite subtly) for not subordinating their work needs to the expectations of others in the family. Women in families are expected to be available to play their family roles on demand on a regular daily basis, not four days a week or every other weekend, although privileged men may participate in family life on their own terms. This is reinforced by schools and other institutions that conform to rigid schedules, not permitting children to stay after midafternoon or offering evening service hours. Only commercial establishments such as stores and banks have changed their hours, enabling mothers who work to shop and bank at odd hours. We can see how ideologies tied to the gendered use of time restrict boundary crossings by women who wish to move into male roles and by men who wish to perform more family roles.

Thus, within the professions and the managerial ranks, men and women are subject to different sets of norms regarding their use of time. These norms are geared to reinforcing gender norms in the occupational setting and to reinforcing appropriate emotion norms to go with them. Men may labor long and hard—with work-associated play included—but women may not. Men may eat dinner and go to sports events with clients and define their activity as work time, often delegating aspects of their work to assistants so that they are free to go, but women feel less free to do this (Epstein et al. 1999).

This is not to say that there are no limitations on male privilege in delegating activities to others, because there are. Men can exercise this freedom when they *conform to traditional gender roles.* As I shall describe later, men may not work in roles outside the occupational setting—as caretakers of children or kin, for example—without facing negative sanctions from their organizations (Williams and Siegal 2003) and derision from peers and others as being less than "real men" (Epstein et al. 1999). Men who transgress female role boundaries by taking on nurturing roles on a systematic basis—for example, working part-time to take care of children—also suffer social disapproval that may prevent them from performing such roles for very long or not at all. The men my colleagues and I interviewed in our study of part-time work in the legal profession (Epstein et al. 1999) complained that it was more difficult for them to negotiate part-time schedules because managers did not consider their requests as legitimate as women's. The same complaint was voiced by the men interviewed for a *New York Times* article on the "fear of taking paternity leave" (Melinda Ligos, "The Fear of Taking Maternity Leave," *New York Times,* May 31, 2000, p. G1). The article reported:

> James M. Strauss did not consider himself a wimp. But Mr. Strauss, a Manhattan lawyer, was not going to take an extended leave of absence when his son Evan was born last June. One of the reasons: He feared that his co-workers would question his machismo. "If I said I was planning to

take more than two weeks off, people would have looked at me askance."
said Mr. Strauss. Instead he took just three days of vacation to help his wife
with their newborn.

The article reported that very few men take advantage of the
previsions in the Family and Medical Leave Act passed in 1993 by
the United States Congress. "While their organizations may profess
to be family friendly, their bosses are giving them the message that
men who take leave are not very manly, or are somehow letting
down the team" (Melinda Ligos, "The Fear of Taking Maternity
Leave," *New York Times,* May 31, 2000, G1). A state trooper who
applied for six weeks' leave to care for his child while his wife was
enrolled in nursing school was told by his supervisors that "a man's
job is to work, not to stay home with the kids." His supervisor
remarked to him that his wife would have to be "in a coma or dead"
for a man to qualify as a primary caregiver (Williams and Siegal
2003). The American Civil Liberties Union has represented state
troopers in South Carolina and Maryland in sex discrimination suits
based on their departments' refusals to grant paternity leave
(Balestier 2000). Other men interviewed for the *New York Times*
article, among them Harvard professors and lawyers, asserted that
requests for family leave evoked threats that the men's careers
would be jeopardized by requests for leave to take on parental
roles. The human resources manager for a major company suggested to an employee that he take a combination of vacation time
and sick leave in order not to have the term "parental leave" put in
his employee record.

In our part-time study, the few men who chose part-time schedules to share child rearing were the victims of informal sanctions
when they went to the playground with their children during the
day. Women viewed them with suspicion; they were avoided because they might be (1) unemployed, (2) gay, (3) on the prowl for
sex. Stay-at-home mothers ignored them and often would not permit their children to play with the men's children. What was condemned as deviant during the week was admired on the weekend,
when fathers who took children to the playground found other
fathers to talk to and were given approval for spelling the mother
for a few hours. The weekend schedule meant they were acting out
a father's role and not a mother's role.

## CONCLUSION

Work and family institutions are predicated on predictability and order. Only certain people from certain groups—usually men in high-level professional or craft jobs—are granted the privilege of responding to time demands that do not occur during regular work hours. Women who cross gender boundaries to work at male-labeled jobs, especially when they work at times women are supposed to be "at home," are often regarded as insufficiently attentive to their children and husbands; some are considered selfish and uncaring. Women who delegate some of their obligations to surrogates (as men do) face disapproval. Similarly, men who take on household responsibilities during time reserved for paid work encounter negative characterizations of their abilities and personalities. And there seem to be many new versions of the old ideologies propounded by voices from the right and the left demanding that women not abandon the traditional "caring" activities that demand intensive commitments of time (Ehrenreich and Hochschild 2003).

Of course, these constraints compete with considerable changes in ideologies that promote equality between the sexes and that have supported a certain number of border crossings. Transgressions and border crossings can be successfully negotiated when men and women are given legitimation for the time allocations in the various roles that they hold. This was clearly demonstrated in the United States military during the recent wars in the Middle East, when women soldiers left their husbands and children for duty far from home with a certain ambivalence but the backing of official United States policy. For them, as for women and men in the civilian world, the problem of coordination becomes one of time management and not time conflict.

Notably, media hysteria about work-family time conflict, the risks presented by "killer nannies" (Glassner 1999), and the harm to children when mothers work that crops up from time to time avoids mention of successful management. Millions of women do accommodate themselves to the role obligations of work and family. They do this by means large and small (Nippert-Eng 1996; Moen 2003). Some do it by the judicious use of surrogates, by activating the participation of their kin networks (Clinton 1996), by accomplishing role obligations at times that seem unusual to most others, by not conforming to faddish ideologies about intensive mothering, and by rising high enough in their careers to behave as men do—delegating responsibility and having other people cover for them, and forcing others to accommodate their schedules. As one woman attorney in my first study of women lawyers (Epstein 1981) put it, "The higher you rise in an organization, the greater the freedom."

Men, too, have been more successful in transgressing gender boundaries as they have accepted the ideology of equality at work and in the home. A number of male attorneys I interviewed pointed out that when they were young and hoping for partnerships they delegated all child care to their wives. A small percentage of these men now were in second marriages and have had a second set of children. They report that they try to spend more time with these children, and make it their business to take them to school and attend school events. They also stand in for their (second) wives who are more likely to have careers of their own. Of course, these are privileged men whose time can be guarded from accountability to others.

There are also cohorts of younger men who subscribe to an ideology of equality and who make the choice at the beginning of their careers to move from large bureaucratic settings to smaller firms in order to have control over their time—time they dedicate to the family. These are, of course, individual adaptations.

It would be fine if workplaces became more flexible and home life were also more accommodating to the schedules of family members. Many western European countries provide universal day care for small children, which permits women to participate in the labor force confident that their children will be well provided for, and this enjoys widespread social approval. Even in the United States, where solutions to time demands must be made by individuals, my research found that people can be innovative and accomplish much if they don't face the opprobrium resulting from norms that wrest from them the freedom to live their lives as idiosyncratically as they wish. It is doubtful, however, that their experience will be the wave of the future. Rather, society is too invested in maintaining boundaries of all sorts, with gender boundaries among the most profound and pervasive. Keeping women and men in their proper gender places is played out in a myriad of ways, and the rules attached to time management are among the most effective in limiting or preventing boundary transgressions. Thus, the widening of the opportunity structure for women, a result of years of political action, legislative activity, and economic growth, is countered by ideological campaigns to prevent women from making full use of their potential for leadership in the economy and the society and for men to share the rewards of family life. The integration of work and family for women and men remains "contested terrain" (Edwards 1979).

## NOTES

1. Consider the recent revelations about the rapes numerous women cadets in the U.S. Air Force Academy have been subjected to (Tom Kenworthy and Patrick O'Driscoll, "Climate Has to Change, Air Force Leader Says," *USA Today,* March 12, 2003).
2. I am grateful to Jean Halley for alerting me to this movement. See also the websites of such organizations as Gentle Christian Mothers, which has links to more than thirty articles on the philosophy and practice of Christian attachment mothering (http://www.gentlemothering.com/topics/), and of the Whole Family Attachment Parenting Association (http://www.motherstuff.com/html/parent-attach.htm).

## REFERENCES

Bailyn, Lotte. 1993. *Breaking the Mold.* New York: Free Press.

Balestier, Bruce. 2000. "Paternity Leave Slowly Catches On." *New York Law Journal* 223(121, June): 24.

Barnett, Rosalind C., and Caryl Rivers. 1997. "Working It Out: Can a Family Wreck Your Career?" *Pittsburgh Post Gazette,* May 4, E-1.

———. 1998. *She Works/He Works: How Two-Income Families are Healthier, Happier, and Better off.* Cambridge, Mass.: Harvard University Press.

Baruch, Grace, and Rosalind Barnett. 1986. "Role Quality: Multiple Role Involvement and Psychological Well-Being in Midlife Women." *Journal of Personality and Social Psychology* 51(3): 578–81

Bourdieu, Pierre. 1984. *Distinction: A Social Critique of the Judgment of Taste.* Cambridge, Mass.: Harvard University Press.

Chetkovich, Carol. 1997. *Real Heat: Gender and Race in the Urban Fire Service.* New Brunswick, N.J.: Rutgers University Press.

Clinton, Hillary Rodham. 1996. *It Takes a Village and Other Lessons Children Teach Us.* New York: Simon & Schuster

Cole, Jonathan, and Harriet Zuckerman. 1991. "Marriage, Motherhood and Research Performance." In *The Outer Circle: Women in the Scientific Community,* edited by Harriet Zuckerman, Jonathan R. Cole, and John T. Bruer. New Haven: Yale University Press.

Coser, Lewis. 1974. *Greedy Institutions: Patterns of Undivided Commitment.* New York: Free Press.

Coser, Rose Laub. 1975. "Stay Home, Little Sheba: On Placement, Displacement, and Social Change." *Social Problems* 22(4): 470–79.

———. 1991. *In Defense of Modernity: Role Complexity and Individual Autonomy.* Palo Alto, Calif.: Stanford University Press.

Coser, Rose Laub, and Lewis Coser. 1974. "The Housewife and the Greedy Institution of the Family." In *Greedy Institutions: Patterns of Undivided Commitment.* New York: Free Press.

Deaux, Kay, and Brenda Major. 1987. "Putting Gender into Context: An Interactive Model of Gender-Related Behavior." *Psychological Review* 94(2): 169–387.

Edwards, Richard. 1979. *Contested Terrain: The Transformation of the Workplace in the Twentieth Century.* London: Heinemann.

Ehrenreich, Barbara, and Arlie Russell Hochschild. 2003. *Global Women: Nannies, Maids, and Sex Workers in the New Economy.* New York: Metropolitan Books.

Epstein, Cynthia Fuchs. 1981. *Women in Law.* New York: Basic Books.

———. 1985. "The Politics of Stress: Public Visions, Private Realities." *American Journal of Psychoanalysis* 45(3): 282–90.

———. 1987. "Multiple Demands and Multiple Roles: The Conditions of Successful Management." In *Spouse, Parent, Worker: On Gender and Multiple Roles,* edited by Faye J. Crosby. New Haven: Yale University Press.

———. 1988. *Deceptive Distinctions.* New York: Russell Sage Foundation.

———. 1992. "Tinkerbells and Pinups." In *Cultivating Distinctions,* edited by Michele Lamont and Michel Fournier. Chicago: University of Chicago Press.

———. 1996. "The Protean Woman: Anxiety and Opportunity." In *Trauma and Self,* edited by Charles B. Strozier and Michael Flynn. New York: Rowman & Littlefield.

Epstein, Cynthia Fuchs, and Robert Sauté, Bonnie Oglensky, and Martha Gever. 1995. "Glass Ceilings and Open Doors: The Mobility of Women in Large Corporate Law Firms." *Fordham Law Review* 56(2): 291–449.

Epstein, Cynthia Fuchs, Carroll Seron, Bonnie Oglensky, and Robert Sauté. 1999. *The Part-Time Paradox: Time Norms, Professional Life, Family, and Gender.* New York: Routledge.

Flanagan, Caitlin. 2004. "How Serfdom Saved the Women's Movement." *The Atlantic* 293(2): 109–28. Available at: http://www.theatlantic.com/issues/2004/03/flanagan.htm (accessed on April 16, 2004).

Foucault, Michel. 1977. *Discipline and Punish*. New York: Vintage.

Glassner, Barry. 1999. *The Culture of Fear: Why Americans Are Afraid of the Wrong Things*. New York: Basic Books.

Goode, William J., 1960. "A Theory of Role Strain." *American Sociological Review* 25(4): 483–96.

Hays, Sharon. 1996. *The Cultural Contradictions of Motherhood*. New Haven: Yale University Press.

Hochschild, Arlie. 1979. "Emotion Work, Feeling, Rules, and Social Structure." *American Journal of Sociology* 85(2): 551–95.

Jacobs, Jerry A., and Kathleen Gerson. 2004. *The Time Divide: Work, Family and Gender Inequality*. Cambridge, Mass.: Harvard University Press.

Lamont, Michele, and Robert Wuthnow. 1990. "Betwixt and Between: Recent Cultural Sociology in Europe and the United States." In *Frontiers of Social Theory: The New Syntheses,* edited by George Ritzer. New York: Columbia University Press.

Lareau, Annette, and Elliot Weininger. 2003. "Social Class Differences in the Pace and Rhythm of Family Life." Paper presented at the Annual Meeting of the Eastern Sociological Society. Philadelphia (February 28, 2003).

Lasch, Christopher. 1977. *Haven in a Heartless World: The Family Besieged*. New York: Basic Books.

Lewis, Michael. 1989. *Liar's Poker: Rising Through the Wreckage on Wall Street*. New York: Norton.

Marks, Stephen. 1977. "Multiple Roles and Role Strain: Some Notes on Human Energy, Time, and Commitment." *American Sociological Review* 42(2): 921–36.

Markus, Hazel M., Marie Crane, Stan Bernstein, and Michael Siladi. 1982. "Self-Schemas and Gender." *Journal of Personality and Social Psychology* 42(1): 38–50.

Merton, Robert K. 1957. *Social Theory and Social Structure*. Glencoe, Ill.: Free Press.

———. 1984. "Socially Expected Durations: A Case Study of Concept Formation in Sociology." In *Conflict and Consensus: A Festschrift in Honor of Lewis A. Coser,* edited by Walter Powell and Richard Robbins. New York: Free Press.

Moen, Phyllis, ed. 2003. *It's About Time: Couples and Careers*. Ithaca, N.Y.: Cornell University Press.

Nippert-Eng, Christina. 1996. *Home and Work: Negotiating Boundaries Through Everyday Life*. Chicago: University of Chicago Press.

Reskin, Barbara, and Irene Padavic. 1988. "Male Supervisors' Resistance to Sex Integration." Paper presented at the annual meeting of the American Sociological Association. Atlanta (August 25).

Sears, William, and Martha Sears. 1993. *The Baby Book: Everything You Need to Know About Your Baby from Birth to Age Two.* Boston: Little, Brown.

Selye, Hans. 1974. *Stress Without Distress.* Philadelphia: Lippencott.

Sieber, Sam. 1974. "Toward a Theory of Role Accumulation." *American Sociological Review* 39(5): 567–78.

Thompson, Jeffrey A., and J. Stuart Bunderson. 2001. "Work/Non-Work Conflict and the Phenomenology of Time: Beyond the Balance Metaphor." *Work and Occupations* 28(1, February): 17–39.

Williams, Joan, and Nancy Siegal. 2003. "The New Glass Ceiling: Mothers— and Fathers—Sue for Discrimination." *Harvard Women's Law Journal* 26 (Spring): 77–162.

Wrigley, Julia. 1995. *Other People's Children.* New York:: Basic Books.

Yarrow, Michael. 1987. "Class and Gender in the Developing Consciousness of Appalachian Coal Miners." Paper presented to the Fifth UMIST-ASTON Annual Conference on Organization and Control of the Labour Process. Manchester, England (April 22 to 24).

Zerubavel, Eviatar. 1981. *Hidden Rhythms.* Chicago: University of Chicago Press.

# Index

348    Index